Walkers', Cyclists' and Horse Riders'

Lightfoot Guide to the Via Francigena

Edition 4

*Vercelli
to
St Peter's Square, Rome
837 Kilometres*

Copyright © 2010 Pilgrimage Publications All rights reserved.
ISBN: 978-2-917183-22-9
Revision 2

The authors have done their best to ensure the accuracy and currency of the information in the LightFoot Guide to the Via Francigena, however they can accept no responsibility for any loss, injury or inconvenience sustained by any traveller as a result of information contained in the guide. Changes will inevitably occur within the lifespan of this edition and the authors welcome notification of such changes and any other feedback that will enable them to enhance the quality of the guide.

About the Authors

We are two very ordinary people who quit the world of business and stumbled on the St James Way during our search for a more viable, rewarding alternative to our previous lifestyle. Since then we have completed four pilgrimages, one of which was particularly tough and finally prompted us to create Pilgrimage Publications and the LightFoot guide series. We have no religious beliefs, but share a 'wanderlust' and need to know about and contribute to the world we occupy.

Pilgrimage Publications is a not-for-profit organisation dedicated to the identification and mapping of pilgrim routes all over the world, regardless of religion or belief. Any revenue derived from the sale of guides or related activities is used to further enhance the service and support provided to pilgrims.

The ethos of Pilgrimage Publications is based on 4 very basic aims:
* To enable walkers, cyclists and riders to follow pilgrim routes all over the world.
* To ensure LightFoot guides are as current and accurate as possible, using pilgrim feedback as a major source of information.
* To use eco-friendly materials and methods for the publication of LightFoot guides and Travel Books.
* To promote eco-friendly travel.

Also by Babette Gallard and Paul Chinn

Riding the Milky Way 2006
Riding the Roman Way 2007
Reflections - A Pictorial Journey Along the via Francigena 2008
LightFoot Guide to the via Francigena - Canterbury to Besançon 2008/9/10/12
LightFoot Guide to the via Francigena - Besançon to Vercelli 2008/9/10/12
Companion to the via Francigena 2010/2011
LightFoot Guide to the via Domitia 2011
LightFoot Companion to the via Domitia 2011
LightFoot Guide to the Three Saints Way - Winchester to Mont St Michel 2008
LightFoot Guide to the Three Saints Way - Mont St Michel to St Jean d'Angely 2008

Tracing Yesterday Using Today's Technology

LightFoot Guides are designed to enable everyone to meet their personal goals and enjoy the best, whilst avoiding the worst, of following ancient pilgrimage routes. Written for Walkers, Cyclists and Horse Riders, every section of this LightFoot guide provides specific information for each group.

The authors would like to emphasise that they have made great efforts to use only public footpaths and to respect private property. Historically, pilgrims may not have been so severely restricted by ownership rights and the pressures of expanding populations, but unfortunately this is no longer the case. Today, even the most free-spirited traveller must adhere to commonly accepted routes. Failure to do so will only antagonise local residents, encourage the closure of routes and inhibit pilgrims following on behind.

Revised editions of this guide will be published each year, but everyone is advised to refer to the relevant update page on the Pilgrimage Publications website - changes will be listed as soon as they are received. www.pilgrimagepublications.com
Please let us know about any changes to the route or inaccuracies within this guide book - mail@pilgrimagepublications.com

Our special thanks go to:

Barbara Edgar, for her tireless and ever vigilant proof-reading.
William Marques, Confraternity of Pilgrims to Rome, for his help and support. http://www.pilgrimstorome.org.uk/
François Louviot, President Association Via Francigena Français, for his support and offer of accommodation information.
Adelaide Trezzini for her contribution to the development and mapping of the via Francigena route. http://www.francigena-international.org/
Openstreetmap: The maps in this book are derived from data (c) Openstreetmap (http://www.openstreetmap.org) and its contributors and are made available under the Creative Commons agreement (http://creativecommons.org/licenses/by-sa/2.0/).
Maperitive for the creation of an indispensable tool used in the drawing of our maps. http://igorbrejc.net/about
Cristina Menghini and the rest of the folks at Movimento Lento for their tackiling the monumental task of signing the via Francigena route in Italy.
http://www.francigena.movimentolento.it

CONTENTS

		Page
LightFoot Guide to the Via Francigena		5
Using Maps and Instructions		6
The Basics in Italy		7
Useful Links		8
Useful Links and Recommended Reading		9
Map symbols		10
SECTION FIFTY-EIGHT	Vercelli to Robbio	11
SECTION FIFTY-NINE	Robbio to Mortara	19
SECTION SIXTY	Mortara to Santuario-Madonna-della-Bozzola	24
SECTION SIXTY-ONE	Santuario-Madonna-della-Bozzola to Pavia	30
SECTION SIXTY-TWO	Pavia to Santa Cristina	38
SECTION SIXTY-THREE	Santa Cristina to Orio Litta	44
SECTION SIXTY-FOUR	Orio Litta to Piacenza	48
SECTION SIXTY-FIVE	Piacenza to Fiorenzuola d'Arda	57
SECTION SIXTY-SIX	Fiorenzuola d'Arda to Fidenza	66
SECTION SIXTY-SEVEN	Fidenza to Costamezzana	74
SECTION SIXTY-EIGHT	Costamezzana to Fornovo di Taro	78
SECTION SIXTY-NINE	Fornovo di Taro to Cassio	87
SECTION SEVENTY	Cassio to Ostello della Cisa	95
SECTION SEVENTY-ONE	Ostello della Cisa to Pontremoli	103
SECTION SEVENTY-TWO	Pontremoli to Villafranca-in-Lunigiana	115
SECTION SEVENTY-THREE	Villafranca-in-Lunigiana to Aulla	125
SECTION SEVENTY-FOUR	Aulla to Sarzana	132
SECTION SEVENTY-FIVE	Sarzana to Massa	141
SECTION SEVENTY-SIX	Massa to Pietrasanta	153
SECTION SEVENTY-SEVEN	Pietrasanta to Lucca	160
SECTION SEVENTY-EIGHT	Lucca to Altopascio	169
SECTION SEVENTY-NINE	Altopascio to San-Miniato	174
SECTION EIGHTY	San-Miniato to Gambassi-Terme	183
SECTION EIGHTY-ONE	Gambassi-Terme to San-Gimignano	189
SECTION EIGHTY-TWO	San-Gimignano to Abbadia-Isola	193
SECTION EIGHTY-THREE	Abbadia-Isola to Siena	204
SECTION EIGHTY-FOUR	Siena to Ponte d'Arbia	213
SECTION EIGHTY-FIVE	Ponte d'Arbia to San-Quirico d'Orcia	220
SECTION EIGHTY-SIX	San-Quirico d'Orcia to Radicofani	227
SECTION EIGHTY-SEVEN	Radicofani to Acquapendente	233
SECTION EIGHTY-EIGHT	Acquapendente to Bolsena	239
SECTION EIGHTY-NINE	Bolsena to Montefiascone	246
SECTION NINETY	Montefiascone to Viterbo	254
SECTION NINETY-ONE	Viterbo to Capranica	261
SECTION NINETY-TWO	Capranica to Campagno-di-Roma	272
SECTION NINETY-THREE	Campagno-di-Roma to La Storta	278
SECTION NINETY-FOUR	La Storta to St Peter's Square, Rome	284
Map Reference List		292
List of churches and religious organisations along the route		295

This book traces the Via Francigena from Vercelli to St Peter's Square, Rome. You will find an introductory section followed by 37 chapters, each of which covers a segment of the route. Each chapter contains:
- A Route Summary
- Detailed instructions
- Map
- Altitude profile
- Address and contact details for accommodation of other facilities

Layout
The entire distance has been divided into manageable sections of approximately 22 kilometres, but accommodation (where it exists) is listed for the entire length of the section so that is up to you and your body where you decide to stop.

Instructions
The entire route has been GPS traced and logged using way point co-ordinates. On this basis, it should be possible to navigate the route using only the written instructions, though a map is provided for additional support and general orientation. Use of a compass is recommended.

Each instruction sheet provides
- Detailed directions corresponding to GPS way point numbers on the map
- Verification Point - additional verification of current position
- Distance (in metres) between each way point
- Compass direstion to next way point
- Waypoint Altitude

Each map provides:
- A north/south visual representation of the route with way point numbers
- Altitude Profile for the section
- Icons indicating places to stay, monuments etc. (see Map symbols)
- Map scale bar

Accommodation Listings:
Accomodation prices are based on one double room per night - accurate at the time of entry, but subject to change. For simplicity, the listing is divided into 3 price bands:

A = (€)65+   B = (€) 30 - 65   C = (€) 0 - 30   D = Donation

In general there are no listings above 70£/€ per night, unless nothing else is available in the area. Accommodation is listed in ascending order (i.e. cheapest first). Prices may or may not include breakfast and some establishments charge a tariff for dogs. In general, dogs are not welcome in Youth or Religious Hostels. Similarly, the general rule for accommodation in Religious Houses is that reservations must be made 24 hours ahead of arrival. The title 'Church or Religious Organisation' is used where it is in a church hall with minimal facilities. At the end of this section you will also find details of churches and religious organisations either in or near towns along the route.

First and most importantly many thanks to those people that have given us feed back from their journeys using the Lightfoot Guides this year.After a long dormant period, significant changes are taking place along the route in France in preparation for progressive adoption of the via Francigena as a GR route (GR145) by the FFRP - La Fédération Francaise de la Randonnée Pédestre.

As we have seen elsewhere, the process is generally the welding together of segments of existing routes, (Grand Randonées –GR) with short link sections and then branding this as the via Francigena. This has the great advantage of further reduction in the use of road sections, the use of established and maintained rights of way and consistent signing. The downside is much more mileage and an even wider skirting of the probable Sigeric route. The changes that we are presently aware of will add around 200km to the existing 837km from Calais to the Swiss border or about an extra 7 days for the average walker. We are very aware that some people will welcome these changes while others will object to the increase in distance. As guide writers we hope to satisfy as many groups as possible. In this edition we identify intersections between the existing route and the emergent GR145 and for the next edition we will survey the signed sections of the GR145 and incorporate them either into the primary route or as fully detailed alternatives.

In Italy, the route is under constant development by many agencies and volunteers and unfortunately not always within an overall framework of signing or routing principles. As a result you may find that the instructions conflict with some signposting. It has been our goal to find a route for walkers that is a compromise between attractiveness, historic authenticity and practicality. We anticipate that horse-riders and cyclists (mountain bikers) will primarily follow the pedestrian route, however we have created some alternatives where there are particular problems for these groups. We have also suggested walkers alternatives when we feel the full route will be either too long or too difficult for some people. Road-bikers may find some parts of the pedestrian route acceptable but overall they are encouraged to plan their routes from an appropriate road map.

The maps include a series of icons indicating the facilities that can be found in each town on the main route or within reasonable reach of the main route. The text for each stage gives complete descriptions of the facilities with address and contact details. We have included an icon for food stores and cafés for the areas outside of Italy. In Italy cafés and food stores are typically found in all but the very smallest villages. The maps show towns and roads within a corridor of about 5 kilometres on either side of the main route. This is provided to help with orientation, but also to allow pilgrims that have gone off-piste to find their way back to the main route.

Each instruction is numbered where the numbers coincide to the GPS Waypoints for those who have downloaded the data from www.pilgrimagepublications.com. Email mail@pilgrimagepublications.com for the necessary password.

The maps all conform to the north up standard with the direction of travel, for those heading to Rome, normally from top left to bottom right - South-Eastwards. The map scale is specific to each map to provide as much information as possible in the available space.

Currency: Euro. Standard banking Hours: 08.30–13.30 and 14.30-16.00, Monday to Friday. Closed on Sundays.

Post Offices - Standard Opening Hours: 08.30-19.30 and 13.45-18.30, Monday to Friday. Branches in smaller towns and villages close for an hour, 13.00-14.00.

Phone booths that still accept coins are hard find. If you're planning to use a public phone purchase of a telephone card is recommended.
Numbers beginning with 800 are free.
170 - English-speaking operator.
176 - International Directory Enquires.
12 - Telephone Directory Assistance Number
112 - Carabinieri (national-level police who also perform military police duties)
113 - Emergency Police Help Number (also ambulance and fire)
115 - Fire Department
116 - A.C.I. (Italian Automobile Club) road assistance.
118 - Medical Emergencies
Note: Italian telephone numbers can include 4, 5, 6, 7, or even 8 digits, so don't automatically assume you have the wrong number if it looks strange. Since December 1998, calls to land lines in most cities, but not all, and all other points in Italy must include a leading '0' regardless of whether the call originates within or outside of Italy. However, the leading '0' is not required with mobile phones. The '0' is shown as (0) throughout the guide, in order to draw your attention to this potential confusion.

Basic Business Hours 08.00-13.00 and 16.00-19.00, Monday to Friday. Shops in smaller towns may close on Saturday afternoons and Monday mornings.

Visting churches and religious sites. Most churches are open in the early morning for Mass and close around noon, opening up again at 16.00 and closing at 19.00 or 20.00. In some remote places, churches only open for early morning and evening services. Opening hours for museums are generally Tuesday to Saturday, 09.00 to 19.00 with a midday break.

All EU citizens are eligible for free health care in Italy, if they have the correct documentation. Non EU Citizens must arrange personal health insurance.

Traditionally Italian food consists of lunch (pranzo) and dinner (cena) starting with antipasto (literally before the meal), a course consisting of cold meats, seafood and vegetables. The next course, primo, involves soup, risotto or pasta, followed by secondo - the meat or fish course, usually served alone. Vegetables - contorni - are ordered and served separately.
Pizza is now a worldwide phenomenon, but Italy remains the best place to eat it.
Italian ice cream (gelato) is justifiably famous and available in every conceivable flavour.

Public Holidays - August, particularly during the weeks either side of Ferragosto (August 15) is a difficult time for travellers, because many towns are deserted, with shops, bars, hotels and restaurants shut.

Italian hotels fall into a number of categories, though the difference between each is gradually decreasing.
Locanda - historically the most basic option, but now tending to charge more for 'traditional' facilities.
Pensione, albergo or hotel - prices vary greatly between tourist hotspots and rural areas. Expect an additional charge for breakfast.
Hostels usually charge 15€. Virtually all hostels (excepting Religious Hostels) are members of the International Youth Hostel Association and you'll need to be a member.
Agritourismo - basically an upmarket B&B in a rural area and usually a working farm (see Travel tips for more information)
Camping in Italy is popular and the sites are generally well equipped.

Pilgrim and Travel Sites

www.Pilgrimstales.com	PILGRIM TALES publishing is passionate about inspiring others with the possibility of discovery, understanding and peace through travel
www.pilgrimstorome.org.uk	Practical information for the pilgrimage to Rome
www.theexpeditioner.com	THE EXPEDITIONER popular travel-themed webzine featuring articles about travel, music and film.
www.eurovia.tv	EUROVIA serves as a platform made by pilgrims, for pilgrims. Everybody is welcome to share their experiences with others, and to contribute their views and opinions. Other pilgrims are always grateful to receive useful tips
www.camminideuropageie.com	An Italian, Spanish, French collaboration
www.culturalroutes.ch	CULTURAL ROUTES OF SWITZERLAND deals with cultural routes in Switzerland and as such has information about the Via Francigena through that country. At time of writing it is in German and French only
www.francigena.eu	EUROPEAN ASSOCIATION webpage. In Italian. Has photos and maps of the route in Italy though they may not have enough detail for walkers
www.giovannicaselli.com/francigena/italy.htm	VIA FRANCIGENA - HIGHWAY TO HEAVEN Website of Giovanni Caselli. In Italian.
www.groups.yahoo.com/group/viafrancigena/	VIA FRANCIGENA YAHOO DISCUSSION GROUP A lively discussion group with a large amount of useful information.
www.pelgrimswegen.nl	DUTCH ASSOCIATION OF PILGRIMS TO ROME Site in Dutch
www.canterbury.gov.uk	CANTERBURY CITY COUNCIL
www.csj.org.uk	CONFRATERNITY OF ST JAMES providing a wealth of information about the many pilgrim routes to Santiago de Compostela in Spain as well as general guidance and advice to pilgrims. It is well worth visiting if this is your first pilgrimage.
www.sixtina.com	ITALIA SIXTINA A French booking service for lodging in convents and monasteries.
www.stjamesirl.com	IRISH SOCIETY OF THE FRIENDS OF ST JAMES The site of the Irish equivalent to the CSJ.
www.francigena-international.org	INTERNATIONAL ASSOCIATION OF VIA FRANCIGENA publishes maps of the route in walking stages as well as route instructions and accommodation lists.
http://www.osun.org/francigena-pdf.html	Files, brochures, articles and on the Via Francigena.
http://vfpilgrims.blogspot.com	Excellent site, full of information, run by a VF pilgrim

Useful Links

General

il Movimento Lento http://www.movimentolento.it/it/

Guida alla Via Francigena di Monica D'Atti e Franco Cinti
http://www.zio-zeb.it/spirito/francigena.html

The Walking Pilgrim - Peter Robbins
http://pilgrim.peterrobins.co.uk/routes/details/francigena_i.html

A source of online and interactive maps in Italy: http://www.pcn.minambiente.it/viewer/

Association International Via Francigena http://www.francigena-international.org/

Confraternita di San Jacopo di Compostella
http://www.confraternitadisanjacopo.it/Francigena/viafrancigena/situazione.htm

Official Italian Tourist Board http://www.italia.it/en/home.html

Italian maps www.igmi.org

Further Reading

Europe's Monastery and Convent Guest Houses	Kevin J. Wright
Guide St. Christophe - Comprehensive Guide for lodging in monasteries and convents (French only)	Available from: GSC, 163 blvd Malesherbes 75859 PARIS CEDEX
The Art of Pilgrimage	Phil Cousineau
Have Saddle Will Travel	Don West
The Essential Walker's Journal	Leslie Sansone
Pilgrimage to Rome in the Middle Ages: Continuity and Change (Studies in the History of Medieval Religion)	Debra J. Birch
The Age of Pilgrimage: The Medieval Journey to God	Jonathan Sumption
The Pilgrim's France - A Travel Guide to the Saints	James & Colleen Heater
Along the Templar Trail	Brandon Wilson
Via Francigena - Impressions of a Pilgrimage	Publisher: Eurovia
The Christian's Guide to Rome	S.G.A Luff
Rome: a pilgrim's companion	David Baldwin (Catholic Truth Society, London)
In Search of a Way: two journeys of spiritual discovery	Gerard Hughes
Pilgrim-Diary, Nikulas of Munkathvera: the Road to Rome	Francis P. Magoun
In Search of a Way	Gerard W Hughes

Useful Links and Recommended Reading

Map Symbols

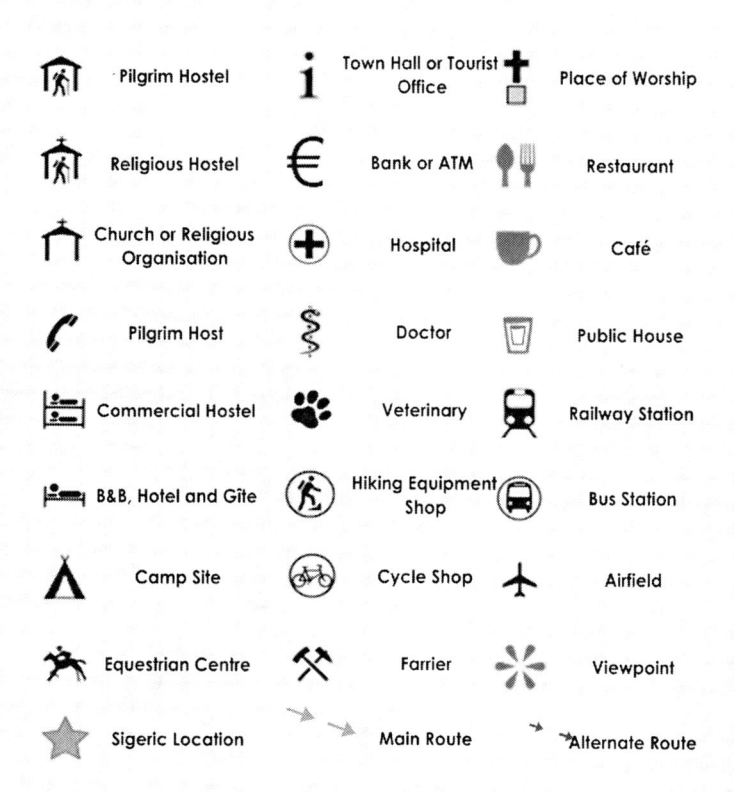

Pilgrim Hostel	Town Hall or Tourist Office	Place of Worship	
Religious Hostel	Bank or ATM	Restaurant	
Church or Religious Organisation	Hospital	Café	
Pilgrim Host	Doctor	Public House	
Commercial Hostel	Veterinary	Railway Station	
B&B, Hotel and Gîte	Hiking Equipment Shop	Bus Station	
Camp Site	Cycle Shop	Airfield	
Equestrian Centre	Farrier	Viewpoint	
Sigeric Location	Main Route	Alternate Route	

The Route

Vercelli
to
St Peter's Square, Rome
837 kilometres

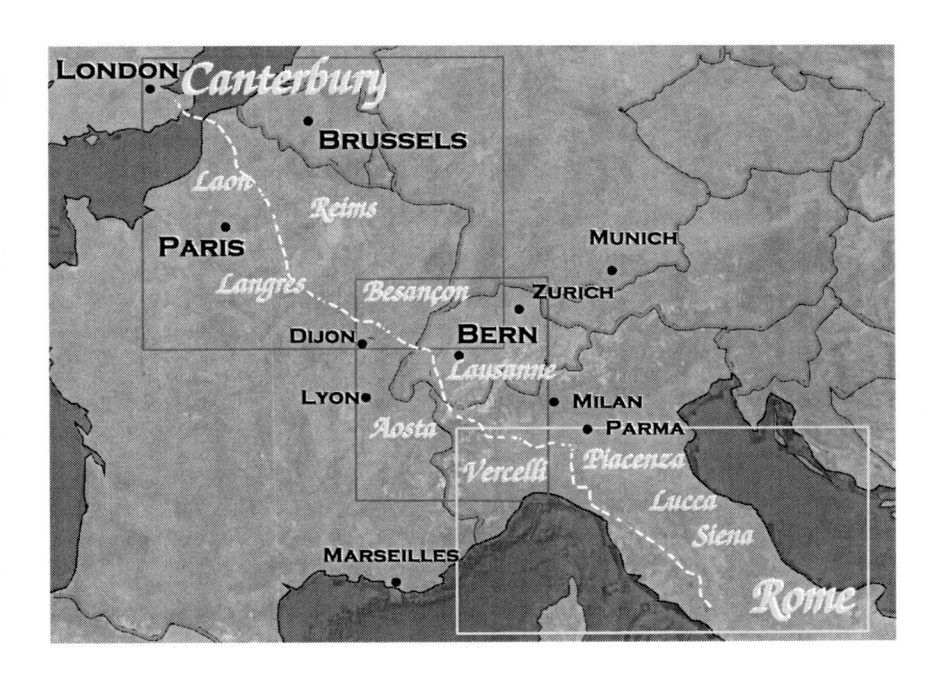

"*Let your mind start a journey thru a strange new world. Leave all thoughts of the world you knew before. Let your soul take you where you long to be...Close your eyes let your spirit start to soar, and you'll live as you've never lived before.*"

Erich Fromm

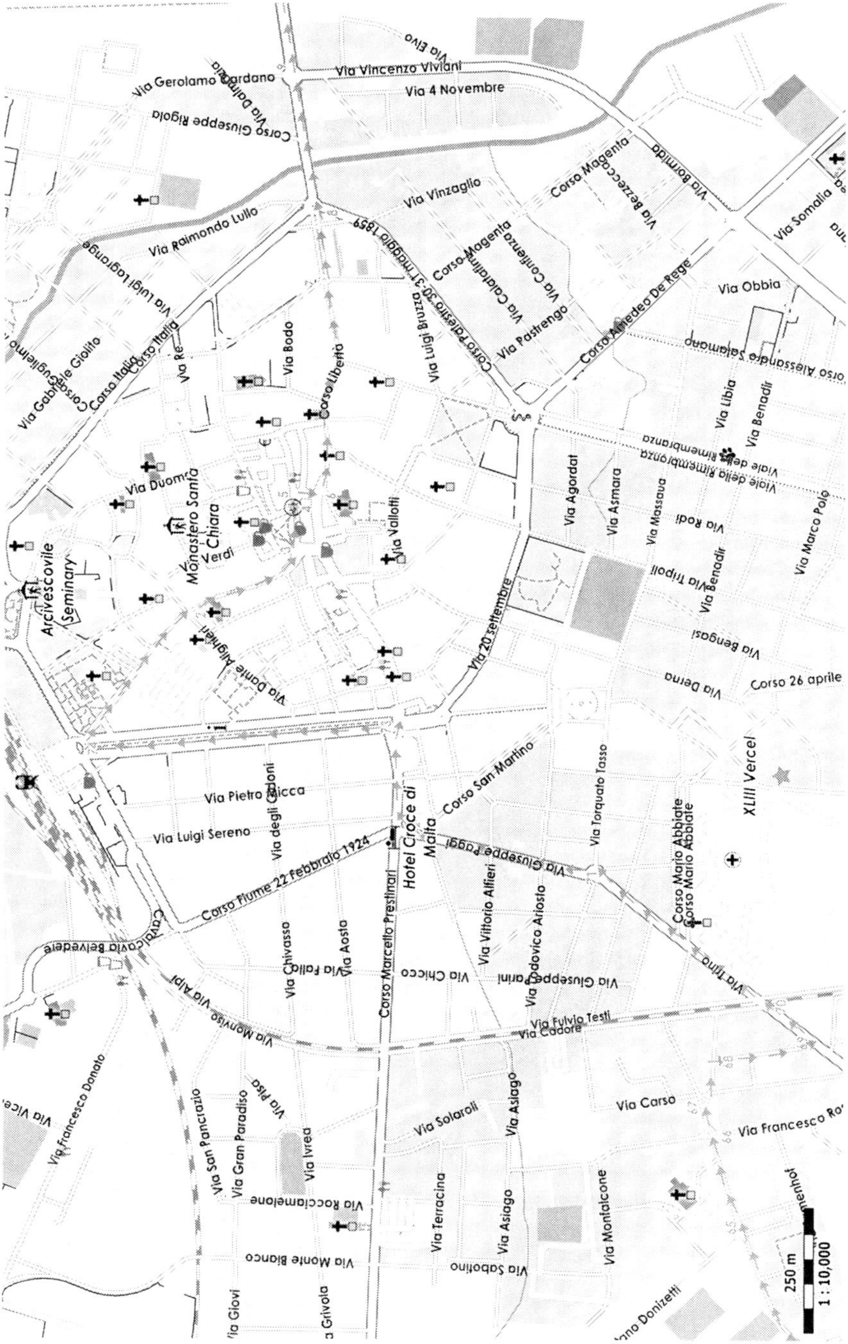

Via Gerolamo Cardano
Via Vincenzo Viviani
Via Elvo
Via 4 Novembre
Corso Giuseppe Rigola
Via Vinzaglio
Corso Magenta
Via Bormida
Via Bezzecca
Via Somalia
Via Raimondo Lullo
Via Luigi Lagrange
Corso Palestro 30-31 maggio 1859
Corso Magenta
Via Calatafimi
Via Confienza
Via Pastrengo
Corso Amedeo De Rege
Via Obbia
Via Luigi Bruzza
Via Bodo
Corso Libertà
Via Re
Corso Italia
Corso Italia
Via Libia
Via Benadir
Viale della Rimembranza
Via Duomo
Monastero Santa Chiara
Verdi
Via Agordat
Via Asmara
Via Massaua
Via Rodi
Via Marco Polo
Via Vallotti
Arcivescovile
Seminary
Via Tripoli
Via Benadir
Via 20 settembre
Via Dante Alighieri
Via Bengasi
Via Derna
Corso 26 aprile
Corso San Martino
Via Torquato Tasso
XLIII Vercel
Via Pietro Micca
Via Luigi Sereno
Hotel Croce di Malta
Via Giuseppe Paggi
Corso Mario Abbiate
Corso Fiume 22 Febbraio 1924
Corso Marcello Prestinari
Via Vittorio Alfieri
Via Lodovico Ariosto
Cavalcavia Belvedere
Via Chivasso
Via Aosta
Via Chicco
Via Giuseppe Parini
Via Trino
Via Alpi
Via Monviso
Via Fulvio Testi
Via Cadore
Via Francesco Donato
Via San Pancrazio
Via Gran Paradiso
Via Pisa
Via Ivrea
Via Solaroli
Via Asiago
Via Carso
Via Terracina
Via Asiago
Via Montalcone
Via Rocciamelone
Via Monte Bianco
Via Sabotino
Via Giovi
250 m
1 : 10,000

Religious Hostel

Convento di Billiemme,Corso Alessandro Salamano, 139,13100 Vercelli(VC),Italy
Tel:+39 0161 250167,Price:D,

Monastero Santa Chiara,Via Feliciano di Gattinara, 10,13100 Vercelli(VC),Italy
Tel:+39 0161 251226,www.serviziocivilevolontario.org/,

Arcivescovile Seminary,Piazza Sant'Eusebio, 10,13100 Vercelli(VC),Italy
Tel:+39 0161 213425,

B&B, Hotel, Gite d'Etape

Albergo delle Miniere,Corso Giacomo Matteotti, 91,13047 San-Germano-Vercellese(VC),Italy Tel:+39 0161 933111,Price:B,

Hotel Croce di Malta,Corso Marcello Prestinari, 2,13100 Vercelli(VC),Italy
Tel:+39 0161 214432,www.secerchitrovi.com/alberghi/vercelli/,Price:B,

Tourist Information

Tourist Office,Corso Giuseppe Garibaldi, 90,13100 Vercelli(VC),Italy
Tel:+39 0161 257899,www.atlvalsesiavercelli.it,

Banks and ATMs

Banca Popolare di Novara,Via Cavour, 9,13047 San-Germano-Vercellese(VC),Italy
Tel:+39 0161 933009,

Biverbanca Cassa di Risparmio,Corso Mario Abbiate, 21,13100 Vercelli(VC),Italy
Tel:+39 0161 210627,www.biverbanca.it,

Banca Sella SPA,Via Castelnuovo delle Lanze, 2,13100 Vercelli(VC),Italy
Tel:+39 0161 211397,www.sella.it,

Travel

Stazione Ferrovie,Piazza Roma, 18,13100 Vercelli(VC),Italy
Tel:+39 06 6847 5475,www.renitalia.it,

Hospital

Ospedali Riuniti,Corso Mario Abbiate, 21,13100 Vercelli(VC),Italy Tel:+39 0161 5931,

Doctor

Salamano - Medico Generico,Piazza Solferino,13100 Vercelli(VC),Italy Tel:+39 0161 260527,

Veterinary

Clinica Veterinaria Sant'Andrea,Viale Rimembranza, 105,13100 Vercelli(VC),Italy
Tel:+39 0161 503331,

Hiking Equipment

Decathlon,Corso Torino,13100 Vercelli(VC),Italy Tel:+39 0161 393687,

Bicycle Shop

Bike Shop di Minola Violino Manuel,Via Francesco Crispi, 22,13100 Vercelli(VC),Italy
Tel:+39 0161 503188,

Stage Fifty-eight Summary: after leaving Vercelli the route follows quiet tracks beside the river Sesia to Palestro. Between Palestro and Robbio intensive farming has made some of the tracks treacherous, particularly in bad weather and it may be necessary to take the longer Alternate Route for riders.

Distance from Canterbury: 1236km   Distance to Saint-Peter's-Square: 838km
Stage Ascent: 52m   Stage Descent: 62m

Waypoint	Distance Between Waypoints (m)	Total (km)	Directions	Verification Point	Compass	Altitude (m)
58.001	0	0,0	From the roundabout in front of the railway station – piazza Roma – take via Galileo Ferraris	Pass the basilica of Sant'Andrea on the left	SE	130
58.002	300	0,4	At the crossroads continue straight ahead	No Entry, towards church	SE	136
58.003	270	0,6	Bear left into piazza Cavour and go straight ahead keeping to the right side of the piazza		E	138
58.004	90	0,7	Bear right on via F. Crispi		E	139
58.005	30	0,7	Turn right	Remain on via Crispi	S	139
58.006	40	0,8	At the end of the road turn left in piazza San Paolo	Corso Libertà	E	139
58.007	500	1,2	At the mini-roundabout at the end of Corso Libertà continue straight ahead	Piazza Modesto Cugnolio, via Francigena sign beside the kiosk ahead	E	131
58.008	140	1,4	At the roundabout continue straight ahead, direction Pavia	Cross bridge over waterway	E	128
58.009	300	1,7	At roundabout go straight ahead, direction Pavia (SS11)	Cross over the Sesia river bridge	E	125
58.010	1000	2,6	After the bend to the left on the main road, turn right on the small road Strada del Boarone	Via Francigena sign	SE	122
58.011	400	3,1	At the fork, bear right towards the river	VF sign	S	120
58.012	600	3,6	At fork, keep right, and then bear left	Pass farm house on your right	S	119
58.013	500	4,1	Cross the bridge and turn left	Pass house on the left	SE	119
58.014	700	4,8	At the crossroads in the track, continue straight ahead		E	119

Vercelli to Robbio 19.16km

14

15

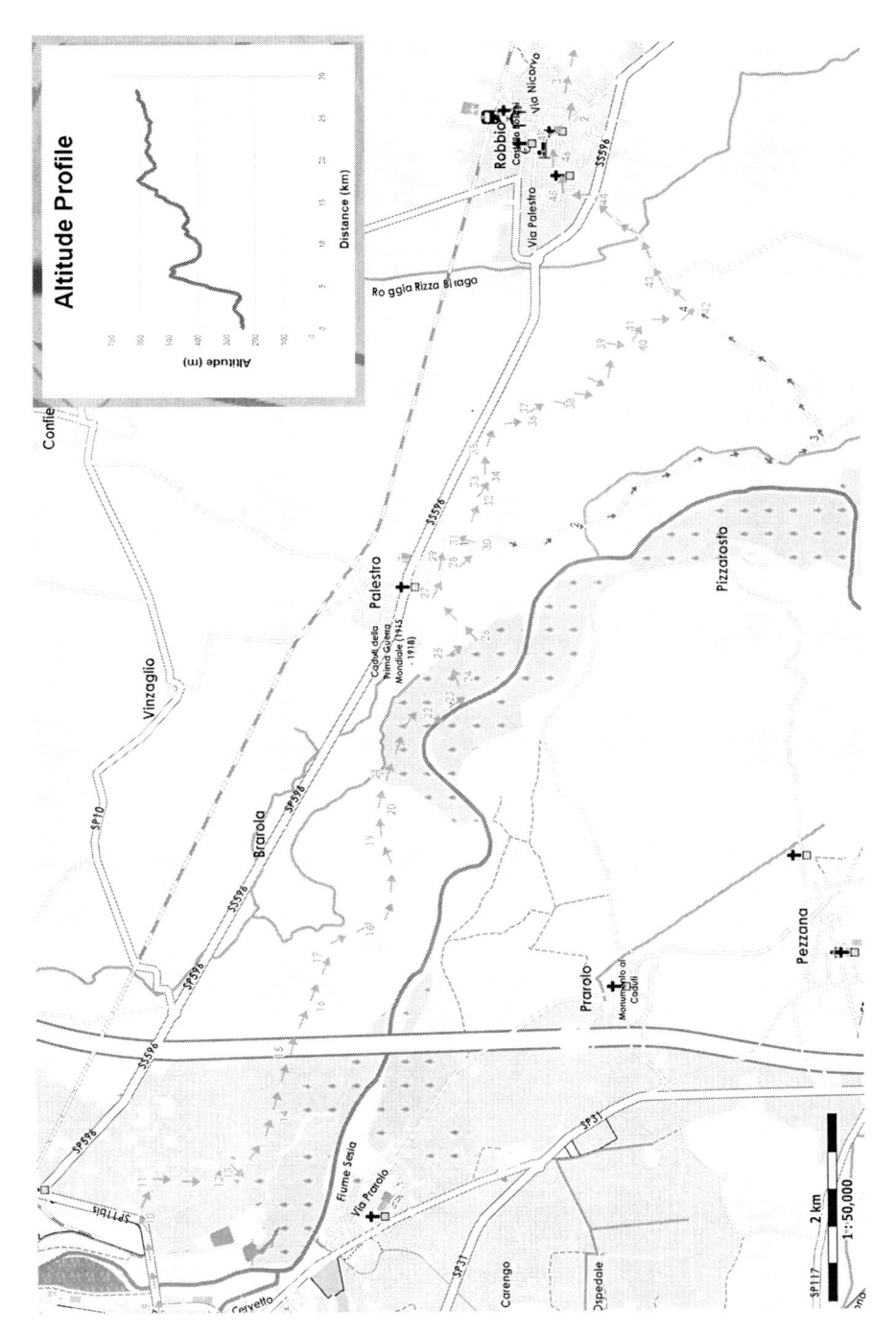

Waypoint	Distance Between Waypoints (m)	Total (km)	Directions	Verification Point	Compass	Altitude (m)
58.015	700	5,5	Continue straight ahead	Under the Autostrada bridge	E	119
58.016	500	6,0	At the crossroads in the track, continue straight ahead		SE	118
58.017	600	6,6	At the crossroads in the track, continue straight ahead		SE	116
58.018	400	7,0	Continue straight ahead	Ignore turning on the left	E	118
58.019	1200	8,2	At the crossroads in the track, continue straight ahead		E	113
58.020	300	8,5	Continue straight ahead	Ignore the track on the left	E	113
58.021	400	8,9	At the crossroads in the track, continue straight ahead		SE	116
58.022	700	9,6	At the crossroads in the track, turn right	Towards the river	S	116
58.023	600	10,3	Take the left fork	Away from the river-side	E	110
58.024	220	10,5	Go straight ahead	Wooden bridge	E	113
58.025	250	10,7	At the crossroads in the track, turn right		SE	116
58.026	300	11,1	At the T-junction, turn left	Towards the village of Palestro	NE	113
58.027	600	11,7	Turn right at the edge of Palestro on SP56 - via Garibaldi	VF sign	E	117
58.028	300	12,0	Cross bridge and proceed straight ahead	VF sign	SE	118
58.029	80	12,1	Turn right direction Rosasco on via Rosasco	VF sign	S	117

Vercelli to Robbio 19.16km

Waypoint	Distance Between Waypoints (m)	Total (km)	Directions	Verification Point	Compass	Altitude (m)
58.030	500	12,5	On the crown of the bend to the right, turn left onto partially visible grass track. Note:- intensive farming has made this track too narrow for riders and uncomfortable for walkers in wet conditions. If in doubt take the Alternate Route	Towards trees	NE	112
58.031	110	12,6	Turn right on the embankment	Trees on left	E	112
58.032	500	13,1	The embankment narrows and becomes a footpath	Beside rice field	SE	115
58.033	280	13,3	Follow the sign to the left		NE	116
58.034	60	13,4	Turn right on the track		E	116
58.035	300	13,7	At the junction continue straight ahead		SE	119
58.036	500	14,2	Take the left fork	Trees on right	SE	116
58.037	230	14,5	At the end of the path beside the trees turn right on the track		S	118
58.038	230	14,7	Follow the sign to the left and immediately turn right	Track zigzags around fields	SE	117
58.039	1300	16,0	Enter into a private property and at the junction after the cascina Bosco dei Cani turn right		S	114
58.040	180	16,1	At the next farm turn left		SE	113
58.041	250	16,4	Crossroads continue straight ahead		S	113
58.042	600	17,0	At the T-junction with the tarmac road turn left on the road. Note:- Alternate Route joins from the right		NE	114
58.043	500	17,4	Continue straight ahead	Direction Robbio	NE	114
58.044	1200	18,6	At the crossroads with the SS596 proceed straight ahead	Towards Robbio centre	N	117
58.045	290	18,9	At crossroads, after passing building material yard, turn right	VF sign, via Rosasco	E	118
58.046	500	19,4	At the crossroads, proceed straight ahead	VF sign, direction Mortara	E	119
58.047	220	19,6	Arrive at Robbio centre	Church of San Pietro and small park on your right		119

Vercelli to Robbio 19.16km

Stage Summary: riders Alternate Route by road, passing through Rivoltella

Stage Descent: 9m   Stage Ascent: 4m

Waypoint	Distance Between Waypoints (m)	Total (km)	Directions	Verification Point	Compass	Altitude (m)
58A1.001	0	0,0	Continue straight ahead on the tarmac road		S	120
58A1.002	1300	1,2	Continue straight ahead on the tarmac road	Ignore track to the river weir on the right	S	119
58A1.003	2900	4,1	Turn left	Into the village of Rivoltella	NE	111
58A1.004	2100	6,2	Continue straight ahead on the tarmac. Note:- Main Route joins from the left			115

Vercelli to Robbio 19.16km

Church or Religious Organisation

Parrocchia di S.Stefano,Via Santo Stefano, 2,27038 Robbio(PV),Italy Tel:+39 0384 670436,
www.pontidiluce.org/public/route_francigena_saint_jacques_saint_francois/lombardia.asp
,Price:D,

B&B, Hotel, Gite d'Etape

Moderno,Via Mazzini, 5,27038 Robbio(PV),Italy Tel:+39 0384 670367,Price:B,

Banks and ATMs

Banca Popolare di Novara,Via Vittorio Veneto, 15/17,27038 Robbio(PV),Italy
Tel:+39 0384 670407,

Stage Fifty-nine Summary: the route continues on level farm tracks between rice fields, with only short stretches on minor roads.

Distance from Canterbury: 1256km   Distance to Saint-Peter's-Square: 818km
Stage Ascent: 17m   Stage Descent: 28m

Waypoint	Distance Between Waypoints (m)	Total (km)	Directions	Verification Point	Compass	Altitude (m)
59.001	0	0,0	At the traffic lights beside the park, Giardini San Pietro, bear right direction Mortara	Via Mortara, pass church on the left	SE	119
59.002	260	0,3	Turn left onto via Roggetta	VF sign	E	118
59.003	400	0,7	At the crossroads with a major road, continue straight ahead beside the sports ground	VF sign, tarmac road becomes a gravel track	SE	118
59.004	1000	1,7	Bear left after crossing a small bridge	VF sign	E	115
59.005	600	2,3	Fork right passing large concrete barn on the right	VF sign	E	115
59.006	1000	3,3	Fork right	VF sign	E	112
59.007	1200	4,5	At the junction with road turn left	VF sign, irrigation ditch on the right	E	112
59.008	400	4,9	Road forks, bear left over bridge	VF sign	NE	110
59.009	200	5,1	At the T-junction, turn right, direction Nicorvo, SP6	VF sign, towards mobile-phone mast	E	110
59.010	1200	6,3	At the T-junction in Nicorvo, turn left	Direction Cilavegna	N	113
59.011	240	6,5	In the centre of Nicorvo with the bell tower on the left, turn right, direction Mortara	VF sign, via Albonese	E	114
59.012	500	7,0	Bear right onto the track. Note:- the route will return to the road 400m ahead		E	111
59.013	400	7,4	Turn left	Towards the road	N	111
59.014	110	7,5	Rejoin the road and turn right		E	111
59.015	400	7,9	Turn right onto the part grassed track between rice fields	VF sign	S	111

Robbio to Mortara 14.3km

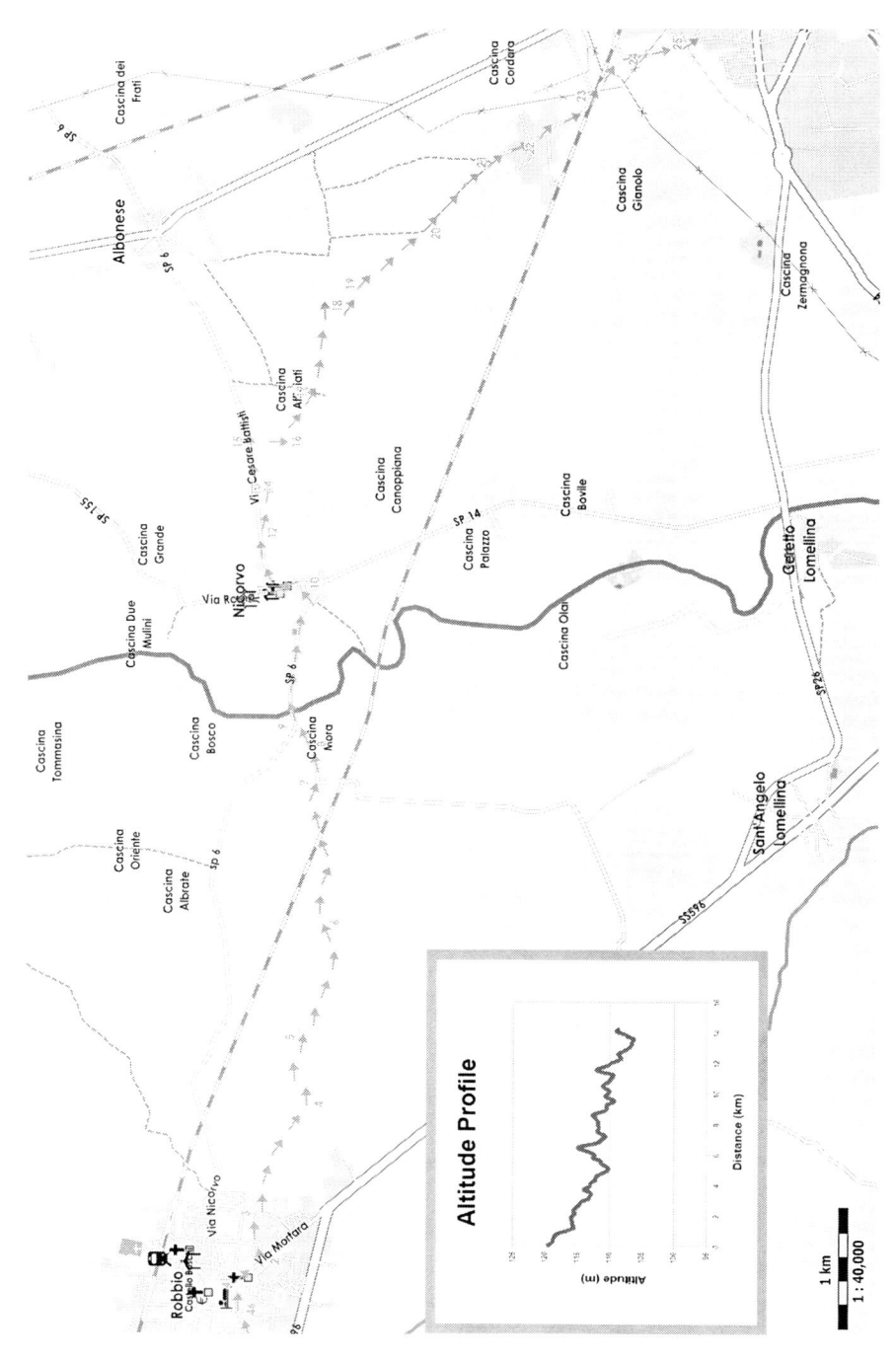

Waypoint	Distance Between Waypoints (m)	Total (km)	Directions	Verification Point	Compass	Altitude (m)
59.016	270	8,2	At the T-junction, turn left	VF sign	SE	111
59.017	500	8,7	Cross the gravel track and continue on the grass track	Large red farm building on the right	E	112
59.018	700	9,4	Turn right to cross over concrete bridge	VF sign	SE	110
59.019	400	9,8	At the crossroads in the track, continue straight ahead	VF sign	SE	110
59.020	700	10,5	Bear right at the T-junction in track	VF sign	SE	110
59.021	800	11,3	Bear right at T-junction in track		SE	109
59.022	210	11,5	Proceed straight ahead and pass through the village of Madonna del Campo	Walled gardens on both sides of the road	SE	111
59.023	800	12,3	Continue straight ahead across the railway tracks. Note:- the route ahead includes a subway under the main railway line. Riders are recommended to bear left at this point and then turn right at the junction with the main road into the centre of the Mortara and the end of the section	VF sign, towards apartment buildings on the horizon	SE	108
59.024	400	12,7	At the junction, continue straight ahead	Concrete barn on the left	S	108
59.025	600	13,2	At the junction bear left towards the railway and the prominent apartment block	Via de Cantiano	SE	106
59.026	400	13,6	At the rear of the railway sidings turn right	Keep railway on the left	S	106
59.027	170	13,8	In the square beside a water-tower continue straight ahead into the No Through Road	Keep railway close on the left	S	107
59.028	230	14,0	Take the pedestrian subway under the railway and continue straight ahead on the far side		NE	108
59.029	300	14,3	Arrive at Mortara centre in front of the railway station	Beside fountain		108

Robbio to Mortara 14.3km

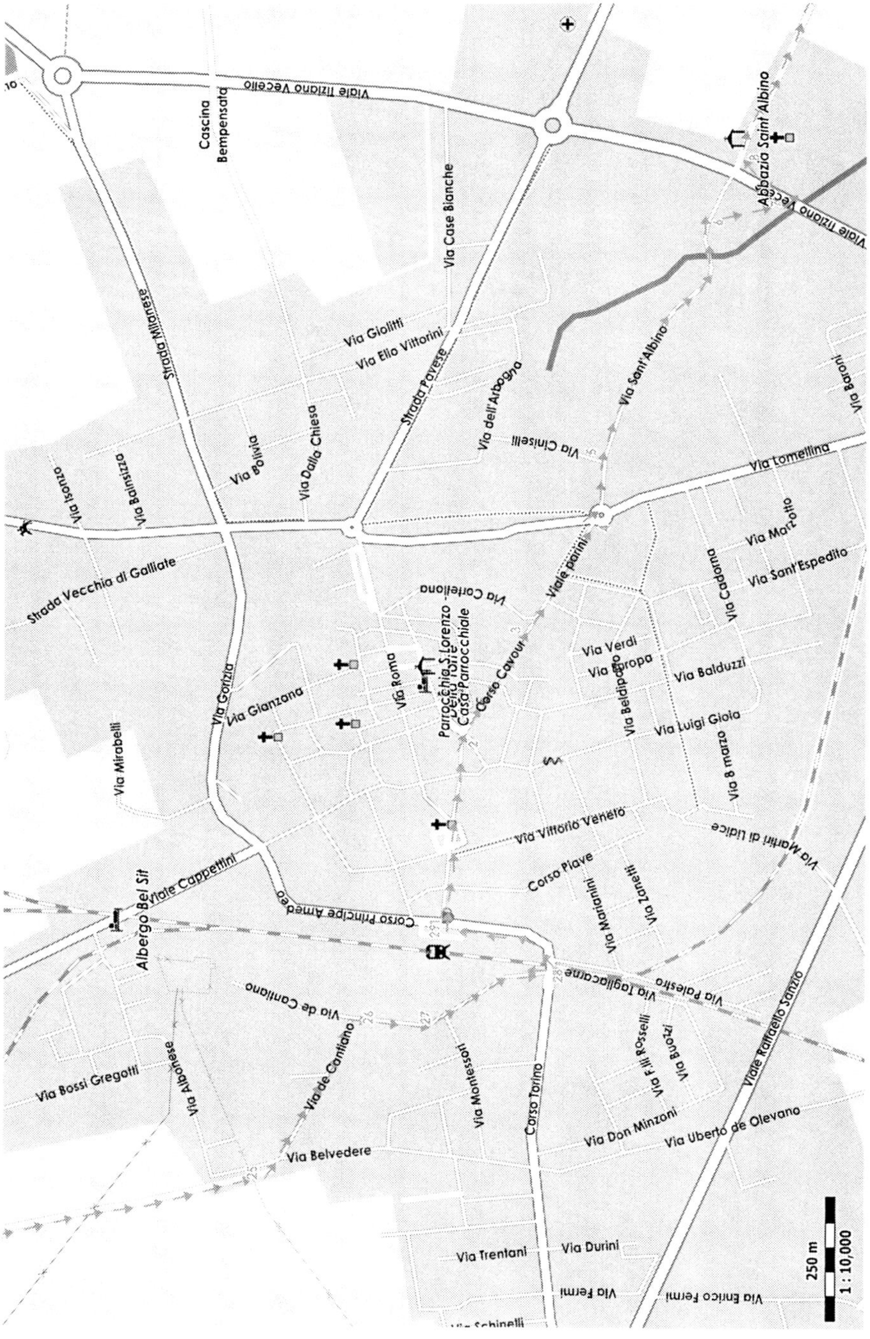
Viale Tiziano Vecellio
Cascina Bempensata
Via Case Bianche
Abbazia Saint'Albino
Strada Milanese
Via Giolitti
Via Elio Vittorini
Strada Pavese
Via dell'Arbogna
Via Sant'Albino
Via Baroni
Via Isonzo
Via Bainsizza
Via Bolivia
Via Dalla Chiesa
Via Cinisello
Via Lomellina
Via Marzotto
Via Sant'Espedito
Via Cadorna
Strada Vecchia di Galliate
Via Cortellona
Viale Parini
Parrocchia S.Lorenzo
Casa Parrocchiale
Corso Cavour
Via Verdi
Via Europa
Via Balduzzi
Via Gorizia
Via Gianzana
Via Roma
Via Beldiporto
Via Luigi Gioia
Via 8 marzo
Via Mirabelli
Via Vittorio Veneto
Via Martiri di Lidice
Albergo Bel Sit
Viale Cappettini
Corso Principe Amedeo
Corso Piave
Via Marianini
Via Zanetti
Via Tagliacarne
Via Palestro
Via de Cantiano
Via Bossi Gregotti
Via Albonese
Via Montessori
Via F.lli Rosselli
Via Buozzi
Viale Raffaello Sanzio
Corso Torino
Via Don Minzoni
Via Uberto de Olevano
Via Belvedere
Via Trentani
Via Durini
Via Fermi
Via Enrico Fermi
250 m
1 : 10,000

Pilgrim Hostel

Francesca & Gianmario Grosso,Via Roma,27020 Nicorvo(PV),Italy
Tel:+39 3383 785706,Mobile:+39 3396 005229,francesca.grosso@guidafrancigena.it,

Church or Religious Organisation

Casa Parrocchiale,Piazza Libertà, 2,27020 Nicorvo(PV),Italy
Tel:+39 0384 524042,Mobile:+39 3391 380537,Price:D,

Parrocchia S.Lorenzo - Casa Parrocchiale,Contrada San Dionigi, 1,27036 Mortara(PV),Italy
Tel:+39 0384 99772,Price:C,

Abbazia Saint Albino,Via Tiziano Vecellio,27036 Mortara(PV),Italy
Tel:+39 0384 295327,Mobile:+39 3477 194503,Price:C,

B&B, Hotel, Gite d'Etape

Albergo Bel Sit,Viale Capettini Arturo e Casare, 58,27036 Mortara(PV),Italy
Tel:+39 0384 295954,www.cozzo.virgilio.it/,Price:C,

Della Torre,Contrada Torre, 7,27036 Mortara(PV),Italy
Tel:+39 0384 90775,www.cozzo.virgilio.it/,Price:B,

Equestrian

Centro Ippico Mortara,Via Parona Cassola, 433,27036 Mortara(PV),Italy
Tel:+39 0384 295988,

Centro Ippico Mortara,Via Parona Cassola, 433,27036 Mortara(PV),Italy
Tel:+39 0384 295988,www.centroippicomortara.it/,

Tourist Information

Municipio di Mortara,Piazza Martiri della Libertà, 21,27036 Mortara(PV),Italy
Tel:+39 0384 256411,

Banks and ATMs

Banca Popolare di Sondrio,Via Roma, 23,27036 Mortara(PV),Italy
Tel:+39 0384 295744,www.popso.it/FixedPages/Common/DoveSiamoFiliali.php/L/IT,

Credito Artigiano,Corso Cavour, 18,27036 Mortara(PV),Italy
Tel:+39 0384 090101,www.creval.it,

Travel

Stazione Ferrovie,Piazza Guglielmo Marconi, 12,27036 Mortara(PV),Italy
Tel:+39 06 6847 5475,www.renitalia.it,

Hospital

Ospedale Asilo,Strada Pavese, 1125,27036 Mortara(PV),Italy Tel:+39 0348 2041,

Doctor

Casale Protti - Studio Medico,Via Goia Luigi, 24,27036 Mortara(PV),Italy
Tel:+39 0384 98640,

Veterinary

Clinica Veterinaria Citta' di Mortara,Strada Per Cascina Cassagalla,27036 Mortara(PV),Italy
Tel:+39 0384 93330,

Robbio to Mortara 14.3km

Stage Sixty Summary: after Mortara the route continues to meander through the rice fields. The route passes through a number of small villages and the pleasant town of Tromello. There are a number of variants of this section which will cross our Main Route and can be confusing. We have chosen a route which passes close beside Abbazia Sant'Albino, and arrives at the Santuario Madonna della Bozzola. The route is reasonably direct and we believe will be maintained by the local via Francigena group.

Distance from Canterbury: 1270km   Distance to Saint-Peter's-Square: 804km
Stage Ascent: 28m   Stage Descent: 40m

Waypoint	Distance Between Waypoints (m)	Total (km)	Directions	Verification Point	Compass	Altitude (m)
60.001	0	0,0	From the railway station in Mortara, go straight ahead on Corso Garibaldi	Railway station directly behind	E	108
60.002	400	0,4	Beside the town hall (municipio) bear right	Corso Cavour	SE	111
60.003	270	0,7	Continue straight ahead on Corso Cavour	Direction Sant'Albino	SE	110
60.004	250	0,9	At the roundabout go straight ahead	Via Sant'Albinio Alcuino, towards water tower	E	108
60.005	180	1,1	Continue straight ahead to join the cycle track	Water tower immediately to the left	SE	106
60.006	600	1,6	Bear right on the cycle track	After crossing waterway	S	104
60.007	170	1,8	Take subway under the main road (SS494) and then immediately turn left	Parallel to the main road	NE	104
60.008	150	1,9	Turn right on the gravel track	Abbazia Sant'Albino on the right	SE	105
60.009	600	2,5	At the junction bear right	Towards the railway track	S	104
60.010	220	2,7	Cross over the railway and turn left	Railway immediately on the left	SE	104
60.011	1200	3,9	At the T-junction beside the irrigation channel turn left	Towards the gas plant	NE	102
60.012	140	4,0	Continue straight ahead. Note:- route variant turns right at this point	Towards gas plant	NE	102

24

25

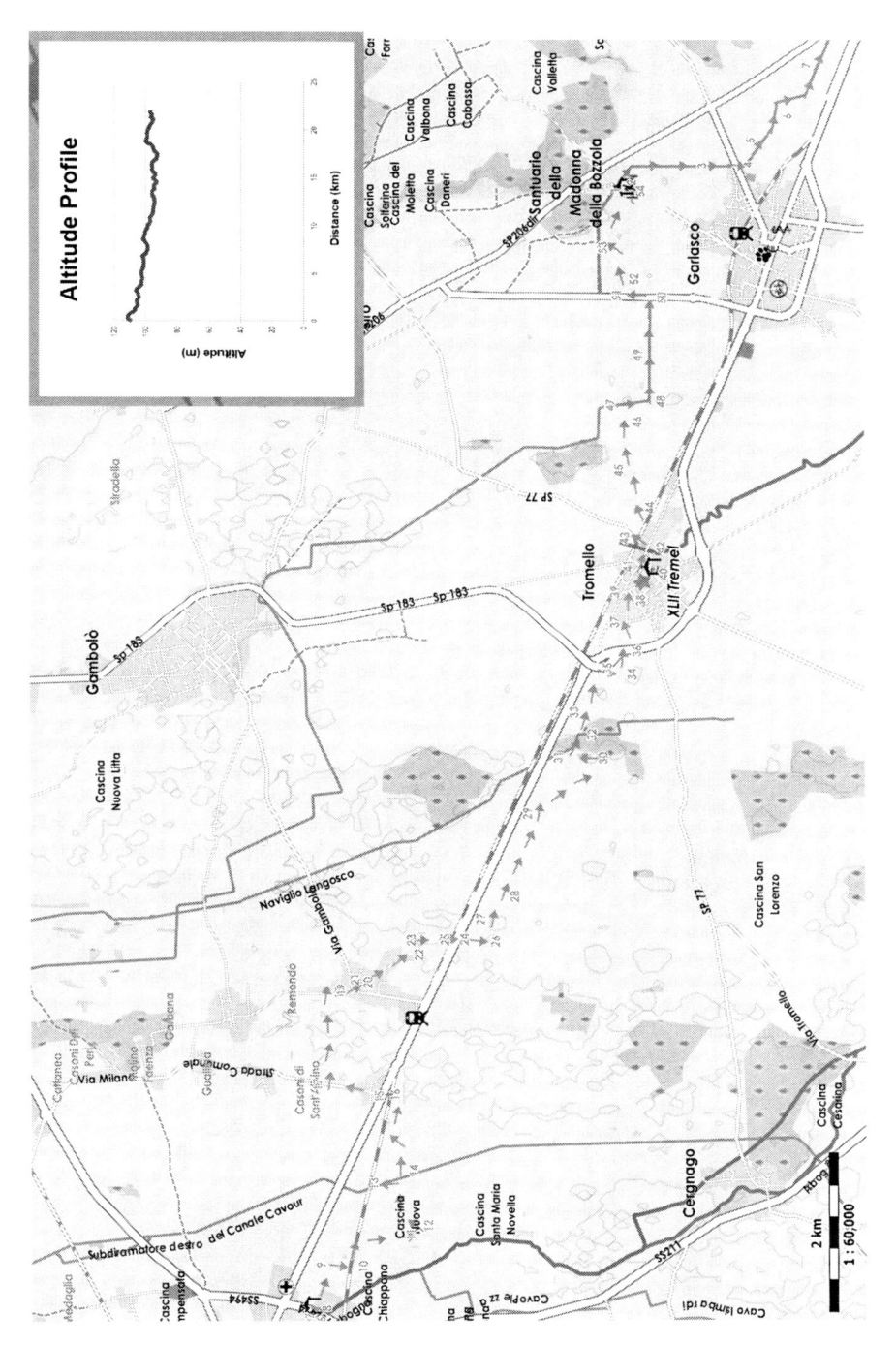

Waypoint	Distance Between Waypoints (m)	Total (km)	Directions	Verification Point	Compass	Altitude (m)
60.013	800	4,8	Following the bend to the left, turn right, cross the bridge over Canal Cavour and bear right	Turning beside the gas plant	SE	102
60.014	260	5,1	Fork left	Over small bridge	E	102
60.015	1100	6,2	At the T-junction turn left	Cross over railway track	N	101
60.016	110	6,3	Cross straight over the main road into the village of Casoni di Sant'Albino	Direction Guallina	N	101
60.017	700	6,9	Shortly after passing house N° 33, turn right onto an unmade road	Cross small bridge	E	101
60.018	1200	8,1	At the T-junction with the road, turn right	Cemetery ahead at the junction	S	99
60.019	300	8,4	At the crossroads, in the centre of Redondo, turn left	Direction Gambolò, bar on the left	E	100
60.020	100	8,5	At the crossroads, turn right on via Arturo Ferrarin	Church on the right, war memorial on the left	S	101
60.021	160	8,7	At the junction continue straight ahead	Via Arturo Ferrarin	SE	101
60.022	600	9,3	Take the left fork	Pass apartments on your left	SE	100
60.023	300	9,6	Take the right fork	Water channel directly on the right	S	99
60.024	400	9,9	Continue straight ahead	Cross railway	S	98
60.025	80	10,0	Recross main road to continue on the track the other side		S	98
60.026	300	10,3	Take the left fork	Towards radio masts	SE	97
60.027	300	10,6	Continue straight ahead	Pass radio towers on the right	SE	97
60.028	300	10,9	Continue straight ahead	Towards large tree on the right	SE	96

Mortara to Santuario-Madonna-della-Bozzola 22.1km

Waypoint	Distance Between Waypoints (m)	Total (km)	Directions	Verification Point	Compass	Altitude (m)
60.029	1100	12,1	Pass beside cascina Roventino, after the arch turn right	Keep farm buildings and irrigation ditch close on the right	SE	94
60.030	1100	13,2	Pass through a clump of trees and at the T-junction turn left		N	95
60.031	250	13,4	At the junction turn sharp right	Parallel to the main road	E	95
60.032	300	13,7	Continue straight ahead	Cross the Langosco canal	E	94
60.033	300	14,0	At the crossroads proceed straight ahead	Towards cascina San Vincenzo	SE	94
60.034	800	14,8	At the T-junction turn left		E	94
60.035	80	14,9	At the junction where the track becomes tarmac continue straight ahead. Note:- at the next Waypoint there is a crash barrier and dangerous road crossing to negotiate. Riders should turn right here and then left at the T-junction and follow the road into the centre of Tromello	Grass track, pass trees on the right	E	95
60.036	220	15,1	Carefully cross the main road (SS596) and continue straight ahead on the track	Towards the bell tower in the village	E	94
60.037	400	15,5	At the crossroads continue straight ahead on the tarmac road	Pass garages on the left	E	94
60.038	280	15,8	At the junction with via Crispi continue straight ahead	Long brick wall to your left	E	95
60.039	110	15,9	At the T-junction, turn right on via Cavour	VF signs	SE	95

Mortara to Santuario-Madonna-della-Bozzola 22.1km

27

Mortara to Santuario-Madonna-della-Bozzola 22.1km

Waypoint	Distance Between Waypoints (m)	Total (km)	Directions	Verification Point	Compass	Altitude (m)
60.040	400	16,3	In piazza Campegi, in the centre of Tromello (XLII), turn left	Via Giovanni Mussini, café on the left	NE	95
60.041	190	16,5	At the traffic lights turn right	Via Guglielmo Marconi, direction Garlasco	SE	95
60.042	260	16,7	After crossing the bridge turn left	Towards Borgo S. Siro	NE	95
60.043	180	16,9	After crossing the railway, turn right	Via Cascinino, VF sign	E	93
60.044	400	17,3	Take the right fork on the track	Valve on the left at the junction	E	92
60.045	500	17,8	At the crossroads, continue straight ahead	Towards power line	E	94
60.046	700	18,4	At the junction continue straight ahead		E	96
60.047	230	18,7	At the canal crossing, turn right	Keep canale Cavour on your left	S	98
60.048	300	19,0	At the junction, keep left	Remain beside the canal	E	99
60.049	600	19,6	Bear left and then right over the canal	Continue with the canal on your right	E	99
60.050	800	20,3	Cross over road and bear left on track with canal on the left	VF sign	N	97
60.051	300	20,6	Fork right away from the canal	VF sign, trees on your left	NE	96
60.052	230	20,9	Take the second turning on the right	VF sign, into trees	E	95
60.053	400	21,3	Turn left and then right	VF sign, trees on the left	E	96
60.054	800	22,1	Arrive at Santuario-Madonna-della-Bozzola	VF sign		96

28

Religious Hostel

Santuario Madonna della Bozzola,Piazzale Santuario, 1,27026 Garlasco(PV),Italy
Tel:+39 0382 822117,Price:D,

Church or Religious Organisation

Parrocchia Sanmartin,Via Branca, 1,27020 Tromello(PV),Italy
Tel:+39 0382 86020,Mobile:+39 3356 609347,Price:D,

B&B, Hotel, Gite d'Etape

Albergo Margherita,Via Don Minzoni, 5,27026 Garlasco(PV),Italy
Tel:+39 0382 822674,hotel.margherita@libero.it,Price:B,

Banks and ATMs

Credito Artigiano,Corso Cavour, 162,27026 Garlasco(PV),Italy
Tel:+39 0382 1759121,www.creval.it/ca/filiali.html,

Banca Popolare di Lodi,Via Biscaldi, 2,27020 Tromello(PV),Italy Tel:+39 0382 809016,

Doctor

Croce - Studio Medico,Corso Cavour, 173,27026 Garlasco(PV),Italy Tel:+39 0382 820191,

Veterinary

Mozzato - Ambulatorio Veterinario,Piazza Garibaldi, 14,27026 Garlasco(PV),Italy
Tel:+39 0382 800553,

Bicycle Shop

Gallottibike di Gallotti Claudio,Via Alagna, 47,27026 Garlasco(PV),Italy
Tel:+39 0382 810483,

Mortara to Santuario-Madonna-della-Bozzola 22.1km

Stage Sixty-one Summary: the section continues on the canal-side before passing through the town of Gropello Cairoli. The route then alternates between country roads and farm tracks before following riverside paths into the centre of Pavia.

Distance from Canterbury: 1292km   Distance to Saint-Peter's-Square: 782km
Stage Ascent: 88m   Stage Descent: 105m

Waypoint	Distance Between Waypoints (m)	Total (km)	Directions	Verification Point	Compass	Altitude (m)
61.001	0	0,0	With the Santuario Madonna della Bozzola behind, turn right to keep the sanctuary on your right	VF sign	NE	96
61.002	180	0,2	Immediately after crossing over the bridge, turn right beside the cana	VF sign, canal on the right	S	98
61.003	1300	1,5	Continue straight ahead with a bridge on the right	VF sign, canal on the right	S	92
61.004	270	1,7	Cross the road and continue on the track beside the canal	Bridge on right	SE	94
61.005	500	2,3	Turn right, cross over bridge, then turn immediately left to skirt the large building on the right	Canal on the left	SE	92
61.006	400	2,6	Beside bridge, continue straight ahead with water on left	VF sign	SE	91
61.007	1000	3,6	Cross over the sluice gate bridge, then cross the bridge to the left and bear right	VF sign, continue with canal on the right	SE	90
61.008	1000	4,5	At the crossroads with the SP206 cross the road and continue on the track beside the canal	Canal on the left	E	89
61.009	300	4,9	At the crossroads, continue straight ahead	Canal on the left	E	88
61.010	200	5,1	Fork right away from the canale Cavour on the lower track direction Gropello Cairoli	VF sign	SE	89
61.011	1000	6,1	Continue straight ahead at the junction	After passing behind the cemetery	SE	89

Santuario-Madonna-della-Bozzola to Pavia 24.8km

31

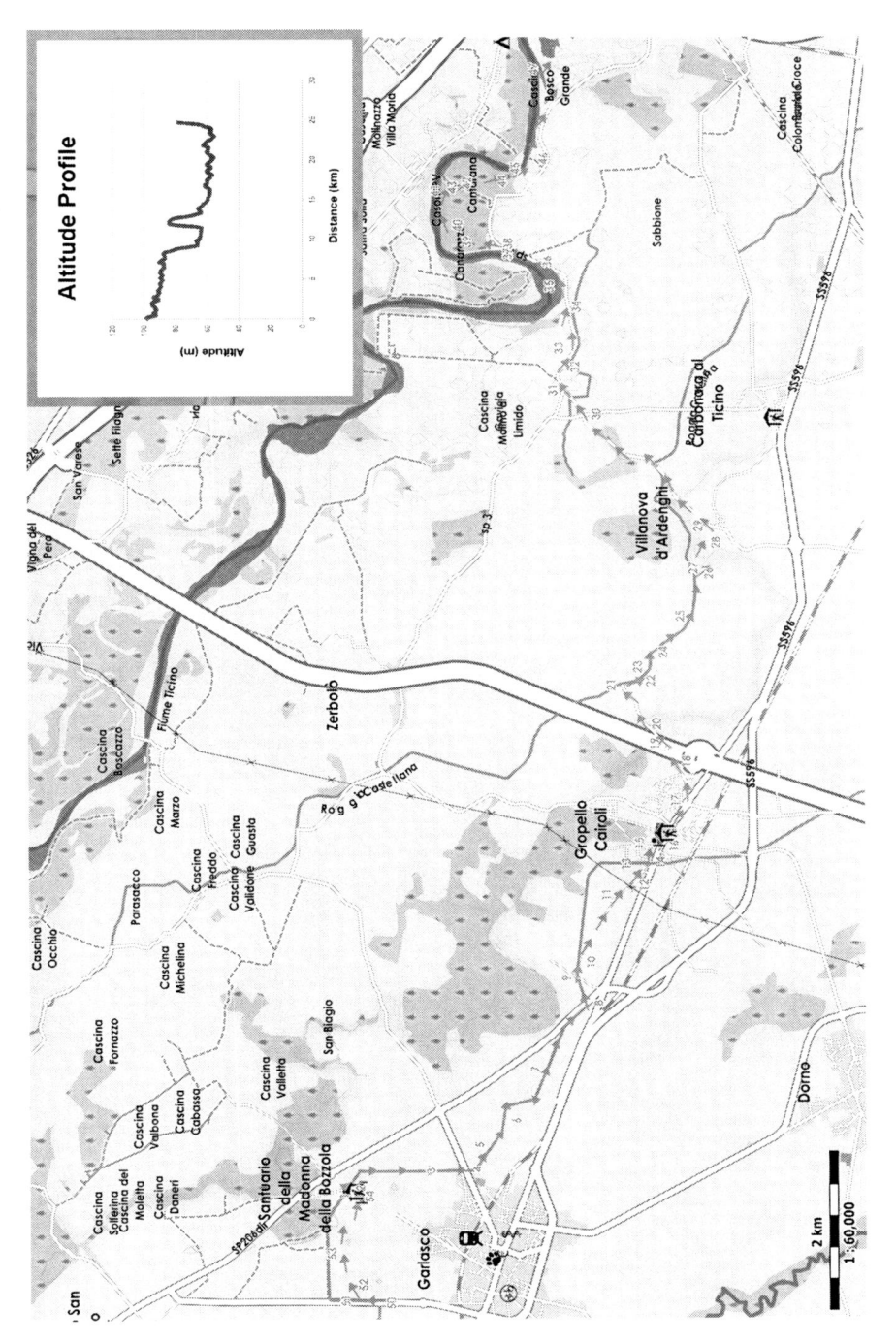

Waypoint	Distance Between Waypoints (m)	Total (km)	Directions	Verification Point	Compass	Altitude (m)
61.012	200	6,3	Fork left on the track	Avoid tarmac road to the right	E	88
61.013	290	6,6	Cross the canal and turn right	Keep canal on the right	S	87
61.014	130	6,7	Take the first turn on the left	Via Verdi	E	87
61.015	260	7,0	At the end of the road, turn right	No Entry sign	S	87
61.016	120	7,1	At the T-junction with the main road, turn left	Chiesa Parrocchiale San Giorgio ahead at the junction	SE	89
61.017	700	7,8	Pass the church of San Rocco (in centre of main road) and immediately bear left on viale C.B. Zanotti	Sign for Centro Ippico Sant'Andrea	E	86
61.018	600	8,3	On leaving the town continue straight ahead on the bridge over the motorway	Pass telephone mast on the right	E	87
61.019	270	8,6	After crossing the bridge bear left on strada del Morgarolo	Factory on the right and motorway on the left	NE	83
61.020	400	8,9	Continue straight ahead	Pass beside Centro Ippico Sant'Andrea	NE	75
61.021	600	9,5	At the junction turn right	Direction cascina Morgarolo	S	65
61.022	190	9,7	On the entrance to the farm turn left, cross over the canal and then immediately turn right between buildings	Proceed with canal close on the right	SE	66
61.023	250	10,0	Take the left fork	Between broad and narrow channels	E	65
61.024	190	10,2	At the fork bear right	Keep irrigation channel close on right	SE	64
61.025	700	10,9	After crossing a bridge bear left	Keep irrigation ditch close on left	E	64
61.026	600	11,4	At the T-junction, turn right, away from the irrigation channel	Bridge on the left at the junction	SE	63

Santuario-Madonna-della-Bozzola to Pavia 24.8km

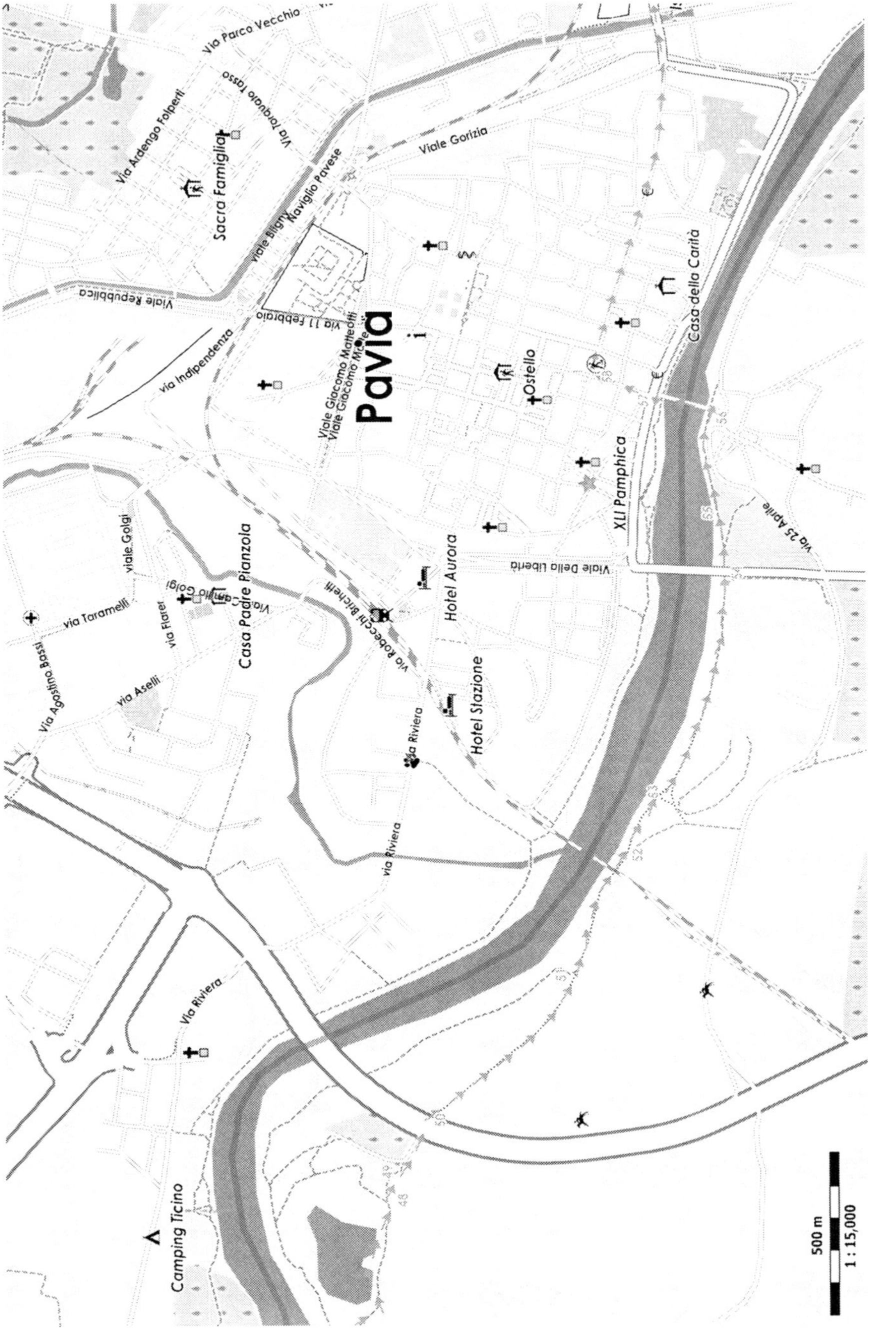
Pavia
Via Parco Vecchio
Via Torquato Tasso
Via Ardengo Folperti
Sacra Famiglia
Viale Gorizia
Naviglio Pavese
Viale Bligny
Viale Repubblica
Via 11 Febbraio
Viale Giacomo Matteotti
via Indipendenza
Ostello
XLI Pamphica
Casa della Carità
Viale Della Libertà
Via 25 Aprile
Hotel Aurora
Hotel Stazione
Via Robecchi Bricchetti
Casa Padre Pianzola
viale Golgi
via Taramelli
Via Agostino Bassi
via Aselli
via Flarer
via Riviera
Via Riviera
Camping Ticino
500 m
1 : 15,000

Waypoint	Distance Between Waypoints (m)	Total (km)	Directions	Verification Point	Compass	Altitude (m)
61.027	150	11,6	At the fork, bear left into Villanova d'Ardenghi on the tarmac road	Uphill between trees	E	66
61.028	400	12,0	Continue straight ahead through the town	Via Pollini	E	83
61.029	230	12,2	At the crossroads turn left on via Roma	Direction Zerbolo	NE	84
61.030	2200	14,4	At the crossroads, continue straight ahead	VF sign	NE	62
61.031	400	14,8	Continue straight ahead on the raised road	Large farm on left, cascina Gaviola	E	60
61.032	300	15,2	Shortly after the bend to the right, descend from the embankment and take the path on the left. Note:- to avoid potentially wet ground, cyclists may wish to remain on the road for the 8.8km to the ponte coperto in Pavia		SE	59
61.033	280	15,4	Turn right to follow the watercourse		E	59
61.034	600	16,0	Continue straight ahead on the path	River Ticino on the left	E	58
61.035	270	16,3	Continue straight ahead on the riverside path		NE	58
61.036	500	16,8	Take the right fork, climb the embankment and continue straight ahead	Keep the river to the left	NE	61
61.037	220	17,0	Bear left to leave the embankment and return to the riverside path	Village of Canarazzo on the right	NE	60
61.038	300	17,3	Cross a car park and at the T-junction turn left and then bear right	Path branches away from the road	N	60
61.039	230	17,6	Take the left fork	Right fork leads to farm buildings	NE	59
61.040	500	18,1	Continue straight ahead	Ignore the turning to the beach on the left	E	56
61.041	500	18,6	At the T-junction bear right and then left		SE	60
61.042	130	18,7	At the T-junction, turn right		SW	60

Santuario-Madonna-della-Bozzola to Pavia 24.8km

Waypoint	Distance Between Waypoints (m)	Total (km)	Directions	Verification Point	Compass	Altitude (m)
61.043	130	18,8	Bear left on the track		S	59
61.044	300	19,2	Continue straight ahead	Ignore the turning towards the river	S	58
61.045	500	19,7	Continue straight ahead on the riverside path		E	59
61.046	140	19,8	Continue straight ahead	Pass beside a restaurant	E	57
61.047	1200	21,0	At the T-junction in the woods turn right	Pass lake on the left	E	60
61.048	600	21,6	Take the right fork		E	59
61.049	100	21,7	Continue straight ahead on the tarmac road	Towards the elevated highway	SE	60
61.050	180	21,9	Proceed under the ring road and continue straight ahead	Road is closed to traffic	SE	62
61.051	600	22,5	Continue straight ahead on the unmade road	Parallel to the river	SE	58
61.052	400	22,9	Continue on the riverside track	Pass under the railway	SE	55
61.053	250	23,1	Continue straight ahead on the riverside path	Ignore the turning to the right	E	56
61.054	700	23,9	Continue straight ahead on the riverside path	Pass under road bridge	E	57
61.055	170	24,0	Pedestrians continue on the riverside path. Cyclists and riders should turn right and take the road to the entrance to the ponte coperto	Borgo Ticino to the right and the ponte coperto directly ahead	E	57
61.056	300	24,3	Climb the steps and cross the covered bridge	No Entry Sign on the bridge	N	62

Santuario-Madonna-della-Bozzola to Pavia 24.8km

Waypoint	Distance Between Waypoints (m)	Total (km)	Directions	Verification Point	Compass	Altitude (m)
61.057	220	24,6	At the traffic lights cross the piazzale Ponte Ticino and take the road ahead	Corso Strada Nuova	NE	68
61.058	200	24,8	Arrive at Pavia (XLI) centre. Note:- if you plan to use the Pò ferry from Corte Sant'Andrea, we recommend that you call well in advance, preferably between 20.00 and 22.00 in the evening and be flexible in the timing of your crossing. In case of difficulties with the ferry we suggest that you plan to stay in Orio Litta to avoid the risk of having to substantially extend your journey to the next stopping place if the ferry does not arrive	Crossroads with Corso Garibaldi	NE	79

Pilgrim Hostel

Sports Hall Pro Loco,Via Roma, 18,27020 Carbonara-al-Ticino(PV),Italy Tel:+39 0382 400425,Price:C,

Ostello,Piazza della Vittoria,27100 Pavia(PV),Italy Tel:+39 0382 597010,

Religious Hostel

Chiesa di S.Giorgio Martire,Via Libertà,27027 Gropello-Cairoli(PV),Italy Tel:+39 0382 815049,Price:D,

Sacra Famiglia,Viale Ludovico il Moro,27100 Pavia(PV),Italy Tel:+39 0382 575381,www.sacrafamigliapv.it/,Price:D,

Istituto S.Giovanni Bosco,Via San Giovanni Bosco, 4,27100 Pavia(PV),Italy Tel:+39 0382 411011,

Casa Padre Pianzola,Viale Camillo Golgi, 49,27100 Pavia(PV),Italy Tel:+39 0382 525581,

Church or Religious Organisation

Casa della Carità,Via Giuseppe Pedotti,27100 Pavia(PV),Italy Tel:+39 0382 23138, Mobile:+39 3334 477119,Price:D,

Parrocchia del S.S.Crocifisso,Via Bartolomeo Suardi,27100 Pavia(PV),Italy Tel:+39 0382 471040,www.sacrafamigliapv.it/,

B&B, Hotel, Gite d'Etape

Alexi's Hotel,Via Cairoli, 12,27027 Gropello-Cairoli(PV),Italy Tel:+39 0382 815391,Price:C,

Hotel Aurora,Viale Vittorio Emanuele II, 25,27100 Pavia(PV),Italy
Tel:+39 0382 23664,www.hotel-aurora.eu/,Price:B,

Hotel Stazione,Via Bernardino de' Rossi, 8,27100 Pavia(PV),Italy
Tel:+39 0382 35477,www.italiainviaggio.eu/hotel/pavia.htm,Price:B,

Camping

Camping Ticino,Via Mascherpa, 16,27100 Pavia(PV),Italy
Tel:+39 0382 527094,info@campingticino.it,www.campingticino.it,

Equestrian

Il Centro Ippico di Pavia,Strada Per il Lido,27100 Pavia(PV),Italy Mobile:+39 3386 065179,

Il Centro Ippico di Pavia,Strada Canarazzo,27100 Pavia(PV),Italy
Tel:+39 0382 308322,www.lombardia-inform.com/,

Tourist Information

Tourist Office,Piazza Italia, 5,27100 Pavia(PV),Italy Tel:+39 0382 597022,

Banks and ATMs

San Paolo,Corso Giuseppe Garibaldi, 52,27100 Pavia(PV),Italy Tel:+39 0382 304401,

Banca Regionale Europea,Piazzale del Policlinico, 5,27100 Pavia(PV),Italy
Tel:+39 0382 527482,

San Paolo,Via Libertà, 108,27027 Gropello-Cairoli(PV),Italy Tel:+39 0382 815701,

Banca Popolare di Sondrio,Piazzale Ponte Ticino, 8,27100 Pavia(PV),Italy
Tel:+39 0382 301759,www.popso.it/FixedPages/Common/DoveSiamoFiliali.php/L/IT,

Travel

Stazione Ferrovie,Piazzale della Stazione, 9,27100 Pavia(PV),Italy
Tel:+39 06 6847 5475,www.renitalia.it,

Hospital

Azienda Ospedaliera,Via Carlo Forlanini, 1,27100 Pavia(PV),Italy Tel:+39 0382 527549,

Doctor

Bolduri - Studio Medico,Via Defendente Sacchi, 25,27100 Pavia(PV),Italy
Tel:+39 0382 33622,

Veterinary

Ambulatorio Veterinario Ticino,Via Riviera, 43,27100 Pavia(PV),Italy Tel:+39 0382 526322,

Hiking Equipment

Rino Sport,Corso Garibaldi Giuseppe, 4,27100 Pavia(PV),Italy Tel:+39 0382 26976,

Bicycle Shop

Bike Corner di Milazzo Luca,Viale Cremona, 186,27100 Pavia(PV),Italy Tel:+39 0382 575040,

Stage Sixty-two Summary: after exiting the centre of Pavia, the route follows suburban roads before negotiating the crossing of the busy ring road. From there the Main Route follows a mix of quiet country roads and white roads making for easy going for all groups.

Distance from Canterbury: 1317km   Distance to Saint-Peter's-Square: 757km

Stage Ascent: 107m   Stage Descent: 116m

Waypoint	Distance Between Waypoints (m)	Total (km)	Directions	Verification Point	Compass	Altitude (m)
62.001	0	0,0	From the crossroads turn right	Corso Garibaldi	E	79
62.002	1000	1,0	At the traffic lights go straight ahead direction Piacenza, San Lazaro	Cross waterway on viale dei Partigiani	E	70
62.003	1200	2,2	At San Pietro in Verzolo continue straight ahead	Pass church on the right	E	75
62.004	400	2,6	Turn right down via Francana	VF sign, kiosk on the corner	SE	67
62.005	700	3,2	Continue straight ahead	Ignore the turning to the left on via Scarenzio	SE	66
62.006	160	3,4	At the end of the road continue straight ahead on the tarmac which quickly becomes an unmade track and winds from left to right and then turns back towards the main toad		NE	65
62.007	300	3,7	At the crossroads at the end of the track take the tarmac road straight ahead	Uphill	NE	67
62.008	90	3,8	At the T-junction turn right on the broader road	Via Montebolone	SE	70
62.009	160	4,0	At the roundabout, continue straight ahead	Church on right	E	75
62.010	130	4,1	At the T-junction, turn right	Pedestrian and cycle path	SE	75
62.011	600	4,7	At the T-junction turn left on strada Scagliona	Factory buildings directly ahead at the junction	SE	69

Pavia to Santa-Cristina 27.9km

39

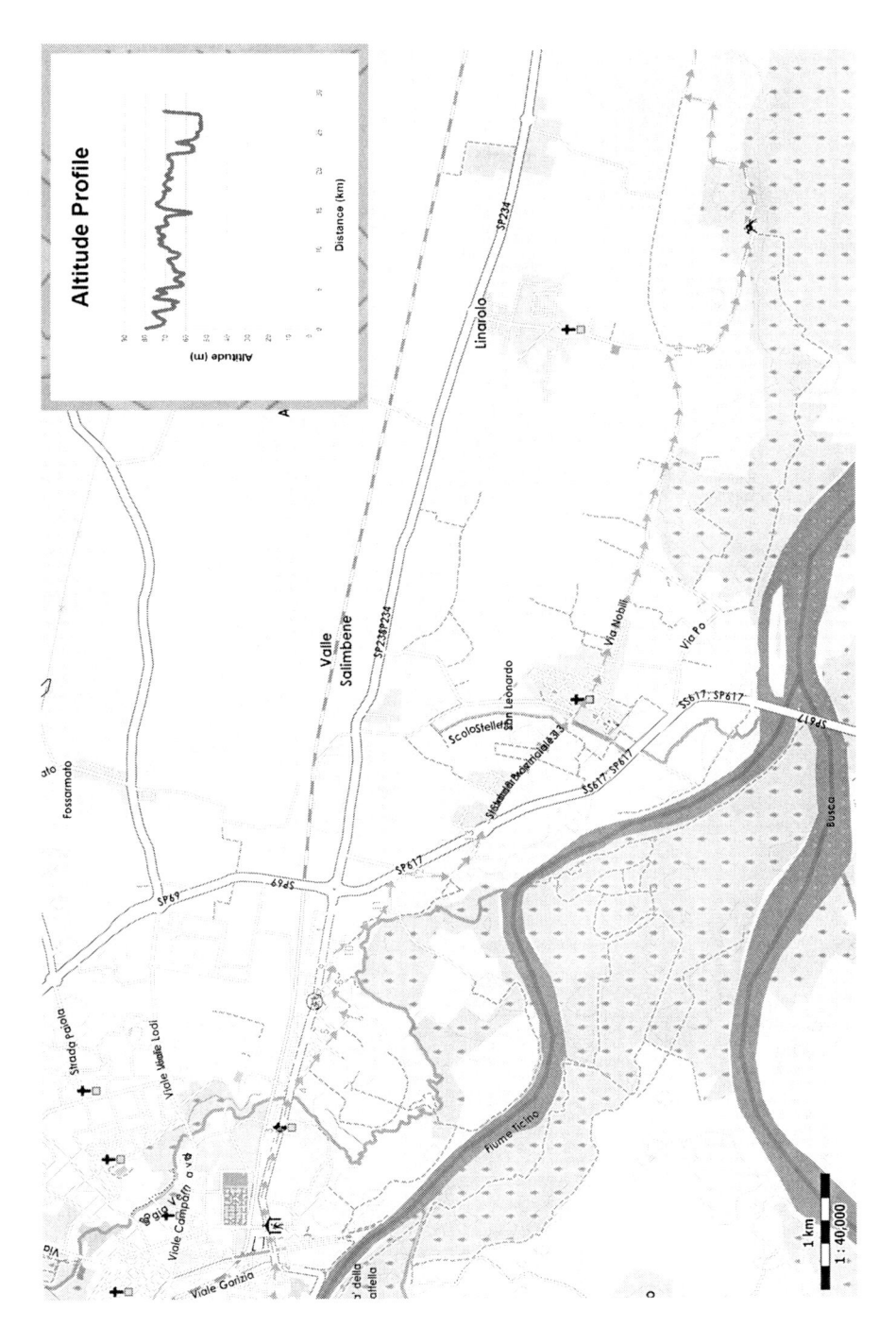

Waypoint	Distance Between Waypoints (m)	Total (km)	Directions	Verification Point	Compass	Altitude (m)
62.012	400	5,1	Bear right	Direction Broni, VF sign	SE	73
62.013	800	5,9	At the roundabout, proceed with care to take the second exit	Direction San Leonardo	E	61
62.014	4700	10,6	After passing through Ospedaletto at the sharp bend to the left, bear right on the tarmac and then turn right on the unmade road	Direction S. Giacomo	S	71
62.015	500	11,0	At the first crossroads turn left and pass through San Giacomo and Santa Margherita	VF sign	E	71
62.016	4000	15,0	Remain on the road into Belgioioso	Factory to the right	N	62
62.017	1100	16,0	In Belgioioso turn right on via P. Nenni	VF sign, direction carabinieri	E	73
62.018	500	16,5	At the T-junction, turn right on SP9 towards Torre de' Negri	Exit Beligioioso	SE	71
62.019	2100	18,6	Pass through Torre de' Negri and on the crown of the right hand bend continue on the road	Ignore the track to the left	S	70
62.020	800	19,3	On the crown of a further bend to the right, bear left on the white road	Direction Cascina Campobello, pass silos on the right	E	68
62.021	700	20,0	At the crossroads with the SP199 continue straight ahead	Towards quarry	E	67
62.022	230	20,2	Besides the quarry buildings, turn left on the gravel track	Skirt the quarry on your right	E	67
62.023	800	21,0	Bear right following the fence		SE	66

Pavia to Santa-Cristina 27.9km

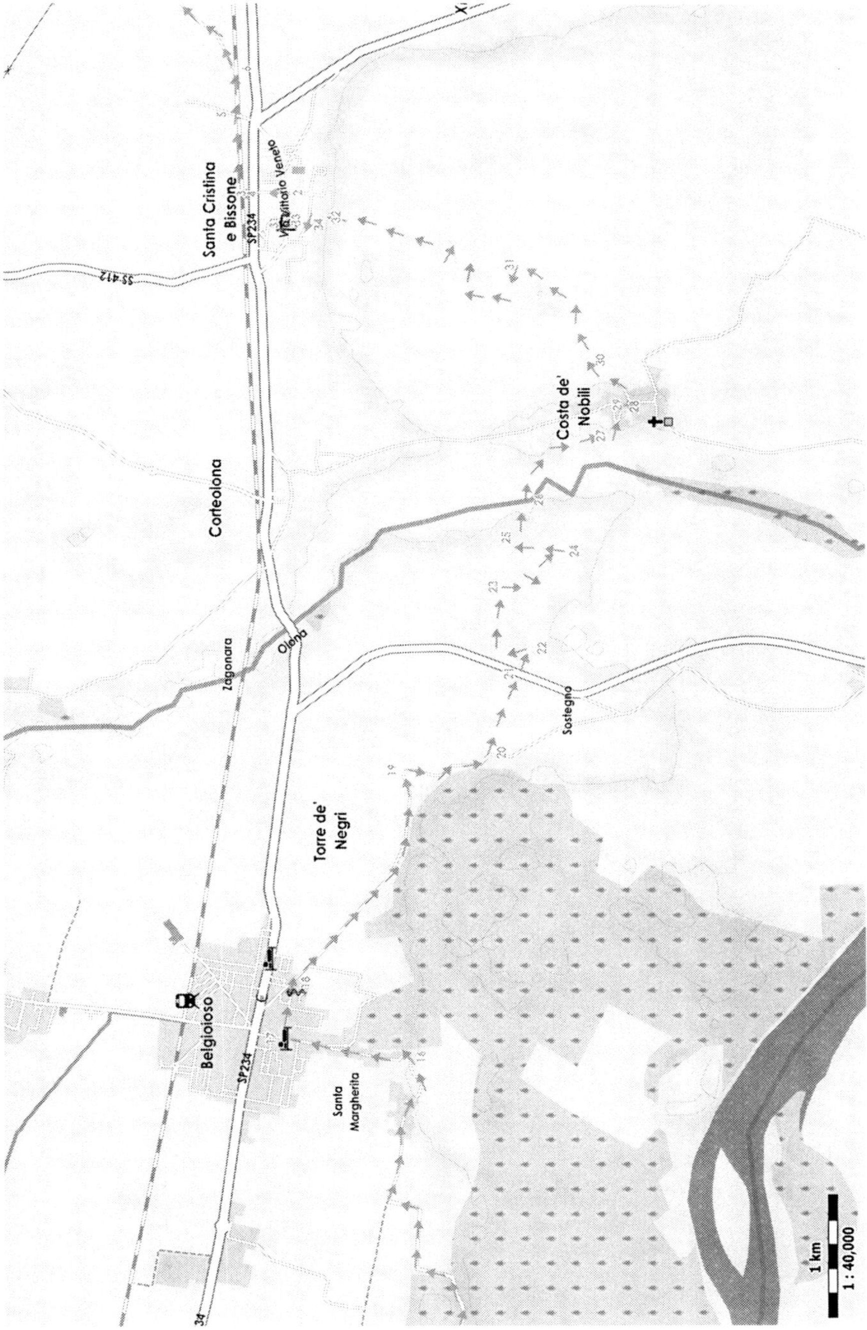
Santa Cristina
e Bissone
SP234
Via Vittorio Veneto
SS412
Corteolona
Costa de'
Nobili
Zagonara
Olona
Sostegno
Torre de'
Negri
Belgioioso
SP234
Santa
Margherita
1 km
1 : 40,000

Waypoint	Distance Between Waypoints (m)	Total (km)	Directions	Verification Point	Compass	Altitude (m)
62.024	700	21,8	At the T-junction turn left	VF sign	N	68
62.025	400	22,2	At the next junction, at the end of the field, continue straight ahead	Slightly downhill	E	68
62.026	300	22,5	Cross the bridge and continue straight ahead on the broad track beside the canal	Woodland to the right and canal close on the left	SE	57
62.027	1000	23,5	Turn left over the next bridge	Via Aldo Moro	E	58
62.028	260	23,7	At the T-junction turn right on the main road into the village of Costa de' Nobili	Via Roma	S	64
62.029	70	23,8	Turn left towards Cascina Padulino	Shortly after turning the tarmac gives way to an unmade road	NE	63
62.030	600	24,4	By the farm entrance continue straight ahead	Farm on the left	NE	55
62.031	1000	25,4	At the T-junction turn left		N	53
62.032	2200	27,5	Continue straight ahead into Santa Cristina	The unmade road returns to the tarmac via Italia	N	62
62.033	120	27,7	At the T-junction turn left	VF sign	NW	68
62.034	60	27,7	Take the next turning to the right	Via Gibelli, VF sign	N	69
62.035	160	27,9	Arrive at Santa-Cristina (XL) centre	Beside the church		70

Pavia to Santa-Cristina 27.9km

Religious Hostel

Parrocchia S.Michele Arcangelo - Abitazione del Parroco,Via Garibaldi, 34,27010 Miradolo-Terme(PV),Italy Tel:+39 0382 77116,Price:D,

Parrocchia di S.Cristina e Bissone,(Don Antonio Pedrazzini),Via Vittorio Veneto, 118,31055 Santa-Cristina(TV),Italy Tel:+39 0382 70106,Mobile:+39 3333 429685, santacristina@parrocchie.diocesi.pavia.it,www.parrocchiasantacristinaebisone.it,Price:D,

B&B, Hotel, Gite d'Etape

Hotel Gulliver,Via Cavallotti, 50,27011 Belgioioso(PV),Italy Tel:+39 0382 969666,Price:B,

La Locanda della Pesa Ristorante Albergo,Via 20 Settembre, 111,27011 Belgioioso(PV),Italy Tel:+39 0382 969073,Price:B,

Equestrian

La Castellana,Frazione San Giacomo,27011 Belgioioso(PV),Italy Tel:+39 0382 970207,

Banks and ATMs

Banca Popolare di Lodi,27010 Miradolo-Terme(PV),Italy Tel:+39 0382 721790,www.poplodi.it,

Istituto Bancario San Paolo di Torino,Piazza Vittorio Veneto, 15,27011 Belgioioso(PV),Italy Tel:+39 0382 969015,

Doctor

Salvi - Studio Medico,Via Amendola, 6,27011 Belgioioso(PV),Italy Tel:+39 0382 970567,

Stage Sixty-three Summary: we again use farm tracks and minor roads over generally level ground.

Distance to Saint-Peter's-Square: 729km Distance from Canterbury: 1345km

Stage Ascent: 39m Stage Descent: 55m

Waypoint	Distance Between Waypoints (m)	Total (km)	Directions	Verification Point	Compass	Altitude (m)
63.001	0	0,0	Facing the church in Santa Cristina turn right and proceed along the main street	Via Vittorio Veneto	E	70
63.002	220	0,2	Turn left on viale Rimembranze	Direction Stazione	N	70
63.003	270	0,5	Cross the main road (SS234) and continue straight ahead	Pedestrian traffic lights	N	67
63.004	100	0,6	Cross the railway line and immediately turn right on the path beside the railway	Open fields to the left and railway to the right	E	67
63.005	700	1,3	Turn right and then immediately left	Between the railway and the irrigation channel	E	67
63.006	400	1,7	Bear left over the irrigation channel		NE	66
63.007	2200	3,8	Cross the main road and continue straight ahead	Pass cemetery on your left	NE	67
63.008	500	4,3	In piazza del Comune in Miradolo Terme, bear right	Via Garibaldi	SE	68
63.009	300	4,6	Bear right	Via Garibaldi	S	69
63.010	90	4,7	Take the first turning to the left and follow the road into open country towards Camporinaldo	Via San Marco	SE	70
63.011	800	5,4	Take the left fork		E	65
63.012	1300	6,7	At the crossroads in the centre of Camporinaldo turn right	Via Cavour	S	69

Santa-Cristina to Orio-Litta 16.7km

45

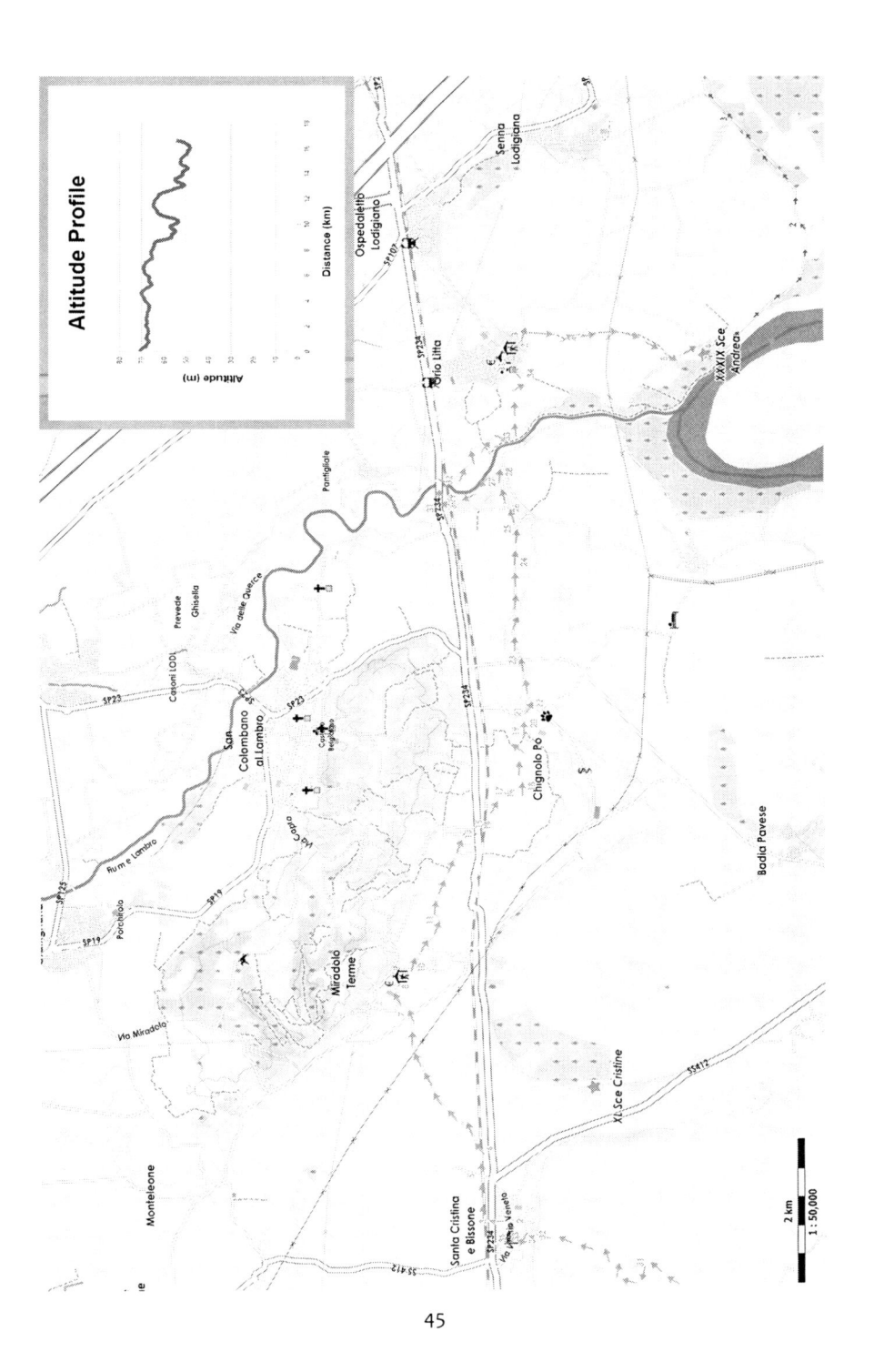

Waypoint	Distance Between Waypoints (m)	Total (km)	Directions	Verification Point	Compass	Altitude (m)
63.013	240	6,9	At the T-junction with the main road turn left and then cross the road using the pedestrian crossing beside the traffic lights and continue along the main road	SS234, via Cremona	E	68
63.014	130	7,1	Turn right on the first track between the fields	Towards the railway	S	67
63.015	140	7,2	Shortly after crossing the railway bear left		SE	66
63.016	500	7,7	Turn right	Towards the canal	S	65
63.017	130	7,8	Turn right	Cross small canal bridge	S	65
63.018	280	8,1	At the T-junction turn left	Initially parallel to canal	E	65
63.019	900	8,9	Continue straight ahead	Towards Chignolo Po	E	57
63.020	110	9,1	Continue straight ahead	Towards the town centre	E	56
63.021	160	9,2	Beside the castle continue straight ahead	Castle to the left	SE	56
63.022	130	9,3	At the traffic lights bear left	Via Garibaldi, towards Lambrinia	E	55
63.023	600	9,9	At the crossroads with the Strada Provinciale continue straight ahead	Towards Lambrinia	E	56
63.024	1400	11,3	Continue straight ahead on the cycle track	Pass cemetery on the right	E	63
63.025	500	11,8	At the fork bear left	Via Mameli	NE	64
63.026	300	12,1	Bear right	Via Bellaria	E	62

Santa-Cristina to Orio-Litta 16.7km

Waypoint	Distance Between Waypoints (m)	Total (km)	Directions	Verification Point	Compass	Altitude (m)
63.027	400	12,5	At the end of the tarmac road turn left and immediately right on the footpath	Near pink house	E	60
63.028	150	12,7	Turn left	Keep canal on your right	NW	57
63.029	700	13,3	Keep left	Remain beside canal	N	52
63.030	270	13,6	Turn left and immediately right towards the main road		NW	54
63.031	70	13,7	Using the guard rail for protection turn right at the T-junction with the main road	SS234, cross over river bridge	E	54
63.032	400	14,1	Immediately after crossing the river bridge, turn right onto the unmade road	Towards railway	SE	51
63.033	1500	15,6	Leave the embankment on the second track to the left	Towards Orio Litta and between fields	E	49
63.034	900	16,5	Beside the first houses in Orio Litta turn left on the tarmac road	Via Roma	NE	50
63.035	200	16,7	Arrive at Orio-Litta centre	Piazza dei Benedettini to the left		54

Santa-Cristina to Orio-Litta 16.7km

Pilgrim Hostel
Palestra Comunale,Piazza Aldo Moro, 2,26863 Orio-Litta(LO),Italy
Mobile:+39 3356 468587,Price:C,

Church or Religious Organisation
Cascina San Pietro,Piazza dei Benedettini,20080 Orio-Litta(LO),Italy
Tel:+39 0377 944436,Price:D,

B&B, Hotel, Gite d'Etape
B&B "la Conchiglia",Cascina Quaino, 4,27013 Chignolo-Po(PV),Italy
Tel:+39 3383 831889,Price:B,

Equestrian
Centro Ippico Visola,Strada dei Boschi, 29,26813 Graffignana(LO),Italy Tel:+39 0371 209237,

Banks and ATMs
Banca Popolare di Lodi,Via Giuseppe Mazzini, 2,26863 Orio-Litta(LO),Italy
Tel:+39 0377 833472,

Doctor
Zucca - Studio Medico,Via 8 Marzo,27013 Chignolo-Po(PV),Italy Tel:+39 0382 723095,

Veterinary
Ambulatorio Veterinario,Via Garibaldi, 138,27013 Chignolo-Po(PV),Italy
Tel:+39 0382 766531,

Stage Sixty-four Summary: the route leads from Orio Litta to the Pò ferry crossing on farm tracks and the Argine. From the ferry dock to the outskirts of Piacenza the route continues on pleasant country roads, but the long entry into Piacenza unfortunately uses the very busy via Emilia Pavese. An Alternate Route along the argine is available for those not able to take the ferry.

Distance from Canterbury: 1361km   Distance to Saint-Peter's-Square: 713km

Stage Ascent: 55m   Stage Descent: 48m

Waypoint	Distance Between Waypoints (m)	Total (km)	Directions	Verification Point	Compass	Altitude (m)
64.001	0	0,0	From piazza dei Benedettini bear right	Via Roma	E	54
64.002	300	0,3	At the T-junction beside Villa Litta bear right	Via Montemalo	SE	59
64.003	200	0,5	At the bottom of the hill bear right on the unmade road	Beside the water course, Cascina Cantarana	S	53
64.004	600	1,1	Take the left fork beside the gas sub-station	Remain beside the water course	S	49
64.005	1600	2,7	At the T-junction turn left on the embankment, Argine, above the river		SE	50
64.006	400	3,1	Turn right	Remain on the embankment	SW	48
64.007	300	3,4	Arrive beside the Pò river ferry (Guado di Sigerico). Note:- the ferry is only suitable for pedestrians or a small number of bikes. Horse riders and those not wishing to take the ferry will need to continue on the Alternate Route	Corte Sant'Andrea (XXXIX) to the left	SE	51
64.008	4400	7,8	After climbing from the ferry landing stage, proceed to the left on the gravel track	Pò on the left	E	48
64.009	700	8,5	At the fork in the track, bear right on grassy track	VF sign	SE	49
64.010	500	9,0	Turn right onto a minor road towards the village of Calendasco	VF sign	S	49

Orio-Litta to Piacenza 21,5km

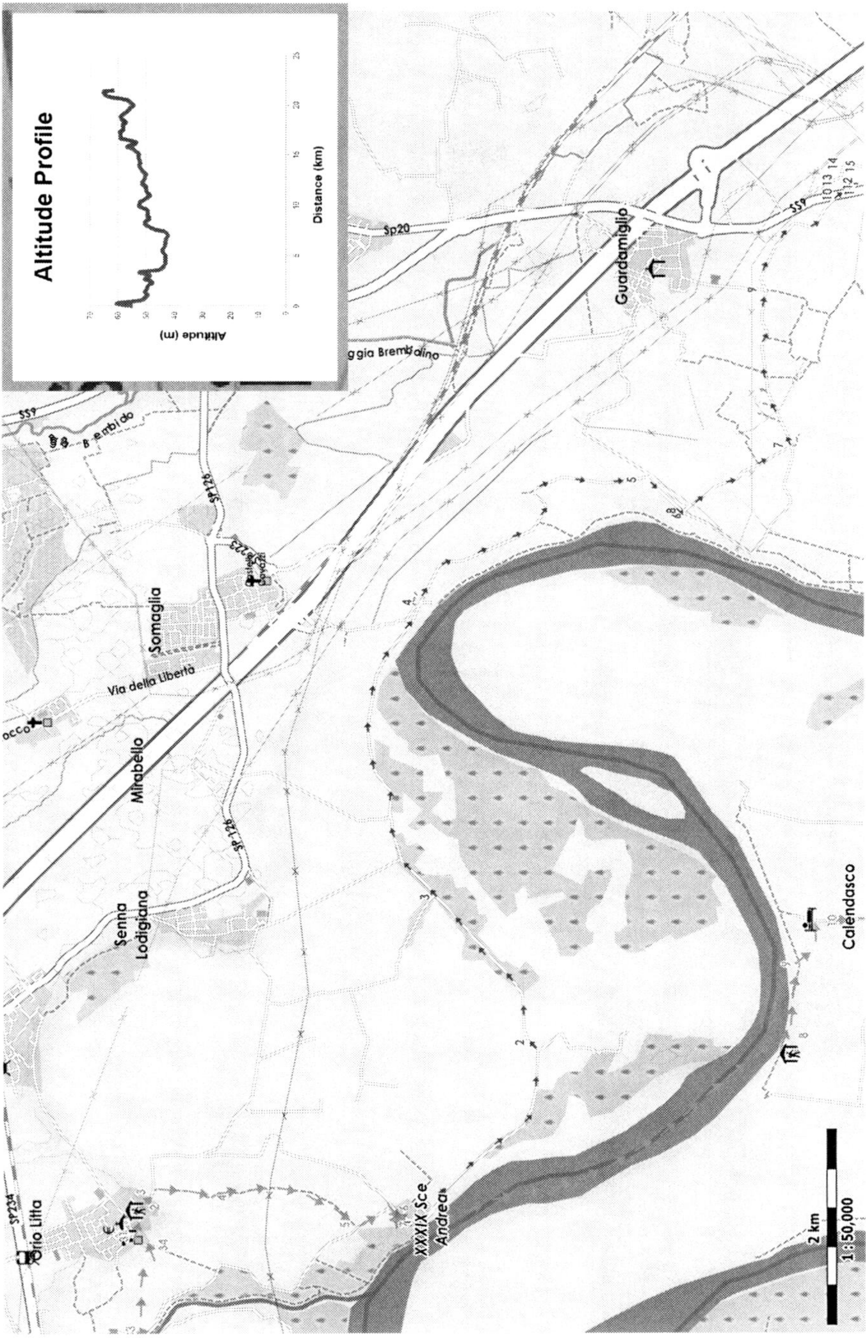
Altitude Profile
Altitude (m)
Distance (km)
Orio Litta
SP234
XXXIX Sce Andrea
Senna Lodigiana
Mirabello
Via della Libertà
Somaglia
SP126
SS9
Brembiolo
Sp20
Guardamiglio
Calendasco
2 km
1:50,000

Waypoint	Distance Between Waypoints (m)	Total (km)	Directions	Verification Point	Compass	Altitude (m)
64.011	900	9,9	At the crossroads, turn left directly in front of a large building - Commune di Calendasco	Via Mazzini	SE	52
64.012	2200	12,1	On the crown of the bend to the right, in the hamlet of Incrociata, turn left	Direction Cotrebbia Nuova, VF sign	SE	51
64.013	2000	14,0	At the fork in Malpaga, bear right	Towards Autostrada, VF sign	S	52
64.014	1600	15,7	After passing under the railway and the road bridges turn immediately right and climb the ramp		W	55
64.015	220	15,9	At the junction with the main road, turn right to cross the bridge and continue on the long straight via Emilia Pavese. Note:- caution narrow pavement over the long bridge beside the very busy road	Direction Piacenza	E	56
64.016	3700	19,6	At the roundabout in piazzale Torino turn left on via XXI Aprile	Fountain in roundabout	NE	55
64.017	300	19,9	At the next roundabout turn right on via Campagna	Pass park and citadel walls on the left	E	54
64.018	900	20,8	In piazza del Borgo go straight ahead	Via Garibaldi	SE	62
64.019	400	21,2	At the crossroads with corso Vittorio Emanuele II, go straight ahead. The Alternate Route joins from the left	Strada Sant'Antonino	SE	65
64.020	270	21,5	Arrive at Piacenza (XXXVIII) centre	Beside the church of Sant'Antonino		61

Orio-Litta to Piacenza 21,5km

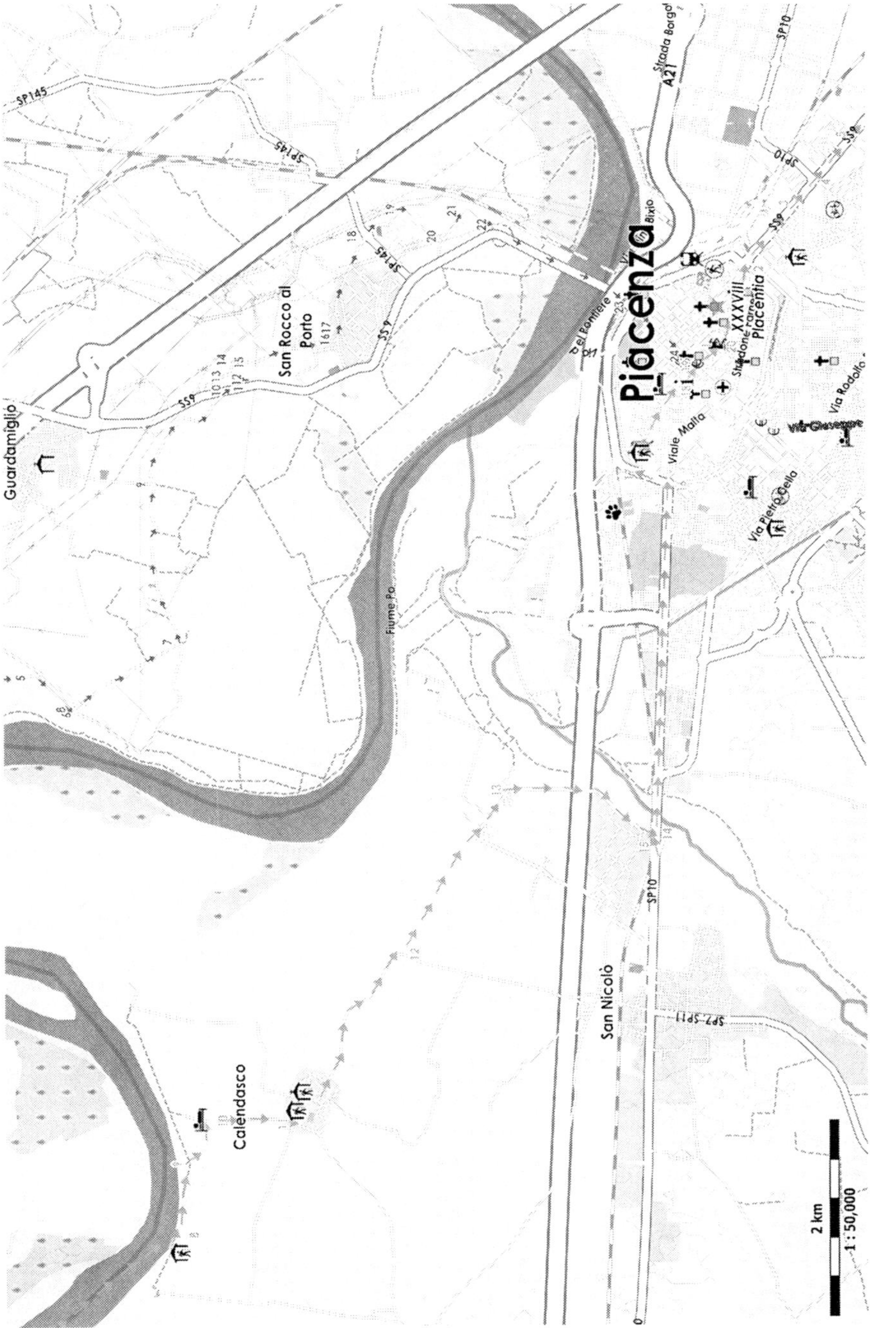
Guardamiglio
San Rocco al Porto
Piacenza
XXXVIII Placentia
Viale Malta
Via Pietro Cella
Fiume Po
Calendasco
San Nicolò
SP145
SS9
SP10
A21
2 km
1 : 50,000

Santuario Santa Maria di Campagna
XXXVIII Placentia
B&B Angela
Pilgrims
250 m
1 : 10,000
Via 21 Aprile
Via Pieve di Roncaglia
Via Cardinale Maculani
Via Alessio Tramello
Via Campagna
Via Trebbia
Via 24 Maggio
Viale Malta
Via Giuseppe Taverna
Via del Castello
Via Maddalena
Via Beverora
Via Venturini
Via Nova
Via Croce
Via San Giovanni
Via del Tempio
Corso Vittorio Emanuele II
Via Santa Franca
Stradone Farnese
Via San Siro
Via San Vincenzo
Via Sopramuro
Via Sant'Antonino
Corso Giuseppe Garibaldi
Via Cittadella
Via Camillo Cavour
Via Roma
Via Borghetto
Via San Marco
Viale Risorgimento
Via X Giugno
Via Giordano Bruno
Via delle Benedettine
Via Abbondanza
Via Abbadia
Via Francesco Alberoni
Via Giambattista Scalabrini
Via Cantarana
Via San Sepolcro
Via San Bartolomeo
Via Degani
Via Pietro Agnelli
Via Umberto Locati
Via Ubaldo Cassina
Via Valente Faustini
Via Mezzanini
Via del Pontiere
Strada della Raffalda
Via Guglielmo Da Saliceto
Via Carlo Maruli
Via Paolo Bozzini
Via Giacomo Puccini

Stage Summary: Alternate Route to Piacenza avoiding the Pò ferry

Stage Ascent: 0m   Stage Descent: 0m

Waypoint	Distance Between Waypoints (m)	Total (km)	Directions	Verification Point	Compass	Altitude (m)
64A1.001	0	0,0	Continue straight ahead	Remain on the Argine	SE	0
64A1.002	2400	2,3	Continue straight ahead on the embankment	Farm on the left	NE	0
64A1.003	1800	4,2	Continue straight ahead on the embankment	Village of Guzzafame on the left	E	0
64A1.004	3500	7,6	At the crossroads, continue straight ahead on the embankment		SE	0
64A1.005	3000	10,6	Bear right on the embankment	Parallel to the road below	SW	0
64A1.006	600	11,2	Beside the village of Valloria, turn sharp left to leave the embankment		SE	0
64A1.007	1400	12,5	At the junction with the embankment, turn left	Follow the embankment	NW	0
64A1.008	10	12,5	Turn right and pass through the centre of Valloria	Via Dante Alighieri	E	0
64A1.009	1700	14,2	Continue straight ahead	Remain on the embankment	SE	0
64A1.010	1400	15,7	Shortly before the T-junction with the main road, turn right on the gravel track	Pass industrial zone on your left	S	0

Alternate Route #64.A1 22.8km

53

Alternate Route #64.A1 22.8km

Waypoint	Distance Between Waypoints (m)	Total (km)	Directions	Verification Point	Compass	Altitude (m)
64A1.011	230	15,9	At the crossroads, turn left, carefully cross the main road and continue straight ahead into the industrial zone	Via Alberelle	E	0
64A1.012	70	16,0	Bear left on the road	Pass between industrial buildings	N	0
64A1.013	210	16,2	Bear right on the road		E	0
64A1.014	200	16,4	Bear right on the road		S	0
64A1.015	150	16,5	Take the left fork		S	0
64A1.016	900	17,4	At the crossroads in San Rocco al Porto, turn left	Via Giovanni Bosco	E	0
64A1.017	130	17,6	Continue straight ahead and skirt San Rocco al Porto on your right	Via Martiri della Libertà	E	0
64A1.018	1000	18,5	At the roundabout, continue straight ahead		SE	0
64A1.019	500	19,1	Bear right	Waterway on the left and industrial buildings on the right	SW	0
64A1.020	500	19,6	At the roundabout, turn left		SE	0
64A1.021	300	19,9	Bear right	Between car park and railway line	SW	0
64A1.022	400	20,3	At the roundabout, continue straight ahead and join the pedestrian path beside the main road	Cross the Pò bridge	SW	0
64A1.023	1600	21,9	At the roundabout, continue straight ahead	Memorial on roundabout	SW	0
64A1.024	800	22,7	Continue straight ahead on via Cavour	Pass Piazza Cavalli on the right	SW	0
64A1.025	160	22,8	At the crossroads, turn left and rejoin the Main Route	Via Sant'Antonio		0

Pilgrim Hostel

Caupona Sigerico,Località Soprarivo, 21,29010 Calendasco(PC),Italy
Tel:+39 0523 771607,Mobile:+39 3886 933850,ser.pe@libero.it,Price:D,

Ostello le Tre Corone,Via Mazzini Nuova, 59,29010 Calendasco(PC),Italy
Tel:+39 0523 772894,Mobile:+39 3341 866556,
mszaniboni@yahoo.co.uk,www.trecorone.it,Price:C,

Ostello Don Zermani,Via Luigi Zoni,29100 Piacenza(PC),Italy
Tel:+39 0523 712319,www.inyourlife.it,Price:B,

Religious Hostel

Parrocchia Corpus Domini,Strada Farnesiana, 24,29122 Piacenza(PC),Italy
Tel:+39 0523 592321,Price:D,

Ostello San Pietro,(Don Pietro Bulla),Via Emilia Parmense, 71,29100 Piacenza(PC),Italy
Tel:+39 0523 614256,Mobile:+39 3331 493595,sanlazzaro@libero.it,Price:D,

Santa Maria Assunta,Via Verdi, 1,29010 Calendasco(PC),Italy Tel:+39 0523 771497,Price:D,

Santuario Santa Maria di Campagna,Piazzale delle Crociate, 5,29121 Piacenza(PC),Italy
Tel:+39 0523 490728,
www.pro.iakke.it/2324473/convento_frati_minori_s_maria_di_campagna.html,

Church or Religious Organisation

San Giovanni Battista,Piazza 4 Novembre,26862 Guardamiglio(LO),Italy
Tel:+39 0377 51020,Price:D,

B&B, Hotel, Gite d'Etape

Pilgrims,Via G.Morigi, 36,29121 Piacenza(PC),Italy Tel:+39 0523 453527,Price:C,

B&B San Raimondo,Via Galileo Galilei,29100 Piacenza(PC),Italy
Tel:+39 0523 380150,Price:B,

B&B Angela,Via Giuseppe Mazzini,29100 Piacenza(PC),Italy Tel:+39 0523 499098,Price:B,

B&B Nicolini,Via Vittorio Cipelli, 41,29100 Piacenza(PC),Italy Tel:+39 0523 606091,Price:B,

Locanda il Masero,Loc.Masero, 2,29010 Calendasco(PC),Italy Tel:+39 0523 772787,Price:A,

Tourist Information

Provincia di Piacenza,Via Giuseppe Garibaldi, 50,29121 Piacenza(PC),Italy
Tel:+39 0523 7951,

Banks and ATMs

Deutsche Bank,Corso Vittorio Emanuele II, 8,29100 Piacenza(PC),Italy Tel:+39 0523 33981,

Unicredit,Largo Cesare Battisti, 26,29100 Piacenza(PC),Italy Tel:+39 0523 308211,

Banca Popolare,Piazzale Medaglie d'Oro, 7,29122 Piacenza(PC),Italy Tel:+39 0523 713081,

Banca di Piacenza,Via Genova, 37,29121 Piacenza(PC),Italy Tel:+39 0523 753401,

Banca di Piacenza,Via Giuseppe Mazzini, 20,29121 Piacenza(PC),Italy Tel:+39 0523 347336,

Travel

Stazione Ferrovie,Piazzale Marconi Snc, C/o C.C.Borgo Fax Hall,29100 Piacenza(PC),Italy
Tel:+39 06 6847 5475,www.renitalia.it,

Hospital

Azienda Unita' Sanitaria Locale di Piacenza,Corso Vittorio Emanuele II, 169,29121
Piacenza(PC),Italy Tel:+39 0523 301111,www.ausl.pc.it,

Hospital

Azienda Unita' Sanitaria Locale di Piacenza,Corso Vittorio Emanuele II, 169,29121 Piacenza(PC),Italy Tel:+39 0523 301111,www.ausl.pc.it,

Doctor

Zucchi Marco,Via Chiapponi, 46,29121 Piacenza(PC),Italy Tel:+39 0523 336921,

Studio Medico Associato Bossalini - Burgazzi - Moschini di G.Bossalini - E.Burgazzi - G.L.Moschini,Via Egidio Gorra, 53,29122 Piacenza(PC),Italy Tel:+39 0523 452538,

Veterinary

Ambulatorio Veterinario,Via Trebbia, 28,29121 Piacenza(PC),Italy Tel:+39 0523 490272,

Hiking Equipment

Vivo,Via Egidio Gorra, 5,29122 Piacenza(PC),Italy Tel:+39 0523 716432,

Eightysix,Via Martiri della Resistenza, 36,29122 Piacenza(PC),Italy Tel:+39 0523 751369,

Hobby Sport,Via Giulio Alberoni, 108,29121 Piacenza(PC),Italy Tel:+39 0523 328607,

Bicycle Shop

Ciclo Point Piacenza di Galante & C.Snc,Via Caduti Sulla strada,29122 Piacenza(PC),Italy Tel:+39 0523 606970,

Tuttociclismo Tizzoni Tuttociclismo di Tizzoni & C.Sas,Via Pietro Cella, 39a,29121 Piacenza(PC),Italy Tel:+39 0523 457578,

Stage Sixty-five Summary: a long section through farmland, finally leaving the rice fields behind. The exit from Piacenza follows the dangerous via Emilia. Thereafter we enter the countryside where again there is the difficulty of navigation with few distinct landmarks but also with a number of river crossings to be negotiated After leaving Piacenza, there are no real opportunities for intermediate stops and so be sure that you have sufficient water and food for the day.

Distance from Canterbury: 1383km Distance to Saint-Peter's-Square: 691km
Stage Ascent: 79m Stage Descent: 56m

Waypoint	Distance Between Waypoints (m)	Total (km)	Directions	Verification Point	Compass	Altitude (m)
65.001	0	0,0	From the church of Sant'Antonino continue straight ahead on via Sant'Antonino and via Scalabrini	Church to the right	E	60
65.002	900	0,9	In piazzale Roma continue straight ahead on the right side of the long, straight, broad road	Via Emilia Parmense	SE	58
65.003	1000	1,8	At the roundabout continue straight ahead on the via Emilia Parmense, SS9	Hotel ahead and cycle track on the right	SE	56
65.004	180	1,9	At the next roundabout continue straight ahead	Direction Parma, spire ahead	SE	55
65.005	700	2,6	Continue straight ahead at the traffic lights	Pass the Parrocchia San Lazzaro on the right	SE	54
65.006	500	3,1	Continue straight ahead at the traffic lights	Via Emilia Parmense, SS9	SE	54
65.007	500	3,5	Continue straight ahead on the pavement	Via Emilia Parmense, SS9	SE	54
65.008	600	4,1	At the junction continue straight ahead on the cycle path	Large commercial centre to the right	SE	57
65.009	250	4,3	With great care cross the major highway intersection and continue straight ahead	Via Emilia Parmense, SS9	SE	57
65.010	1000	5,3	Turn right to leave the via Emilia Parmese	Towards office complex	S	58
65.011	140	5,4	At the roundabout, turn left	Follow pedestrian	SE	58

Piacenza to Fiorenzuola-d'Arda 31.9km

XXXVIII
Placentia

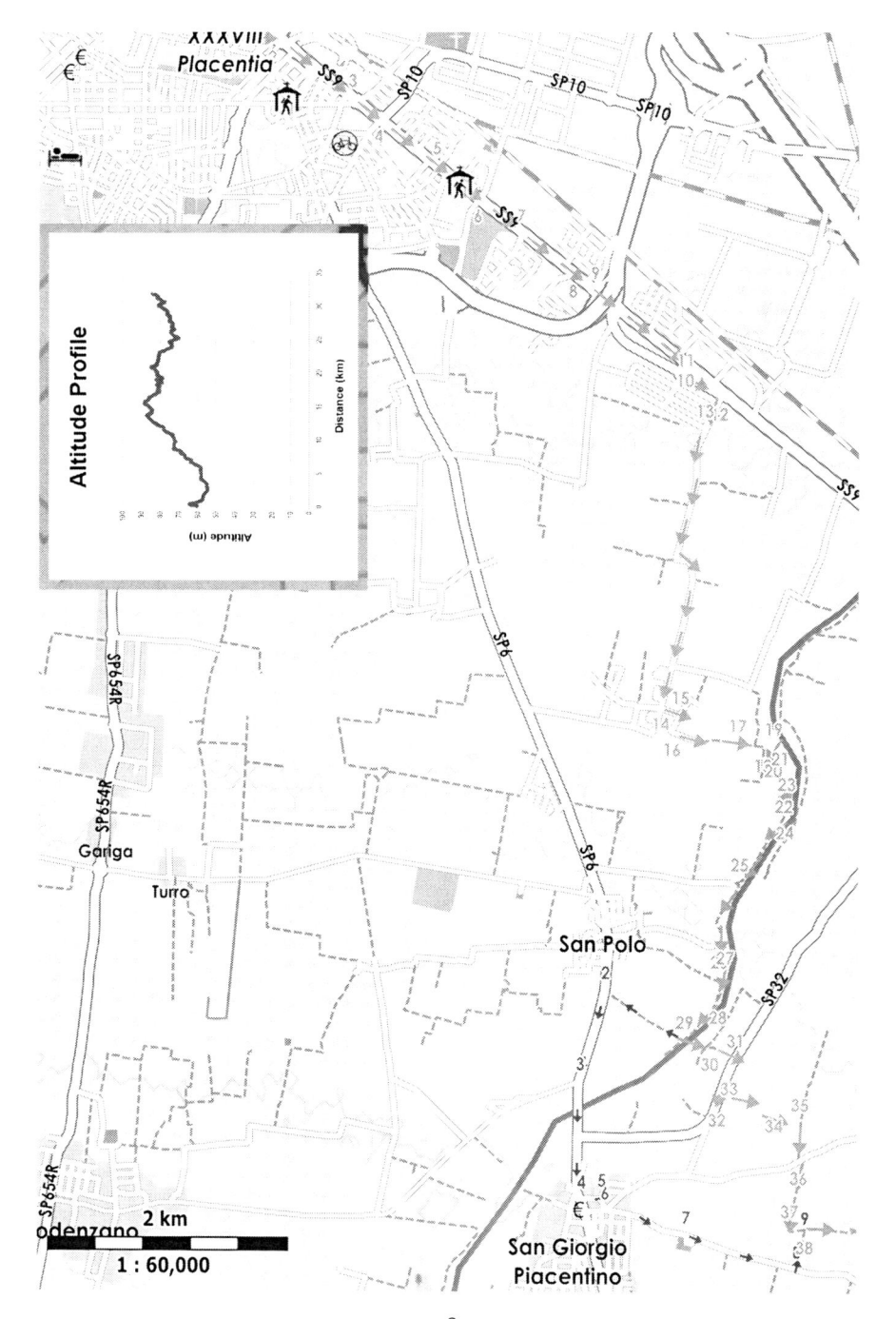

Altitude Profile

Gariga
Turro

San Polo

San Giorgio
Piacentino

odenzano 2 km
1 : 60,000

Waypoint	Distance Between Waypoints (m)	Total (km)	Directions	Verification Point	Compass	Altitude (m)
65.012	300	5,8	Bear right on the cycle track		SW	58
65.013	300	6,1	Bear left on the cycle track over the ditch and continue straight ahead on the country road	Pass telephone mast on your right!	S	58
65.014	2600	8,7	At the first crossroads in the hamlet of I Vaccari turn left on the road	Via L Rocci to the right at the junction	SE	72
65.015	180	8,8	At the T-junction turn right	Via G. Seti, VF sign	SW	72
65.016	160	9,0	At the T-junction, turn left on the tarmac road	Strada I Vaccari	E	72
65.017	600	9,6	Continue straight ahead on the white road	Farm buildings to the right	E	72
65.018	220	9,8	Continue straight ahead on the track	Metal gate	E	71
65.019	100	9,9	Turn right onto a partially obscured path into the trees	Path leads beside the river – torrente Nure	S	71
65.020	50	9,9	Fork left	VF sign	S	71
65.021	220	10,2	Fork left		S	72
65.022	100	10,3	At the junction, keep left	VF sign	S	72
65.023	130	10,4	Take the right fork	River visible on the left	S	72
65.024	120	10,5	Keep left on the path	Remain beside the river	SW	73
65.025	700	11,2	At the next intersection turn left	Remain beside the river, farm on your right	S	76
65.026	600	11,8	At the T-junction with the white road turn left	Remain beside the river, VF sign	S	77
65.027	300	12,1	Continue straight ahead	Between the fields and the river	S	79

Piacenza to Fiorenzuola-d'Arda 31.9km

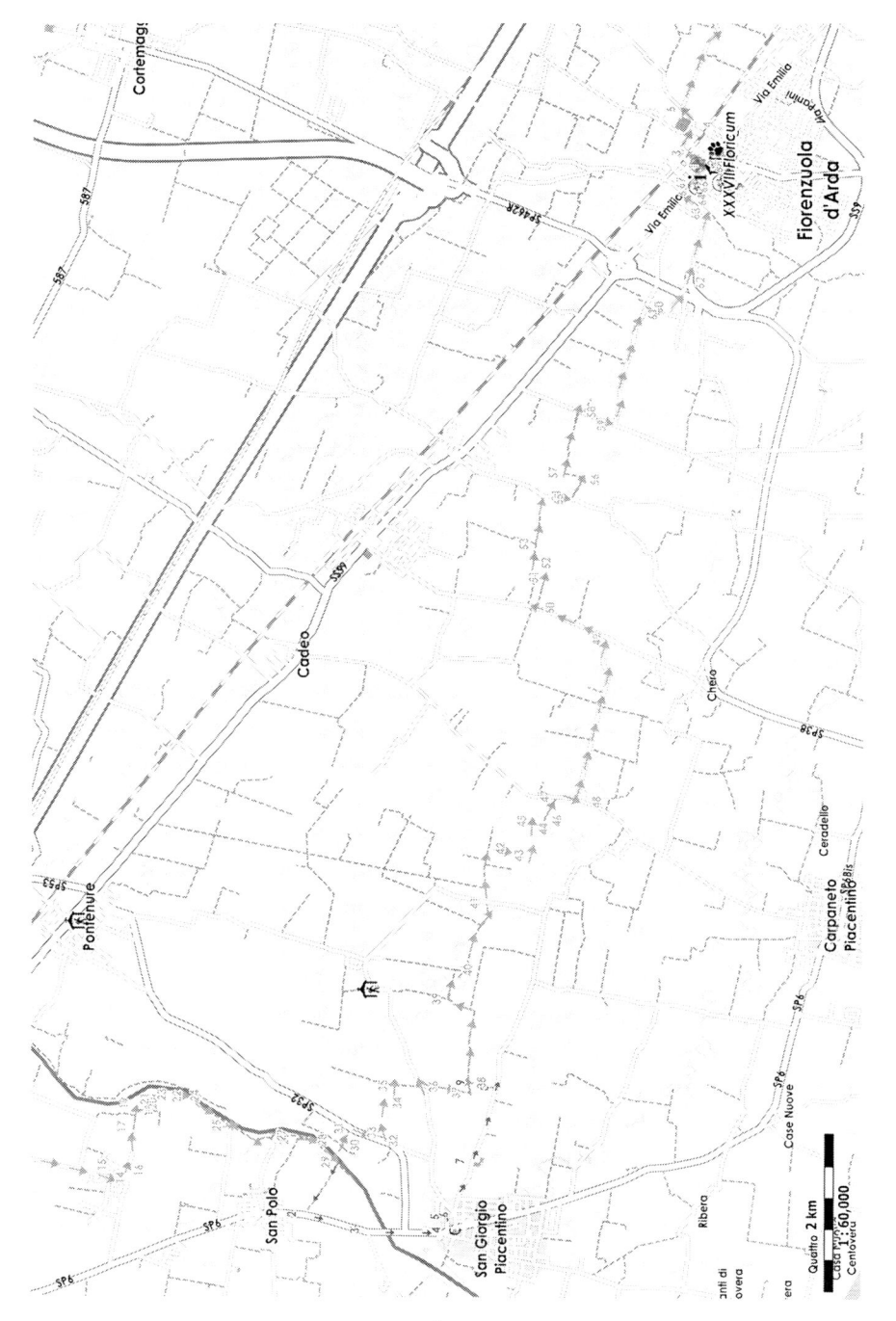

Waypoint	Distance Between Waypoints (m)	Total (km)	Directions	Verification Point	Compass	Altitude (m)
65.028	240	12,3	Turn left and then right	Remain beside the river	SW	81
65.029	500	12,8	At the crossroads turn left. Note:- there have been considerable earth works on the river banks, if the river crossing is not passable follow the Alternate Route to the right	Across the river ford	E	84
65.030	240	13,0	On the far side of the river, continue straight ahead	Towards the main road	SE	84
65.031	240	13,3	At the T-junction with the main road, turn right		S	85
65.032	400	13,7	Turn left, towards the farm	Strada privata	E	86
65.033	100	13,8	Pass through the farm buildings, turn left and then immediately right on the track		E	87
65.034	500	14,2	At the T-junction turn right	Remaining on the track	SE	84
65.035	300	14,5	At the T-junction turn right	Tarmac road	S	84
65.036	300	14,9	At the next T-junction turn left and then immediately right onto a white road	Località Montanaro	S	85
65.037	700	15,5	Turn left	Cascina del Lupo to the right	E	88
65.038	140	15,6	At the junction, continue straight ahead on the tarmac. Note:- Alternate Route joins from the right		E	87
65.039	1300	16,9	At the junction, next to a farm, turn right on the white road	At the end of the tarmac section	E	81
65.040	400	17,3	At the T-junction turn right		SE	80

Piacenza to Fiorenzuola-d'Arda 31.9km

61

Waypoint	Distance Between Waypoints (m)	Total (km)	Directions	Verification Point	Compass	Altitude (m)
65.041	1100	18,3	At the crossroads, continue straight ahead	Shortly after passing Castello di Paderna	E	80
65.042	700	19,1	After passing driveways on the right and left, turn right on the track	Towards trees	S	81
65.043	600	19,6	At the T-junction, turn left	Pass trees on your right	E	81
65.044	400	19,9	Bear right	Across the field	E	81
65.045	110	20,0	Turn right	Pass trees on your left, towards farm	S	81
65.046	140	20,2	At the T-junction, turn left	Farm on the right at the junction	SE	81
65.047	400	20,5	At the T-junction with the main road, turn right		S	82
65.048	300	20,9	On the entry to the hamlet of Zena, turn left	Towards Chero	E	84
65.049	2200	23,0	At the T-junction turn left. Note:- beware of the traffic	Strada Zappellazzo	NE	80
65.050	1000	24,0	After passing the tower in Zappellazzo turn right on the tarmac road		E	73
65.051	400	24,4	At the end of the tarmac road ford the torrente Chero and turn left on the track	Keep trees to the left and cultivated field to the right	NE	74
65.052	290	24,7	Turn right passing a barrier	Track between fields	E	74
65.053	250	25,0	Continue straight ahead on the white road	Ignore the turning to the left	E	71

Piacenza to Fiorenzuola-d'Arda 31.9km

Waypoint	Distance Between Waypoints (m)	Total (km)	Directions	Verification Point	Compass	Altitude (m)
65.054	600	25,6	At the T-junction with the tarmac road, turn right	Keep trees to the left	S	72
65.055	400	26,0	Take the next turning to the left	Towards the trees and fording torrente Chiavenna	SE	74
65.056	290	26,2	Shortly after the ford turn left	Between fields, with trees on the left	N	73
65.057	260	26,5	Bear right	Pass between two farms	E	72
65.058	800	27,3	At the T-junction with the tarmac road, turn right		S	73
65.059	500	27,8	Immediately after passing farm buildings, close on the left side of the road, turn left on the unmade road	Strada Vicinale della Felina	E	74
65.060	1600	29,4	Turn right on the tarmac road	VF sign	S	76
65.061	240	29,6	Bear left and then take the left fork		SE	78
65.062	500	30,1	At the road junction after the underpass continue straight ahead	VF sign	E	80
65.063	900	31,1	Follow the main road to the left	Enter Fiorenzuola-d'Arda	NE	80
65.064	300	31,4	Turn right on the cycle track	Cross the bridge over the river Arda	SE	81
65.065	130	31,5	Bear left towards the main road		NE	81
65.066	50	31,5	Take the pedestrian crossing over the main road and turn right towards the centre of the town	SS9	SE	81
65.067	110	31,6	Continue straight ahead on the main street	Corso Giuseppe Garibaldi	SE	82
65.068	260	31,9	Arrive at Fiorenzuola-d'Arda (XXXVII) centre	Crossroads with via della Liberazione		83

Piacenza to Fiorenzuola-d'Arda 31.9km

Stage Summary: Alternate Route bypassing river crossing

Stage Ascent: 17m   Stage Descent: 13m

Alternate Route #65-A1 4.9km

Waypoint	Distance Between Waypoints (m)	Total (km)	Directions	Verification Point	Compass	Altitude (m)
65A1.001	0	0,0	Turn right	Towards the farm	NW	84
65A1.002	800	0,8	At the T-junction with the main road	Turn left	S	86
65A1.003	800	1,6	Continue straight ahead	Direction San Giorgio	S	92
65A1.004	1000	2,6	Shortly after entering San Giorgio, turn left on via Garibaldi	Elaborately decorated house on the right at junction	E	100
65A1.005	180	2,8	Turn right	Via Manzoni	S	99
65A1.006	110	2,9	At the T-junction, turn left		E	98
65A1.007	700	3,6	Continue straight ahead on the road	Pass the cemetery on the right	E	96
65A1.008	1000	4,6	Take the next turning on the left		N	89
65A1.009	290	4,9	At the T-junction, turn right and rejoin the Main Route			88

Religious Hostel

Parrocchia di San Fiorenzo,Piazza Molinari Fratelli, 15,29017 Fiorenzuola-d'Arda(PC),Italy Tel:+39 0523 983401,parrocchiasanfiorenzo@tin.it,Price:D,

Oratorio S.Pietro Apostolo,Piazza Re Amato,29010 Pontenure(PC),Italy Tel:+39 0523 511342,Price:D,

Strada Valconasso 10,29010 Pontenure Pc,Italy,Frazione Valconasso,29010 Pontenure(PC),Italy Tel:+39 0523 517110,Price:B,

B&B, Hotel, Gite d'Etape

Albergo Concordia,Via 20 Settembre, 54,29017 Fiorenzuola-d'Arda(PC),Italy Tel:+39 0523 984841,Price:B,

Tourist Information

Comune di Fiorenzuola d'Arda,Corso Giuseppe Garibaldi, 53,29017 Fiorenzuola-d'Arda(PC),Italy Tel:+39 0523 9891,

Banks and ATMs

Banca Farnese,Via Risorgimento,29017 Fiorenzuola-d'Arda(PC),Italy Tel:+39 0523 985053,

Banca Nazionale del Lavoro,Via Scapuzzi, 2,29017 Fiorenzuola-d'Arda(PC),Italy Tel:+39 0523 983626,

Banca di Piacenza,Via Patrioti, 9,29019 San-Giorgio-Piacentino(PC),Italy Tel:+39 0523 377219,

Hospital

Ospedale Civile,Via Roma, 35,29017 Fiorenzuola-d'Arda(PC),Italy Tel:+39 0523 9890,

Doctor

Bazzani - Medico Chirurgo,Piazza Molinari Fratelli, 5,29017 Fiorenzuola-d'Arda(PC),Italy Tel:+39 0523 983411,

Anelli - Medico Chirurgo,Piazza Verdi,29017 Fiorenzuola-d'Arda(PC),Italy Tel:+39 0523 981770,

Veterinary

Carolfi - Veterinario,Via Mischi, 7,29017 Fiorenzuola-d'Arda(PC),Italy Tel:+39 0523 984494,

Hiking Equipment

Ivan Sport,Via Brunani, 14,29017 Fiorenzuola-d'Arda(PC),Italy Tel:+39 0523 982748,

Bicycle Shop

Bici Sprint di Graffi,Viale Giacomo Matteotti, 52,29017 Fiorenzuola-d'Arda(PC),Italy Tel:+39 0523 943165,

Cigala Cicli di Stori Sergio,Viale Giacomo Matteotti, 5,29017 Fiorenzuola-d'Arda(PC),Italy Tel:+39 0523 941730,

Stage Sixty-six Summary: a gentle stage on level ground generally using country roads
Distance from Canterbury: 1415km   Distance to Saint-Peter's-Square: 659km
Stage Ascent: 54m   Stage Descent: 60m

Waypoint	Distance Between Waypoints (m)	Total (km)	Directions	Verification Point	Compass	Altitude (m)
66.001	0	0,0	From the centre of Fiorenzuola, near N° 55 Corso Garibaldi, turn left onto the narrow street	Via della Liberazione	NE	83
66.002	90	0,1	At the crossroads, continue straight ahead	Direction Busseto, VF sign	NE	81
66.003	210	0,3	Pass under the railway and bear right on the road	Viale dei Tigli	E	76
66.004	400	0,7	Bear left on the pavement on the left side of the road	Pass beside the cemetery	NE	75
66.005	250	1,0	Just after the cemetery, cross the road and turn right	Towards agriturismo Battibue	E	71
66.006	2200	3,1	At the T-junction at the end of the road turn right	Towards farm on the left of the road	S	62
66.007	500	3,6	Turn left on the road	Towards Chiaravalle, VF sign	E	66
66.008	1500	5,1	Continue straight ahead on the pathway on the left side of the road	Pass cemetery on the left	E	57
66.009	800	5,8	Continue straight ahead	Towards the Abbey courtyard	E	54
66.010	110	6,0	In front of the Abbey of Chiaravalle de Colomba bear left to follow the road	Towards Busseto	NE	54
66.011	700	6,7	Continue straight ahead	Cross Autostrada bridge	E	49
66.012	1600	8,2	Bear left on the road and ignore the junction to the right	Beside Cascina Ongina	N	52
66.013	300	8,5	Continue straight ahead on strada Borre	Beside the entrance to the village of San Rocco	N	53
66.014	230	8,8	Turn right	Before reaching church	E	52

Fiorenzuola-d'Arda to Fidenza 22.3km

66

67

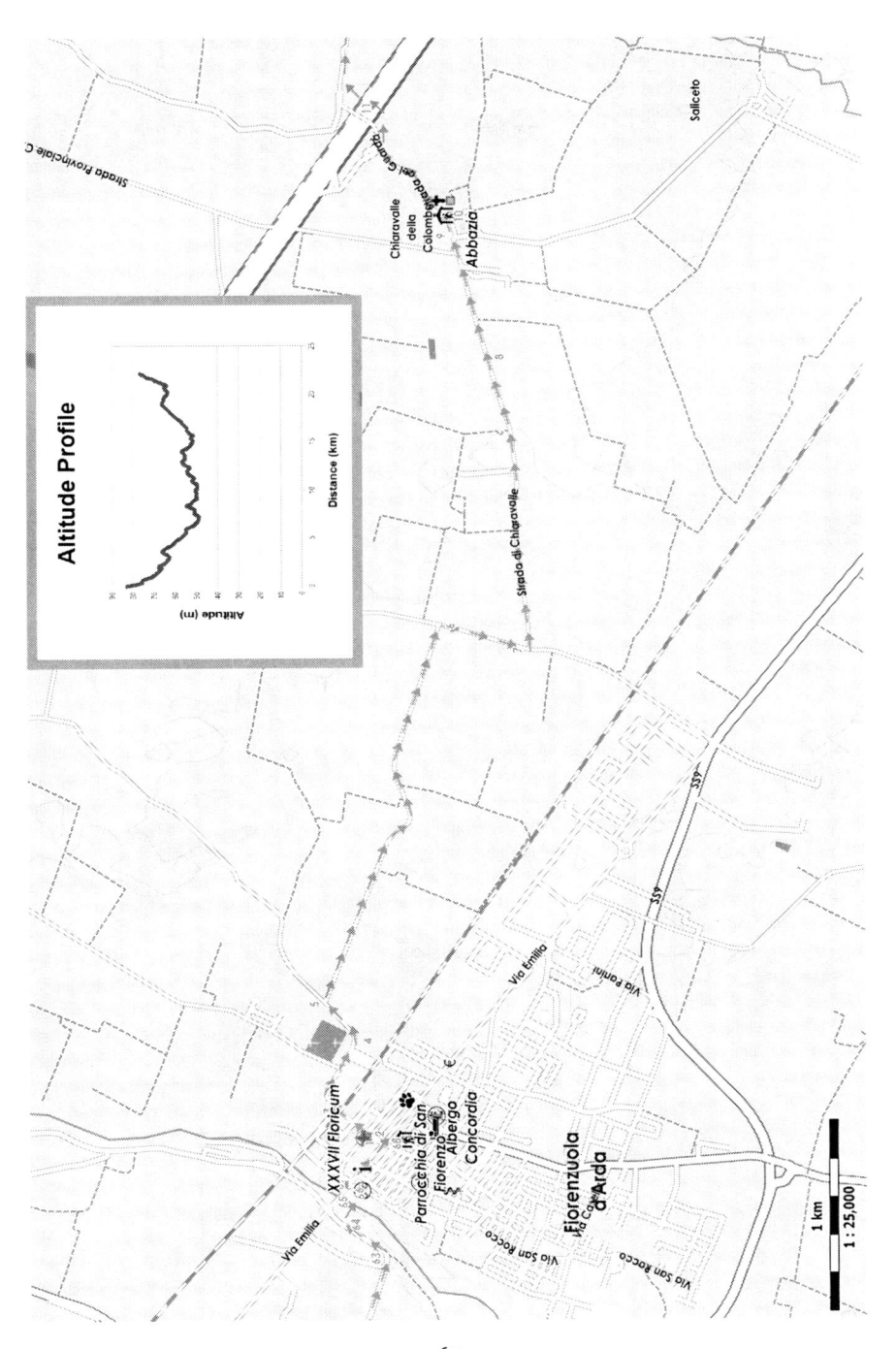

Waypoint	Distance Between Waypoints (m)	Total (km)	Directions	Verification Point	Compass	Altitude (m)
66.015	700	9,4	At the T-junction at the end of the road turn left	Industrial area ahead at junction	N	49
66.016	140	9,6	Take the next turn to the right	Strada Orsi	SE	50
66.017	400	10,0	Bear right on the tarmac	Pass barn on the right	S	50
66.018	140	10,1	Bear left on the unmade road	Entrance to farm on the right	E	50
66.019	600	10,7	At the crossroads, turn right	Bridge ahead	SW	49
66.020	900	11,6	Continue straight ahead on strada Fossa Superiore	Ignore the turning on the tarmac road to the left	S	52
66.021	400	12,0	At the T-junction with a tarmac road turn left	Strada Portone	E	54
66.022	1500	13,4	At the T-junction, turn left	Direction Fidenza	NE	55
66.023	100	13,6	At the traffic lights, turn right	Direction Fidenza	SE	55
66.024	240	13,8	After rounding the first bend turn left	Towards Bastelli	E	55
66.025	130	13,9	At the T-junction turn right	Towards Bastelli	E	56
66.026	900	14,9	Continue straight ahead on the long straight road	Cross railway	E	52
66.027	1200	16,0	At the T-junction turn right	Towards Bastelli	S	53
66.028	1000	17,0	In hamlet of Bastelli with silos on the right, turn left	Towards Soragna	SE	56
66.029	120	17,1	Turn right on the road	Towards Fidenza	S	56

Fiorenzuola-d'Arda to Fidenza 22.3km

Waypoint	Distance Between Waypoints (m)	Total (km)	Directions	Verification Point	Compass	Altitude (m)
66.030	1900	19,0	Turn left	Towards Fidenza	E	66
66.031	400	19,4	At the crossroads, continue straight ahead	Direction Fidenza	E	65
66.032	500	19,9	Continue straight ahead	Cross Ponte Sigerico	SE	64
66.033	400	20,3	Keep right on the main road		SW	63
66.034	700	20,9	Continue straight ahead	Pass under highway	SW	64
66.035	700	21,6	At the traffic lights turn right under the railway	Car park on the left at the junction	S	70
66.036	130	21,8	After emerging from under the railway, turn right direction Duomo	Pass Hotel Astoria on the left	W	73
66.037	400	22,2	Continue straight ahead at the roundabout and then quickly bear left towards the old city gate	Piazza Grandi, large VF sign on entry to piazza	SW	76
66.038	100	22,3	Arrive at Fidenza (XXXVI) centre	Piazza Cremoni, beside the Duomo		77

Florenzuola-d'Arda to Fidenza 22.3km

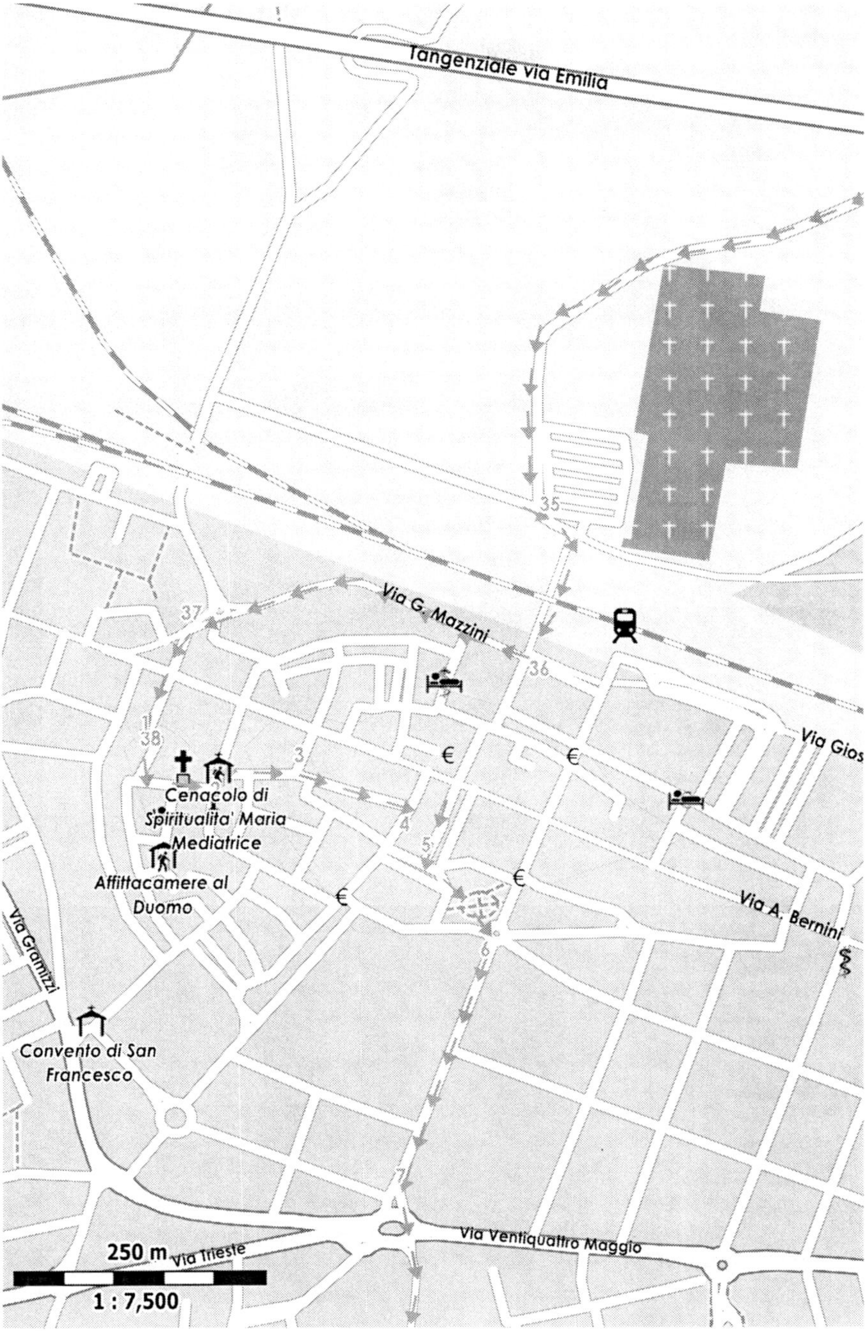
Tangenziale via Emilia
35
Via G. Mazzini
37
36
38
3
Via Gios
Cenacolo di Spiritualita' Maria Mediatrice
Affittacamere al Duomo
4
5
Via A. Bernini
Via Gramizzi
6
Convento di San Francesco
7
Via Ventiquattro Maggio
250 m
Via Trieste
1 : 7,500

Pilgrim Hostel

Affittacamere al Duomo,Via Arnaldo Da Brescia, 2,43036 Fidenza(PR),Italy Tel:+39 0524 523930,Price:B,

Religious Hostel

Abbazia,Chiaravalle della Colomba,29010 Alseno(PC),Italy Tel:+39 0523 940132,Price:D,

Parrocchia di S.Tommaso Becket,Via Cabriolo,43036 Fidenza(PR),Italy Tel:+39 9052 481912,Mobile:+39 3294 130656, parrocchiadicabriolo@libero.it,cabriolo.altervista.org,Price:D,

Cenacolo di Spiritualita' Maria Mediatrice,Via Micheli, 19,43036 Fidenza(PR),Italy Tel:+39 0524 528070,

Church or Religious Organisation

Convento di San Francesco,Via Lorenzo Berzieri,43036 Fidenza(PR),Italy Tel:+39 2035 520118,Price:D,

B&B, Hotel, Gite d'Etape

Pizzeria Ristorante Albergo Ugolini,Via Cornini Malpeli, 90,43036 Fidenza(PR),Italy Tel:+39 0524 83264,Price:C,

Affittacamere al Duomo Pizzati Renato - Affittacamere,Via Arnaldo Da Brescia, 2,43036 Fidenza(PR),Italy Tel:+39 0524 523930,Price:C,

Hotel Ponte,43036 Fidenza(PR),Italy Tel:+39 0524 522115,Price:B,

Hotel Astoria,Via Gandolfi, 5,43036 Fidenza(PR),Italy Tel:+39 0524 524314,Price:A,

Equestrian

Centro Ippico Montevalle – Castelnuovo Fogliani,Strada di Montevalle,29010 Alseno(PC),Italy Tel:+39 0523 1880990,

Tourist Information

Associazione Europea delle Vie Francigene,Piazza Duomo,43036 Fidenza(PR),Italy Tel:+39 7513 517380, segreteriagenerale@associazioneviafrancigena.it,www.viafrancigena.eu,

Banks and ATMs

Banca Popolare di Vicenza,Via Malpeli Cornini, 13,43036 Fidenza(PR),Italy Tel:+39 0524 528180,

Banca di Piacenza,Via Benedetto Bacchini, 2/4,43036 Fidenza(PR),Italy Tel:+39 0524 533436,

Banca Popolare,Piazza Giuseppe Garibaldi, 24,43036 Fidenza(PR),Italy Tel:+39 0524 523928,

Credito Emiliano,Via Antonio Gramsci, 49,43036 Fidenza(PR),Italy Tel:+39 0524 528461,

Banca Monte Parma,Via Ventiquattro Maggio, 66,43036 Fidenza(PR),Italy Tel:+39 0524 522178,

Unicredit,Via Agostino Berenini, 57,43036 Fidenza(PR),Italy Tel:+39 0524 202011,

Banca Cremonese,Via 24 Maggio,43036 Fidenza(PR),Italy Tel:+39 0524 533309,

Banca Monte dei Paschi di Siena,Via Antonio Gramsci, 1,43036 Fidenza(PR),Italy Tel:+39 0524 528361,

Banca Popolare di Lodi,Via Malpeli Cornini, 56,43036 Fidenza(PR),Italy Tel:+39 0524 520274,

Travel

Stazione Ferrovie,Via Giuseppe Mazzini,43036 Fidenza(PR),Italy Tel:+39 06 6847 5475,www.renitalia.it,

Hospital

Fidenza San Secondo,Via Don Tincati, 5,43036 Fidenza(PR),Italy Tel:+39 0524 515111,www.ausl.pr.it/page.asp?IDCategoria=625&IDSezione=3930,

Doctor

Medical Center Srl,Via Andrea Costa, 3,43036 Fidenza(PR),Italy Tel:+39 0524 528110,

Lannutti Ferdinando,43036 Fidenza(PR),Italy Tel:+39 0524 523476,

Veterinary

Cattivelli - Medico Veterinario,Frazione Fornio,43036 Fidenza(PR),Italy Tel:+39 0524 60171,

Hiking Equipment

Fitness,Via 24 Maggio,43036 Fidenza(PR),Italy Tel:+39 0524 84328,

Fiorenzuola-d'Arda to Fidenza 22.3km

Stage Sixty-seven Summary: after leaving Fidenza the well marked route begins to climb into the beautiful, rolling foothills of the Appenines. The section is largely conducted on small country roads and tracks, but can be challeging in hot weather.

Distance from Canterbury: 1437km   Distance to Saint-Peter's-Square: 637km

Stage Ascent: 152m   Stage Descent: 88m

Waypoint	Distance Between Waypoints (m)	Total (km)	Directions	Verification Point	Compass	Altitude (m)
67.001	0	0,0	From piazza Cremoni beside the Duomo pass in front of the church and turn left to skirt the church	Church on the left	SE	77
67.002	120	0,1	At the rear of the church turn right	Pedestrian zone, via Micheli. VF sign	E	79
67.003	80	0,2	Continue straight ahead across the small square and take via Antini	VF sign	E	80
67.004	110	0,3	Continue straight ahead in piazza del Palazzo, pass under the porch and turn right	Via Amendola	S	81
67.005	90	0,4	Bear left across the small park	Keep playground on your left	SE	80
67.006	90	0,5	At the roundabout turn right into the tree lined street	Via Gramsci	S	80
67.007	290	0,8	At the roundabout, cross the main road – via 24 Maggio – and bear a little to the left towards the trees	Via Caduti di Cefalonia	S	78
67.008	900	1,7	At the roundabout continue straight ahead on the cycle track	Sports ground to the right before the roundabout	S	77
67.009	300	2,0	Continue straight ahead keeping to the left side of the road		S	79
67.010	180	2,2	Continue straight ahead. Note:- at the cost of bypassing Piave Cabriolo (dedicated to Thomas Becket), 500m may be saved by turning left across the fields and rejoining the Main Route at the next road crossing	Footpath sign and small wooden bridge on the left	S	79
67.011	230	2,4	Shortly after passing farm on the left, bear left on the tree lined track	VF sign	SE	80
67.012	400	2,8	Bear right into the trees	Towards Pieve di Cabriolo	S	82

Fidenza to Costamezzana 11.7km

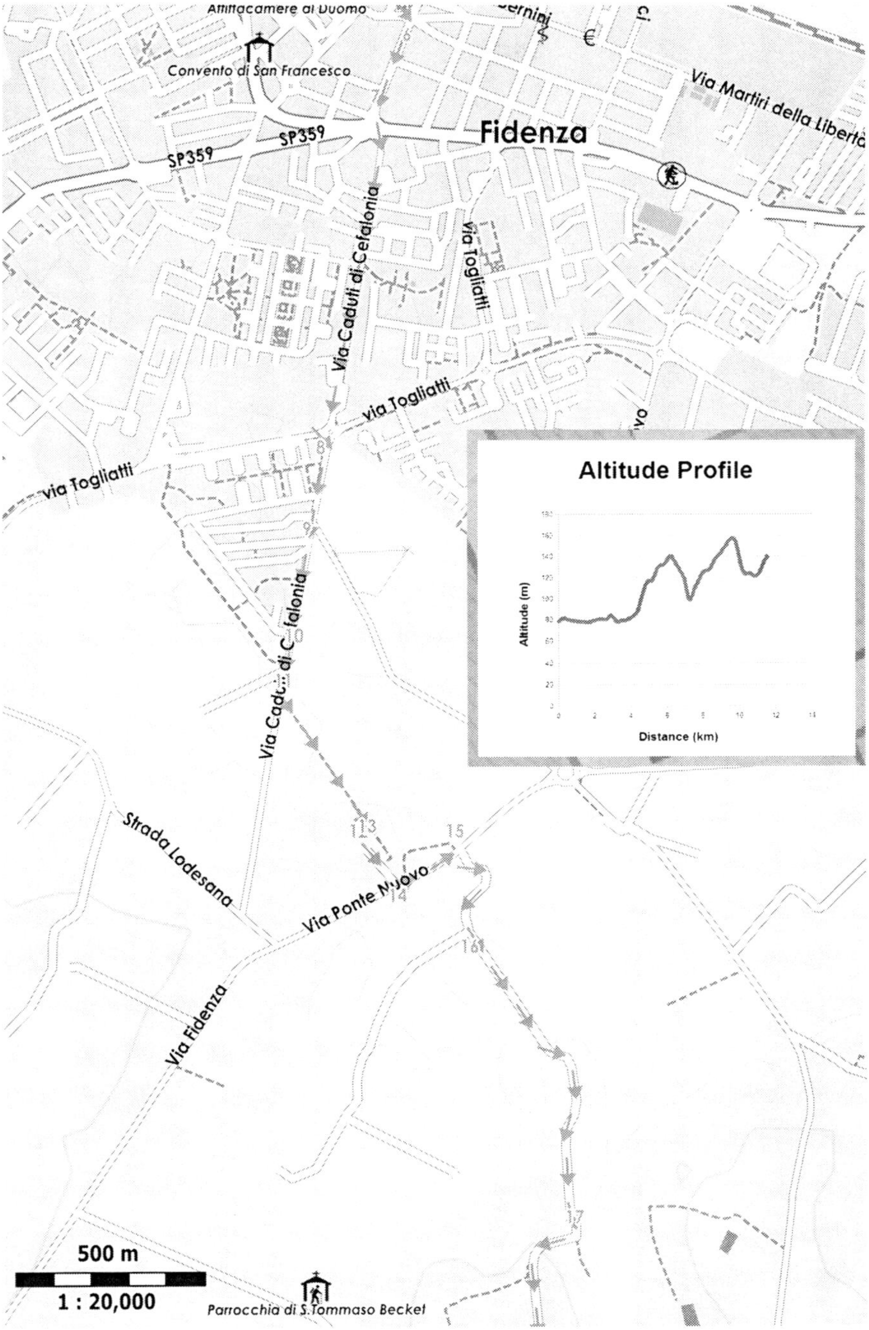

Affittacamere al Duomo
Convento di San Francesco
Via Martiri della Libertà
Fidenza
SP359
SP359
Via Caduti di Cefalonia
Via Togliatti
via Togliatti
via Togliatti
Altitude Profile
Altitude (m)
Distance (km)
Strada Lodesana
Via Ponte Nuovo
Via Fidenza
500 m
1 : 20,000
Parrocchia di S.Tommaso Becket

Santa Margherita

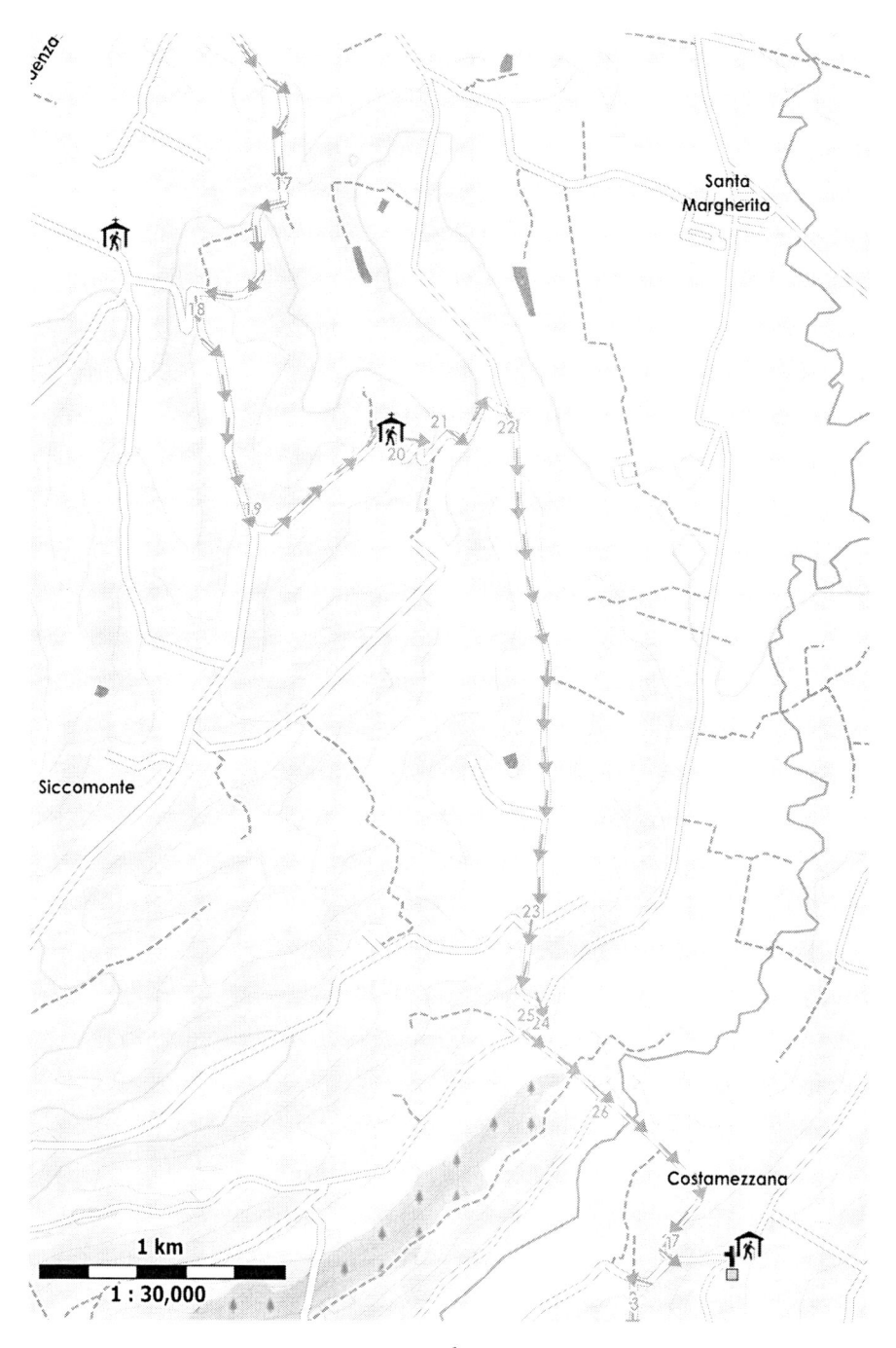

Siccomonte

Costamezzana

1 km
1 : 30,000

Waypoint	Distance Between Waypoints (m)	Total (km)	Directions	Verification Point	Compass	Altitude (m)
67.013	80	2,9	Turn left on the tarmac driveway	Bell tower on your right at the junction	SE	83
67.014	170	3,1	At the T-junction with the main road, turn left	Pass cheese producer on left	NE	81
67.015	170	3,2	Take the first turning to the right	Towards trees, VF sign	S	78
67.016	280	3,5	Continue straight ahead on the unmade road	Ignore the turning to the right	S	78
67.017	1000	4,5	Turn right towards the hilltop	Via Cabriolo	SW	90
67.018	700	5,2	At the junction with a tarmac road – on a sharp bend – turn left	Uphill, towards the top of the ridge	S	116
67.019	1100	6,2	Turn left	Towards Siccomonte	NE	140
67.020	800	7,0	In front of the Chiesa di Siccomonte turn right then left on the grassy path, downhill	Keep church to the left	E	117
67.021	180	7,2	Leave the grass and turn left on the road		NE	102
67.022	400	7,6	At the T-junction at the top of the hill, turn right on the tarmac road	Direction Tabiano, VF sign	S	109
67.023	2200	9,8	Take the left fork	Towards Pieve Cusignano, VF sign	S	154
67.024	400	10,2	At the T-junction, at the bottom of the hill, turn right, towards Costamezzana	Osteria on your left at the junction	SW	128
67.025	130	10,3	Turn left	Towards Costamezzana	SE	124
67.026	400	10,7	Keep left	Towards Costamezzana, VF sign	SE	123
67.027	1000	11,7	Arrive at Costamezzana	Village centre ahead		140

Fidenza to Costamezzana 11.7km

Pilgrim Hostel

Ostello Comunale di Costamezzana,Via All'Isola, 1,43015 Noceto(PR),Italy
Tel:+39 0521 629149,Price:C,PR,

Religious Hostel

Casa di Preghiera S.Giovanni Battista,Frazione Siccomonte,43036 Fidenza(PR),Italy
Tel:+39 9052 463408,Mobile:+39 3492 825720,www.siccomonte.135.it,Price:C,

Stage Sixty-eight Summary: the route continues to climb and fall on farm tracks and some small roads. Great care needs to be exercised on the final approach to Fornovo where the traffic can be heavy on the river bridge.

Distance from Canterbury: 1449km   Distance to Saint-Peter's-Square: 625km

Stage Ascent: 400m   Stage Descent: 393m

Waypoint	Distance Between Waypoints (m)	Total (km)	Directions	Verification Point	Compass	Altitude (m)
68.001	0	0,0	From the junction at the entrance to Costamezzana, turn towards the Castello	Note:- at the time of writing there is a VF sign pointing the wrong way	SW	140
68.002	200	0,2	At the crossroads, just before reaching the farm, turn left	Via Costa Canali, VF sign	S	140
68.003	190	0,4	Take the narrow road to the left	Towards the Hostaria Castello, VF sign	S	151
68.004	1000	1,4	Beside the Castello di Costamezzana bear left and immediately right	Keep trees close on your right, VF sign	SW	216
68.005	700	2,0	At the junction in the tracks, continue straight ahead between the vines	Farm immediately on the left	SW	248
68.006	500	2,6	At the T-junction, turn left on the tarmac road	Towards the houses on the sky-line	S	284
68.007	110	2,7	At the T-junction turn right	Leaving via Costa Canali	SW	288
68.008	700	3,3	On the crown of the bend to the right, take the track downhill to the left	VF sign, towards small wood	SE	276
68.009	700	4,0	Beside the first farm, continue straight ahead	VF sign	E	223
68.010	270	4,3	Bear right towards the road below		S	193
68.011	140	4,4	At the T-junction turn left on the grass track		E	193
68.012	80	4,5	At the junction with the tarmac road, continue straight ahead, then bear right downhill	Pass house on your left	SE	193

Costamezzana to Fornovo-di-Taro 22.3km

79

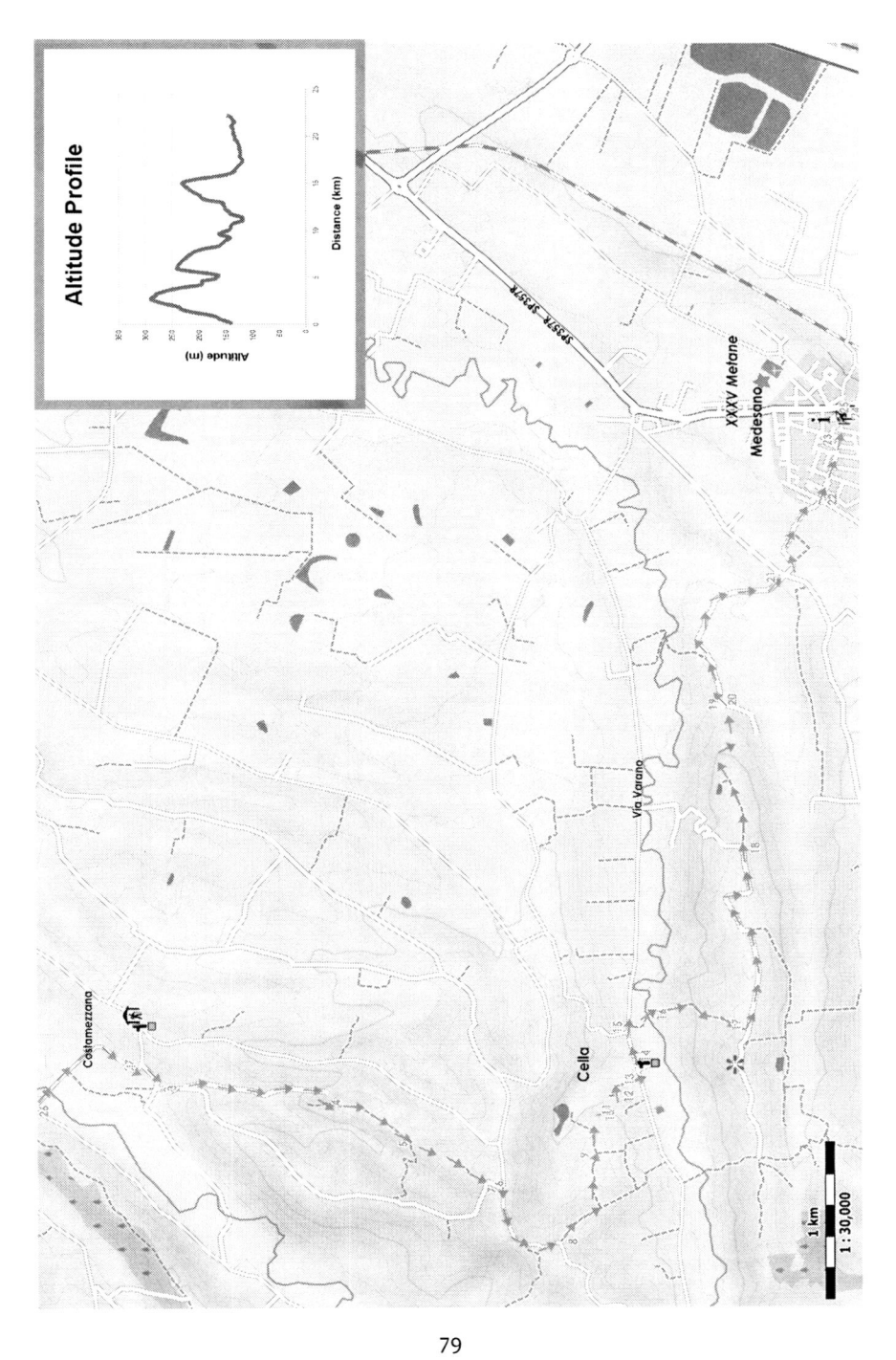

Waypoint	Distance Between Waypoints (m)	Total (km)	Directions	Verification Point	Compass	Altitude (m)
68.013	230	4,7	At the T-junction with the main road, turn left and follow the pavement on the left	Car parks on the right and left at junction	E	184
68.014	160	4,9	In the centre of Cella, cross the road and continue straight ahead with care on the other side	Restaurant on the left	E	168
68.015	190	5,1	Just after slight bend to the right in the road, turn right on the track	VF sign, house on the right	SE	164
68.016	190	5,3	Cross the river ford and continue straight ahead	Between fields and steeply uphill	S	163
68.017	700	6,0	At the T-junction, after a steep climb, turn left on a tarmac road	Large house on the hilltop to the right at the junction	E	240
68.018	1400	7,3	At a bend in the road to the left, continue straight ahead on an unmade road	Pass between farm buildings, VF sign	E	220
68.019	1000	8,3	At the T-junction, turn left on the track	Towards farm	NE	165
68.020	50	8,4	With the farm directly ahead, turn right		SE	162
68.021	1200	9,5	At the crossroads, at the top of the hill, in the hamlet of Arduini, continue straight ahead	VF sign, via Giuseppe Verdi	SE	159
68.022	600	10,2	At the roundabout, at the entry to Medesano (XXXV), continue straight ahead	Via Giuseppe Verdi, towards spire, VF sign	E	141
68.023	400	10,6	At the crossroads with via Dante Alighieri, continue straight ahead	Footpath and cycleway on the right	E	139
68.024	170	10,7	Before reaching the main road turn right. Note:- riders should continue to the main road to avoid a flight of steps	Towards the church, VF sign	SE	136

Costamezzana to Fornovo-di-Taro 22.3km

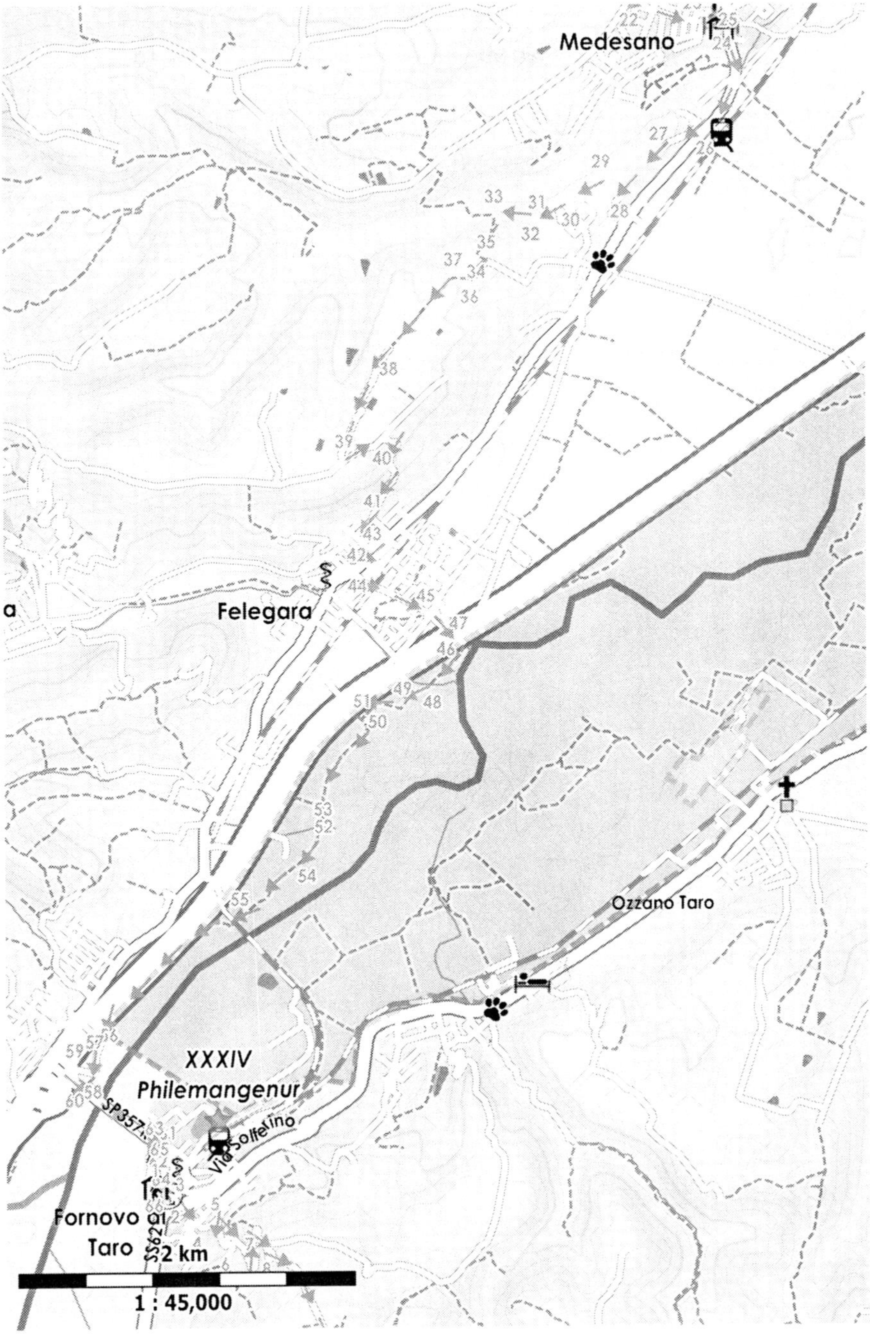
Medesano
Felegara
Ozzano Taro
XXXIV
Philemangenur
Via Solferino
SP357
SS62
Fornovo di
Taro
2 km
1 : 45,000

Costamezzana to Fornovo-di-Taro 22.3km

Waypoint	Distance Between Waypoints (m)	Total (km)	Directions	Verification Point	Compass	Altitude (m)
68.025	90	10,8	Pass beside the church and turn right on the main road to leave the town	SP357R, pavement protected by crash barrier	S	132
68.026	600	11,5	Just before the gantry for the exit from Medesano, turn right onto a small road	VF sign, road quickly bears left	SW	120
68.027	300	11,8	Continue straight ahead on the track between the buildings	Track skirts field to the right	SW	140
68.028	400	12,1	Turn right towards the woods	Fence on the left	NW	146
68.029	140	12,3	Turn left in front of the woods		SW	150
68.030	230	12,5	Continue straight ahead	Tree lined track	SW	151
68.031	230	12,7	Take the right fork slightly downhill		NW	154
68.032	80	12,8	After a short descent take the faint pathway across the ditch to the left	Pass hedge on your right	W	154
68.033	230	13,0	At the T-junction at the end of the field, turn left on the broad track	Uphill	SW	159
68.034	260	13,3	Bear left on the track		SE	188
68.035	70	13,4	Turn right on the tarmac road	Uphill towards the houses	SW	191
68.036	150	13,5	Beside the farm bear right on the grassy track		W	195
68.037	100	13,6	Bear left on the track		SW	196
68.038	600	14,2	Continue straight ahead	Driveway to a house on the right	S	214
68.039	800	15,0	At the T-junction, turn left	Shrine on the left	NE	231

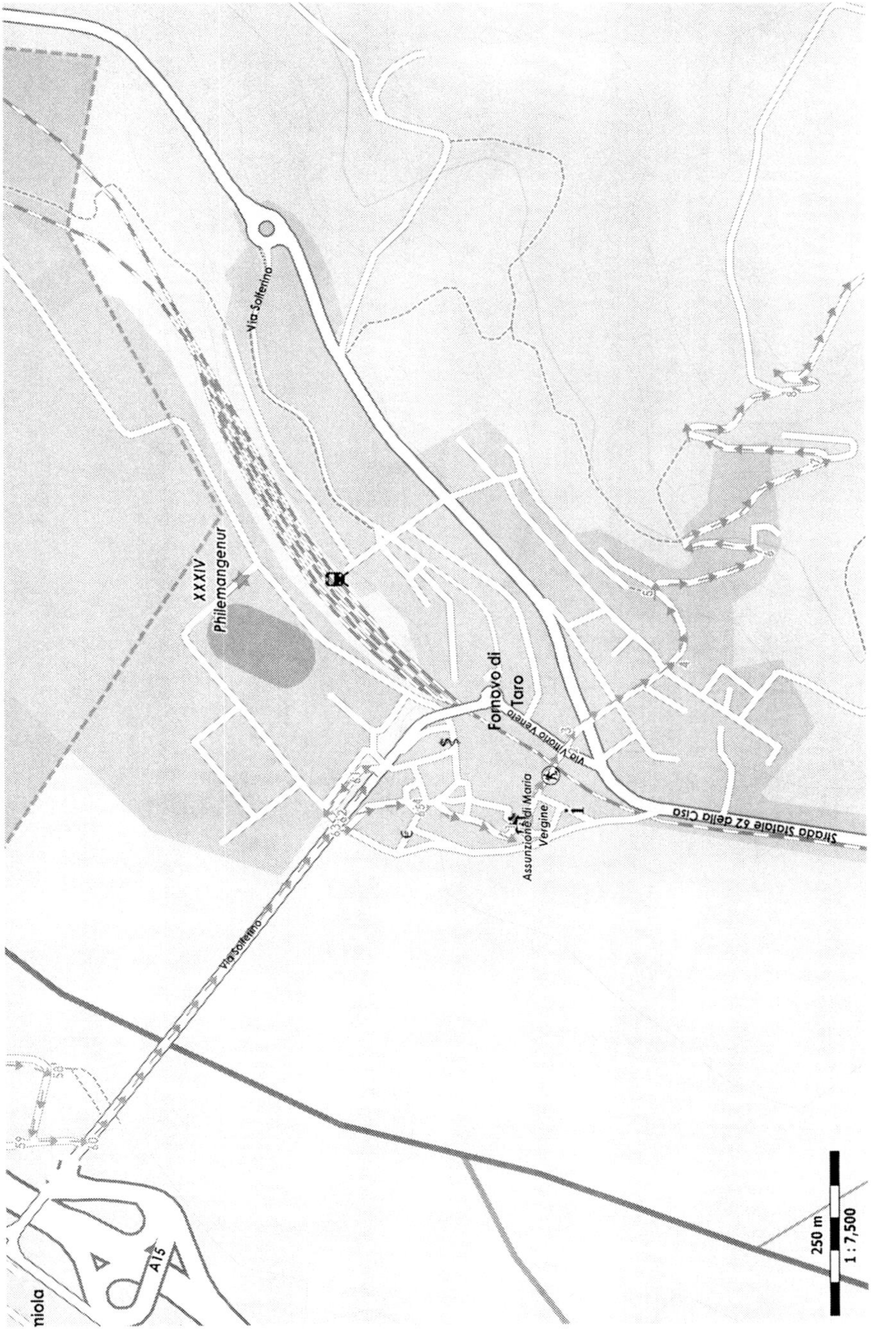
Via Solferino
XXXIV
Philemangenur
Fornovo di
Taro
Via Vittorio Veneto
Assunzione di Maria
Vergine
Strada statale 62 della Cisa
Via Solferino
A15
niola
250 m
1 : 7,500

Waypoint	Distance Between Waypoints (m)	Total (km)	Directions	Verification Point	Compass	Altitude (m)
68.040	280	15,3	Turn right on the tarmac road	Steep descent	S	220
68.041	600	15,9	On the crown of a bend to the left, on the entry Felegara, turn right	Via Damiano Chiesa	SW	151
68.042	160	16,1	At the T-junction, turn left, downhill	Via Campioni	SE	141
68.043	150	16,2	At the T-junction with the main road, turn right	Via Repubblica towards the pharmacy, VF sign	SW	135
68.044	130	16,3	At the roundabout with a fountain, turn left. Note:- the riverside path ahead involves a number of water crossings. Cyclists may wish to continue straight ahead on the busy road to rejoin the Main Route on the bridge over the river Taro	Via G. Picelli, VF sign	SE	133
68.045	500	16,9	At the roundabout continue straight ahead	Via Pattigna	SE	126
68.046	160	17,0	Bear right on the track under the Autostrada	Chain barrier across track and VF sign	SE	123
68.047	120	17,1	At the exit from the underpass, turn right and immediately left	Initially with the river close on the left	SW	120
68.048	300	17,5	Ford the stream and bear right		SW	118
68.049	250	17,7	Take the right fork		W	121
68.050	150	17,9	Turn left on the footpath	Parallel to the Autostrada	SW	122
68.051	140	18,0	At the T-junction, turn left		SW	122

Costamezzana to Fornovo-di-Taro 22,3km

Waypoint	Distance Between Waypoints (m)	Total (km)	Directions	Verification Point	Compass	Altitude (m)
68.052	700	18,7	At the junction in the tracks, continue straight ahead		S	123
68.053	120	18,8	Cross a small ditch and continue straight ahead	Close beside the river	SW	124
68.054	200	19,0	Continue straight ahead		SW	124
68.055	600	19,5	Cross the stream, pass under the railway bridge and bear right	Keeping the quarry on the left	SW	129
68.056	1000	20,6	Take the left fork away from the motorway and close beside the quarry	Beside Fornace Grigolin and further barrier	S	135
68.057	280	20,9	On reaching the football field, continue straight ahead	Keep football field to the right	S	136
68.058	80	20,9	Turn right	Keep football field on the right	W	137
68.059	110	21,0	At the T-junction, turn left		S	139
68.060	80	21,1	At the T-junction with the main road, turn left and cross the bridge over the river Taro. Note:- take great care as there is frequently heavy traffic on the bridge and only a narrow pavement	Towards Fornovo di Taro, bar opposite the junction	SE	139
68.061	700	21,8	At the end of the bridge turn sharp left	VF sign	NW	137
68.062	110	22,0	At the bottom of the hill turn left, piazza Mercato	Pass under the bridge	SW	138
68.063	40	22,0	Immediately after passing under the bridge turn left	Via Pietro Zuffardi	SE	138
68.064	100	22,1	At the end of the road turn right and immediately left in the small piazza		S	141
68.065	50	22,1	Bear right across piazza Giacomo Matteotti	Direction Duomo, via 20 Settembre	S	142
68.066	130	22,3	Arrive at Fornovo-di-Taro (XXXIV) centre	Piazza IV Novembre in front of Duomo		147

Religious Hostel

Assunzione di Maria Vergine,Piazza 4 Novembre,43045 Fornovo-di-Taro(PR),Italy Tel:+39 0525 2218,Price:D,

Church or Religious Organisation

Parrocchia San Pantaleone - Circolo Don Bosco,Via Conciliazione, 2,43014 Medesano(PR),Italy Tel:+39 0525 422136,dontorri@libero.it,Price:D,

B&B, Hotel, Gite d'Etape

Centrale,Via Giuseppe Verdi, 2a,43048 Medesano(PR),Italy Tel:+39 0525 430127,

Hotel Grillo,Strada Cisa, 22,43045 Fornovo-di-Taro(PR),Italy Tel:+39 0525 2680,

Tourist Information

Associazione Turistica Pro Loco,Via dei Collegati, 19,43045 Fornovo-di-Taro(PR),Italy Tel:+39 0525 2599,

Comune di Medesano,Piazza Guglielmo Marconi, 6,43014 Medesano(PR),Italy Tel:+39 0525 422711,

Banks and ATMs

Banca Monte dei Paschi di Siena,Piazza del Mercato, 10,43045 Fornovo-di-Taro(PR),Italy Tel:+39 0525 30290,

Banca Reggiana,Via Giuseppe Verdi, 4a,43014 Medesano(PR),Italy Tel:+39 0525 422011,www.bancareggiana.it,

Travel

Stazione Ferrovie,Via Antonio Gramsci, 22,43045 Fornovo-di-Taro(PR),Italy Tel:+39 06 6847 5475,www.renitalia.it,

Doctor

Simsmieh - Medico Chirurgo,Via Grazia Deledda, 12,43040 Medesano(PR),Italy Tel:+39 0525 430716,

Barbarese - Ambulatorio,Via Nazario Sauro, 5,43045 Fornovo-di-Taro(PR),Italy Tel:+39 0525 39917,

Veterinary

Associazione Veterinaria il Castello,V.Carnevala, 18,43014 Medesano(PR),Italy Tel:+39 0525 420280,

Clinica Veterinaria,Strada della Cisa, 23,43045 Fornovo-di-Taro(PR),Italy Tel:+39 0525 400393,

Hiking Equipment

City Sport,Via 24 Maggio, 16,43045 Fornovo-di-Taro(PR),Italy Tel:+39 0525 401053,

Stage Sixty-nine Summary: the climb to the summit of the Cisa Pass begins on minor roads before taking to forest and mountain tracks. Some of these are narrow, steep and over broken ground. The route includes a number of short stretches on the SS62, which is a favourite with high-speed motorcycle groups particularly on Sundays and holidays.

Distance from Canterbury: 1471km   Distance to Saint-Peter's-Square: 603km

Stage Ascent: 1046m   Stage Descent: 396m

Waypoint	Distance Between Waypoints (m)	Total (km)	Directions	Verification Point	Compass	Altitude (m)
69.001	0	0,0	From the Duomo in Fornovo, take via XXIV Maggio	VF sign, pass Duomo on the left	SE	148
69.002	130	0,1	Cross piazza Tarasconi and continue straight ahead	Kiosk on the right, pedestrian zone	SE	155
69.003	50	0,2	Cross the main road (SS62) and continue straight ahead on via Guglielmo Marconi	Pass bank on the right	SE	158
69.004	170	0,4	At the end of the pavement bear left on the road uphill	Via Guglielmo Marconi	E	170
69.005	130	0,5	Follow the road as it turns right and winds up the hill	Via Guglielmo Marconi	SE	181
69.006	180	0,7	Bear left on the road		SE	194
69.007	400	1,1	Continue to follow the road to the left as it climbs the hill	Avoid road to right	NE	222
69.008	400	1,4	Continue straight ahead	Direction Caselle, VF sign	SE	247
69.009	1000	2,5	At the fork in Caselle bear right and downhill	Narrow road, shrine on the left	S	312
69.010	600	3,0	Bear right and downhill on the tarmac road	House on the hill to your left	S	261
69.011	500	3,5	Take the right fork downhill	Towards the main road	SW	196

Fornovo-di-Taro to Cassio 20.8km

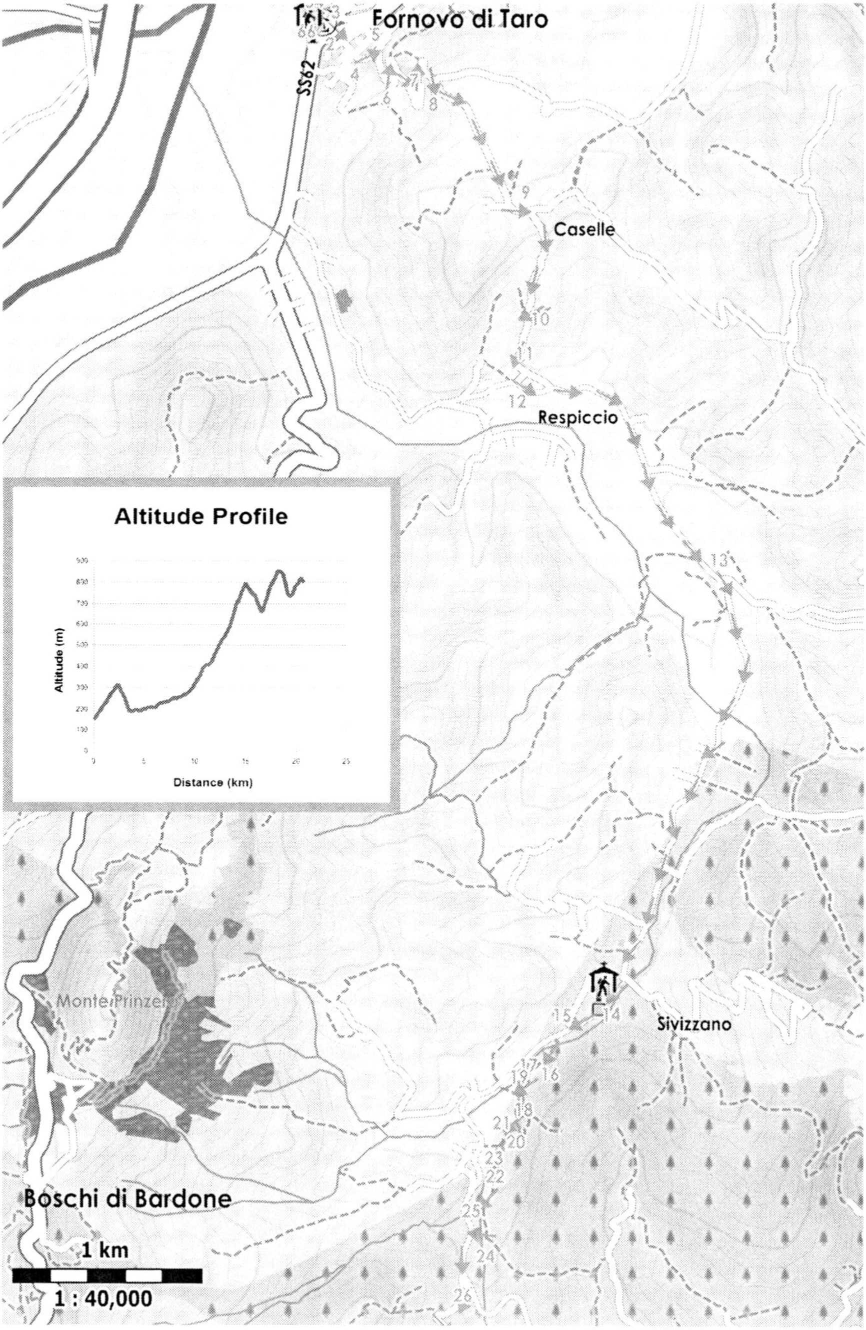

Fornovo di Taro
SS62
Caselle
Respiccio
Altitude Profile
Altitude (m)
Distance (km)
Sivizzano
Monte Prinzera
Boschi di Bardone
1 km
1 : 40,000

Waypoint	Distance Between Waypoints (m)	Total (km)	Directions	Verification Point	Compass	Altitude (m)
69.012	80	3,6	At the T-junction at the bottom of the hill turn left on the main road, SP39	Metal fence on embankment on your left	SE	192
69.013	1700	5,3	Continue straight ahead on strada Val Sporzona	Ignore left turn to San Vitale	S	205
69.014	2500	7,8	Continue straight ahead on the SP39	Village of Sivizzano to the right	SW	247
69.015	400	8,1	Bear left on the track. Note:- the track includes a number of river crossings and may be difficult for cyclists, who may refer to remain on the road	VF sign, direction Campo Sportivo	SW	251
69.016	130	8,3	After crossing the river and passing a group of buildings on your left, turn right	Faint track on the edge of the field with trees close on your right	SW	251
69.017	210	8,5	At the T-junction with broader track, turn right	Towards the river	SW	255
69.018	50	8,5	Cross the river and continue straight ahead		SW	256
69.019	50	8,6	At the T-junction, turn left		S	257
69.020	160	8,7	Bear right	River close on the left	SW	260
69.021	140	8,9	Take the right fork, then bear left	House on the hill to the right	S	264
69.022	90	9,0	Take the left fork, cross the river and continue straight ahead	Uphill	S	266
69.023	140	9,1	Bear right on the faint track	Field on your left, trees on right	S	269
69.024	400	9,4	Turn right. Note:- riders ford the river	Over footbridge	NW	278
69.025	100	9,5	At the T-junction with the road, turn left	Bungalows ahead at the junction	S	284

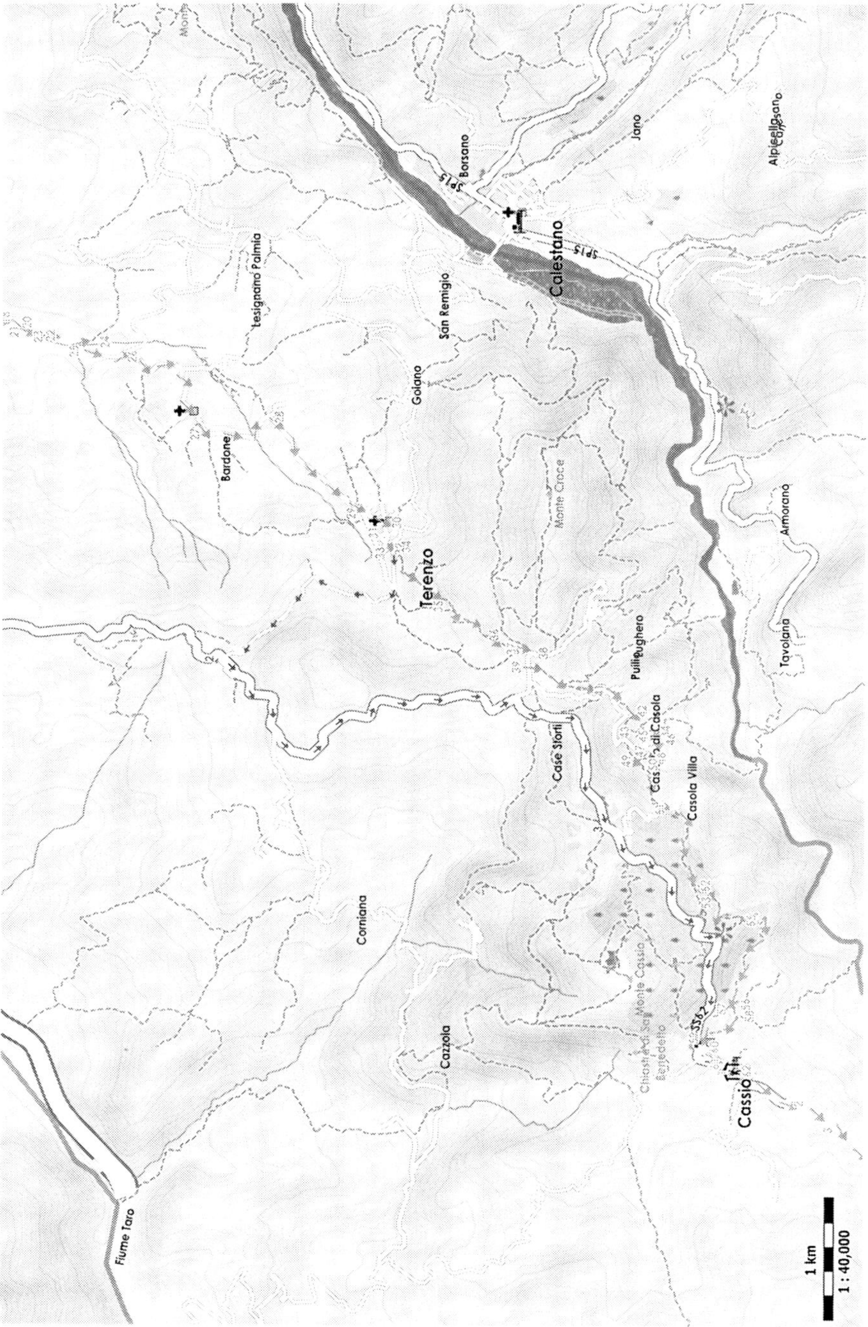
Fiume Taro
Cazzola
Corniana
Cassio
Monte Cassio
Case Storti
Casola Villa
Terenzo
Bardone
Lesignano Palmia
Golano
San Remigio
Monte Croce
Calestano
Borsano
SP15
Jano
Armorano
Tavolana
1 km
1 : 40,000

Waypoint	Distance Between Waypoints (m)	Total (km)	Directions	Verification Point	Compass	Altitude (m)
69.026	260	9,8	Fork right on the road	VF sign, direction Bardone	SW	301
69.027	1300	11,1	After passing through Bardone bear left	Strada Ca'di Bardone to the right	S	404
69.028	600	11,7	Bear right up the hill	Ca'di Fucinello to the left	SW	423
69.029	1200	12,9	Fork left into Terenzo	VF sign, strada della Posta	SW	534
69.030	170	13,0	At the T-junction, in front of the Piave di Terenzo turn right	Strada della Posta	W	546
69.031	90	13,1	Fork left up a small paved passageway	VF sign	W	554
69.032	140	13,3	At the T-junction, turn left uphill	VF sign, via Capoluogo	SW	567
69.033	150	13,4	Turn left at the top of the hill. Note:- the route ahead is off-road and strenuous with steep climbs over broken ground. Cyclists are advised to turn right on the Alternate Route joining the SS62	VF sign	E	582
69.034	60	13,5	Turn right onto an unmade road	VF sign	SW	588
69.035	700	14,2	Continue straight ahead on the track	Fence on your right	SW	704
69.036	400	14,6	Continue straight ahead towards the top of the hill		S	751
69.037	400	15,0	Bear right on the widening track	Large VF sign on left	SW	789
69.038	60	15,1	At the T-junction, turn right onto a minor road	VF sign, towards large pylon	W	789
69.039	120	15,2	Just after passing the house on the left, turn left on the grassy path	VF sign, towards church tower	S	783

Fornovo-di-Taro to Cassio 20.8km

Waypoint	Distance Between Waypoints (m)	Total (km)	Directions	Verification Point	Compass	Altitude (m)
69.040	600	15,7	Continue straight ahead on the track	Citi di Bardone route	S	746
69.041	200	15,9	In Castello di Casola cross the tarmac road and continue straight ahead	Downhill	SW	739
69.042	240	16,2	Cross the track and continue straight ahead on the faint path	Between the trees	W	711
69.043	300	16,5	Fork right	Towards the houses	S	670
69.044	120	16,6	Turn right between the houses in Villa di Casola	Strada Vici Villa	SW	661
69.045	40	16,6	Continue straight ahead on the tarmac and then bear right	Towards fork	SW	661
69.046	50	16,7	Take the left fork	VF sign	NW	663
69.047	110	16,8	Continue straight ahead at the crossroads	Strada della Fontana, VF sign	NW	675
69.048	90	16,9	Proceed straight ahead onto a small track	Uphill	N	689
69.049	80	17,0	At the T-junction turn left	VF sign	W	701
69.050	30	17,0	Turn left onto the grassy track	VF sign	SW	706
69.051	600	17,5	Cross the unmade road and continue straight ahead on the footpath	VF sign	W	785
69.052	700	18,3	Immediately after a bend in the track, turn left on the footpath. Note:- the pathway ahead is not suitable for cyclists or riders, they and walkers wishing for a shorter and easier route, should turn right and remain on the broad track to the main road, then turn left and follow the main road for 1km to Cassio	Signpost to Cassio	SW	850

Waypoint	Distance Between Waypoints (m)	Total (km)	Directions	Verification Point	Compass	Altitude (m)
69.053	270	18,5	At a crossroads in the tracks, continue straight ahead on the footpath following the sign		SW	847
69.054	400	18,9	Join a broader track and bear left		S	810
69.055	170	19,1	Turn right on the footpath		W	773
69.056	900	19,9	Join a track and continue straight ahead	Uphill	W	781
69.057	40	20,0	Continue straight ahead	Ignore turnings on both sides	W	784
69.058	70	20,1	Join a broadening track and turn to the right		NW	787
69.059	300	20,4	Take the right fork	Enter Cassio	NW	811
69.060	100	20,5	Turn left along the main street through Cassio	Pieve di Cassio ahead	SW	816
69.061	270	20,8	At the end of the street turn right and then left on the main road – SS62	Towards the old hostel	SW	802
69.062	80	20,8	Arrive at Cassio	Beside Ostello di Cassio		797

Fornovo-di-Taro to Cassio 20.8km

93

Stage Summary: the Alternate Route allows cyclists and those not wishing to deal with the steepest climbs over broken ground to follow the main road to Cassio.

Stage Ascent: 478m   Stage Descent: 260m

Alternate Route #69.A1 9.7km

Waypoint	Distance Between Waypoints (m)	Total (km)	Directions	Verification Point	Compass	Altitude (m)
69A1.001	0	0,0	Turn right on the road	Strada Terenzo-Calestano	NW	583
69A1.002	2100	2,1	At T-junction turn left on the main road	SS62 direction Cassio and Berceto	SW	657
69A1.003	4800	6,9	Continue straight ahead on the main road		SW	876
69A1.004	2800	9,7	Arrive in Cassio and rejoin the Main Route			800

Pilgrim Hostel

Ostello di Cassio,Loc.Cassio via Nazionale,43040 Terenzo(PR),Italy
Tel:+39 0525 64521,Price:A,

Religious Hostel

Parrocchia di S.Margherita - Abitazione del Parroco,(Pietro Adorni),Località Sivizzano Centro, 18,43045 Fornovo-di-Taro(PR),Italy Tel:+39 0525 56258,
Mobile:+39 3497 839051,Price:C,

B&B, Hotel, Gite d'Etape

Hotel Mantovani,Via Mazzini, 2,43030 Calestano(PR),Italy Tel:+39 0525 52118,Price:B,

Affittacamere Da Veronica,Via Nazionale 51 Loc.Cassio,43040 Terenzo(PR),Italy
Tel:+39 0525 526002,Mobile:+39 3204 480116,albergo-bonora@hotmail.it,Price:B,

Stage Seventy Summary: the route initially follows the SS62 before making diversions onto forest and farm tracks and descending into the centre of the town of Berceto. After Berceto there is the choice of climbing along the forest tracks or remaining on the shorter route beside the SS62.

Distance from Canterbury: 1492km   Distance to Saint-Peter's-Square: 582km

Stage Ascent: 618m   Stage Descent: 414m

Waypoint	Distance Between Waypoints (m)	Total (km)	Directions	Verification Point	Compass	Altitude (m)
70.001	0	0,0	Continue straight ahead on the SS62	Ostello on your right	SW	796
70.002	500	0,5	On a bend in the road to the left take the footpath to the right	Second track on right after strada Perdella	SW	769
70.003	500	1,0	Rejoin the main road and continue straight ahead on the right side of the road	Km 75, SS62	SW	743
70.004	2400	3,4	On the crown of the bend to the right take the small tarmac road to the left. Note:- heavily packed bike riders may prefer avoid the steep tracks ahead and remain on the road	Sign Cavazzola di Sopra 700m	S	745
70.005	400	3,8	After a stretch on a level track, turn right	Steep forest track uphill	SW	771
70.006	500	4,2	Bear left on the track		SW	862
70.007	170	4,4	At the fork in the tracks, keep right	Downhill	SW	879
70.008	160	4,6	Take the left fork		S	893
70.009	180	4,8	Join a track and bear left	Under the electricity lines	SW	908
70.010	120	4,9	Turn right into the main street	Castellonchio	W	910
70.011	70	4,9	Bear left, downhill	Church to the right	S	907
70.012	500	5,4	Before the exit from the town take the left fork	Right fork leads back to the main road	S	902
70.013	270	5,7	Continue straight ahead on the unmade road		S	913

Cassio to Ostello-della-Cisa 17km

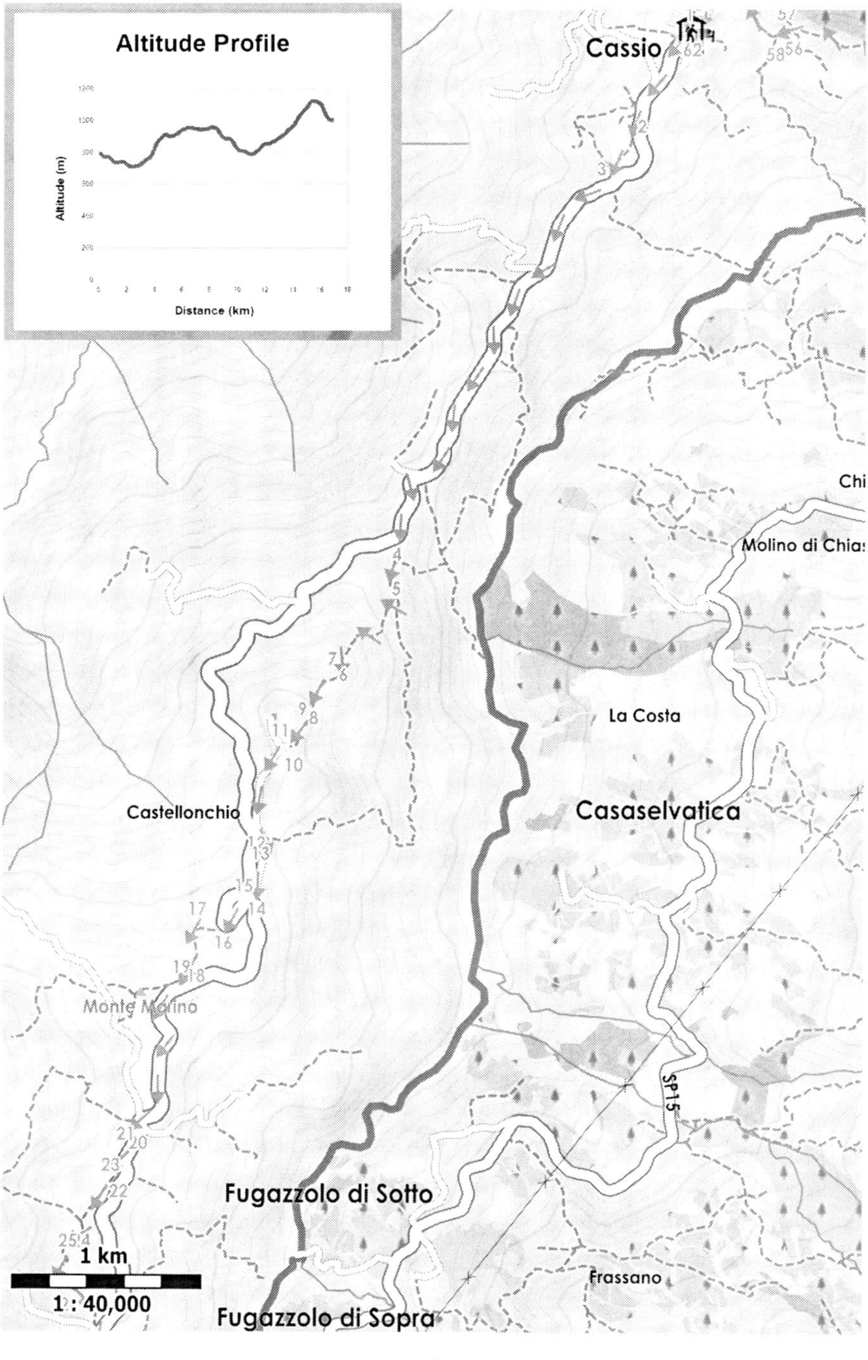
Altitude Profile
Altitude (m)
Distance (km)
Cassio
Chi
Molino di Chias
La Costa
Castellonchio
Casaselvatica
Monte Marino
SP15
Fugazzolo di Sotto
Frassano
Fugazzolo di Sopra
1 km
1 : 40,000

Waypoint	Distance Between Waypoints (m)	Total (km)	Directions	Verification Point	Compass	Altitude (m)
70.014	120	5,8	Take the right fork	On the footpath	SW	922
70.015	100	5,9	At the junction with the main road turn right, cross over and continue on the left side of the road	SS62	SW	929
70.016	170	6,0	On the crown of the next bend, turn left on the track	Into the woods	W	937
70.017	160	6,2	In the middle of the woods take the left fork		S	941
70.018	180	6,4	Bear right	Ignore the turning to the left	SW	951
70.019	180	6,6	Rejoin the main road and turn right remaining on the right side of the road	SS62 (VI	S	952
70.020	900	7,5	Bear right on the track into the woods. To avoid obstacles in the path, cyclists and riders should remain on the road	Beside the turning for Pagazzano	SW	940
70.021	170	7,6	Continue straight ahead over the stile on the path through the woods	Main road close on the left	S	942
70.022	130	7,8	Continue straight ahead	Path joins a track	SW	942
70.023	80	7,9	Continue straight ahead	Track broadens into a road	SW	943
70.024	260	8,1	Bear left towards the radio mast	Across stile	S	953
70.025	260	8,4	After a short paved section turn right on the footpath		S	953
70.026	220	8,6	Bear right on the track		SE	941
70.027	230	8,8	Pass through the cattle gate and continue on the path	Towards the main road	S	909

Cassio to Ostello-della-Cisa 17km

Berceto
Albergo Ristorante Vittoria Da Rino

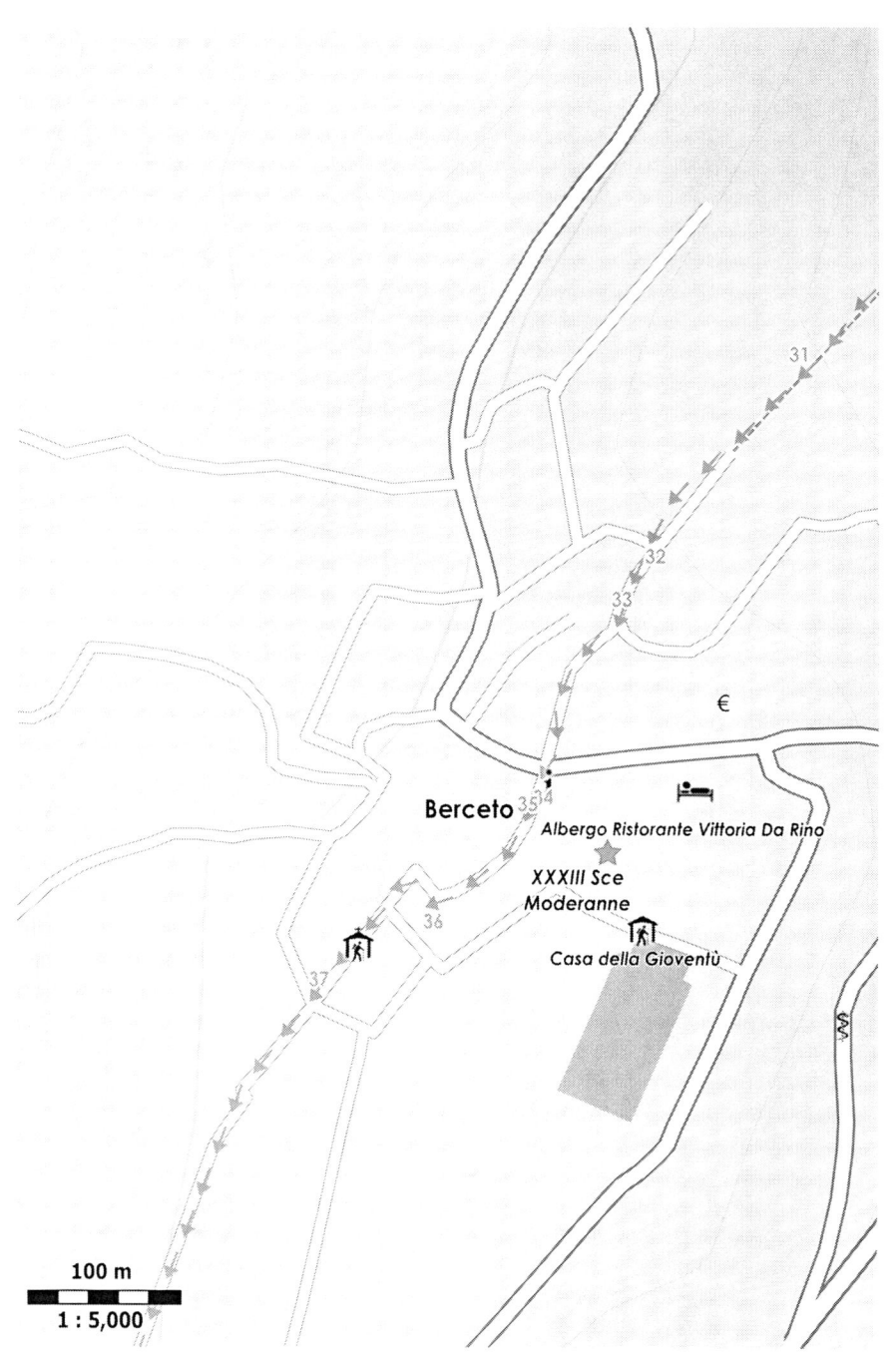

XXXIII Sce Moderanne

Casa della Gioventù

100 m
1 : 5,000

Waypoint	Distance Between Waypoints (m)	Total (km)	Directions	Verification Point	Compass	Altitude (m)
70.028	80	8,9	Bear right on the main road remaining on the right side	SS62 (IV	S	899
70.029	300	9,2	As the road bears left, bear right on the footpath	Towards Berceto below	S	883
70.030	500	9,7	Take the right fork	Downhill, towards Berceto	SW	865
70.031	180	9,9	Continue straight ahead on the tarmac	Via Ripasanta	SW	839
70.032	160	10,0	Continue straight ahead	Castle to the left	S	820
70.033	60	10,1	In Largo Castello continue towards the centre of the town on the paved road	Via Rossi	SW	814
70.034	130	10,2	At the crossroads of via Martiri Libertà and via P.M. Rossi in the centre of Berceto (XXXIII), take via Romea	Pass in front of the Duomo	S	808
70.035	30	10,3	Continue on via Romea	Information Office to the left	SW	807
70.036	90	10,3	At the end of the small cobbled street in piazzale le Baruti, turn right and then immediately left	Via al Seminario, VF sign	SW	806
70.037	120	10,5	Proceed straight ahead onto via E. Colli	VF sign	SW	805
70.038	700	11,1	At T-junction with main road turn right and almost immediately left onto a gravel track	VF sign	SW	785
70.039	600	11,7	At the fork, bear right	VF sign	SW	821
70.040	400	12,0	Fork right at the top of the rise	VF sign	S	850

Cassio to Ostello-della-Cisa 17km

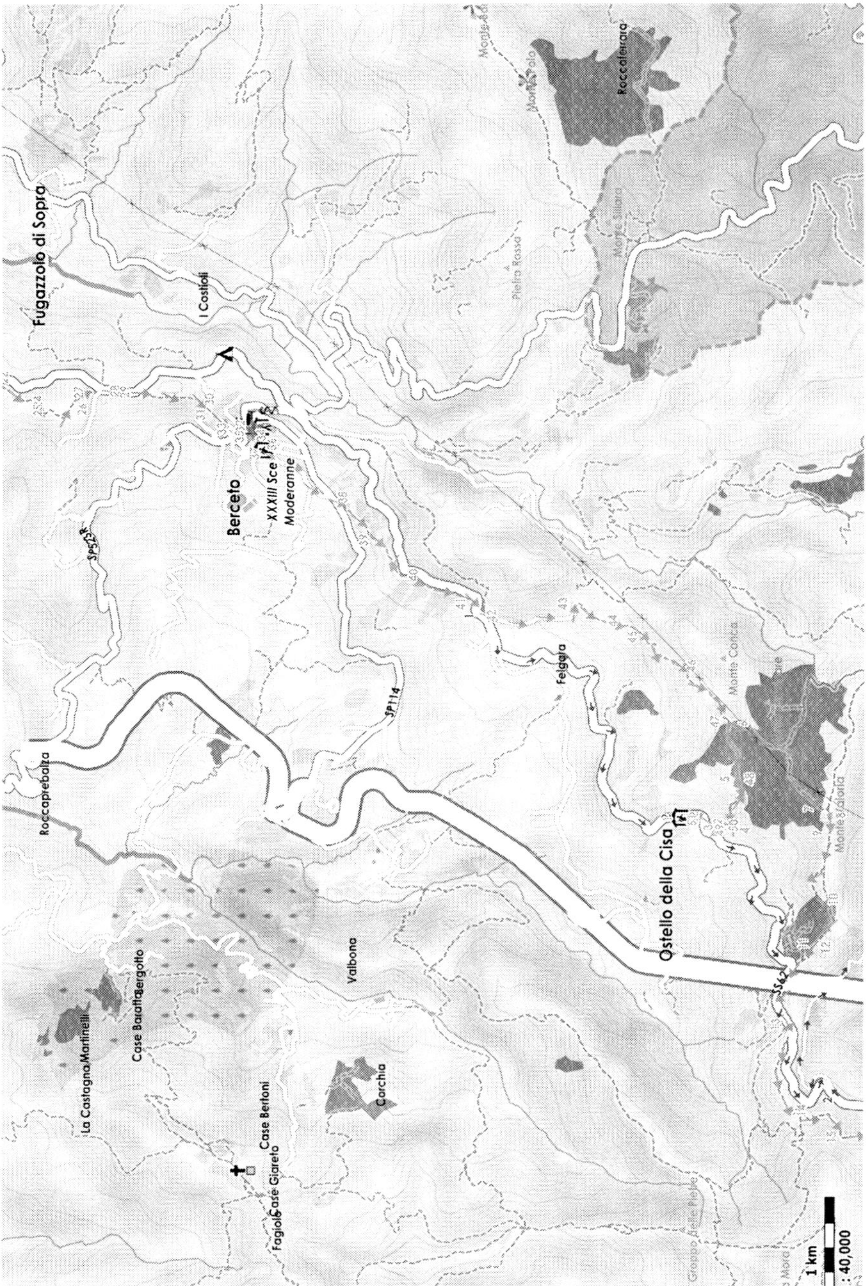
Fugazzolo di Sopra
I Castioli
Berceto
XXXIII Sce
Moderanne
SP513R
SP114
Roccaprebalza
Felgara
Monte Conca
Ostello della Cisa
SS62
Roccaferrara
Monte Sillara
Pietra Rossa
Valbona
Bergotto
Case Baratta
La Castagna Martinelli
Case Bertoni
Case Giareto
Fagiolo
Corchia
1 km
1 : 40,000

Waypoint	Distance Between Waypoints (m)	Total (km)	Directions	Verification Point	Compass	Altitude (m)
70.041	700	12,7	Track emerges onto a small tarmac area, continue straight ahead	VF sign, old factory on right	SW	867
70.042	140	12,8	Cross the main road and continue straight ahead towards Monte Valoria. Note:- to avoid climbing on further forest tracks which include stiles follow the Alternate Route by turning right on the SS62	VF sign	S	874
70.043	900	13,7	Take the right fork	Farm Felgara to the left	SW	939
70.044	260	14,0	On the crown of a bend to the left bear right on the track	Uphill	S	958
70.045	400	14,4	Continue straight ahead	Altitude 1000m	SW	1012
70.046	500	14,9	Take the right fork		SW	1063
70.047	700	15,5	Turn right. Note:- if you wish to bypass the hostel continue straight ahead and follow the instructions for the next section	Follow sign for the VF hostel	W	1121
70.048	500	16,0	Keep left		W	1105
70.049	500	16,5	Turn sharp right		N	1028
70.050	100	16,6	Bear left		N	1013
70.051	220	16,8	At the T-junction with the main road, turn right	Follow road downhill and across the river	N	1000
70.052	200	17,0	Arrive at Ostello-della-Cisa	Hostel on the left		1000

Cassio to Ostello-della-Cisa 17km

Stage Summary: the Alternate Route allows cyclists and those not wishing to deal with further forest tracks to proceed on the main road.

Stage Ascent: 122m   Stage Descent: 9m

Waypoint	Distance Between Waypoints (m)	Total (km)	Directions	Verification Point	Compass	Altitude (m)
70A1.001	0	0,0	Turn right onto on the SS62	VF sign points ahead	SW	869
70A1.002	3100	3,1	Arrive beside Ostello della Cisa at the end of the section	Hostel on the right		981

Alternate Route #70.A1 3.1km

Pilgrim Hostel

Casa della Gioventù,Via Martino Iasoni,43042 Berceto(PR),Italy Tel:+39 0525 60087,Price:D,

Ostello via Francigena,Frazione Passo Cisa,43042 Berceto(PR),Italy Tel:+39 0525 629072,forestalepassocisa@libero.it ,Price:C,

Religious Hostel

Santuario di Berceto,Via Seminario,43042 Berceto(PR),Italy Tel:+39 0525 60071, Mobile:+39 3479 776652,berceto@seminariovescovile.parma.it,Price:A,

B&B, Hotel, Gite d'Etape

Albergo Ristorante Vittoria Da Rino,Via Guglielmo Marconi, 5,43042 Berceto(PR),Italy Tel:+39 0525 64703,Price:B,

Camping

Camping I Pianelli,Località I Pianelli, 146,43042 Berceto(PR),Italy Tel:+39 0525 64521,

Tourist Information

Ufficio Turistico,Via Romea, 5,43042 Berceto(PR),Italy Tel:+39 0525 629027,

Banks and ATMs

Banca Monte Parma,Vicolo Marina,43042 Berceto(PR),Italy Tel:+39 0525 629011,

Doctor

Croce Rossa Italiana - Delegazione,Salita P.Silva,43042 Berceto(PR),Italy Tel:+39 0525 60040,

Stage Seventy-one Summary: this is a long and strenuous section with few intermediate facilities. The "Ministry Route" remains largely off-road, but after a pleasant descent from the pass summit, again climbs over the 700m Crocetta pass.

Distance from Canterbury: 1509km   Distance to Saint-Peter's-Square: 565km

Stage Ascent: 591m   Stage Descent: 1348m

Waypoint	Distance Between Waypoints (m)	Total (km)	Directions	Verification Point	Compass	Altitude (m)
71.001	0	0,0	With the Ostello-della-Cisa directly behind you, turn right on the road	Uphill	S	1000
71.002	210	0,2	After crossing the river, turn left on the path. Note:- if the traffic conditions permit, the route can be reduced by 2km by remaining on the road to the summit of the pass	Uphill into the woods	S	998
71.003	190	0,4	Bear right		S	1009
71.004	120	0,5	Turn sharp left		E	1026
71.005	500	1,0	Bear right		E	1104
71.006	500	1,5	At the T-junction, turn right	Uphill	SW	1126
71.007	1200	2,6	Near the summit of Valoria take the right fork	Towards the summit	SW	1199
71.008	80	2,7	At the summit take the path to the right	Along the ridge	W	1192
71.009	160	2,9	Continue straight ahead	Ignore the turning to the right	W	1176
71.010	600	3,5	Continue straight ahead	Cross the stile	W	1132
71.011	500	3,9	After a steep descent, continue straight ahead	Cross a second stile	NW	1081
71.012	40	4,0	Join a track and bear right		W	1073

Ostello-della-Cisa to Pontremoli 24.1km

104

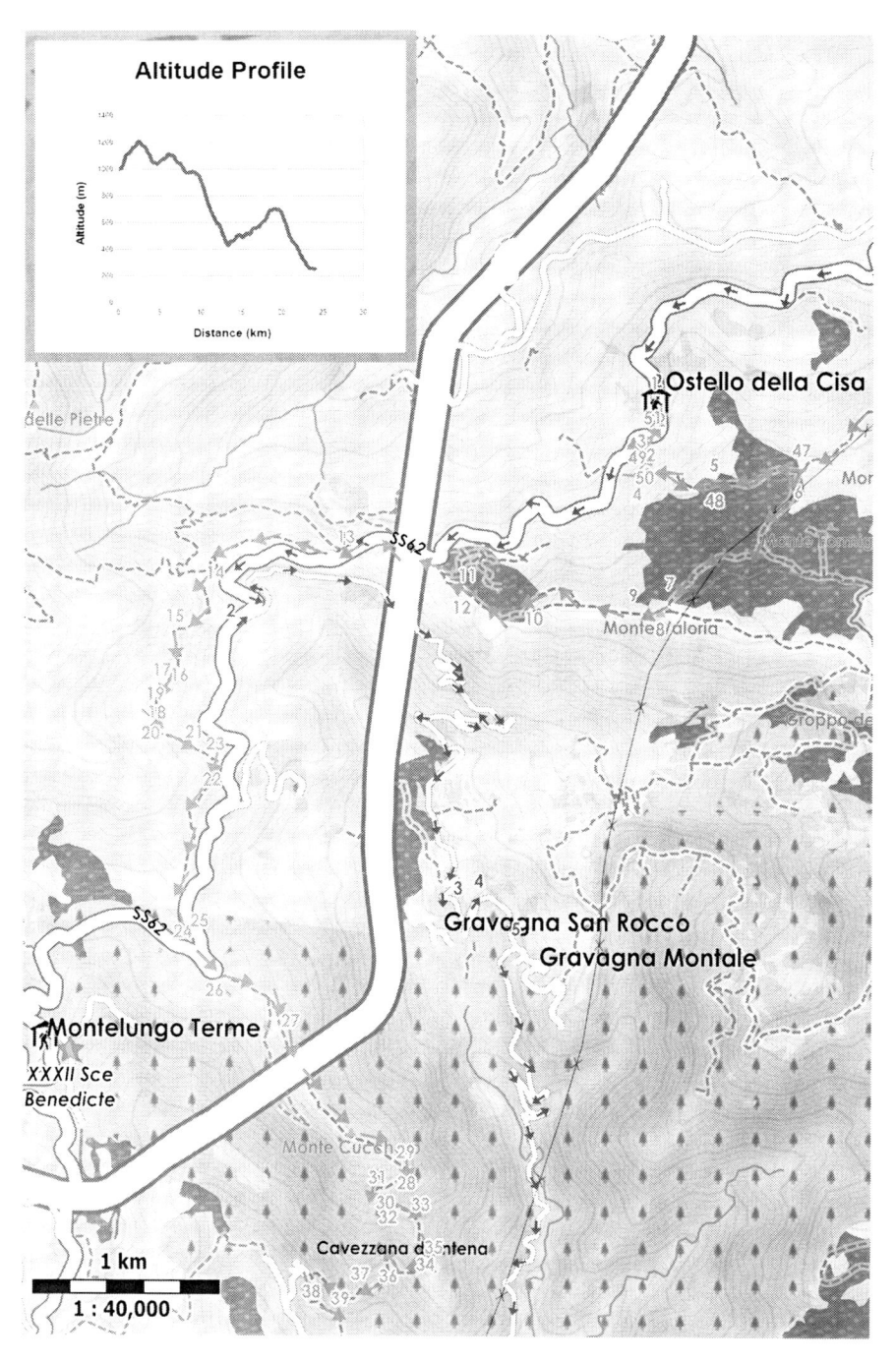

Waypoint	Distance Between Waypoints (m)	Total (km)	Directions	Verification Point	Compass	Altitude (m)
71.013	800	4,7	At the summit of the Cisa Pass, cross the main road and bear right on the footpath. The Alternate Route offers a pleasant descent to Pontremoli on generally quiet roads and may be preferred by cyclists and horse riders. The Main Route includes sometimes difficult water crossings as well as steep descents and steps. Note:- there are many intersecting CAI routes using red and white signs and so be sure to check for the pilgrim on the signs	Parallel to the steps to the church	W	1036
71.014	800	5,5	At an intersection between 3 tracks, take the left track	Downhill, red and white sign	SW	1070
71.015	600	6,1	Continue straight ahead across the stream	Cairn ahead	S	1108
71.016	140	6,2	Take the left fork	Downhill	SW	1106
71.017	200	6,4	Bear right and cross the stream	Continue on the small track	SW	1098
71.018	50	6,5	Bear left, cross the stream and a small grassy area and bear right	Re-enter woods	S	1097
71.019	110	6,6	Turn right on the forest road	Red and white sign	SW	1098
71.020	30	6,6	Turn left on another forest road	Cross another stream	SE	1099
71.021	400	7,0	At a T-junction of forest-tracks, turn right		SE	1062
71.022	110	7,1	Ignore a turning to the right and continue straight ahead	Downhill	E	1048
71.023	20	7,1	Turn right on the path	Gentle descent, parallel to the main road below	S	1047

Ostello-della-Cisa to Pontremoli 24.1km

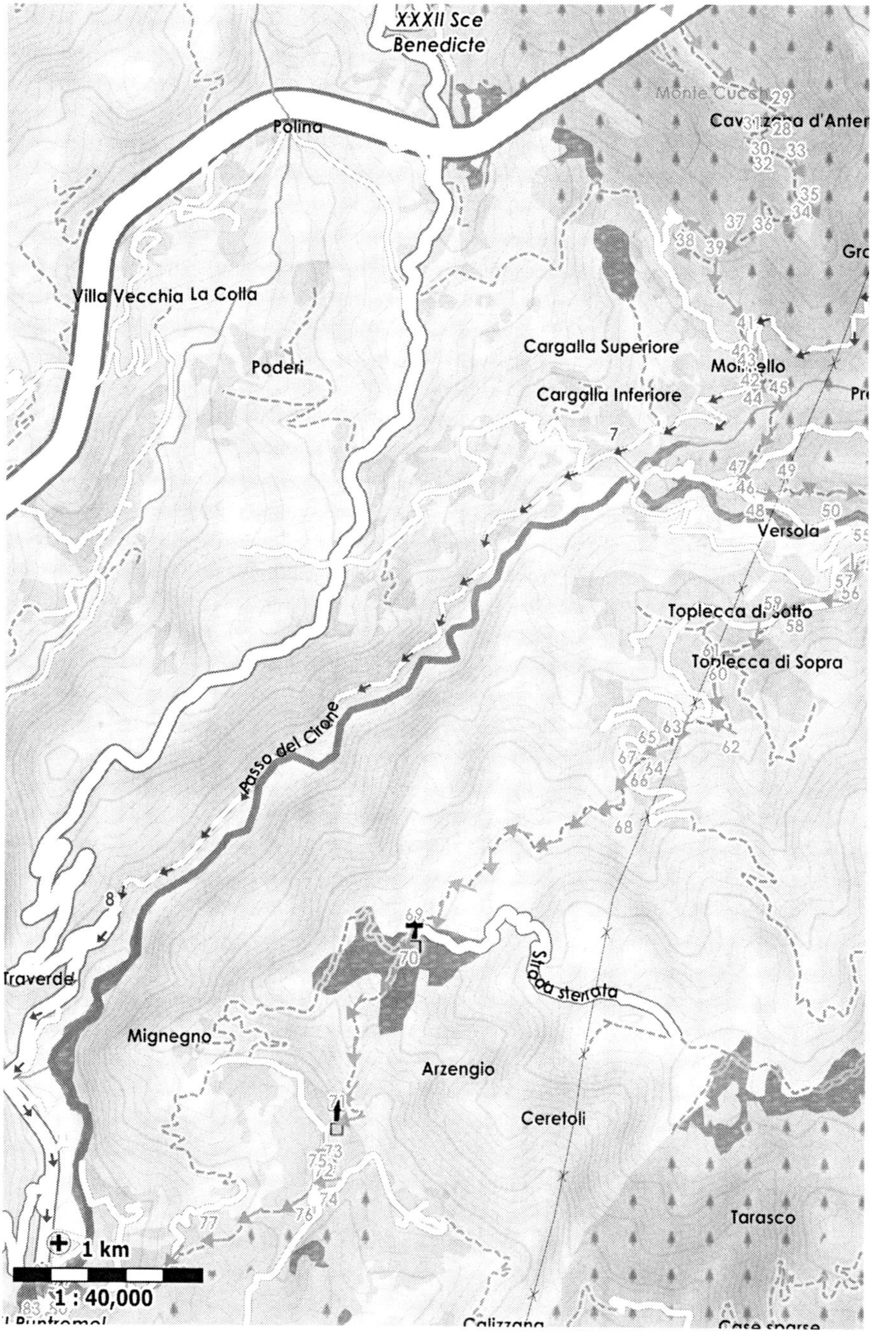
XXXII Sce Benedicte
Monte Cucch
Polina
Villa Vecchia
La Colla
Poderi
Cargalla Superiore
Cargalla Inferiore
Versola
Toplecca di Sopra
Passo del Cirone
Traverde
Mignegno
Arzengio
Ceretoli
Strada sterrata
Tarasco
1 km
1 : 40,000

Waypoint	Distance Between Waypoints (m)	Total (km)	Directions	Verification Point	Compass	Altitude (m)
71.024	900	8,0	The path enters a track, bear right down the hill	Parallel and closer to the main road	SE	985
71.025	190	8,2	At the junction with the main road bear right on the road	SS62 - Km53	SE	971
71.026	200	8,4	On the apex of the next bend, bear left on the unmade road. Note:- to visit Montelungo (XXXII) follow the main road with care. The main road continues to Pontremoli	Via Francigena sign	SE	968
71.027	600	9,1	Pass a radio mast and continue straight ahead	Descend in open space between woods	SE	975
71.028	1000	10,1	Continue straight ahead	Ignore the turning to the right	S	907
71.029	40	10,1	At the T-junction with a broader track, turn right	Downhill	SW	901
71.030	140	10,2	At the fork in the tracks, bear right	Follow the larger track	SW	880
71.031	140	10,4	At a T-junction in the tracks, bear left	Downhill	E	856
71.032	50	10,4	Continue straight ahead	Ignore turning to the right	SE	848
71.033	240	10,7	Continue straight ahead	Ignore the turning to the left and to the right	S	794
71.034	130	10,8	Continue straight ahead downhill	Ignore the turning to the right	SE	764
71.035	190	11,0	At a turn in the track continue straight ahead on the path	Into the woods	W	731
71.036	400	11,3	Continue straight ahead	Ignore the turning to the right	SW	681
71.037	300	11,6	At a fork in the tracks, take the right fork		W	640

Ostello-della-Cisa to Pontremoli ≥4.1km

XXXI Puntremel

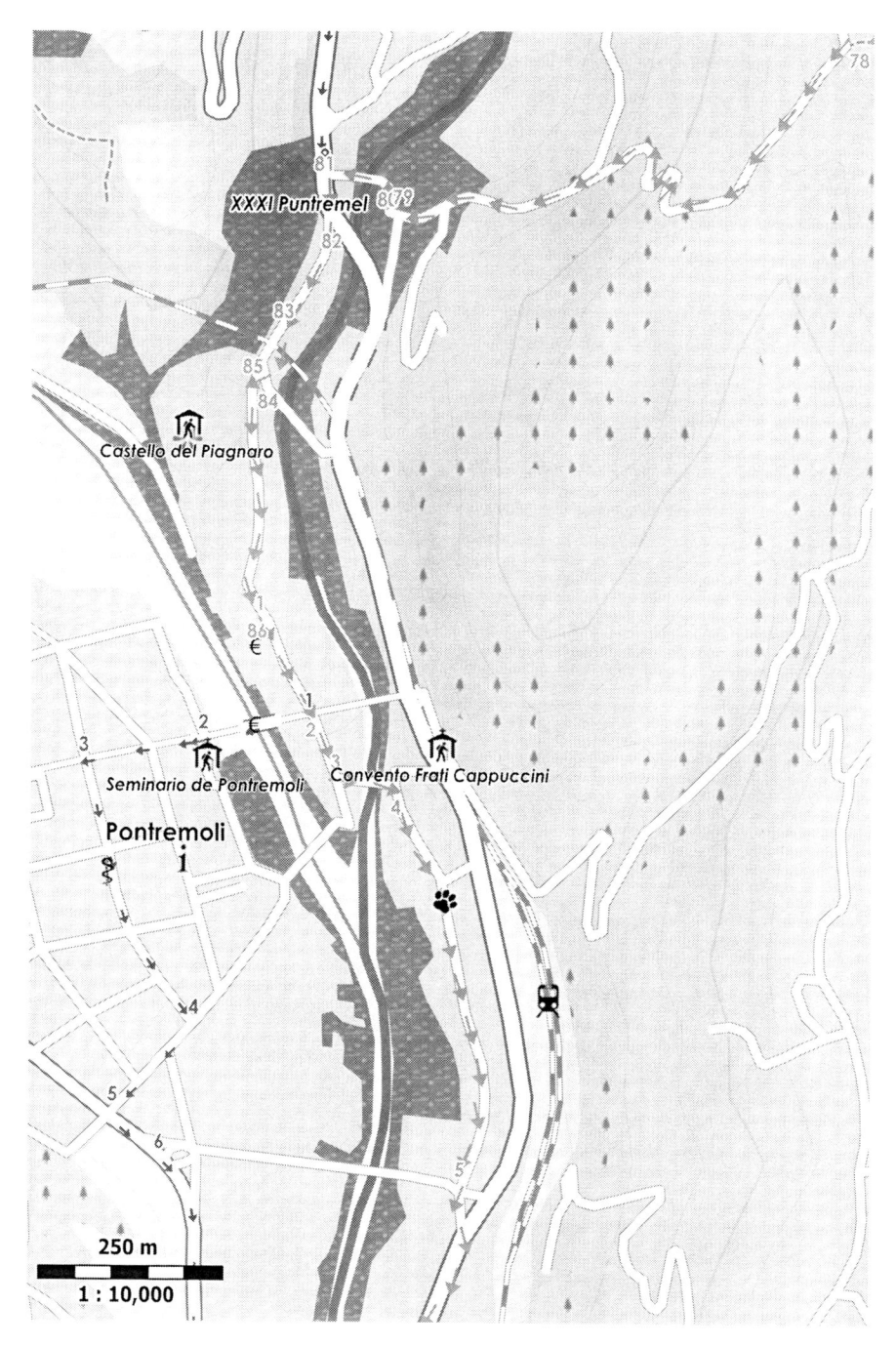

Castello del Piagnaro

Seminario de Pontremoli   Convento Frati Cappuccini

Pontremoli

250 m
1 : 10,000

Waypoint	Distance Between Waypoints (m)	Total (km)	Directions	Verification Point	Compass	Altitude (m)
71.038	400	12,0	At a T-junction with a grassy track, turn left	Church ahead, ignore VF sign to the right	SE	598
71.039	400	12,3	At the fork in the tracks, take the right fork	Downhill	S	581
71.040	500	12,8	Continue straight ahead on the tarmac road	Enter Groppoli	SE	511
71.041	60	12,8	At the intersection with the tarmac road continue straight ahead on the cobbled road	Pass between houses	S	501
71.042	120	13,0	Continue straight ahead	Narrow cobbled path	S	483
71.043	100	13,1	At the exit from Gropolli take the left fork		E	467
71.044	40	13,1	At the junction with the main road turn right and immediately left on the track. Note:- to reduce total distance by 2.5km and avoid further off-road tracks and the climb over the Crocetta pass continue to the right on the road and join the Alternate Route	Vines and wooden fence on the right	SE	460
71.045	300	13,4	Continue straight ahead and take the difficult ford across the Civasola torrente	Uphill	SW	427
71.046	400	13,8	At the intersection with the tarmac road, turn right and immediately left onto a footpath	Steep descent into Previdè	SW	457
71.047	110	14,0	On reaching Previdè turn left onto the tarmac and then immediately left again	Towards the village centre	E	456
71.048	110	14,1	At the exit from the village take the left fork, uphill on the grass track	Shrine on the left	E	455
71.049	180	14,2	Take care to locate an indistinct junction and bear right over a dry wall	Between the olive trees	E	468

Ostello-della-Cisa to Pontremoli 24.1km

Waypoint	Distance Between Waypoints (m)	Total (km)	Directions	Verification Point	Compass	Altitude (m)
71.050	270	14,5	After an uphill section take a footpath to the right	Across the hillside	E	493
71.051	400	14,9	Continue straight ahead	Enter Groppodalosio	E	503
71.052	100	15,0	In the centre of the village turn right	Down a flight of steps	SW	497
71.053	140	15,1	Continue straight ahead	Over the old river Magra bridge	SW	486
71.054	290	15,4	Join a tarmac road and turn right	Towards the village of Casalina	SW	494
71.055	70	15,5	Bear left away from the road on a footpath		SW	499
71.056	150	15,6	At the first junction in Casalina continue straight ahead	On the paved road	S	508
71.057	150	15,8	Continue straight ahead	Pass an old mill	W	515
71.058	270	16,0	Continue straight ahead	Tarmac road	SW	508
71.059	160	16,2	Bear left on the well signed path	Into the woods	SW	515
71.060	400	16,6	Join the track and bear left		SW	554
71.061	80	16,6	At a bend to the left in the track, continue straight ahead on the path		S	555
71.062	400	17,0	Cross a ditch and turn sharply to the right		W	557
71.063	400	17,4	After a steep climb turn right on the track	Towards the village	W	580
71.064	100	17,5	At the junction with the tarmac road turn left on the road	Uphill	SW	588

Waypoint	Distance Between Waypoints (m)	Total (km)	Directions	Verification Point	Compass	Altitude (m)
71.065	50	17,6	Bear left on a footpath	Skirt the village of Toplecca di Sopra	SW	593
71.066	40	17,6	At the T-junction turn left		SW	596
71.067	120	17,8	Cross the tarmac road and continue straight ahead		S	603
71.068	180	17,9	Continue straight ahead	Over the bridge	SW	609
71.069	1700	19,7	At the summit of the Crocetta pass, after a long climb, continue straight ahead on the track	Pass beside the chapel	SW	691
71.070	40	19,7	Take the grass track to the left and downhill	Towards the village of Arzengio	S	690
71.071	1300	21,0	At the first houses in Arzengio, take the tarmac road to the left		SW	486
71.072	220	21,2	Take the first turning to the left	Skirt the village, with the village centre on the hilltop to the right	SE	461
71.073	140	21,4	On the far side of the village take the small path to the left	Between the olive trees	S	452
71.074	70	21,4	At the next junction turn right on the path	Across the hillside	W	448
71.075	60	21,5	Cross the tarmac road and take right fork on the small road beside the house	Initially parallel to the tarmac road on the left	SW	444
71.076	130	21,6	Continue straight ahead	The road becomes a track	SW	435
71.077	600	22,2	Continue straight ahead	Ignore the turning to the right	SW	365
71.078	180	22,4	Continue straight ahead	Tarmac road	W	343

Ostello-della-Cisa to Pontremoli 24.1km

Waypoint	Distance Between Waypoints (m)	Total (km)	Directions	Verification Point	Compass	Altitude (m)
71.079	900	23,3	At the T-junction turn right		NW	258
71.080	50	23,4	Continue straight ahead over the old bridge over the Magra	Towards the hospital	W	255
71.081	80	23,5	Pass through the archway and at the junction with the main road turn left	SS62, VF sign	S	253
71.082	60	23,5	At the fork in the road, bear right. Note:- to avoid a pedestrian subway bear left on the main road and then turn right to the centre of Pontremoli	Via di Porta Parma	SW	253
71.083	180	23,7	Bear right and continue straight ahead through the underpass	Beneath railway	S	253
71.084	80	23,8	Turn right after coming up from the underpass and go around the mini roundabout	VF sign, shrine directly in front	W	253
71.085	20	23,8	Go under the archway – Porta Parma – and into the narrow street ahead	Via Garibaldi	S	253
71.086	300	24,1	Arrive at Pontremoli centre (XXXI)	Piazza della Repubblica		243

Ostello-della-Cisa to Pontremoli 24.1km

Stage Summary: the Alternate Route, after a short stretch on the main road, follows quiet country roads for much of its length before rejoining the SS62 2km before the entry to Pontremoli. The route is recommended for cyclists.

Stage Ascent: 162m   **Stage Descent: 936m**

Waypoint	Distance Between Waypoints (m)	Total (km)	Directions	Verification Point	Compass	Altitude (m)
71A1.001	0	0,0	Continue straight ahead on the main road	Church on the right	SW	1031
71A1.002	1100	1,2	Turn left away from the SS62. Note:- to visit Montelungo (XXXII) follow the main road with care. The main road continues to Pontremoli	Direction Gravagna	SE	1021
71A1.003	5400	6,5	At the bottom of the hill continue straight ahead into the village of Gravagna San Rocco	VF sign	E	706
71A1.004	230	6,8	At the bottom of the hill continue straight ahead	VF sign	SE	696
71A1.005	400	7,2	Fork right before entering Gravagna Montale	Large house directly in front	S	689
71A1.006	4900	12,0	Continue straight ahead on the road	Main Route crosses from the right	SW	456
71A1.007	1200	13,2	A the T-junction turn right	Towards Pontremoli	SW	396
71A1.008	4100	17,3	At the T-junction, turn left and proceed with caution on the potentially busy road	SS62, downhill, towards Pontremoli	S	358
71A1.009	2400	19,7	Rejoin the Main Route and continue straight ahead on the road	Towards the centre of Pontremoli		257

Alternate Route #71.A1 19.7km

Pilgrim Hostel

Castello del Piagnaro,Via dei Voltoni,54027 Pontremoli(MS),Italy
Tel:+39 0187 831439,istruzione@comune.pontremoli.ms.it,Price:C,

Casa Alpina San Benedetto,(Signora Rita),54020 Montelungo(MS),Italy
Tel:+39 3391 741919,Price:C,

Religious Hostel

Seminario de Pontremoli,Piazza San Francesco,54027 Pontremoli(MS),Italy
Tel:+39 3386 876886,Mobile:+39 3345 446198,Price:D,

Convento Frati Cappuccini,Via dei Cappuccini, 2,54027 Pontremoli(MS),Italy
Tel:+39 0187 830395,adfini@yahoo.it,Price:D,PR,

Prioria Sant'Andrea Apostolocasa Canonica,Località Scorcetoli,54023 Filattiera(MS),Italy
Tel:+39 0187 457191,luciofilippi@treemmei.com,

Church or Religious Organisation

Prioria Sant'Andrea Apostolo, Località,Scorcetoli,54023 Filattiera(MS),Italy
Tel:+39 0187 457191,luciofilippi@treemmei.com,Price:D,

Tourist Information

Comune di Pontremol,Via Generale Reisoli, 11,54027 Pontremoli(MS),Italy
Tel:+39 0187 830056,

Banks and ATMs

Banca Monte dei Paschi di Siena,Via Pietro Bologna, 10,54027 Pontremoli(MS),Italy
Tel:+39 0187 461542,

Banca Monte dei Paschi di Siena,Via Pietro Bologna, 10,54027 Pontremoli(MS),Italy
Tel:+39 0187 461542,

Travel

Stazione Ferrovie,Piazzale Bruno Raschi,54027 Pontremoli(MS),Italy Tel:+39 06 6847 5475,www.renitalia.it,

Hospital

Ospedale Civile Sant'Antonio Abate,Via Nazionale,54027 Pontremoli(MS),Italy Tel:+39 0187 46211,

Doctor

Arrighi - Medico Chirurgo,Via Pirandello, 46,54027 Pontremoli(MS),Italy Tel:+39 0187 831252,

Veterinary

Ballestracci Natale,Via Mazzini, 56,54027 Pontremoli(MS),Italy Tel:+39 0187 833204,

Bicycle Shop

El Nino Cicli di Ambrosini Fabrizio,Via Europa, 74,54027 Pontremoli(MS),Italy
Tel:+39 0187 830457,

Stage Seventy-two Summary: the Main Route is another strenuous section with mixed conditions varying from busy and potentially dangerous roads near Pontremoli to challenging tracks through hilly woodland. A cycle route is available on generally level ground on the western side of the Magra.

Distance from Canterbury: 1533km   Distance to Saint-Peter's-Square: 541km
Stage Ascent: 190m   Stage Descent: 303m

Waypoint	Distance Between Waypoints (m)	Total (km)	Directions	Verification Point	Compass	Altitude (m)
72.001	0	0,0	Continue across piazza della Repubblica and into the narrow street ahead	Via Armani	SE	243
72.002	160	0,2	At the crossroads continue straight ahead. Note:- to use the Cycle Route turn right and continue over the bridge on the Alternate Route	Via Cavour	S	240
72.003	100	0,3	Turn left and cross the river bridge	Ponte Cesare Battisti	E	238
72.004	80	0,3	Pass through the archway and turn right	Via Mazzini	S	237
72.005	600	0,9	At the crossroads continue straight ahead to join the main road, remain on the right-hand side	VF sign, direction Aulla	S	228
72.006	700	1,6	Continue straight ahead	Pass beside the church of San Lazzaro	SE	230
72.007	130	1,7	Cross the road and bear left on the narrow paved street	Via Santissima Annunziata	E	227
72.008	180	1,9	Return to the main road, turn left and continue with care	Direction Massa on the SS62	SE	222
72.009	1200	3,1	Continue straight ahead on the SS62	Direction Villafranca, VF sign	SE	204
72.010	800	3,9	Turn left off the main road	VF sign, pass shop on your right	E	197
72.011	140	4,1	Take the right fork onto the gravel track	VF sign, large drainage ditch to your right	SE	197
72.012	500	4,5	At the junction with a minor road turn sharp left on the road	VF sign, towards railway	NE	198

Pontremoli to Villafranca-in-Lunigiana 18.2km

116

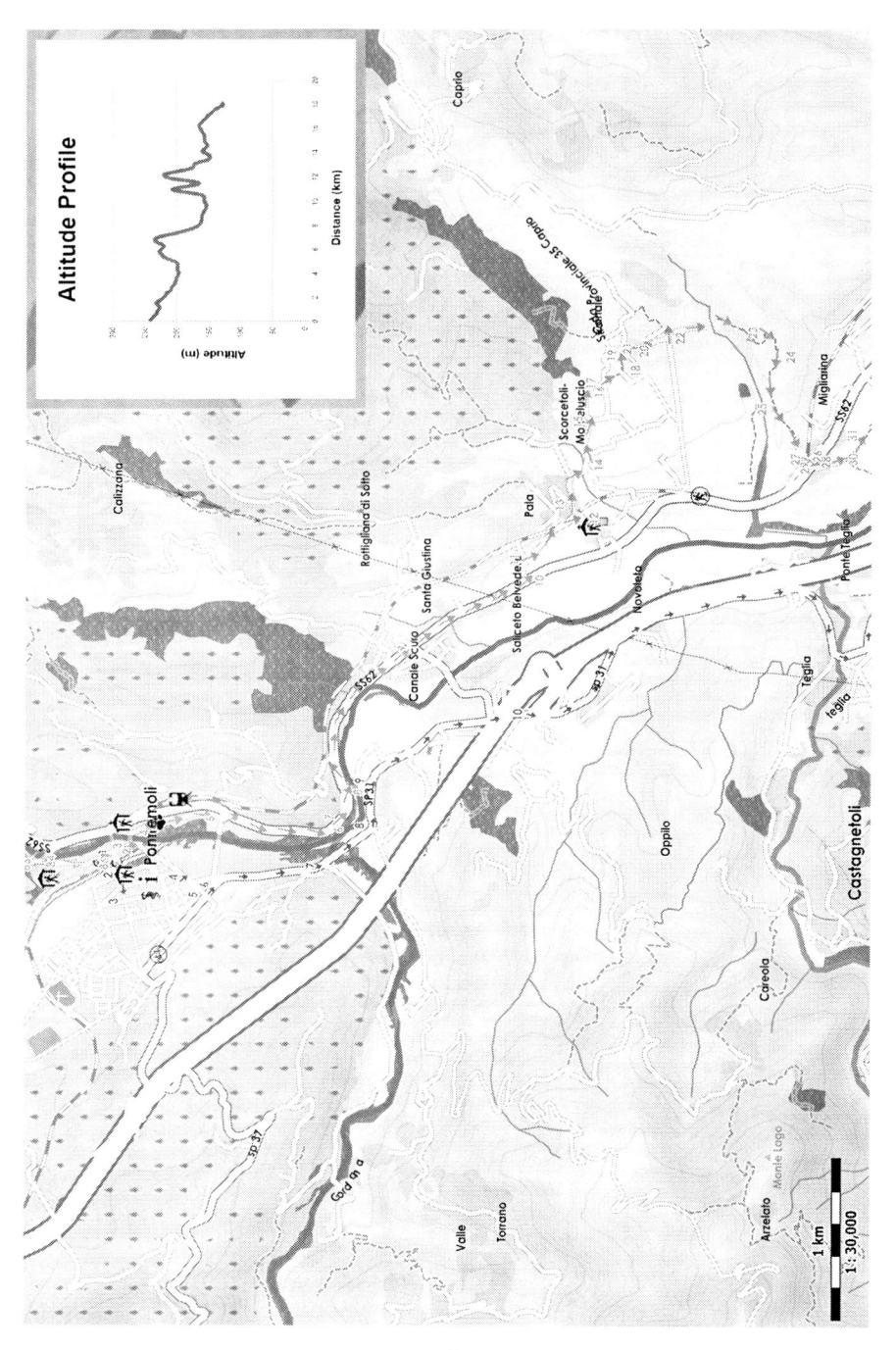

Waypoint	Distance Between Waypoints (m)	Total (km)	Directions	Verification Point	Compass	Altitude (m)
72.013	110	4,6	Take the right fork	Direction Ponticello	E	198
72.014	300	4,9	Continue straight ahead	Up the hill	E	200
72.015	280	5,2	Bear left on the road	Direction Canale, VF sign	E	213
72.016	200	5,4	Continue to the right on the road	VF sign	SE	220
72.017	120	5,5	At the crossroads, continue straight ahead on the gravel track	VF sign	SE	222
72.018	150	5,7	At the T-junction with a minor road, turn left	VF sign	E	225
72.019	100	5,8	At the road junction, cross over and pass on the left side of the church	Borgo de Ponticello, red and white sign	SE	227
72.020	60	5,8	Pass under an archway and turn right	Volta a Crociera	S	227
72.021	50	5,9	Bear left	Pass under a second arch	S	226
72.022	190	6,1	At the crossroads take the second turning on the left	VF sign, track crosses river and climbs ridge	S	223
72.023	800	6,8	Turn sharp right	VF sign	SW	234
72.024	160	7,0	Take the right fork onto the grassy track	VF sign	W	231
72.025	400	7,4	Take the left fork	Line of trees and fence on the left, VF sign	SW	203
72.026	300	7,7	Pass under the railway		SW	180
72.027	20	7,7	Bear left and then turn right in a narrow passageway	Red and white signs	SW	180
72.028	50	7,8	Cross straight over the main road and continue straight ahead	VF sign	SW	177

Pontremoli to Villafranca-in-Lunigiana 18.2km

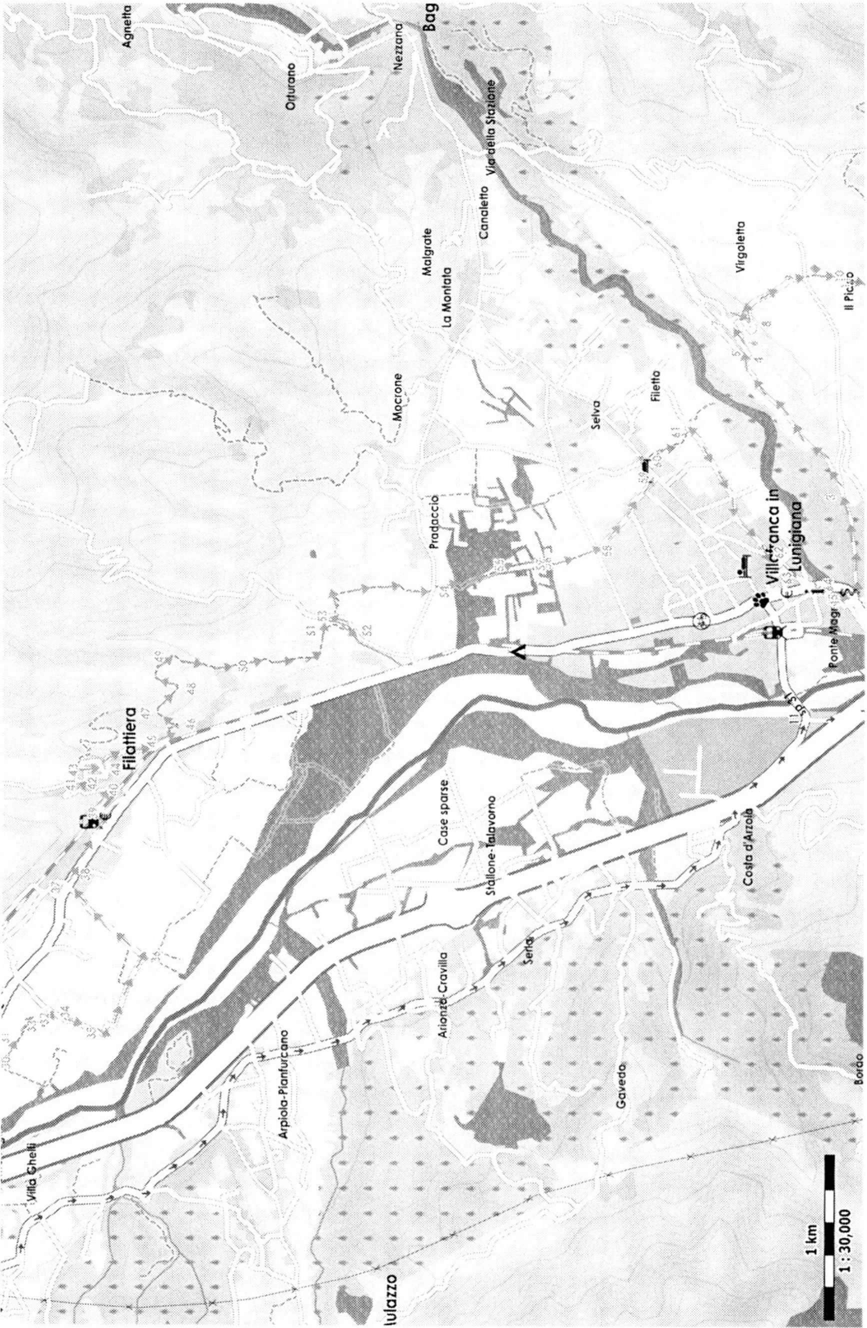
Agnetta
Orturano
Nezzana
Via della Stazione
Canaletto
Malgrate
La Montata
Virgoletta
Mocrone
Selva
Filetta
Pradaccio
Lunigiana
Filattiera
Case sparse
Stallone-Talavorno
Costa d'Arzola
Serra
Arionzo-Cravilla
Arpiola-Pianfurcano
Gaveda
Bordo
Villa Ghelli
1 km
1 : 30,000

Waypoint	Distance Between Waypoints (m)	Total (km)	Directions	Verification Point	Compass	Altitude (m)
72.029	40	7,8	Turn left between houses	Red and white CAI signs	S	174
72.030	160	8,0	At the fork in the track, bear left	Yellow VF sign, vines on your left	SE	167
72.031	190	8,2	At the end of the vines on your left, continue straight ahead on the faint track	Line of trees on your right	SE	164
72.032	170	8,3	At the T-junction, turn right	Towards farm buildings	SW	162
72.033	90	8,4	Turn left	Keep farm buildings to the right	SE	161
72.034	100	8,5	At the T-junction with the tarmac road turn right		SW	161
72.035	400	8,9	Facing a house turn left, road quickly turns right then left	Yellow VF sign	SE	160
72.036	600	9,4	At the T-junction, turn left	Farm on your left	NE	154
72.037	600	10,0	At the T-junction with the main road, turn right	Towards the church – Pieve di Sorano	E	157
72.038	90	10,1	Take the left fork and leave the SS62	Direction Biglio	SE	157
72.039	400	10,5	Turn left under the railway bridge	Brown VF sign	E	160
72.040	210	10,8	Turn right up a flight of steps. Note:- riders should remain on the road and bear right into the centre of the village		N	181
72.041	120	10,9	Continue straight ahead	Beside the square	N	198
72.042	20	10,9	At the road junction turn right	Towards the square in the centre of Filattiera	SE	200
72.043	110	11,0	Turn right to leave the square	Pass café immediately on your left	S	207

Pontremoli to Villafranca-in-Lunigiana 18.2km

Waypoint	Distance Between Waypoints (m)	Total (km)	Directions	Verification Point	Compass	Altitude (m)
72.044	100	11,1	At the end of the road take the left fork	Through archway, brown VF sign	SE	203
72.045	400	11,5	At the T-junction turn left and then right over a bridge and up the hill on a stony track	Railway bridge on the right at the junction	SE	165
72.046	180	11,7	Bear left towards the chapel on the brow of the hill	Yellow VF sign	NE	179
72.047	140	11,9	Take the right fork	Yellow VF sign and red and white signs	SE	200
72.048	210	12,1	Take the left fork	Into the trees	E	217
72.049	300	12,4	Turn right towards the pylon	Yellow VF sign	S	212
72.050	400	12,7	Continue straight ahead		S	179
72.051	700	13,4	Turn right beside the river	Red and white signs	S	153
72.052	230	13,7	At the road junction, turn left	Brown VF sign	NE	148
72.053	180	13,8	Turn right off the road	Brown VF sign	S	149
72.054	800	14,6	At the junction with the road turn left and then immediately right	Brown VF sign, electricity station on the left	S	152
72.055	600	15,1	Continue straight ahead on the narrow track	Trees on the right, field on the left	S	156
72.056	100	15,2	Continue straight ahead	Between the trees	S	156
72.057	130	15,4	Bear left onto the road	Golf course on the right	S	156

Pontremoli to Villafranca-in-Lunigiana 18.2km

Waypoint	Distance Between Waypoints (m)	Total (km)	Directions	Verification Point	Compass	Altitude (m)
72.058	270	15,6	At the crossroads in Filetto, continue straight ahead	Via San Genesio	SE	158
72.059	600	16,2	At the end of the road, turn left	Into Filetto old town	NE	164
72.060	120	16,4	Immediately after leaving the old town, turn right	Via del Canale	SE	164
72.061	400	16,7	At the T-junction, turn right	Parallel to the river and wooded ridge	SW	159
72.062	900	17,6	At the T-junction, turn left	Via Chiusura	SW	138
72.063	270	17,9	Bear left across piazza della Resistenza	Towards the main road	SW	129
72.064	90	18,0	Cross the main road and bear left across the piazza Aeronautica to take the old bridge over the river	Into the old town of Villafranca	SW	127
72.065	220	18,2	Arrive at Villafranca-in-Lunigiana old town centre	Beside the church		130

Pontremoli to Villafranca-in-Lunigiana 18.2km

Stage Summary: the Alternate Route to Terrarossa on the outskirts of Aulla, follows the Cycle Route on the western side of the river Magra and avoids the potentially dangerous SS62. The section to Ponte Magra (near Villafranca) is generally flat, before a stiff climb to Lusuolo

Stage Ascent: 227m   Stage Descent: 396m

Alternate Route #72.A1 21.5km

Waypoint	Distance Between Waypoints (m)	Total (km)	Directions	Verification Point	Compass	Altitude (m)
72A1.001	0	0,0	At the crossroads turn right and cross the river bridge	Via Pietro Bologna	W	240
72A1.002	140	0,1	At crossroads on the far side of the bridge, continue straight ahead	Via Roma	W	242
72A1.003	170	0,3	At the crossroads, turn left	Via Pirandello	SE	246
72A1.004	400	0,7	At the T-junction turn right	Strada di Maggio Galante	SW	239
72A1.005	170	0,9	At the crossroads, turn left onto via Europa and via Groppomontone	Factory building straight ahead	SE	239
72A1.006	100	1,0	Bear right on via Groppomontone	Keep river and bridge to the left	S	237
72A1.007	700	1,7	Continue straight ahead, cross the bridge over the Magra tributary	Via Antonino Siligato	SE	229
72A1.008	400	2,1	At the fork, bear left remaining beside the river	Direction La Spezia	E	222
72A1.009	270	2,3	Bear right on SP31	Between the hill and the river plane	SE	233
72A1.010	1100	3,4	Continue straight ahead, direction Villafranca	Motorway entrance on the left	SE	233

Waypoint	Distance Between Waypoints (m)	Total (km)	Directions	Verification Point	Compass	Altitude (m)
72A1.011	9000	12,4	In Ponte Magra, turn right onto via Pontemagra. Note:- to rejoin the Main Route, turn left and cross the bridge into the centre of Villafranca	Proceed with river Magra on the left	S	125
72A1.012	1900	14,4	Take the left fork	Towards Autostrada	S	188
72A1.013	1800	16,1	At the junction with the main road, turn left	Towards Lusuolo, SP61	S	178
72A1.014	2300	18,4	Bear left remaining on the road	Beside Autostrada on via Osca	SE	98
72A1.015	900	19,3	Bear right into Barbarasco	Via Chiesa	SW	109
72A1.016	100	19,4	At the T-junction in Barbarasco, turn left	SP23, via Roma	SE	110
72A1.017	1500	20,9	After crossing the river, continue straight ahead	Via Barbarasco	SE	73
72A1.018	260	21,2	At the T-junction, turn right	Via Nazionale, direction Aulla	SE	74
72A1.019	300	21,5	With the park on your left, rejoin the Main Route and continue straight ahead	Via Nazionale		71

Alternate Route #72.A1 21.5km

B&B, Hotel, Gite d'Etape

Villa Magnolia,Viale Italia, 33,54028 Villafranca-In-Lunigiana(MS),Italy
Tel:+39 0187 495563,Price:B,

Albergo Manganelli,Piazza San Nicolò, 5,54028 Villafranca-In-Lunigiana(MS),Italy
Tel:+39 0187 493062,Price:B,

Appartamenti Gredo,Piazza Immacolata, 30,54028 Villafranca-In-Lunigiana(MS),Italy
Mobile:+39 3498 487416,Price:A,

Camping

Camping il Castagneto,Via Nazionale,54028 Villafranca-In-Lunigiana(MS),Italy
Tel:+39 0187 493671,

Tourist Information

Comune di Villafranca In Lunigiana,Via Monsignor Razzoli, 2,54028 Villafranca-In-Lunigiana(MS),Italy Tel:+39 0187 493013,

Banks and ATMs

Banca Toscana,Via Chiusura, 22,54028 Villafranca-In-Lunigiana(MS),Italy
Tel:+39 0187 493018,

Banca Monte dei Paschi di Siena,Via Ponte Provinciale, 41,54023 Filattiera(MS),Italy
Tel:+39 0187 458540,

Doctor

Natali - Medico Chirurgo,Via Baracchini, 53,54028 Villafranca-In-Lunigiana(MS),Italy Tel:+39 0187 494193,

Veterinary

Ambulatorio Medico Veterinario,Via Aldo Moro, 2,54028 Villafranca-In-Lunigiana(MS),Italy
Tel:+39 0187 495193,

Hiking Equipment

Bortolasi,Via Provinciale, 2,54023 Filattiera (MS),Italy Tel:+39 0187 458017,

Bicycle Shop

Dueruote di Pagani Emanuele Sas,Via Aldo Moro, 94,54028 Villafranca-In-Lunigiana(MS), Italy Tel:+39 0187 495811,

Pontremoli to Villafranca-In-Lunigiana 18.2km

Stage Seventy-three Summary: the route leaves Villafranca on a minor road before taking to woodland tracks. The route rejoins the busy SS62 between Terrarosa and Aulla.

Distance from Canterbury: 1551km Distance to Saint-Peter's-Square: 523km
Stage Ascent: 235m Stage Descent: 308m

Waypoint	Distance Between Waypoints (m)	Total (km)	Directions	Verification Point	Compass	Altitude (m)
73.001	0	0,0	Cross the piazza, turn left and leave the old town	After passing the church	S	131
73.002	40	0,1	Cross the main road and turn left onto via della Libertà	Direction Virgoletta, SP26, VF sign	E	133
73.003	700	0,8	Fork left	Direction Virgoletta	NE	171
73.004	1100	1,8	Fork right	Direction Virgoletta Centre	SE	176
73.005	40	1,8	Turn left up the narrow alleyway in the direction of the Church	Shrine on left	NE	178
73.006	90	1,9	Turn right	Pass between houses and valley bottom	NE	182
73.007	140	2,1	Turn right and leave the village	Pass natural water source on the left	S	187
73.008	190	2,3	Bear left continuing up the hill	Via delle Fontane	SE	195
73.009	500	2,8	At the crossroads, continue straight ahead towards the cemetery	Red and white painted sign	S	213
73.010	150	2,9	Road becomes a track, continue straight ahead with the football pitch on the left	Red and white painted sign	S	213
73.011	200	3,1	Fork left downhill onto a narrow grassy track	Garden on the right	SW	206
73.012	100	3,2	Continue straight ahead	Ignore turning to the right	SW	201
73.013	240	3,4	Fork left across the stream and continue on the narrow track	Red and white painted sign	SE	193

Villafranca-in-Lunigiana to Aulla 14.8km

126

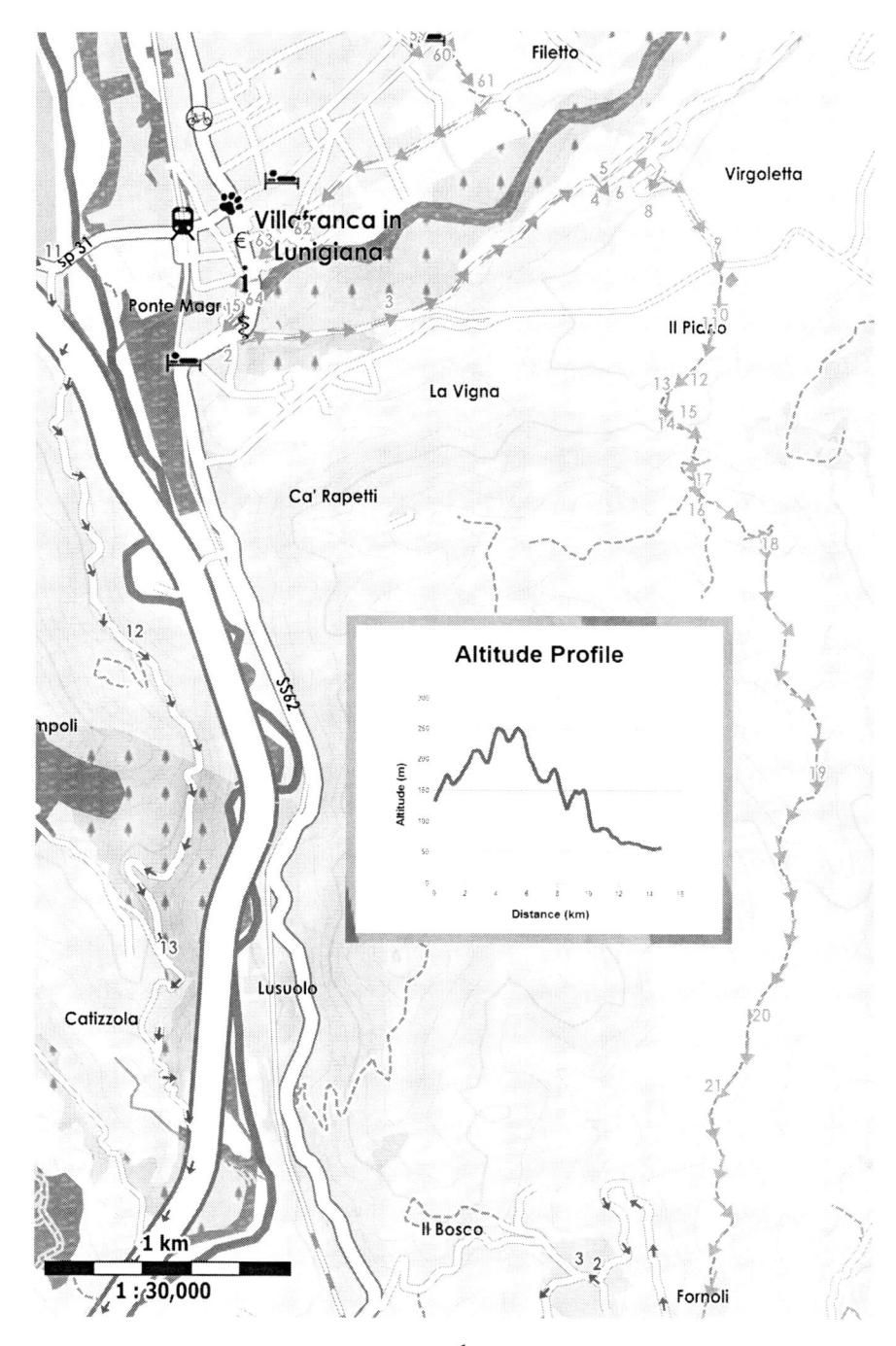

Waypoint	Distance Between Waypoints (m)	Total (km)	Directions	Verification Point	Compass	Altitude (m)
73.014	30	3,5	After crossing the stream take the right fork		SE	194
73.015	180	3,6	Take the right fork up the hill	Red and white painted sign	S	205
73.016	400	4,1	Turn left at the top of the hill	Wooden balustrade on left	SE	246
73.017	40	4,1	Fork left	Continue downhill	SE	248
73.018	400	4,5	Turn sharp right at the T-junction		S	245
73.019	1300	5,7	At the fork bear right	Red and white painted sign	S	243
73.020	1000	6,7	Continue straight ahead	Roman road	SW	173
73.021	500	7,2	Bear left	Following the red and white signs	S	164
73.022	1100	8,3	At the T-junction with the minor road, bear left direction La Valle del Sole. Note:- horse riders should take the Alternate Route to the right to avoid a treacherous pathway and steps	House directly in front	S	143
73.023	40	8,4	Skirt the house and turn right on a gravel track	Red and white painted sign	SW	140
73.024	30	8,4	Turn right to go between two buildings, then immediately turn left	Red and white painted sign	W	138
73.025	400	8,8	After a steep ascent and a rough flight of steps, bear left with an old building immediately on the left and a wall on right	Red and white painted sign	W	128
73.026	70	8,9	Turn left onto the road	Up the hill	SW	133

Villafranca-in-Lunigiana to Aulla 14.8km

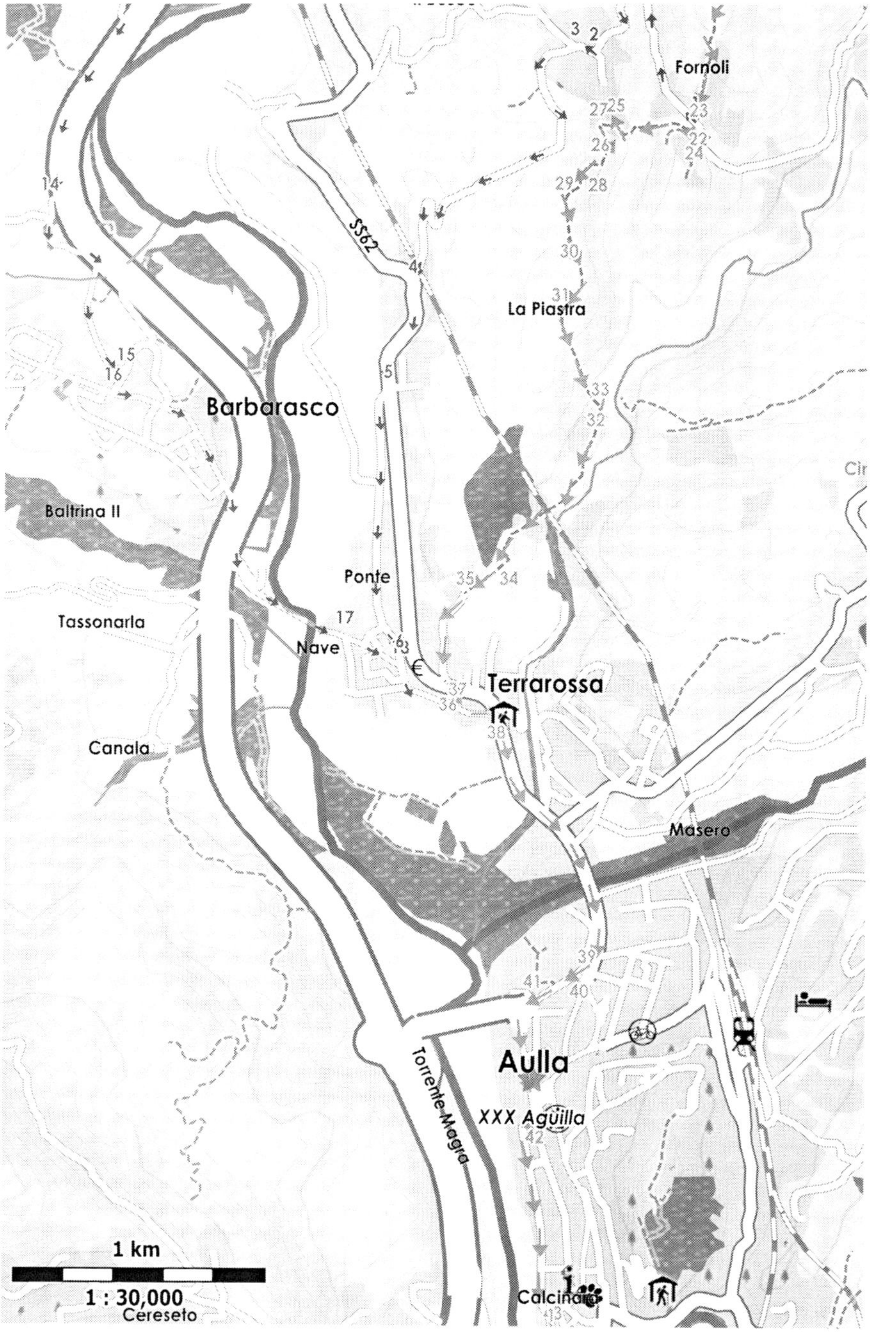
Fornoli
La Piastra
SS62
Barbarasco
Baltrina II
Ponte
Tassonarla
Nave
Terrarossa
Canala
Masero
Aulla
XXX Aguilla
Torrente Magra
Calcinara
1 km
1 : 30,000
Cereseto

Waypoint	Distance Between Waypoints (m)	Total (km)	Directions	Verification Point	Compass	Altitude (m)
73.027	30	8,9	Turn left up the steep narrow track	VF sign	S	135
73.028	190	9,1	Bear right on track	Red and white painted sign	SW	144
73.029	210	9,3	Turn left at the T-junction	Private property on the right	S	148
73.030	130	9,4	Take the right fork		S	145
73.031	400	9,8	Take the left fork		S	148
73.032	400	10,2	Bear right	In the clearing	SE	98
73.033	40	10,2	Bear right on the broader track	White house directly on the left	SW	94
73.034	800	11,0	Take the right fork	Red and white painted sign	SW	88
73.035	230	11,2	Track emerges onto a minor tarmac road – via dei Pini, continue straight ahead	Cemetery on right	S	88
73.036	400	11,7	At the crossroads with the SS62, continue straight ahead	VF sign, via dei Pini	SE	74
73.037	100	11,8	At the T-junction, turn left. Note:- Alternate Routes join from the right	VF sign	E	74
73.038	160	11,9	At the junction with the SS62, turn right and proceed with care on the main road	Pass Castello on your left	S	72
73.039	1200	13,1	Shortly after passing a Tabacchi on your left, turn right into a pedestrian tunnel under the railway	VF sign	W	63

Villafranca-in-Lunigiana to Aulla 14.8km

Waypoint	Distance Between Waypoints (m)	Total (km)	Directions	Verification Point	Compass	Altitude (m)
73.040	30	13,1	After emerging from the tunnel, turn left onto viale Lunigiana	VF sign	SW	63
73.041	220	13,4	Bear left away from the motorway entrance	Viale Lunigiana	S	62
73.042	500	13,9	At the major crossroads, turn right and bear left still on viale Lunigiana	VF sign, proceed beside the river	S	58
73.043	1000	14,8	Arrive at Aulla (XXX) centre beside Abbazia di San Caprasio	Bridge over the river Magra to your right		58

Alternate Route #73.A1 4.7km

Stage Summary: the Alternate Route allows riders to avoid a flight of steps and a steep descent but at the cost of some additional distance on the main road

Stage Ascent: 30m   Stage Descent: 89m

Waypoint	Dist	Total	Directions	Verification Point	Compass	Altitude
73A1.001	0	0,0	Take the road to the right	Direction Finoli	NW	141
73A1.002	1400	1,4	At the T-junction in Fornoli, turn right	Via dell'Ardito	W	155
73A1.003	90	1,5	At the fork bear left	Via dell'Ara	SW	157
73A1.004	1600	3,1	At the T-junction with the main road turn left	SS62, via Cisa	S	90
73A1.005	500	3,5	Turn right	Via Camposagna	S	87
73A1.006	1200	4,7	Join the Cycle Route from Pontremoli and continue straight ahead to rejoin the Main Route beside the park in the centre of Terrarossa	Direction Aulla, via Nazionale		82

Pilgrim Hostel

Castello Malaspina,Via Nazionale Cisa,54019 Terrarossa(MS),Italy
Tel:+39 0187 474942,Mobile:+39 3289 438652,Price:C,

Fortezza "la Brunella",Parco della Brunella,54011 Aulla(MS),Italy
Tel:+39 0187 409077,coopnatur@libero.it,Price:C,

Religious Hostel

Abbazia di San Caprasio,(Don Giovanni Perini),Piazza Abbazia,54011 Aulla(MS),Italy
Tel:+39 0187 420148,Mobile:+39 3396 380331,cultura@comune.aulla.ms.it,Price:D,

B&B, Hotel, Gite d'Etape

B&B Casa Barani,Via Sprini,54011 Aulla(MS),Italy Mobile:+39 3474 657930,Price:B,

Equestrian

Agricamping Ulivetta,Via Molesana,54016 Licciana-Nardi(MS),Italy
Mobile:+39 3472 343196,

Equiluna - Oasi di Cavalli e Persone,Località la Praduscella,54013 Moncigoli(MS),Italy
Mobile:+39 3389 111770,

Tourist Information

Pro Loco,Piazza Gramsci, 24,54011 Aulla(MS),Italy Tel:+39 0187 421439,

Banks and ATMs

Cassa di Risparmio di Carrara,Viale Resistenza, 43,54011 Aulla(MS),Italy
Tel:+39 0187 420297,

Banca Toscana,Viale Resistenza, 52,54011 Aulla(MS),Italy Tel:+39 0187 420224,

Cassa di Risparmio,Strada Statale della Cisa, 55,54016 Licciana-Nardi(MS),Italy
Tel:+39 0187 421371,

Travel

Stazione Ferrovie,Piazza Roma, 18,54011 Aulla(MS),Italy
Tel:+39 06 6847 5475,www.renitalia.it,

Doctor

Peselli - Studio Medico,Piazza della Vittoria, 7,54011 Aulla(MS),Italy Tel:+39 0187 495002,

Veterinary

Crespo - Studio Veterinario,Via Nazionale, 26,54011 Aulla(MS),Italy Tel:+39 0187 421967,

Hiking Equipment

Bortolasi,Via Nazionale, 196B,54011 Aulla(MS),Italy Tel:+39 0187 422544,

Bicycle Shop

Bi.Ciclo di Petacchi Elisabetta e C.Snc - Ingrosso e Dettaglio Biciclette,Via Cerri,54011 Aulla(MS),Italy Tel:+39 0187 408020,

Villafranca-in-Lunigiana to Aulla 14.8km

Stage Seventy-four Summary: this is another rugged segment over the final ridge before the coastal plain. The Alternate Routes offer options for all groups to bypass the most difficult sections and also to visit Santo Stefano di Magra (XXIX).

Distance from Canterbury: 1566km   Distance to Saint-Peter's-Square: 508km

Stage Ascent: 575m   Stage Descent: 605m

Aulla to Sarzana 16.4km

Waypoint	Distance Between Waypoints (m)	Total (km)	Directions	Verification Point	Compass	Altitude (m)
74.001	0	0,0	With the bridge over the river Magra behind and Abbazia di San Caprasio to your left, bear right	Piazza Abazzia, direction La Spezia	SE	58
74.002	80	0,1	At the T-junction, turn right, pass under the arch and then turn left	Towards riverside, red and white signs	SE	58
74.003	50	0,1	At the riverside, turn left direction Massa and La Spezia	Piazza L. Corbani, keep river to the right	NE	57
74.004	120	0,3	At the T-junction, turn right and cross river bridge	SS62, direction La Spezia	S	57
74.005	180	0,4	At the end of the bridge, turn left across a disused railway line and then bear left	Direction Bibola, VF sign	E	62
74.006	200	0,6	Bear right away from the larger road. Note:– the Alternate Route to the left offers a longer but easier option for all groups and is recommended for cyclists and horse-riders	Via Prascara	S	81
74.007	60	0,7	Bear left on the footpath	Beside the wall	S	88
74.008	400	1,1	Cross the track and continue ahead up the hill	Beside the vineyard	S	155
74.009	90	1,2	At the junction with the road turn right and immediately left on the steep footpath	Into the woods	SE	170
74.010	600	1,8	At the T-junction with the track turn right		S	256

133

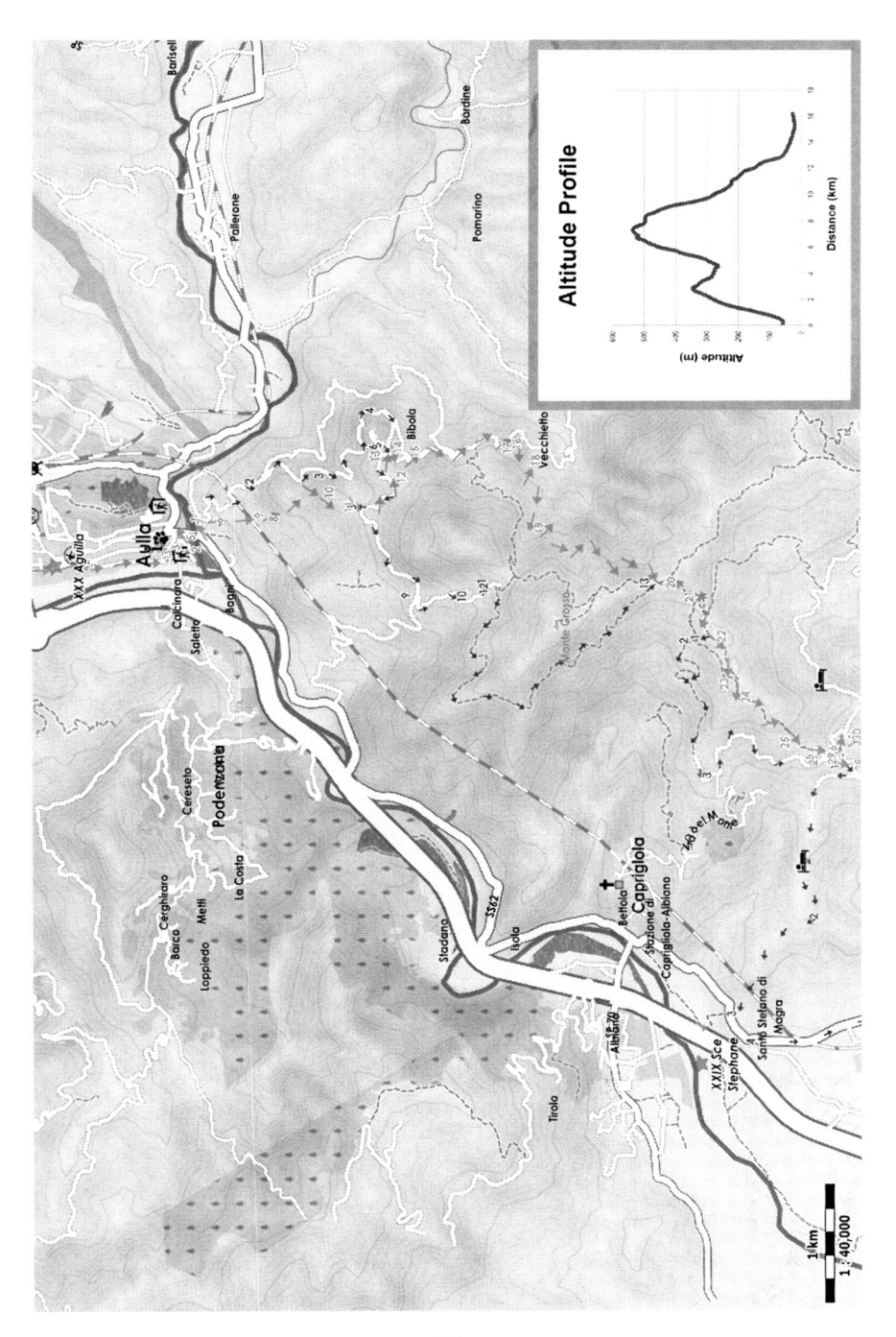

Waypoint	Distance Between Waypoints (m)	Total (km)	Directions	Verification Point	Compass	Altitude (m)
74.011	500	2,3	In the clearing continue straight ahead on the broad track over the crossroads - the Alternate Route crosses the Main Route and continues to the right	Uphill towards Bibola	SE	298
74.012	500	2,8	Approaching the top of the hill take the footpath to the right		E	345
74.013	200	3,0	Rejoin the broad track and turn right downhill	The village of Bibola is on the hilltop to the left	E	336
74.014	90	3,1	Take the next turning to the right and then immediately right again on the unmade road	Across the hillside towards Vecchietto	S	330
74.015	500	3,6	Bear right on the tarmac	Towards Vecchietto	S	299
74.016	900	4,4	Take the right fork into the village of Vecchietto	VF sign, towards bell tower	S	269
74.017	180	4,6	Turn right under the archway	Red and white stripe sign, via Fontana	W	264
74.018	140	4,7	On the edge of the village, bear right on the track, beside the olive grove	Climbing into the forest	W	277
74.019	1000	5,7	Take the steep footpath to the right	In the clearing	SW	395
74.020	1500	7,2	At the crossroads continue straight ahead on the forest track – the Alternate Route joins from the right	At the top of the hill	S	534
74.021	400	7,6	Continue straight ahead. Note:- the turning to the left leads to a viewpoint overlooking La Spezia and the coast		W	517

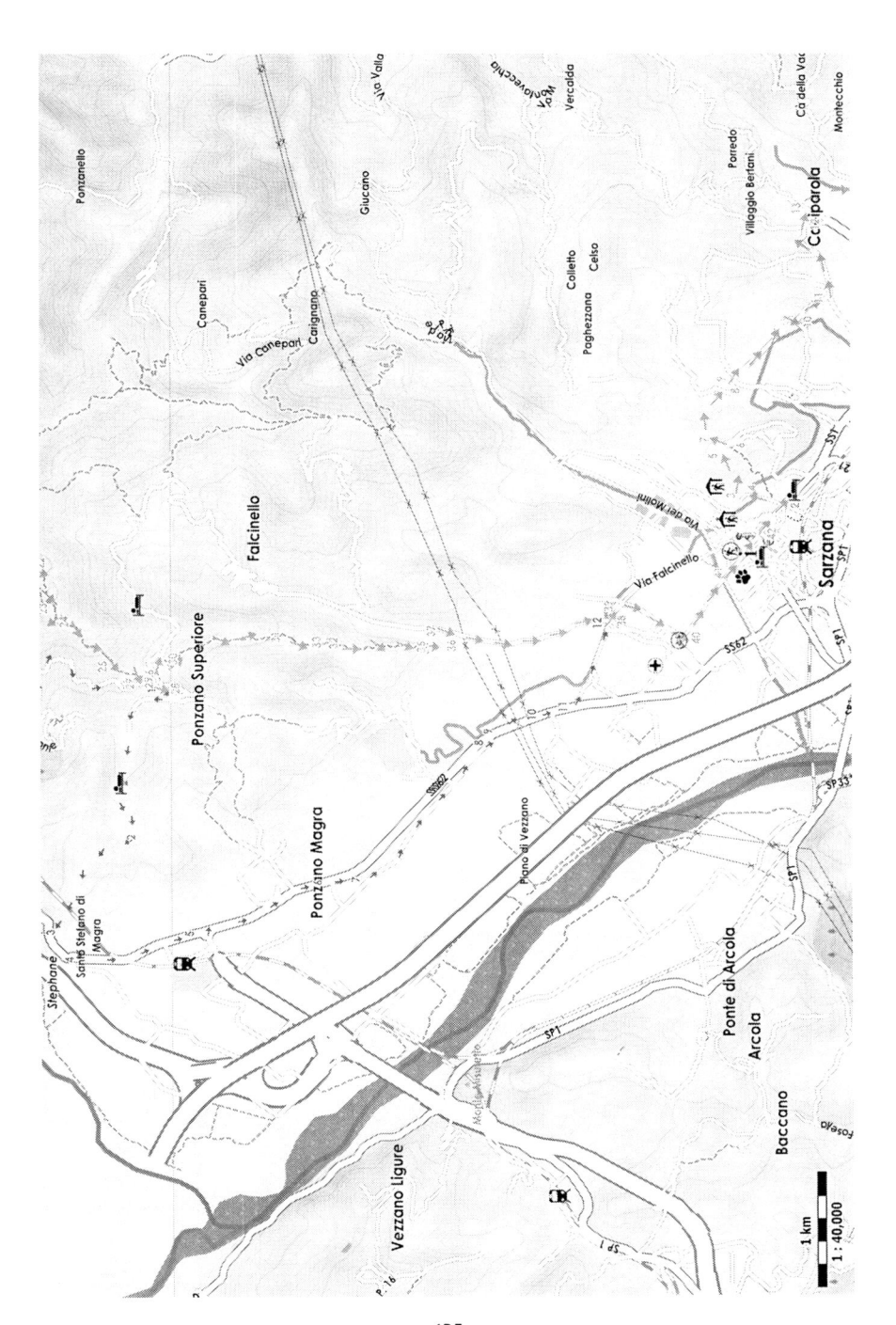
Ponzanello
Canepari
Via Canepari
Carignano
Giucano
Via Valla
Vercalda
Colletto
Celso
Paghezzana
Porredo
Villaggio Bertani
Cà della Vac
Montecchio
Falcinello
Via dei Molini
Via Falcinello
Sarzana
SS62
SP1
SS1
Ponzano Superiore
Ponzano Magra
Piano di Vezzano
SP33
Santo Stefano di Magra
Stephane
Ponte di Arcola
Arcola
Baccano
SP1
Vezzano Ligure
1 km
1 : 40,000

Waypoint	Distance Between Waypoints (m)	Total (km)	Directions	Verification Point	Compass	Altitude (m)
74.022	400	8,0	Go straight ahead onto narrow track - the descent on the Main Route is over broken ground and is unsuitable for bikes and difficult for horses. The Alternate Route leaves to the right and descends on a broader easier track		SW	495
74.023	500	8,5	Continue straight ahead down a narrow track	VF sign direction Sarzana	W	483
74.024	130	8,6	Fork left		SW	466
74.025	800	9,4	At the junction, continue straight ahead	Between olive groves towards Ponzano Superiore	S	359
74.026	220	9,6	Turn right onto a small tarmac road	Downhill	SW	318
74.027	90	9,7	Turn left	Enter Ponzano Superiore	S	305
74.028	190	9,9	Turn left in piazza Aia di Croce direction Sarzana - the pathway ahead has narrow sections over broken ground with steep descents and bypasses Santo Stefano di Magra (XXIX). Cyclists and those wishing to visit Santo Stefano should bear right on the Alternate Route	Via Cesare Orsini	NE	285
74.029	60	10,0	Road becomes a grassy track following the line of the ridge	Red and white stripe sign	E	281

Aulla to Sarzana 16.4km

Waypoint	Distance Between Waypoints (m)	Total (km)	Directions	Verification Point	Compass	Altitude (m)
74.030	230	10,2	Turn right onto a minor road and proceed downhill on via Cattarello	Red and white stripe sign	S	264
74.031	1300	11,4	Fork right	Up the hill	S	196
74.032	300	11,8	Bear right at the top of the hill	Archaeological dig site	S	182
74.033	70	11,8	After passing the dig, bear right	Down the hill	S	176
74.034	800	12,6	Take the lower track to the left	Red and white stripe sign	S	104
74.035	200	12,8	Turn left onto the small tarmac road		S	71
74.036	50	12,9	Turn left at the T-junction	Via Lago	E	66
74.037	140	13,0	In the valley turn right at the T-junction, direction Sarzana	Red and white stripe sign, via Falcinello	S	57
74.038	1500	14,5	After crossing a small bridge, turn left at the crossroads - the Alternate Route rejoins from the right	Bar and shop on the left, VF sign	SE	28
74.039	180	14,7	Turn right	Via Turi	SW	27
74.040	600	15,3	At the crossroads, turn left	Via Cisa, VF sign	SE	20
74.041	700	16,0	Go straight ahead to enter Sarzana old town	Pass through Porta Parma	SE	24
74.042	400	16,4	Arrive at Sarzana centre	Beside the church of Santa Maria		28

Aulla to Sarzana 16.4km

Alternate Route #74.A1 10.2km

Stage Summary: the Alternate easier route takes a quiet road and broad gravel tracks over the ridge

Stage Ascent: 592m   Stage Descent: 134m

Waypoint	Distance Between Waypoints (m)	Total (km)	Directions	Verification Point	Compass	Altitude (m)
74A1.001	0	0,0	Bear left on the road over a small bridge	Direction Bibola	SE	79
74A1.002	1100	1,1	Fork right up the hill	Woodland to the right	S	169
74A1.003	800	1,9	Remain on the road to Bibola	Pass VF sign	SE	228
74A1.004	1100	3,0	Fork right on the road	Direction Bibola	W	297
74A1.005	400	3,3	Turn right at the top of the hill in the direction of Bibola	VF sign	N	330
74A1.006	40	3,4	At T-junction turn left	Away from the hill-top centre of Bibola	W	331
74A1.007	90	3,5	Bear right onto the track	VF sign	NW	334
74A1.008	800	4,3	At fork in track bear left		SW	302
74A1.009	1100	5,4	Turn left onto a minor road and proceed uphill	Towards quarry	S	342
74A1.010	700	6,0	Bear right with the quarry directly on your left		SE	413
74A1.011	230	6,3	At fork bear right	Away from quarry	W	448
74A1.012	60	6,3	At T-junction turn right		S	454
74A1.013	3900	10,2	At the crossroads in the tracks, rejoin the Main Route and turn right			537

Alternate Route #74.A2 3.5km

Stage Summary: the Alternate Route allows cyclists and riders to avoid a difficult descent over broken ground.

Stage Ascent: 36m   Stage Descent: 219m

74A2.001	0	0,0	Turn right		N	490
74A2.002	90	0,1	At the junction, bear right		W	472
74A2.003	2000	2,1	Take the left fork	Pass la Volpara restaurant - provides excellent regional food	S	329
74A2.004	1400	3,5	At the junction, rejoin the Main Route and turn right	Into the village of Ponzano Superiore		308

Alternate Route #74.A3 9.6km

Stage Summary: the Alternate Route passes through Santo Stefano di Magra (XXIX), but includes approximately 5km on the busy SP62

Stage Ascent: 30m   Stage Descent: 287m

Waypoint	Distance Between Waypoints (m)	Total (km)	Directions	Verification Point	Compass	Altitude (m)
74A3.001	0	0,0	In piazza Aia di Croce bear right on the road	Proceed down the hill on via Antonio Gramsci	W	285
74A3.002	2000	2,0	400 metres after third right-hand hairpin turn sharp right leaving the road. Note:- this is a difficult turning to spot	Via Brigate Alpine	NW	149
74A3.003	1400	3,5	At the T-junction at the entry to Santo Stefano di Magra (XXIX), turn left	Via Roma	SW	57
74A3.004	290	3,7	At the T-junction, turn left	SP62, via Cisa Sud	S	52
74A3.005	1100	4,8	At the roundabout, continue straight ahead	SP62, via Cisa Sud	S	26
74A3.006	1200	6,0	At broad junction in Ponzano Magra bear right on the smaller road	Via Cisa Vecchio	S	25
74A3.007	300	6,4	After passing under the railway, join via Seconda Piano Vezzano and proceed straight ahead	Keep railway to the left	SE	22
74A3.008	1600	8,0	At the mini-roundabout, turn left, cross the railway and immediately turn right at the roundabout	Rejoin SS62	SE	19
74A3.009	140	8,1	With a bridge over the road ahead, bear left to leave the main road	Uphill	S	22
74A3.010	400	8,5	At the T-junction with the SS62, turn left	Enter Sarzana	S	21
74A3.011	270	8,8	At the fork, bear left on the small road	Via San Gottardo	E	18
74A3.012	800	9,6	At the crossroads, continue straight ahead and rejoin the Main Route	Bar ahead on the left		28

Pilgrim Hostel

Centro di Crescita Comunitaria,Via Giosuè Carducci, 5,19038 Sarzana(SP),Italy
Tel:+39 1876 112718,mariagrazia.v@consorziocometa.org,Price:D,

Religious Hostel

Convento San Francesco,(Don Renzo Cortese),Via San Francesco,19038 Sarzana(SP),Italy
Tel:+39 0187 614227,Price:C,

B&B, Hotel, Gite d'Etape

Hotel la Trigola,Via Antonio Gramsci, 63,19037 Santo-Stefano-di-Magra(SP),Italy
Tel:+39 0187 630292,Price:B,

B&B la Costa Bed and Breakfast, la Spezia,Via Mario Baria, 11,19037 Santo-Stefano-di-Magra(SP),Italy Mobile:+39 3339 999870,Price:B,

B&B - il viale,Viale Giuseppe Mazzini, 75,19038 Sarzana(SP),Italy
Tel:+39 0187 610866,Mobile:+39 3337 705145,
info@ilvialedivaleria.it,www.ilvialedivaleria.it,Price:B,

Albergo la Villetta,Via Sobborgo Emiliano, 24a,19038 Sarzana(SP),Italy
Tel:+39 0187 620195,Price:A,

Equestrian

River Ranch Sarzana,Via Navonella,19038 Sarzana(SP),Italy Mobile:+39 3382 979071,

Tourist Information

Comune di Sarzana,Via Antonio Bertoloni, 1,19038 Sarzana(SP),Italy Tel:+39 0187 614300,

Banks and ATMs

Unicredit Banca,Via Sobborgo Emiliano, 32,19038 Sarzana(SP),Italy
Tel:+39 0187 029411,www.unicreditbanca.it/?ucid=LEC-GMAP_163,

Travel

Stazione Ferrovie,Piazza Guido Jurgens, 20,19038 Sarzana(SP),Italy
Tel:+39 06 6847 5475,www.renitalia.it,

Hospital

Presidio Ospedaliero San Bartolomeo,Via Cisa,19038 Sarzana(SP),Italy Tel:+39 0187 6041,

Doctor

Battistini - Studio Medico,Via Domenico Fiasella, 30,19038 Sarzana(SP),Italy
Tel:+39 0187 622138,

Veterinary

Studio Medico Veterinario,Via Paganino Da Sarzana,19038 Sarzana(SP),Italy
Tel:+39 0187 621726,

Hiking Equipment

Alberti,Via Circonvallazione, 10,19038 Sarzana(SP),Italy Tel:+39 0187 627387,

Bicycle Shop

Bike Station Srl,Via Cisa, 142,19038 Sarzana(SP),Italy Tel:+39 0187 916668,

Stage Seventy-five Summary: this section is largely undertaken on suburban roads before climbing onto tracks and narrow roads through the vineyards before entering Massa. The Alternate Route from Luni to Pietrasanta provides an opportunity to stroll beside the Mediterranean beaches, avoids some dangerous stretches of road and reduces the total distance to Pietrasanta.

Distance from Canterbury: 1582km   Distance to Saint-Peter's-Square: 492km

Stage Ascent: 403m   Stage Descent: 360m

Waypoint	Distance Between Waypoints (m)	Total (km)	Directions	Verification Point	Compass	Altitude (m)
75.001	0	0,0	Continue along via Giuseppe Mazzini	Church of Santa Maria on the left	SE	28
75.002	300	0,3	At the roundabout, turn left on the narrow via San Francesco	Pass bar on your right	N	22
75.003	400	0,7	Shortly after the road bends to the left, turn right on the small road towards the hillside	Red and white sign, pass small shrine in the house on your left	E	25
75.004	70	0,8	Bear right on the track	Towards the fortress on the hilltop	NE	32
75.005	400	1,1	Bear right	Keep the fortress of Sarzanello immediately on the left	E	79
75.006	100	1,2	Turn left on the cobbled road	Continue to skirt the fortress	NE	84
75.007	120	1,3	At the junction, turn right downhill on via Montata di Sarzanello	Red and white sign	E	79
75.008	600	1,9	At the Stop sign, continue straight ahead	Over the bridge	SE	27
75.009	140	2,0	At the T-junction bear left	Via Canalburo	SE	24
75.010	800	2,8	Bear left and remain on via Canalburo	Ignore turning to the right with bridge over the road	SE	23
75.011	400	3,2	At the T-junction, turn left	Red and white sign and bus stop (Fermata) on the left	E	42
75.012	800	4,0	At the complex junction continue straight ahead on via Caniparola	Pass small parking area on your left	E	61

Sarzana to Massa 27.6km

142

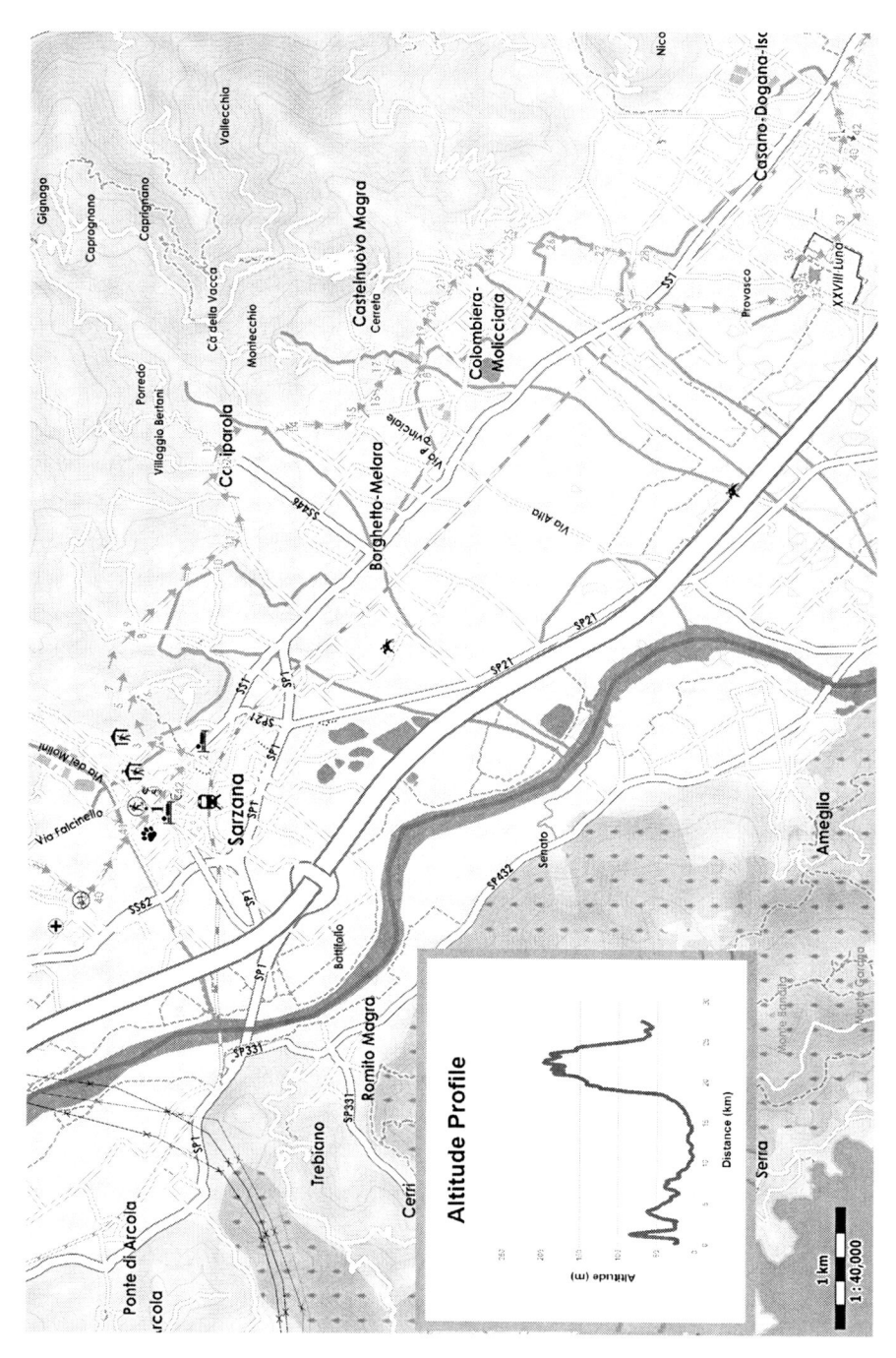

Waypoint	Distance Between Waypoints (m)	Total (km)	Directions	Verification Point	Compass	Altitude (m)
75.013	150	4,1	On the apex of a bend to the left continue straight ahead on the small road	Pass archway on your right	S	61
75.014	700	4,8	At the T-junction, turn right and then immediately left on via Montecchio and enter Colombiera	Olive grove on the left at the junction	S	45
75.015	800	5,5	At the crossroads turn left on via Provinciale	Direction Castelnuovo Magra - Centro Historico	E	31
75.016	100	5,6	Turn right on via Paradiso	Red and white sign, electricity sub-station on the right	SE	30
75.017	400	6,0	Turn right on via Bologna	Red and white sign	SW	29
75.018	220	6,2	At the crossroads, turn left	Towards parking area and dyke	E	22
75.019	500	6,7	At the crossroads, turn left	Beside school, red and white sign	NE	26
75.020	210	6,9	At the crossroads, turn right	Via Pedemontana, red and white sign	SE	36
75.021	400	7,3	At the crossroads, continue straight ahead on via Molino del Piano	Pharmacy on your right	E	39
75.022	100	7,4	At the crossroads, turn right on via Olmarello	Road bears left after the turn	SE	38
75.023	180	7,5	Immediately before reaching the river, bear right and take the grass track	Over the old river bridge	SE	34
75.024	80	7,6	At the junction with the road, turn right	Red and white sign	SE	35
75.025	400	8,1	Turn right on the narrow via Corta	Red and white sign	SW	29
75.026	160	8,2	Immediately after crossing the water channel, turn left on the grass track	Red and white sign, keep waterway on your left	S	21

Sarzana to Massa 27.6km

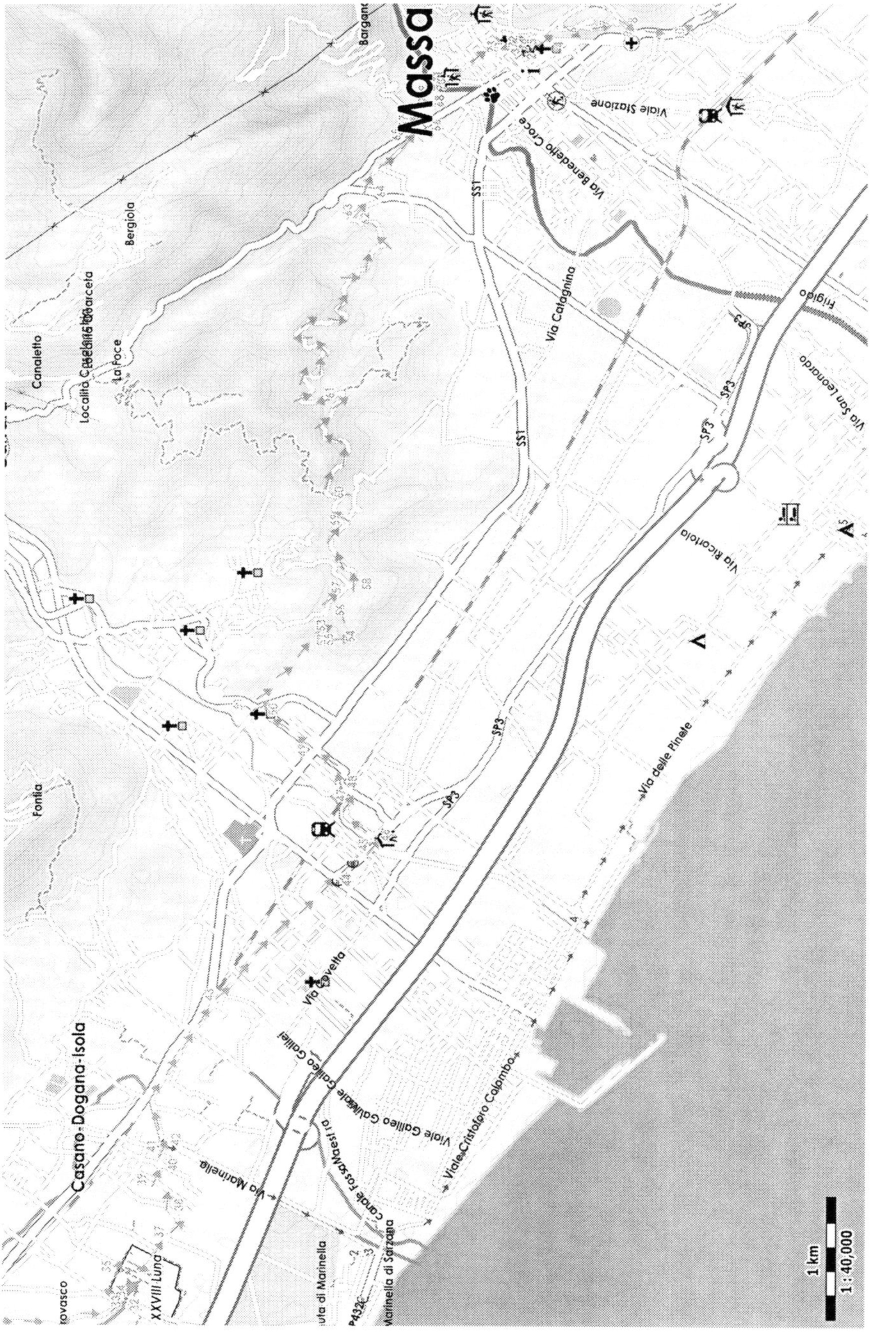
Massa
Bergiola
Canaletto
La Foce
Fontia
Casano-Dogana-Isola
Viale Stazione
Via Benedetto Croce
Via Catagnina
Frigido
Via San Leonardo
Via Ricortola
Via delle Pinete
Via Covetta
Via Marinella
Viale Galileo Galilei
Viale Cristoforo Colombo
Marinella di Sarzana
SS1
SP3
1 km
1 : 40,000

Waypoint	Distance Between Waypoints (m)	Total (km)	Directions	Verification Point	Compass	Altitude (m)
75.027	700	8,9	At the road junction, continue straight ahead on the grass track	Bridge on the left	S	19
75.028	160	9,1	At the next road junction, turn right	Enter Palvotrisia	W	18
75.029	400	9,4	At the Stop sign, continue straight ahead	No through road	W	11
75.030	120	9,5	At the T-junction with the very busy via Aurelia, cross the pedestrian crossing and turn left. Continue with care on the right hand side of the road	Towards traffic lights	SE	10
75.031	120	9,6	Beside the traffic lights, turn right and pass under the railway	Red and white sign, via Provasco	S	9
75.032	1300	11,0	At the junction with the main road continue straight ahead	Towards the archaeological site of Luni (XXVIII)	SE	2
75.033	70	11,0	At the entrance to the site, turn left and follow the path around the site	Keep the site on the right	NE	3
75.034	190	11,2	At the end of the fence turn right	Keep the site on the right	SE	5
75.035	230	11,5	Cross via Luni and take the footpath ahead and slightly to the right	Footpath quickly turns right	S	7
75.036	260	11,7	Turn left on the road	Via Appia	SE	5
75.037	400	12,1	Continue straight ahead	Luni amphitheatre on the left, red and white sign	E	3
75.038	270	12,4	Take the right fork	Via Appia	NE	5
75.039	260	12,6	Turn right on via Marina	Red and white sign	E	8
75.040	140	12,8	At the crossroads, continue straight ahead	No Entry sign	E	9

Sarzana to Massa 27.6km

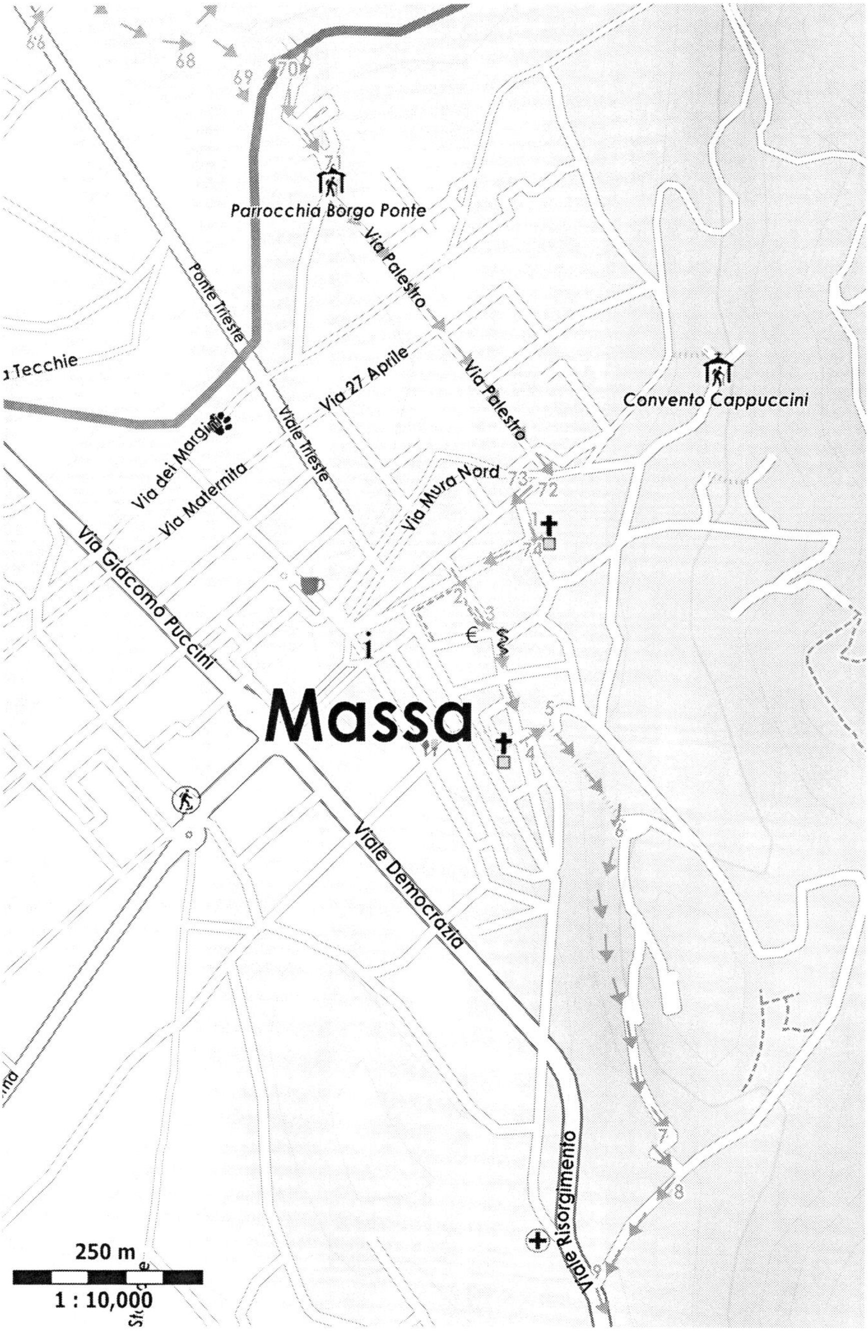
Parrocchia Borgo Ponte
Via Palestro
Ponte Trieste
Via Palestro
Convento Cappuccini
Via 27 Aprile
Viale Trieste
Via dei Margini
Via Maternita
Via Mura Nord
Via Giacomo Puccini
Massa
Viale Democrazia
Viale Risorgimento
250 m
1 : 10,000

Waypoint	Distance Between Waypoints (m)	Total (km)	Directions	Verification Point	Compass	Altitude (m)
75.041	150	12,9	At the T-junction, cross the road and take the footbridge over the waterway	Red and white sign. Note: - turning right and joining the Alternate Route along the coast road, will give the opportunity to put your toes in the Mediterranean Sea, shorten the distance to Pietrasanta by 5km and provide relief from further climbing	E	9
75.042	50	13,0	Bear left on the road	Via del Parmignola, beside the waterway and then the railway track	E	9
75.043	1400	14,3	At the crossroads continue straight ahead	Railway bridge on the left	SE	4
75.044	1300	15,6	At the roundabout, continue straight ahead	Via Giovan-Pietro, pass bar on the right	SE	9
75.045	500	16,1	After crossing the bridge bear left on via Luigi Farini	Fortress to the right – Torre di Castruccio	E	11
75.046	80	16,2	On the crown of the bend to the right, turn left on the narrow road	No Entry sign	NE	12
75.047	500	16,6	At the T-junction, turn left	Over level crossing	NE	15
75.048	160	16,8	At the crossroads, turn right	Marble yard on the right	NE	16
75.049	400	17,2	At the traffic lights, continue straight ahead	Tyre stor on the left	NE	20
75.050	600	17,7	Cross the via Provinciale Nazzano and continue straight ahead	Direction Bonascola	NE	28
75.051	150	17,9	Turn right uphill	Via Forma Bassa	SE	32

Sarzana to Massa 27.6km

Waypoint	Distance Between Waypoints (m)	Total (km)	Directions	Verification Point	Compass	Altitude (m)
75.052	700	18,6	Continue straight ahead on the track		SE	54
75.053	240	18,8	Turn right	Into the woods	W	89
75.054	120	19,0	Turn left	Towards the farm	SW	98
75.055	40	19,0	Turn left beside the farm and then left again uphill	Towards the electricity pylon and between the vines	NE	101
75.056	400	19,4	At the top of the ridge turn right on the road, via Forma Alta	Vines on the right	SE	124
75.057	270	19,7	At the road junction, continue straight ahead	Metal fence and vines to the right	SE	140
75.058	50	19,7	At top of the hill, turn left on the narrow road	Along the ridge	E	141
75.059	700	20,4	Bear left	Quarry on the right	NE	148
75.060	400	20,8	Bear right on the white road, via dell'Uva	Between the vines	E	172
75.061	1200	22,0	Berside the restaurant, turn sharp left, uphill	Via dell'Uva	E	170
75.062	3200	25,2	At the end of the road, turn sharp right		SE	73
75.063	110	25,4	Cross the main road and take the smaller road opposite	Via Ponte del Vescovo, No Entry	E	67
75.064	150	25,5	At the T-junction, turn left into piazza della Libertà and then immediately right	Via San Vitale	SE	64

Sarzana to Massa 27.6km

Waypoint	Distance Between Waypoints (m)	Total (km)	Directions	Verification Point	Compass	Altitude (m)
75.065	600	26,1	At the T-junction with the main road, turn right	Via Foce, Mirteto sign on the left	SE	62
75.066	140	26,3	Turn left opposite the pharmacy	Direction Lavacchio, via Frangola	NE	64
75.067	70	26,3	Take the first turning to the right	Via Ortola	SE	65
75.068	190	26,5	Turn left and then right	Take the bridge over the stream	SE	62
75.069	180	26,7	At the T-junction turn left	Keep, river on the right	NE	56
75.070	80	26,8	Turn right over the bridge	Continue on via Ponte Vecchio	S	55
75.071	220	27,0	Bear right and immediately take the left fork	Via Palestro towards the centre of Massa	SE	59
75.072	500	27,5	At the mini roundabout continue straight ahead on via Cavour	No Entry sign, Seminary on the left	SW	69
75.073	50	27,6	Turn left	Towards the Duomo	S	70
75.074	50	27,6	Arrive at Massa centre	Beside the Duomo		71

Sarzana to Massa 27.6km

Stage Summary: the Alternate Route, shorter by 5km to Pietrasanta, provides relief from further climbs and descents by following the broad promenade beside the beach before turning inland to find the centre of Pietrasanta. It is easy going for cyclists and riders. There are numerous camp sites, hotels and restaurants beside the route.

Stage Ascent: 72m   Stage Descent: 69m

Waypoint	Distance Between Waypoints (m)	Total (km)	Directions	Verification Point	Compass	Altitude (m)
75A1.001	0	0,0	At the T-junction, turn right on via del Parmignola	Towards Autostrada	SW	8
75A1.002	1900	1,9	At the crossroads, turn left towards the sea	Via della Repubblica	S	2
75A1.003	120	2,0	At the T-junction with the main road, turn left on the road	Cross the waterways on the SP432 and enter Marina di Carrara	SE	2
75A1.004	3300	5,3	After passing through Marina di Carrara, bear left to turn inland and remain on the main road	Viale delle Pinete, coast road dead ends at a boat marina	SE	3
75A1.005	4000	9,3	At the roundabout, turn right towards the sea	Via Casola, direction Viareggio	SW	2
75A1.006	230	9,5	Turn left, continue with sea on right	Pass through Marina di Massa	SE	0
75A1.007	1500	11,0	At the roundabout continue straight ahead. Note:- to regain the Main Route in Massa centre turn left and follow viale Roma	Direction Forte dei Marmi	SE	1
75A1.008	9900	20,9	Shortly after crossing the waterway and before the traffic lights in Fiumetto	Hotel Coluccini on the left	NE	1
75A1.009	100	21,0	Cross the road and continue straight ahead into the car park		NE	2
75A1.010	60	21,0	Continue straight ahead on the broad track	Keep kiosks on your right	NE	3

Alternate Route #75.A1 25.2km

Waypoint	Distance Between Waypoints (m)	Total (km)	Directions	Verification Point	Compass	Altitude (m)
75A1.011	1600	22,6	Beside the roundabout with a slender stone sculpture in the centre, continue straight ahead at the pedestrian crossing and follow the cycle track	Direction Pietrasanta	NE	1
75A1.012	1400	23,0	At the traffic lights, take the pedestrian crossing and continue straight ahead on the cycle track	Tree lined road towards the hills	NE	7
75A1.013	700	24,7	At the T-junction turn left on the cycle track	Direction Seravezza, pass commercial centre on the left	NW	8
75A1.014	260	24,9	At the roundabout take the cycle track beside the first exit and pass under the railway	Via Vincenzo Santini, direction Pietrasanta centre	N	7
75A1.015	270	25,2	At the T-junction turn right to join the Main Route	Via Marconi		11

Alternate Route #75.A1 25.2km

151

Pilgrim Hostel

Casa di Accoglienza Caritas,Via Godola, 5,54100 Massa(MS),Italy
Tel:+39 0585 792909,Mobile:+39 3395 829566,buragino@tin.it,Price:D,

Religious Hostel

Parrocchia S.Pietro Apostolo,Piazza Finelli,54033 Carrara(MS),Italy
Tel:+39 0585 857203,Mobile:+39 3388 333413,alpi500@interfree.it,Price:D,

Convento Cappuccini,Piazza San Francesco, 3,54100 Massa(MS),Italy
Tel:+39 9058 542181,Price:D,

Parrocchia Borgo Ponte,Via San Martino, 1,54100 Massa(MS),Italy
Tel:+39 0585 42282,info@sanmartinoalborgo.org,

Camping

Camping Luni,Via Luni, 16,54100 Marina-di-Massa(MS),Italy Tel:+39 0585 869278,

Equestrian

Centro Ippico il Falco,Viale 25 Aprile,19038 Sarzana(SP),Italy Mobile:+39 3334 703446,

Tourist Information

Comune di Massa,Piazza del Teatro, 1,54100 Massa(MS),Italy Tel:+39 0585 8811,

Banks and ATMs

Banca di Roma,Piazza Aranci,54100 Massa(MS),Italy Tel:+39 0585 811574,

Banca Monte dei Paschi di Siena,Via Roma, 77,54038 Montignoso(MS),Italy
Tel:+39 0585 349400,

Banca Monte dei Paschi di Siena,Via della Chiesa, 16,19038 Sarzana(SP),Italy
Tel:+39 0187 649775,

Cassa di Risparmio di Carrara,Via Roma, 3,54033 Carrara(MS),Italy Tel:+39 0585 775053,

Banca Carige,Viale 20 Settembre, 209/21,54033 Carrara(MS),Italy Tel:+39 0585 856227,

Travel

Stazione Ferrovie,Piazza 4 Novembre, 32,54100 Massa(MS),Italy
Tel:+39 06 6847 5475,www.renitalia.it,

Hospital

Ospedale Generale,Via Carlo Orecchia,54100 Massa(MS),Italy
Tel:+39 0585 4931,www.usl1.toscana.it,

Ospedale,Via Aurelia Sud,54100 Montepepe(MS),Italy
Tel:+39 0585 493617,www.ftgm.it,

Doctor

Beeli - Ambulatorio Medico,Piazza Mercurio,54100 Massa(MS),Italy Tel:+39 0585 41137,

Veterinary

Busti - Ambulatorio Veterinari,Via dei Margini, 3,54100 Massa(MS),Italy
Tel:+39 0585 47531,

Hiking Equipment

Articoli Sportivi,Via Giovanni Pascoli, 5,54100 Massa(MS),Italy Tel:+39 0585 40914,

Bicycle Shop

Brewo Srl,Via Azeglio Petracci, 13,54038 Montignoso(MS),Italy Tel:+39 0585 821296,

Stage Seventy-six Summary: the route leaves Massa on the very busy via Aurelia, before returning to narrow and potentially dangerous hillside roads and then descending to the industrial zone for the entry to the attractive town of Pietrasanta.

Distance from Canterbury: 1610km   Distance to Saint-Peter's-Square: 464km

Stage Ascent: 259m   Stage Descent: 308m

Waypoint	Distance Between Waypoints (m)	Total (km)	Directions	Verification Point	Compass	Altitude (m)
76.001	0	0,0	With the Duomo behind go straight ahead on via Dante Alighieri	Towards piazza Aranci	SW	71
76.002	120	0,1	Immediately on entry to piazza Aranci turn left	Trees and obelisk on the right	SE	71
76.003	90	0,2	At the exit from the piazza, bear left and immediately right	Keep the palazzo immediately on you right	S	71
76.004	160	0,4	Keep to the left side of piazza Mercurio and turn left to climb the steps. Note:- to avoid the steps continue straight ahead on via Mario Bigini and via Prado	Via Bigini on the right	NE	73
76.005	30	0,4	At the T-junction with the road, turn right	Via Piastronata	SE	75
76.006	160	0,6	Beside Chiesa della Madonna del Carmine, bear right on via Santa Chiara	Keep Castello Malaspina high on your left	S	86
76.007	500	1,0	At the T-junction, turn left on the small road	Via Grondini	SE	78
76.008	30	1,1	At the T-junction with the larger road, turn right	Via del Bargello	SW	75
76.009	200	1,3	At the crossroads turn left and proceed with caution on the pavement beside the main road	Pizzeria on the left	S	61
76.010	220	1,5	Take the left fork	Remain beside the main road	SE	50
76.011	1400	2,9	After passing the hospital on the left, bear left away from the via Aurelia	Via Carlo Sforza, No Entry	SE	42

Massa to Pietrasanta 16.4km

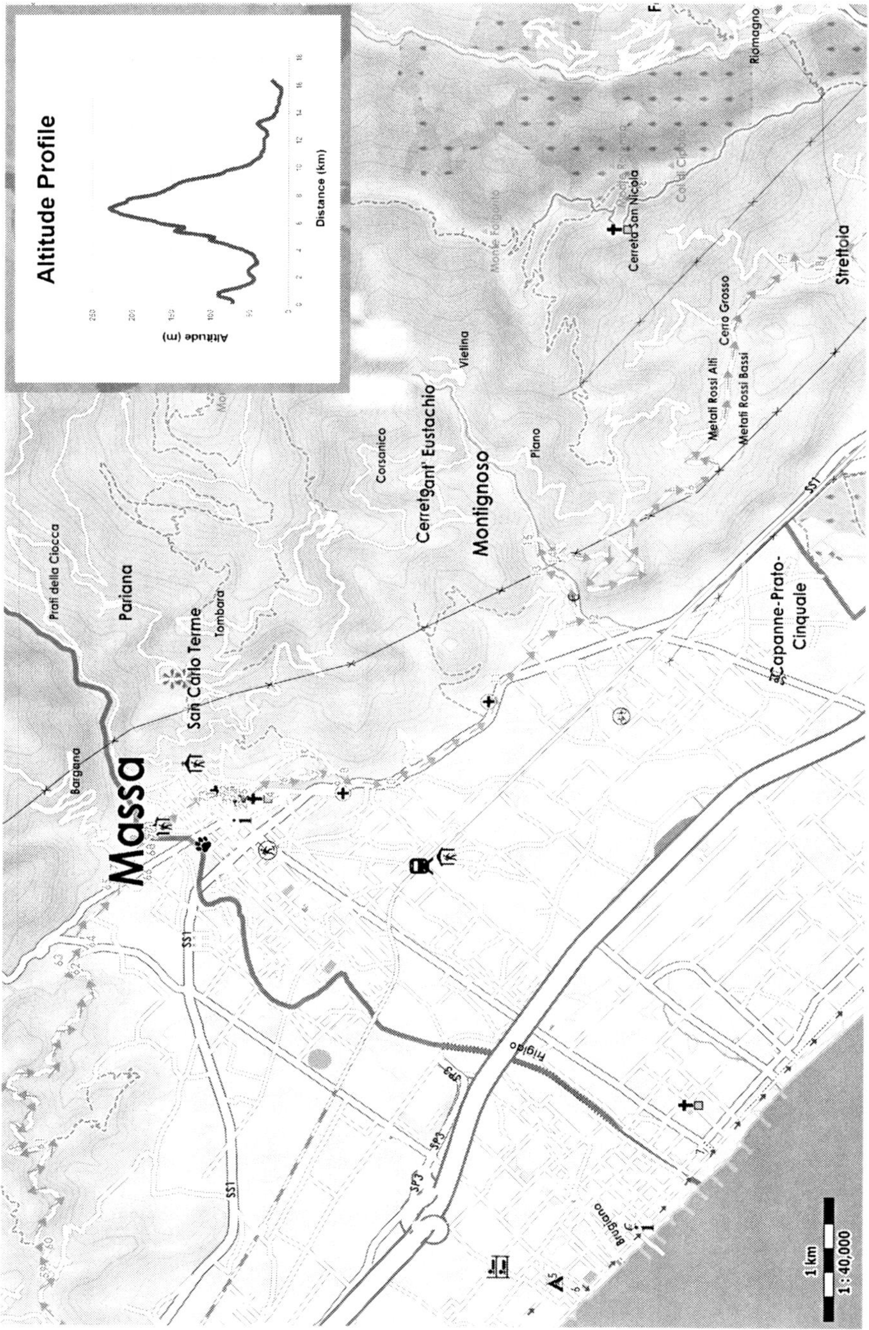
Altitude Profile
Altitude (m)
Distance (km)
Massa
Bargena
San Carlo Terme
Tombara
Pariana
Prati della Ciocca
Corsanico
Cerreto
Sant' Eustachio
Montignoso
Vietina
Piano
Cerreto San Nicola
Cerro Grosso
Metati Rossi Alti
Metati Rossi Bassi
Strettoia
Riomagno
Capanne-Prato-Cinquale
Frigido
Brugiano
SS1
SP3
1 km
1 : 40,000

Waypoint	Distance Between Waypoints (m)	Total (km)	Directions	Verification Point	Compass	Altitude (m)
76.012	800	3,7	At the end of the road, turn left	Concrete wall ahead, No Entry sign	NE	46
76.013	500	4,2	Turn right across the road and then left	Pass car park on the left, river immediately to your right	NE	68
76.014	160	4,3	Cross the footbridge and turn left. Note:- horse-riders should take the road bridge 150m ahead	Via Bottaccio	E	76
76.015	160	4,5	At the end of the road turn right up the hill	Via Patatina, pass Fortezza Aghinolfi on the hilltop	S	85
76.016	2600	7,1	Keep right on the road	Avoid left fork, uphill	SE	227
76.017	2700	9,8	After crossing the stream, keep right on the road	Avoid left turn, via Montebello	SW	80
76.018	120	9,9	Bear left on the road	Pass piazza di Strettoia on your right	SE	73
76.019	1500	11,4	After passing house number 273 on your right, turn left	Via Pigone, No Entry	E	31
76.020	190	11,6	At the T-junction, turn right	Via della Chiusa	SE	31
76.021	180	11,7	At the crossroads, continue straight ahead	Via della Pace	SE	31
76.022	50	11,8	Take the next turning to the left	Towards modern church	NE	31
76.023	70	11,9	At the crossroads bear right and diagonally cross the car park	Keep church to your left	E	31
76.024	60	11,9	In the opposite corner of the car park, bear right on the short track	Sculptures on your left	SE	31
76.025	30	11,9	At the T-junction, turn left	Via del Popolo	NE	31

Massa to Pietrasanta 16.4km

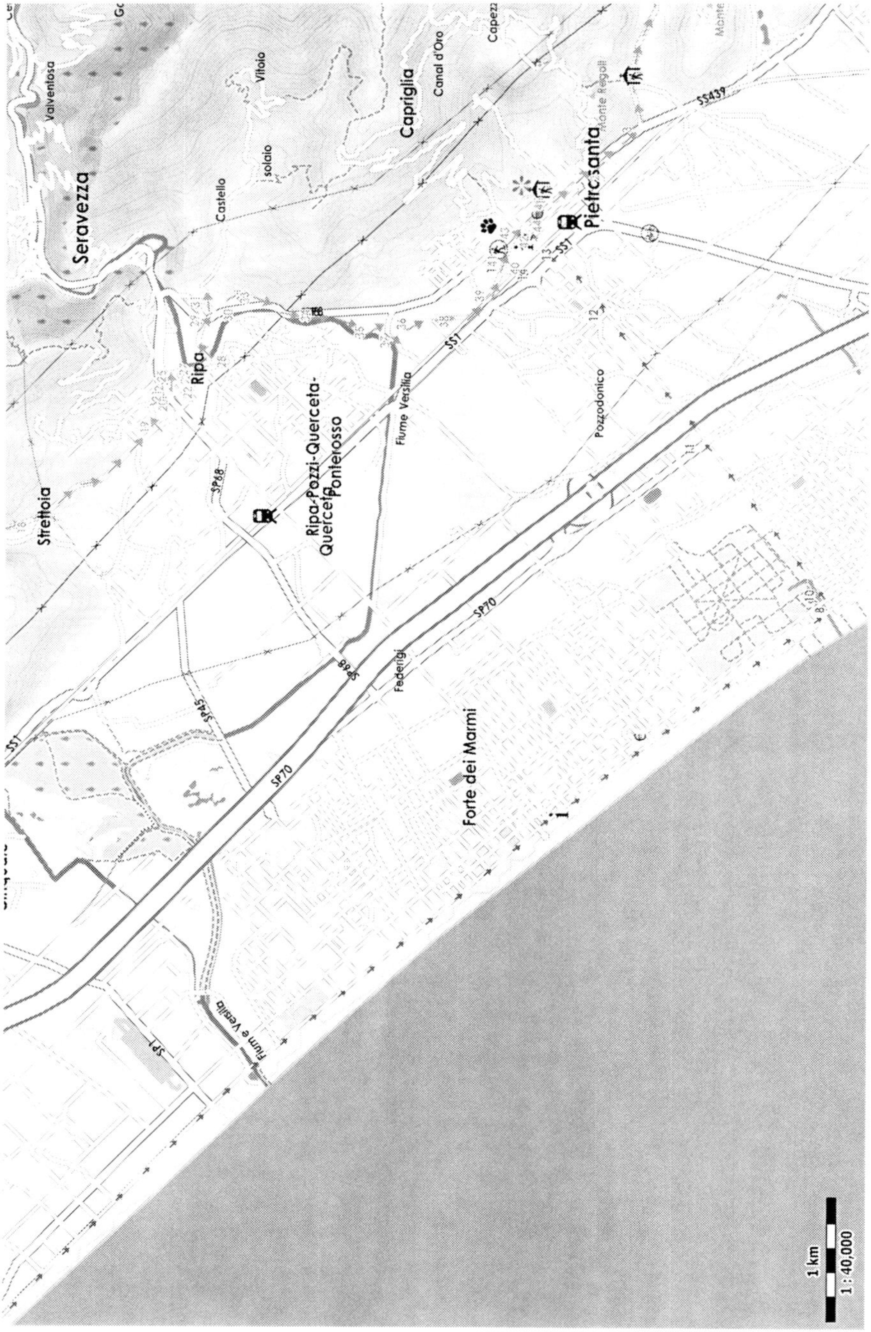
Seravezza
Valventosa
Vitoio
Castello
Solaio
Capriglia
Canal d'Oro
Ripa
Strettoia
Ripa-Pozzi-Querceta-Ponterosso
Querceta
Pietrasanta
Monte Regali
Fiume Versilia
Pozzodonico
Forte dei Marmi
Federigi
SS1
SP68
SP45
SP70
SS439
1 km
1 : 40,000

Waypoint	Distance Between Waypoints (m)	Total (km)	Directions	Verification Point	Compass	Altitude (m)
76.026	30	12,0	At the T-junction with the larger road, turn right	Via del G. Alessandrini	S	31
76.027	200	12,2	At the traffic lights bear left with great care on the walled road	Keep river immediately to your left	SE	30
76.028	100	12,3	Continue straight ahead	Take the bridge over the river	E	28
76.029	400	12,7	At the Stop sign, turn right on the road	Pass church on your left	SE	28
76.030	70	12,7	Take the next turning to the left	Direction Solaio	NE	29
76.031	130	12,9	At the crossroads turn right	Narrow bridge	S	32
76.032	180	13,0	Facing the water fountain, turn right	Via Pozzone	S	36
76.033	240	13,3	Take the right fork	Via Pozzone	SW	39
76.034	400	13,6	Cross the SP8 and bear left on the grass track beside the river	River on the right	S	23
76.035	700	14,3	Bear left and descend from the river-side track	Pass beside a Marble depot	SE	15
76.036	150	14,4	At the T-junction, turn right	Towards the river and electricity pylon	SW	14
76.037	180	14,6	Turn left on via Torraccia	Pass wood yard on the right	SE	12
76.038	400	15,0	Continue straight ahead	Via Torracia	SE	12
76.039	600	15,5	Bear left	Away from railway	E	9
76.040	240	15,7	Continue straight ahead on the cycle track beside the road. The Alternate Route joins from the right	Via Marconi	E	9
76.041	70	15,8	Continue straight ahead	Direction Centro	E	10
76.042	170	16,0	In piazza Matteotti bear slightly right towards the centre of Pietrasanta	Pass gladiator sculpture on your left	SE	14
76.043	80	16,1	Continue straight ahead	Car park on your left	SE	16
76.044	50	16,1	Continue straight ahead into the pedestrian zone	Pass mirrored sculpture, via Mazzini	SE	17
76.045	300	16,4	Arrive at Pietrasanta centre	Piazza Duomo		22

Massa to Pietrasanta 16.4km

157

Religious Hostel

Casa Diocesana "la Rocca",(Sour Irene),Via della Rocca,55045 Pietrasanta(LU),Italy Tel:+39 0584 793093,casarocca@tiscali.it,Price:C,

Pieve di San Giovanni e Santa Felicita,(Don Marco Marchetti),Valdicastello,55045 Pietrasanta(LU),Italy Tel:+39 0584 772009,

Commercial Hostel

Ostello Turimar,Via Bondano, 64,54100 Massa(MS),Italy Tel:+39 0585 243282,info@ostelloturimar.com,www.ostelloturimar.com,Price:B,

B&B, Hotel, Gite d'Etape

Locanda le Monache,Piazza 29 Maggio, 36,55041 Camaiore(LU),Italy Tel:+39 0584 984282,Price:A,

Camping

Campeggio Citta' di Massa,Via delle Pinete, 136,54100 Massa(MS),Italy Tel:+39 0585 869361,

Tourist Information

Agenzia Per il Turismo,Lungomare Vespucci, 24,54100 Massa(MS),Italy Tel:+39 0585 240063,

Ufficio Turistico,Viale Achille Franceschi, 8,55042 Forte-dei-Marmi(LU),Italy Tel:+39 0584 80091,

Comune di Camaiore,Piazza San Bernardino, 1,55041 Camaiore(LU),Italy Tel:+39 0584 9860,

Comune di Pietrasanta,Piazza Matteotti, 29,55045 Pietrasanta(LU),Italy Tel:+39 0584 7951,

Banks and ATMs

Banca Versilia Lunigiana e Garfagnana,Piazza,23814 29-Maggio-27(LC),Italy Tel:+39 0584 984857,www.bccversilia.it,

Banca Monte dei Paschi di Siena,Via Giosuè Carducci, 25,55042 Forte-dei-Marmi(LU),Italy Tel:+39 0584 78351,

Banca di Credito Cooperativo della Versilia,Via Giuseppe Mazzini,55045 Pietrasanta(LU),Italy Tel:+39 0584 72110,www.bccversilia.it,

Cassa di Risparmio di Lucca,Piazza Betti,54100 Massa(MS),Italy Tel:+39 0585 244045,

Travel

Stazione Ferrovie,Piazza Stazione Ferrovie Dello Stato, 1,55045 Pietrasanta(LU),Italy Tel:+39 06 6847 5475,www.renitalia.it,

Hospital

Ospedale Versilia,Via Aurelia, 335,55041 Camaiore(LU),Italy Tel:+39 0584 6051,www.usl12.toscana.it,

Doctor

Ceolin - Ambulatorio,Viale Guglielmo Oberdan, 59,55045 Pietrasanta(LU),Italy Tel:+39 0584 72176,

Centro Medico Campus Maior,Via Oberdan Guglielmo, 39,55041 Camaiore(LU),Italy Tel:+39 0584 984009,

Veterinary

Cure Primarie Versilia Societa' Cooperativa,Via Martiri di Sant'Anna, 10,55045 Pietrasanta(LU),Italy Tel:+39 0584 71563,

Dalle Luche - Medico Veterinario,Via Andreuccetti, 7,55041 Camaiore(LU),Italy Tel:+39 0584 983560,

Hiking Equipment

Sporty,Via Pietro Tabarrani, 14,55041 Camaiore(LU),Italy Tel:+39 0584 989204,

Pianeta Sport,Via Provinciale Vallecchia, 23,55045 Pietrasanta(LU),Italy Tel:+39 0584 71481,

Bicycle Shop

Aliverti,Via Aurelia Sud, 47,55045 Pietrasanta(LU),Italy Tel:+39 5841 962090,

Stage Seventy-seven Summary: take care on the main road as you leave Pietrasanta. Farm tracks leads and very small roads lead over the Monteggiori ridge to the canal-side track to attractive town of Camaiore. The route then climbs on farm tracks parallel to the main road to Montemagno. The route returns to the main road before returning to farm and forest tracks at Valpromaro. The route approaches Lucca along a riverside track before finally entering the walled city.

Distance from Canterbury: 1626km Distance to Saint-Peter's-Square: 448km

Stage Ascent: 450m Stage Descent: 451m

Waypoint	Distance Between Waypoints (m)	Total (km)	Directions	Verification Point	Compass	Altitude (m)
77.001	0	0,0	From piazza Duomo in Pietrasanta take via Giuseppe Garibaldi	Beside the Duomo	SE	22
77.002	300	0,3	At the junction, proceed straight ahead with care on the main road	SP439, direction Lucca	SE	22
77.003	600	0,9	Beside the cemetery turn left, on via Valdicastello Carducci	Sign post chiesa and VF map	E	23
77.004	1300	2,2	Turn right	Via Regnalla, road bends to the left	SE	51
77.005	400	2,6	Take the second right after the bend	Uphill	S	63
77.006	100	2,7	Take the right fork	Keep industrial building on your left	S	71
77.007	180	2,8	Pass beside the factory and a quarry and take the footpath to the right through the woods	Towards the brow of the hill	S	97
77.008	290	3,1	Bear right on the footpath at the end of the woods and proceed directly downhill		S	88
77.009	200	3,3	Turn right and immediately left	Follow via Cannoreto between the houses	S	62
77.010	400	3,7	At the junction with the main road turn left and immediately right	Strada di Monteggiori	S	55
77.011	60	3,8	Bear left onto a small footpath	White arrow	SE	51
77.012	170	4,0	Close beside the farm buildings, turn right on the track		S	32

Pietrasanta to Lucca 32.1km

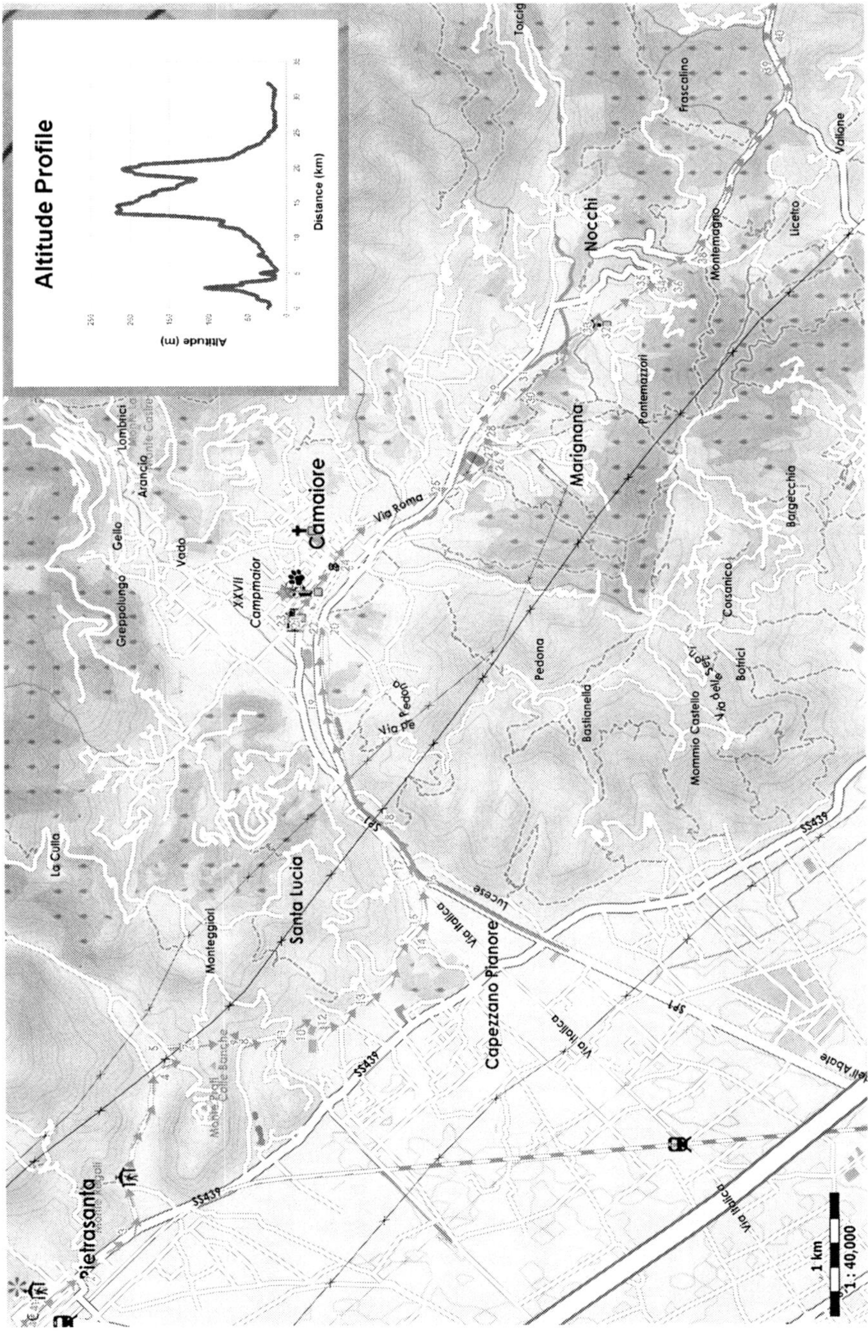

Altitude Profile
Altitude (m)
Distance (km)
Pietrasanta
Santa Lucia
Camaiore
XXVII Campmaior
Capezzano Pianore
Marignana
Nocchi
Pontemazzori
Montemagno
Frascalino
Vallone
Liceto
Bargecchia
Corsanico
Bozzano
Mommio Castello
Bastianella
Pedona
Montegiori
La Culla
Greppolungo
Gello
Vado
Arancio
Lombrici
Via Roma
Via Italica
Lucese
SP1
SS439
Torcigliano
1 km
1 : 40,000

Waypoint	Distance Between Waypoints (m)	Total (km)	Directions	Verification Point	Compass	Altitude (m)
77.013	700	4,6	At the crossroads with via Selvaiana continue straight ahead	Map on your right at the junction	SE	15
77.014	600	5,2	Bear left	Via Dietro Monte	SE	23
77.015	260	5,4	At the junction turn left	Towards the main road	E	12
77.016	300	5,8	At the traffic lights continue straight ahead beside the main road SP1	Towards Camaiore	NE	14
77.017	140	5,9	Cross the main road and take the bridge over the canal, via della Capanne. Then turn left to follow the grass path on the canal-side	Canal on your left	NE	15
77.018	600	6,4	Continue straight ahead beside the canal	Pass canal bridge on the left	NE	20
77.019	1000	7,5	Continue straight ahead on the road beside the canal, via Virgilio Boschi	Pass football ground on the left	E	32
77.020	600	8,1	Take the bridge to the left, cross the main road and continue straight ahead	Direction Centro, via Carignoni	NE	30
77.021	120	8,2	At the T-junction, turn left	Direction Centro	NW	31
77.022	80	8,3	Before reaching the petrol station turn right	Piazza 29 Maggio	NE	31
77.023	80	8,4	Arrive in Camaiore (XXVII) centre with the church directly ahead, take the second turn to the right	Via Vittorio Emanuele	SE	32
77.024	600	8,9	At the end of the road continue straight ahead across piazza Carlo Romboni and join via Roma	Long tree lined road	SE	35
77.025	1200	10,1	At the junction with the SP1, cross over the main road and take the minor road over the bridge	Towards the sports ground "Tori"	SE	46

Pietrasanta to Lucca 32.1km

Monsagrati
SP1
Orbicciano
Migliano
Bartoli
Fibbialla
Gualdo
Stabbiano
Chiatri
Al Mutino
Monti di Chiatri
Bozzano
Quiesa
SS439
Maggiano
Alla Bidia
San Macario in Monte
San Macario in Piano
Farneta
Al Generale
Strada Provinciale 24 di Sant'Alessio
1 km
1 : 40,000

Waypoint	Distance Between Waypoints (m)	Total (km)	Directions	Verification Point	Compass	Altitude (m)
77.026	400	10,4	Continue straight ahead on the footpath	Sports ground to the left	SE	54
77.027	170	10,6	At the T-junction with the tarmac road turn left	Frazione Marignana	NE	54
77.028	280	10,9	Just before reaching the canal, turn right on the road	Keep canal to the left	SE	55
77.029	400	11,3	As the road enters a farm turn right on the track	Towards the woods	SW	61
77.030	100	11,4	Turn left on the footpath	Between the woods and a field	SE	65
77.031	240	11,6	Beside the farm buildings, cross the tarmac driveway and bear right on the track	Beside the woods	SE	78
77.032	700	12,3	Turn left on the track	Towards the church	SE	81
77.033	70	12,4	At the T-junction with the road, turn left and immediately right	Pass the church on the right	SE	80
77.034	600	12,9	After passing a large country house, bear left onto the track	Keep house on right	SE	115
77.035	70	13,0	Turn right onto the SP1	Uphill	SW	121
77.036	130	13,1	On the apex of the bend to the left, turn right up the stony track. Note: - the track ahead may be overgrown, to avoid this remain on the main road until rejoining the Main Route on the entry Montemagno	VF sign	E	133
77.037	190	13,3	Continue straight on, up the narrow pathway	Beside electricity substation	SE	169
77.038	200	13,5	Turn right onto the main road – SP1 and enter Montemagno	Bar and restaurant on left and right	SE	208

Pietrasanta to Lucca 32.1km

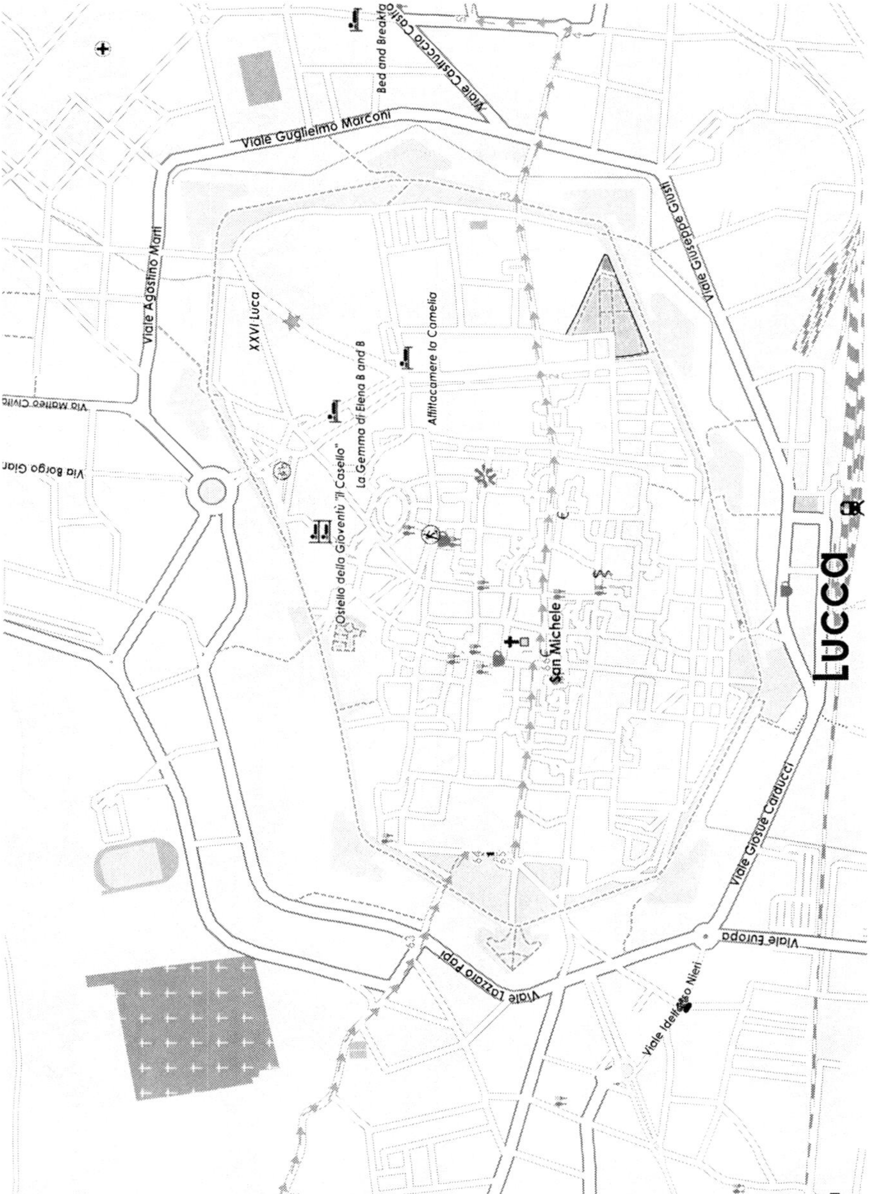

Lucca
Viale Guglielmo Marconi
Viale Giuseppe Giusti
Viale Agostino Marti
XXVI Luca
Affittacamere la Camelia
La Gemma di Elena B and B
Ostello della Gioventù "il Casello"
San Michele
Viale Giosuè Carducci
Viale Europa
Viale Lazzaro Papi
250 m
1 : 10,000

Waypoint	Distance Between Waypoints (m)	Total (km)	Directions	Verification Point	Compass	Altitude (m)
77.039	1800	15,3	Bear right off the main road onto the unmade road	Pass the restaurant "Purgatorio"	E	191
77.040	300	15,7	Return to the main road and bear right	16	E	187
77.041	1300	16,9	Bear right on a minor road into Valpromaro	VF sign	E	160
77.042	600	17,5	After passing through the village turn right onto track between houses	VF sign	E	139
77.043	1000	18,4	At the T-junction, turn right onto the minor road	VF sign, direction Piazzano	S	115
77.044	200	18,6	Just before the road turns to the left, turn right onto a gravel track. Note:- the off-road section is steep over broken ground. Cyclists should remain on the road to Piazzano	VF sign	S	131
77.045	600	19,2	At the T-junction with a minor road turn left	Via delle Gavine	NE	191
77.046	60	19,2	Right fork into Piazzano	VF sign, via della Chiesa XII	E	194
77.047	600	19,8	At the crossroads in centre of Piazzano turn right	VF sign	SE	209
77.048	300	20,1	On leaving the village, continue straight ahead on the road	Pass the church on the left	SE	194
77.049	400	20,5	Bear right on the track. Note:- cyclists continue straight ahead on the road to the T-junction	Pass cemetery on your right	S	185
77.050	80	20,6	At the junction in the tracks continue straight ahead	Downhill	S	179

Pietrasanta to Lucca 32.1km

Waypoint	Distance Between Waypoints (m)	Total (km)	Directions	Verification Point	Compass	Altitude (m)
77.051	800	21,3	At the T-junction with the road, turn left	Across the stream	SE	77
77.052	300	21,7	Continue straight ahead on via delle Gavine. Cyclists rejoin from the road on the left	VF sign, stream on the right	SE	68
77.053	2800	24,4	At the Stop sign in Alla Bidia bear right on the large road	Sign to Piazzano on your left at the junction	S	24
77.054	700	25,1	On entering San Macario Piano, turn left on the narrow street, in the direction of the church	VF sign, via della chiesa Ventitreesima	SE	21
77.055	800	25,9	Bear right on the road	Embankment on your left	SE	13
77.056	260	26,2	At the crossroads, continue straight ahead onto a small road skirting the village	VF sign, towards church	S	15
77.057	500	26,6	At the crossroads, turn left over the river bridge	VF sign, Ponte San Pietro	E	14
77.058	160	26,8	Immediately after crossing the bridge, turn left onto a small tarmac riverside road	VF sign, keep river close on your left	E	15
77.059	3100	29,9	Fork right onto the tarmac road	VF sign, No Entry ahead	S	16
77.060	400	30,3	At the crossroads, turn left	VF sign, keep football ground on the right	E	14
77.061	200	30,5	At the end of the football ground, turn right onto a small tarmac road	VF sign	S	15
77.062	250	30,8	At the T-junction with via dei Cavalletti, turn left	VF sign, keep park on the right	SE	15
77.063	600	31,4	At the traffic lights, cross the road and pass under the arch into walled centre of Lucca	VF sign	SE	17
77.064	200	31,6	At the T-junction, turn right on piazza Giuseppe Verdi	Pass the ancient Porta San Donata on your right	S	18
77.065	100	31,7	Take the first left turn	Towards Ostello S. Frediano, No Entry	E	19
77.066	400	32,1	Arrive at Lucca (XXVI) centre in piazza San Michele	Church to the left		22

Pietrasanta to Lucca 32.1km

Religious Hostel

San Martino,Valpromaro,55041 Camaiore(LU),Italy Tel:+39 0584 956028, Mobile:+39 3276 948204,mario.andreozzi46@alice.it,Price:D,

Convento Cappuccini,Via della Chiesa Ventunesima, 87,55100 Lucca(LU),Italy Tel:+39 0583 341426,Mobile:+39 3391 118421,Price:D,

Commercial Hostel

Ostello della Gioventù "il Casello",Via della Cavallerizza,55100 Lucca(LU),Italy Tel:+39 0584 461007,ostello.sanfrediano@virgilio.it,www.ostellolucca.it,Price:C,

B&B, Hotel, Gite d'Etape

La Gemma di Elena B and B,Via della Zecca, 33,55100 Lucca(LU),Italy Tel:+39 0583 496665,Mobile:+39 3202 346331,lagemma@interfree.it,Price:B,

Affittacamere la Camelia,Piazza San Francesco, 35,55100 Lucca(LU),Italy Tel:+39 0583 467088,Mobile:+39 3394 840178,info@affittacamerelacamelia.com,Price:B,

Bed and Breakfast Butterfly,Via Nicola Barbantini, 87,55100 Lucca(LU),Italy Mobile:+39 3207 257112,info@butterflybb.it,Price:B,

Tourist Information

Azienda di Promozione Turistica,Piazzale Giuseppe Verdi,55100 Lucca(LU),Italy Tel:+39 0583 469964,

Banks and ATMs

Banca Monte dei Paschi di Siena,Piazza Bernardini, 4,55100 Lucca(LU),Italy Tel:+39 0583 9665,

Unicredit,Piazza San Michele, 47,55100 Lucca(LU),Italy Tel:+39 0583 4971,

Travel

Stazione Ferrovie,Piazzale Bettino Ricasoli, 169,55100 Lucca(LU),Italy Tel:+39 06 6847 5475,www.renitalia.it,

Hospital

Presidio Ospedaliero,Via Dell'Ospedale, 238,55100 Lucca(LU),Italy Tel:+39 0583 9701,

Doctor

Puccetti - Medico Chirurgo Studio,Via del Battistero, 18,55100 Lucca(LU),Italy Tel:+39 0583 494139,

Veterinary

Ambulatorio Veterinario,Viale Idelfonso Nieri, 131,55100 Lucca(LU),Italy Tel:+39 0583 581936,

Hiking Equipment

Tuttosport,Via Antonio Mordini, 25,55100 Lucca(LU),Italy Tel:+39 0583 91600,

Bicycle Shop

Cicli Bizzarri,Piazza Santa Maria, 32,55100 Lucca(LU),Italy Tel:+39 0583 496682,

Stage Summary: the route to Altopascio is substantially undertaken on the tarmac, with sections on major roads.

Distance from Canterbury: 1658km   Distance to Saint-Peter's-Square: 415km

Stage Ascent: 55m   Stage Descent: 59m

Waypoint	Distance Between Waypoints (m)	Total (km)	Directions	Verification Point	Compass	Altitude (m)
78.001	0	0,0	From piazza San Michele, take via Roma and then via San Croce	Keep church to the left	E	22
78.002	600	0,6	Proceed through archway, Porta San Gervasio and across the canal onto via Elisa	VF sign	E	20
78.003	400	1,0	After passing through the triple arched Porta Elisa, continue straight ahead across the main road onto viale Luigi Cadoma	VF sign, direction Pontedera	E	20
78.004	400	1,3	At the T-junction, turn left onto via di Tiglio	Towards the domed Santuario di S. Gemma	N	18
78.005	210	1,5	Turn right onto via Romana	Towards the hotels	E	18
78.006	800	2,4	Continue straight ahead at the roundabout	Petrol station on right	E	16
78.007	600	3,0	Turn right onto the small road, via dei Paladini	VF sign, pass doorway with crucifix on your left	E	16
78.008	1500	4,5	At the Stop sign, continue straight ahead on via Vecchia Romana	VF sign, pass the church of San Michele on the left	E	17
78.009	400	4,9	At the crossroads with the main road, continue straight ahead on the small road	VF sign, pass house N° 1241 on your left	E	16
78.010	270	5,1	At the next crossroads, continue straight ahead on the small road	VF sign, enter Capannori	E	16
78.011	400	5,5	After passing the cemetery on the right, turn left in front of shrine	VF sign	E	15

Lucca to Altopascio 18.1km

169

170

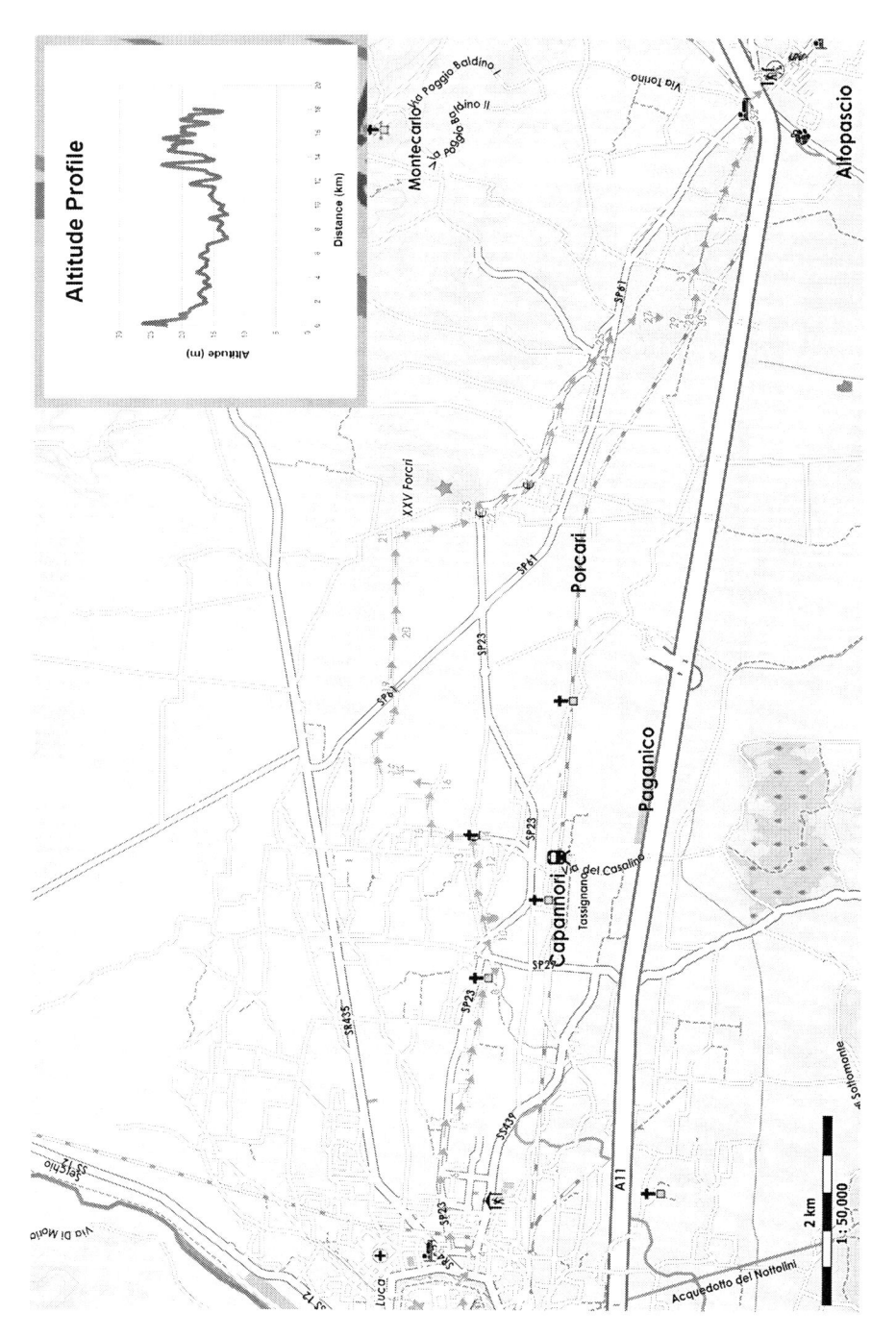

Waypoint	Distance Between Waypoints (m)	Total (km)	Directions	Verification Point	Compass	Altitude (m)
78.012	500	6,0	Beside the church of San Rocco, turn left	Pass walled garden on your left	N	16
78.013	90	6,1	At the Stop sign, turn right	Pass house N° 82 on your right	E	16
78.014	250	6,3	At the crossroads, turn left. Note:- the route can be reduced by approximately 2km by proceeding carefully straight ahead on via Romana to Pocari (XXV)	Via del Popolo, church of San Quirico ahead at the junction	N	15
78.015	500	6,8	At the T-junction, turn right	Via dei Colombini, towards Municipio	E	15
78.016	600	7,3	Turn left on the small road, via del Fontana	Pass the sports ground on the left	NE	12
78.017	400	7,7	Turn left	Keep drainage ditch on your left	N	13
78.018	300	8,0	At the T-junction, turn right	Pass house N° 46 on your right	E	14
78.019	1000	9,0	At the junction with the main road, SP61, turn left and immediately right	Over bridge, towards industrial buildings	E	15
78.020	700	9,7	At the roundabout, turn right and then left on the road	Via Ciarpi, enter Porcari	E	13
78.021	1100	10,7	Just after crossing the stream turn right	Via Pacconi	S	15
78.022	900	11,6	At the T-junction, turn left	Via Capannori, towards post office	E	15

Lucca to Altopascio 18.1km

Waypoint	Distance Between Waypoints (m)	Total (km)	Directions	Verification Point	Compass	Altitude (m)
78.023	130	11,7	In the centre of Porcari (XXV) turn right at the traffic lights	Direction Altopascio, pass church on the hill to the left	SE	18
78.024	2200	13,9	Immediately after entering Turchetto, bear right on the small road	Towards industrial area, VF sign	SE	15
78.025	300	14,2	At the junction with a major road, cross straight over onto via Pistoresi-Tappo-Turchetto	VF sign, pass supermarket on your left	SE	16
78.026	400	14,6	Turn right onto the track towards trees	Commercial building on left at junction	S	21
78.027	260	14,8	Continue straight ahead onto a gravel track	VF sign	S	21
78.028	180	15,0	Continue straight ahead	Pass the cemetery on the left	S	21
78.029	100	15,1	Turn left at the end of the wall	VF sign	SE	21
78.030	40	15,1	Follow the road keeping the church to your left	Via Chiesa	E	20
78.031	500	15,7	At the crossroads, proceed straight ahead into Badia Pozzeveri on via Catalani	VF sign, small shrine to the right	E	22
78.032	1900	17,6	At the T-junction with the SP3, turn right to go under the road bridge	VF sign, towards the bell-tower in Altopascio	SE	18
78.033	500	18,1	Arrive at Altopascio	Beside Chiesa di San Jacopo		18

Lucca to Altopascio 18.1km

Pilgrim Hostel

Magione Cavalieri del Tau,Office of Tourism - piazza Garibaldi, 10,55011 Altopascio(LU),Italy Tel:+39 0583 216525,Mobile:+39 3346 821060, turismo@comune.altopascio.lu.itwebwww.altopasciocultura.it/lospitalit_dei_pellegrini_-124-It.html,Price:D,

B&B, Hotel, Gite d'Etape

Hotel Da Paola,Via Francesca Romea, 24,55011 Altopascio(LU),Italy Tel:+39 0583 276453,Price:B,

Bed&Breakfast il Ponte,Via Sarzanese, 11,55056 Lucca(LU),Italy Tel:+39 0583 329815,Mobile:+39 3496 128128,receptionilpontelucca@gmail.com,Price:B,

Hotel Astoria,Via Roma, 86,55011 Altopascio(LU),Italy Tel:+39 0583 264746,info@hotelastoria-altopascio.com,Price:A,

Cavalieri del Tau,Via Gavinana,55011 Altopascio(LU),Italy Tel:+39 0583 25263,info@cavalierideltau.it,www.cavalierideltau.it,Price:A,

Tourist Information

Comune di Altopascio,Piazza Vittorio Emanuele, 24,55011 Altopascio(LU),Italy Tel:+39 0583 216455,

Banks and ATMs

Banca Toscana,Via Per Corte Giusti,55012 Capannori(LU),Italy Tel:+39 0583 433050,

Unicredit,Via Cavour, 1,55011 Altopascio(LU),Italy Tel:+39 5831 797411,

Banca Toscana,Via Firenze, 81a,55011 Altopascio(LU),Italy Tel:+39 0583 241105,

Banca Monte dei Paschi di Siena,Viale Guglielmo Marconi, 3,55016 Porcari(LU),Italy Tel:+39 0583 297585,

Cassa di Risparmio di Lucca,Via Capannori, 79,55016 Porcari(LU),Italy Tel:+39 0583 298531,

Travel

Gal Galilei Airport,56121 Pisa(PI),Italy Tel:+39 0508 49111,www.pisa-airport.com,

Doctor

Urbani - Medico Chirurgo,Via Roma, 5,55011 Altopascio(LU),Italy Tel:+39 0583 25962,

Veterinary

Bianchi - Medico Veterinario,Via Bientina, 67,55011 Altopascio(LU),Italy Tel:+39 0583 25463,

Hiking Equipment

Crazy Sport,Via Cavour, 12,55011 Altopascio(LU),Italy Tel:+39 0583 264750,

Bicycle Shop

Jolly Bike di Fornari Andrea,Via delle Cerbaie, 16,55011 Altopascio(LU),Italy Tel:+39 0583 216591,

Stage Seventy-nine Summary: the route follows the highways to Galleno before discovering an ancient stretch of the via Francigena leading to the hilltop paths of the Cerbaie. From Ponte a Cappiano the route follows the canal to Fucecchio before crossing the valley of the river Arno and climbing to the historic hilltop town of San Miniato. there are ample stopping places en route.

Distance from Canterbury: 1677km   Distance to Saint-Peter's-Square: 397km

Stage Ascent: 274m   Stage Descent: 170m

Waypoint	Distance Between Waypoints (m)	Total (km)	Directions	Verification Point	Compass	Altitude (m)
79.001	0	0,0	With chiesa di San Jacopo to your left, continue on the road between the shops	Via Cavour	SE	18
79.002	160	0,2	Bear right on via Cavour, direction Fucecchio	VF sign, keep small building with arched portico to the left	SE	20
79.003	1400	1,5	At the roundabout, continue straight ahead on via Romana, SP3, direction Fucecchio	VF signs, large commercial buildings on left	SE	22
79.004	2900	4,4	Fork right onto the unmade road	The ancient via Francigena	S	33
79.005	800	5,2	Continue straight ahead	Cross the small bridge	SE	20
79.006	400	5,6	Arrive in Galleno and continue straight ahead on the main road	Via Romana Lucchese, direction Fucecchio	SE	35
79.007	1000	6,7	Bear right at the major road junction	Direction Fucecchio	SE	38
79.008	110	6,8	Shortly after crossing a bridge, turn right on the track	Pass house on your left	S	36
79.009	60	6,8	Take the left fork	Towards the woods	SE	37
79.010	500	7,4	Cross over the driveway and continue straight ahead	Equestrian centre on the right	SE	51
79.011	50	7,4	Keep left on the track into the woods	Downhill	SE	50
79.012	200	7,6	At the T-junction with the road, turn right		SE	41

Altopascio to San-Miniato 25.5km

175

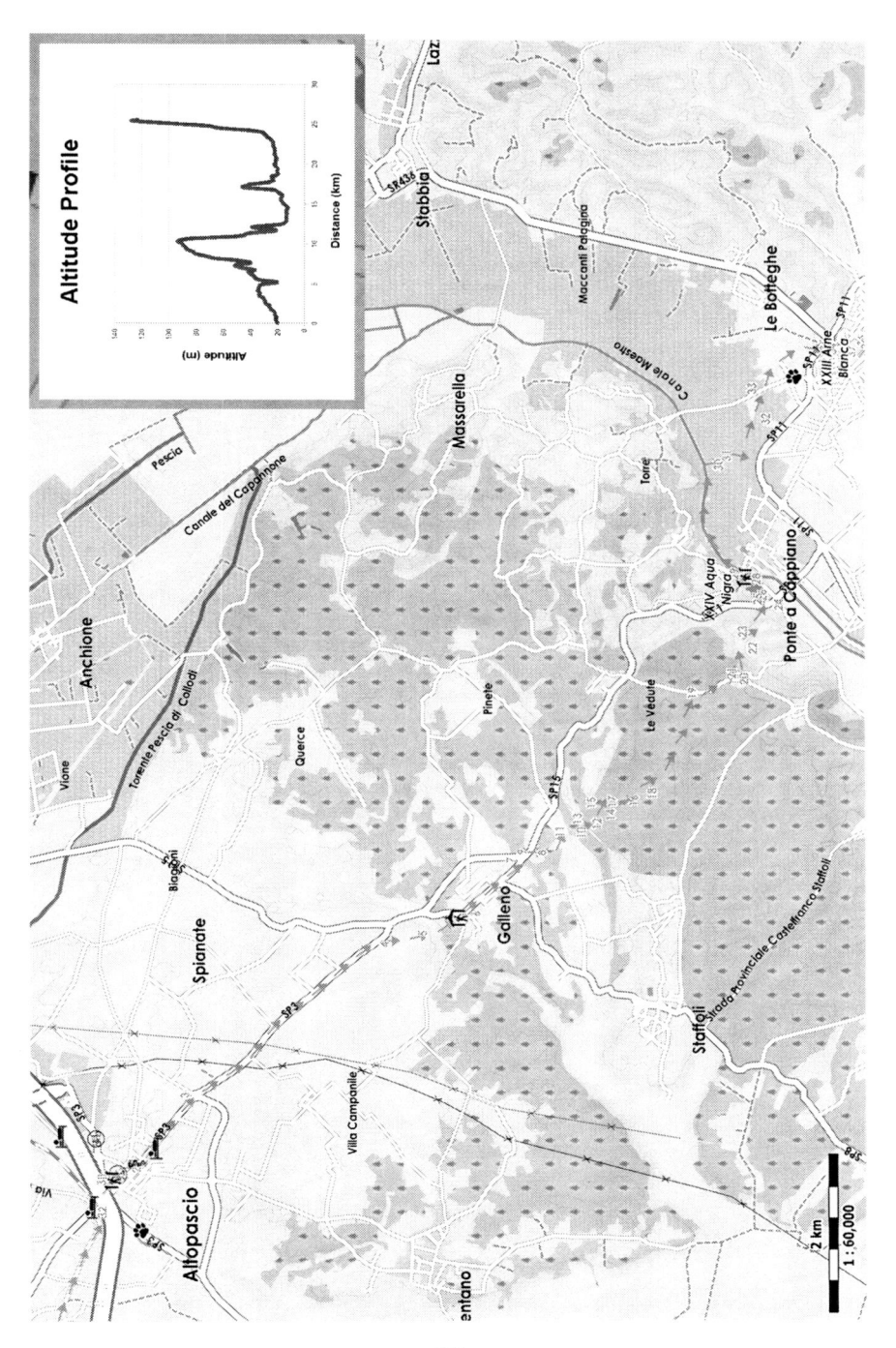

Waypoint	Distance Between Waypoints (m)	Total (km)	Directions	Verification Point	Compass	Altitude (m)
79.013	100	7,7	Shortly after passing the buildings on the left, join a white road and continue straight ahead		SE	39
79.014	130	7,8	Turn left at the next junction	In the woods	SE	42
79.015	170	8,0	Brear right, uphill	Pond on the left	S	50
79.016	220	8,2	At the first junction after a short climb, continue straight ahead		S	64
79.017	40	8,3	At the next junction bear left		SE	66
79.018	220	8,5	Join a broader track and bear slightly left	Pass horse track below on the left	SE	72
79.019	1600	10,1	At the T-junction with a busy tarmac road, bear right on the SP 61	Pass grove of trees on your right	SE	90
79.020	400	10,4	Take the left fork on the narrow, busy road, via di Poggio Adorno	Direction Santa Croce	SE	93
79.021	230	10,7	After the first bend to the left, turn sharp left on the track downhill into the woods	VF sign	E	85
79.022	400	11,0	Take the right fork on the track	Pond on the right	SE	48
79.023	280	11,3	Bear left on the road	Via De Medici	E	43
79.024	500	11,8	Cross the busy SP11 and continue straight ahead	VF sign	SE	21
79.025	60	11,8	Turn sharp left up the hill	Pass walled garden on your right	N	22
79.026	280	12,1	Cross the open space beside the vineyard and continue down the hill on the track	Towards the village	NE	38

Altopascio to San-Miniato 25.5km

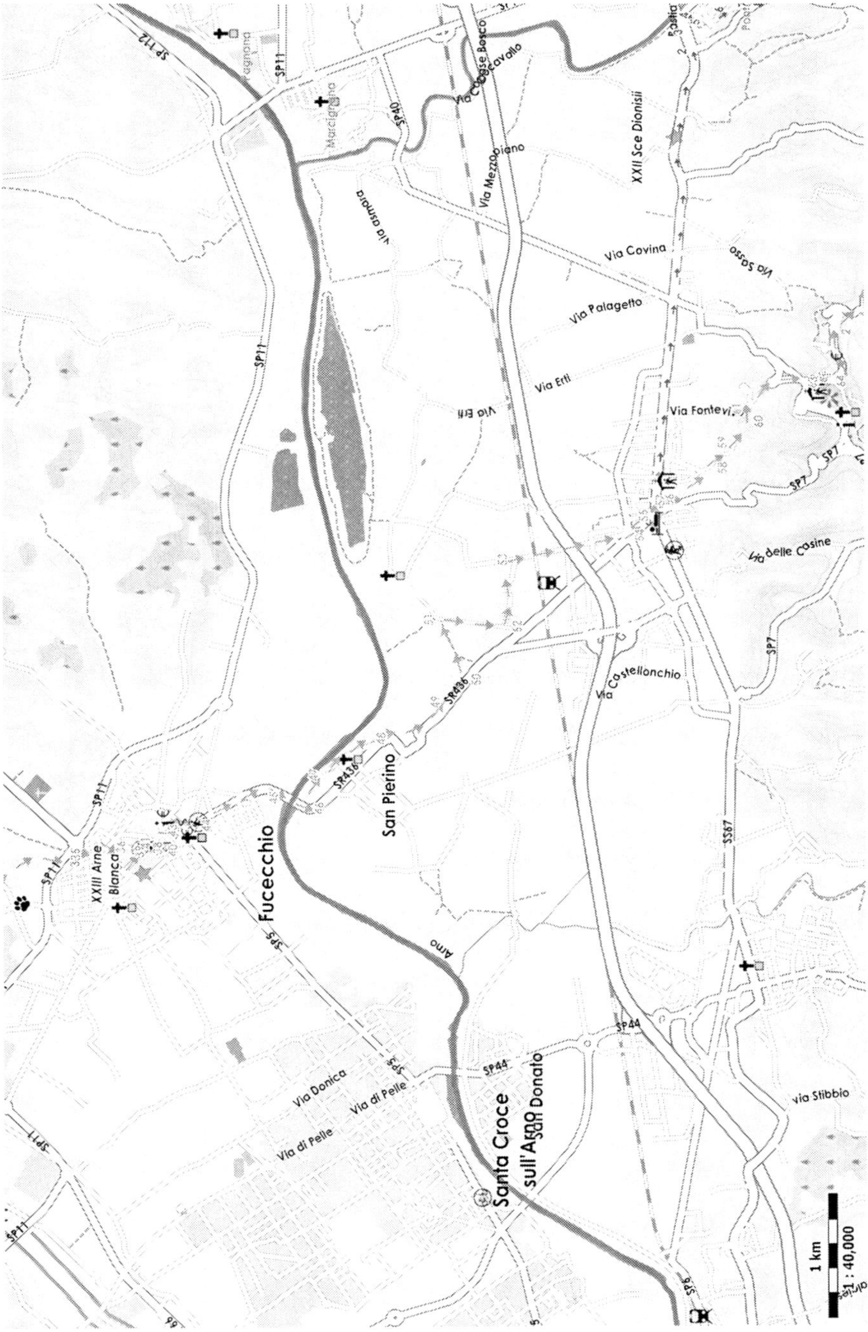
Fucecchio
San Pierino
Santa Croce
sull'Arno
San Donato
Arno
XXIII Arne Bianca
XXII Sce Dionisii
Via Donica
Via di Pelle
Via di Pelle
Via Mezzopiano
Via Covina
Via Palagetto
Via Erti
Via Erti
Via Fontevi.
Via Sasso
Via delle Casine
Via Castellonchio
Via Stibbio
SP11
SP5
SR436
SP44
SS67
SP7
SP40
SP6
1 km
1 : 40,000

Altopascio to San-Miniato 25.5km

Waypoint	Distance Between Waypoints (m)	Total (km)	Directions	Verification Point	Compass	Altitude (m)
79.027	190	12,3	Bear right on the road	Enter Ponte a Cappiano (XXIV)	SE	31
79.028	110	12,4	Cross piazza A. Donnini and continue straight ahead	Towards the covered bridge	SE	21
79.029	60	12,5	Cross the bridge and turn left down the steps into the car park and continue along the banks of the canal. Note:- riders should continue to the end of the bridge and then turn sharp left	Canal immediately to the left	E	17
79.030	1600	14,1	Shortly after the canal begins to bend to the left, turn right away from the canal-side onto another embankment	Right angle to canal	S	13
79.031	400	14,5	Cross the waterway and turn left - riders can continue on the left bank to the next Waypoint where they can cross on a more substantial bridge	Waterway on the left	E	12
79.032	600	15,1	Cross the road and continue straight ahead on the embankment	VF sign, keep waterway on your left	E	15
79.033	400	15,5	Cross another road and continue straight ahead on the embankment	Pass industrial complex on the right	SE	16
79.034	1000	16,4	Cross the SP11 and continue on the small road opposite, via Ponte del Rio	No Entry, pass roundabout on the left	S	18
79.035	230	16,7	Cross viale Napoleone Buonaparte and continue straight ahead	Via Sotto la Valle, VF sign	S	20
79.036	170	16,8	Take the next turning to the right	Via Sant'Antonio, VF sign	SW	25
79.037	230	17,1	At the T-junction, turn left into the centre of Fucecchio (XXIII)	VF sign, pass house N° 69 on your right	SE	43
79.038	180	17,2	After passing piazza S Lavagnini on the left, take the next turning to the right	Via G. di San Giorgio	SW	45

Waypoint	Distance Between Waypoints (m)	Total (km)	Directions	Verification Point	Compass	Altitude (m)
79.039	70	17,3	Cross piazza Garibaldi and take the small road straight ahead. Note:- horse and bike riders bear left into piazza Veneto to avoid a flight of steps	Parking area on your left	S	43
79.040	60	17,4	Turn left	Pass church on the left	E	42
79.041	70	17,4	Descend steps and cross piazza Vittorio Veneto and bear right down the hill	Via del Cassero	E	41
79.042	80	17,5	In the next square turn right	Via Donateschi	S	39
79.043	200	17,7	Continue straight ahead across piazza G. Montanelli and take via N. Sauro	Statue to your right, VF sign	SE	28
79.044	70	17,8	At the crossroads, continue straight ahead on the road	Direction San Miniato	S	25
79.045	800	18,6	Continue straight ahead. Note:- caution narrow pavements on the bridge	River Arno	SW	21
79.046	180	18,8	At the end of the bridge, turn sharp left and then right through the industrial area	Trees and river on the left	SE	19
79.047	400	19,2	Continue straight ahead on the footpath	On the embankment beside the river	SE	20
79.048	500	19,6	Bear right on the track	Away from the river	SE	20
79.049	700	20,4	Continue straight ahead between the embankment and the busy road	Main road on your right	SE	21
79.050	220	20,6	Turn left on the track into the fields	Pass garden allotments on the right	E	20
79.051	600	21,1	At the T-junction with a road, turn right, towards the main road	Pass house N° 12 on your left	S	21

Altopascio to San-Miniato 25.5km

Waypoint	Distance Between Waypoints (m)	Total (km)	Directions	Verification Point	Compass	Altitude (m)
79.052	500	21,6	Immediately after passing house N° 28, turn left on the small road	San Miniato visible on the hilltop to the right	E	21
79.053	600	22,2	At the T-junction, turn right	Towards the railway	S	23
79.054	900	23,1	At the roundabout, cross grass verge and continue straight ahead	Direction San Miniato, tree lined road	SE	25
79.055	290	23,4	At the traffic lights turn left	Pass Tabacchi on the left	E	27
79.056	130	23,6	Turn right on the small road. Note:- to visit the Sigeric location – Borgo Santo Genesio(XXII) - continue straight ahead on the Alternate Route on the main road	Pass the church on your left	S	28
79.057	130	23,7	Bear left on the embankment		SE	29
79.058	400	24,1	At the T-junction with the road, turn right	Via Pozzo, pass house N° 58 on your right	SE	34
79.059	300	24,4	At the end of via Pozzo continue straight ahead on the footpath	Pass house N° 89 on your left	SE	54
79.060	190	24,6	Continue straight ahead on the road	Downhill	E	65
79.061	130	24,7	At the junction with the main road, turn right uphill	Enter San Miniato	SE	68
79.062	500	25,2	Fork left onto viale Giacomo Matteotti	Enter the historic centre	S	114
79.063	180	25,4	Bear left onto via San Francesco	Chiesa di San Francesco on your right at the junction	SE	127
79.064	20	25,4	Take the left fork		SE	127
79.065	70	25,5	Arrive at San-Miniato old town	In piazza Buonaparte		122

180

Stage Summary: the Alternate Route bypasses the historic centre of San Miniato to allow a visit to the location of Borgo Santo Genesio (XXII). The route initially follows the busy road from San Miniato Basso towards Ponte a Elsa before climbing to rejoin the Main Route near Calenzano.

Stage Ascent: 132m   Stage Descent: 18m

Waypoint	Distance Between Waypoints (m)	Total (km)	Directions	Verification Point	Compass	Altitude (m)
79A1.001	0	0,0	Continue straight ahead on SP40	Direction Ponte a Elsa	E	28
79A1.002	3700	3,7	At the entry to Ponte a Elsa bear right on via Nazionale. Note:- the chapel of San Genesio (XXII) and an archaeological dig is to the left	Towards bus stops	E	31
79A1.003	180	3,9	Bear right uphill on the small road	Via Poggio a Pino	E	33
79A1.004	160	4,0	Continue uphill on the small road		SW	40
79A1.005	120	4,2	At the Stop sign, continue straight ahead	Church on the right	SE	46
79A1.006	220	4,4	Fork right	Uphill	S	57
79A1.007	210	4,6	At the Stop sign, turn left	SS67, direction Calenzano	S	62
79A1.008	1700	6,2	Bear left on the main road to rejoin the Main Route	Downhill		142

Alternate Route #79.A1 6.2km

181

Pilgrim Hostel

Ostello Ponte dè Medici – Ponte-a-Cappiano,Via Cristoforo Colombo, 237,50054 Fucecchio(FI),Italy Tel:+39 0571 297831,pontemedici@ponteverde.it,Price:C,

Religious Hostel

San Pietro Apostolo,Via della Chiesa In Galleno,50054 Fucecchio(FI),Italy Tel:+39 0571 299931,mbroti@tin.it,Price:D,

Misericordia San Miniato Basso,(Mario Giugni),Via Torta, 10,56028 San-Miniato(PI),Italy Tel:+39 0571 419455,mario.giugni@libero.it,Price:D,

Convento San Francesco,Piazza San Francesco, 1,56028 San-Miniato(PI),Italy Tel:+39 0571 43398,Price:C,

B&B, Hotel, Gite d'Etape

Albergo Elio,Via Tosco-Romagnola Est, 485,56028 San-Miniato(PI),Italy Tel:+39 0571 42010,Price:B,

Tourist Information

Associazione Turistica Pro Loco,Corso Giuseppe Garibaldi, 2,56028 San-Miniato(PI),Italy Tel:+39 0571 42233,

Comune di Fucecchio,Via la Marmora, 34,50054 Fucecchio(FI),Italy Tel:+39 0571 20681,

Banks and ATMs

Cassa di Risparmio,Piazza Giuseppe Montanelli, 27,50054 Fucecchio(FI),Italy Tel:+39 0571 24711,

Banca Nazionale del Lavoro,Via Trieste, 19,50054 Fucecchio(FI),Italy Tel:+39 0571 260342,

Banca Cr Firenze Filiale di San Miniato Basso,Piazzale della Pace, 9,56028 San-Miniato(PI),Italy Tel:+39 0571 419211,

MPS Banca,Largo Loris Malaguzzi, 9,56028 San-Miniato(PI),Italy Tel:+39 0571 498959,

Hospital

Ospedale San Pietro Igneo,Piazza Spartaco Lavagnini,50054 Fucecchio(FI),Italy Tel:+39 0571 7051,

Doctor

Mattaliano - Studio Medico,Corso Giacomo Matteotti,50054 Fucecchio(FI),Italy Tel:+39 0571 22308,

Buggiani - Studio Medico,Piazza Sandro Pertini,56028 San-Miniato(PI),Italy Tel:+39 0571 419449,

Veterinary

Ambulatorio Veterinario,Via di Burello, 8,50054 Fucecchio(FI),Italy Tel:+39 0571 242838,

Hiking Equipment

Trekking e Sport,Piazza Sandro Pertini,56028 San-Miniato(PI),Italy Tel:+39 0571 400499,

Maracana' Sport,Via Roma, 7,50054 Fucecchio(FI),Italy Tel:+39 0571 20968,

Bicycle Shop

Cicli Barone di Carmelo Barone,Via Provinciale Francesca Sud, 99,56029 Santa-Croce-Sull'Arno(PI),Italy Tel:+39 0571 360675,

Stage Eighty Summary: the route follows a mix of country roads and broad tracks over the rolling Tuscan hills. The section can be challenging in the summer heat with few opportunities for water stops.

Distance from Canterbury: 1702km Distance to Saint-Peter's-Square: 372km
Stage Ascent: 522m Stage Descent: 344m

Waypoint	Distance Between Waypoints (m)	Total (km)	Directions	Verification Point	Compass	Altitude (m)
80.001	0	0,0	Bear left in piazza Buonaparte and follow via Paolo Maioli	Statue of Leopold II on your right	E	118
80.002	400	0,4	Turn right on via Vicolo Borghizzi and almost immediately turn left through an archway. Note:- the pathway ahead involves a flight of steps - horse and bike riders are advised to remain on the road towards Calenzano	VF sign	SE	114
80.003	90	0,5	Turn right down a small brick passage separated by metal balustrades	VF sign	SE	114
80.004	130	0,6	At the T-junction with the road, turn right - riders rejoin from the left	Direction Calenzano	SE	115
80.005	1900	2,5	Fork left, via Castelfiorentino	VF sign, church on right	E	147
80.006	800	3,3	Fork right downhill	Direction Castelfiorentino, VF sign	SE	145
80.007	50	3,3	At the junction, turn right - Alternate Route rejoins from the left	VF sign	SE	142
80.008	1800	5,1	Following a sharp bend to the left, turn right and right again onto a gravel track	VF sign	S	126
80.009	1100	6,2	Fork right	VF sign	W	134
80.010	100	6,3	Fork left up the hill towards trees	VF sign	SW	139
80.011	250	6,5	At the T-junction, turn left	VF sign	S	160

San-Miniato to Gambassi-Terme 23.7km

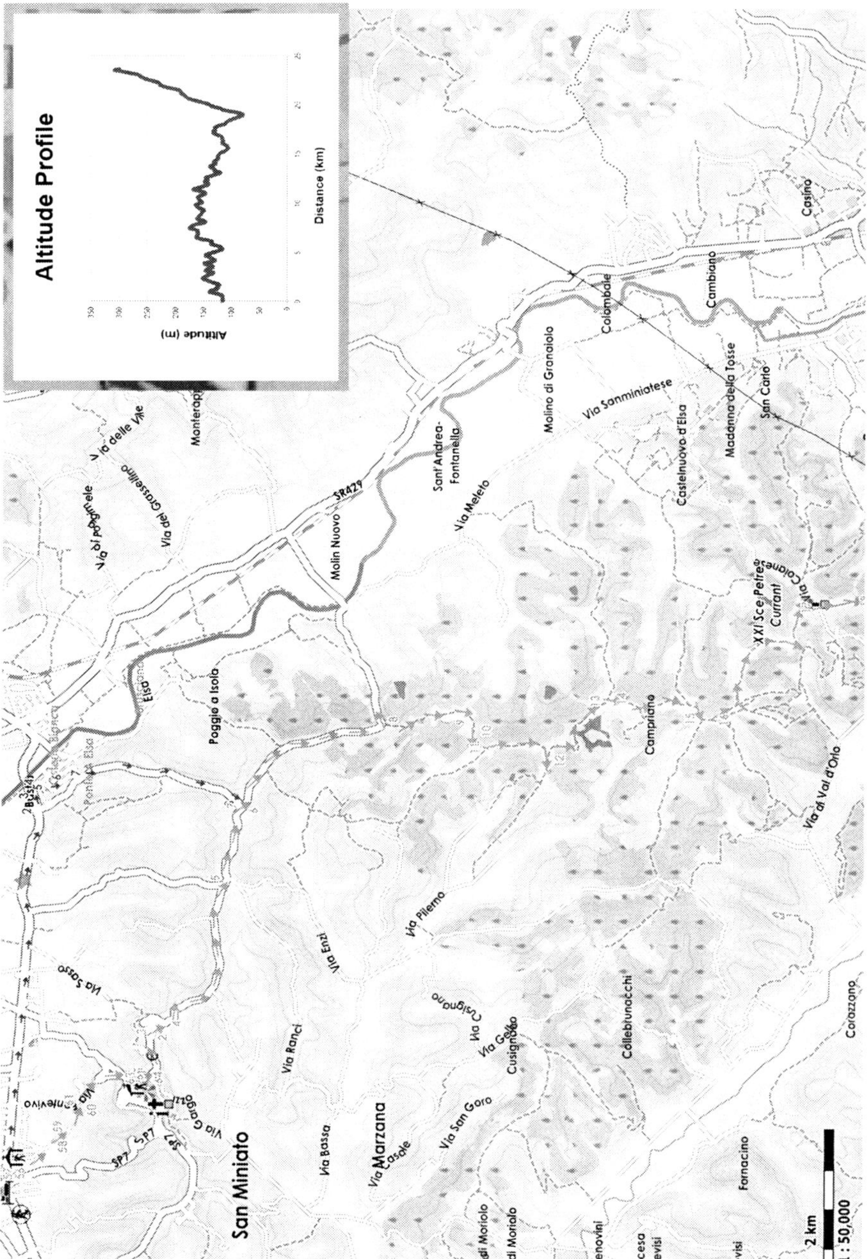
Altitude Profile
Altitude (m)
Distance (km)
San Miniato
SP7
Via Sasso
Via Bassa
Via Ranci
Via Enzi
Via Pilerno
Marzana
Via San Goro
Via Gello
Cusignano
Collebrunacchi
Corazzano
Fornacino
Balconevisi
Fondo Scesa
Balconevisi
Bottega Genovini
Casotti di Moriolo
Campriano
Via di Val d'Orlo
Poggio a Isola
Elsa
Molin Nuovo
SR429
Sant'Andrea-
Fontanella
Via Meleto
Molino di Granaiolo
Via Sanminiatese
Castelnuovo d'Elsa
Madonna della Tosse
San Carlo
Colombaie
Cambiano
Casino
2 km
1 : 50,000

Waypoint	Distance Between Waypoints (m)	Total (km)	Directions	Verification Point	Compass	Altitude (m)
80.012	800	7,3	Turn sharp left up the hill	VF sign	SE	159
80.013	1100	8,4	Turn left with a house directly on the right	VF sign	SE	155
80.014	40	8,4	Fork right onto on via di Meleto, with a farmhouse on right	VF sign	S	157
80.015	1100	9,5	Turn onto the furthest left of the tracks via della Poggiarella	VF sign	S	151
80.016	90	9,6	Take the left fork		SE	155
80.017	1900	11,5	At the crossroads in Coiano (XXI) continue straight ahead, via Coianese	VF sign	S	167
80.018	400	11,8	Continue straight ahead on a slightly wider gravel track	VF sign	SE	147
80.019	900	12,7	Fork right down the hill	VF sign	S	143
80.020	220	12,9	Fork left up the hill	VF sign	SE	131
80.021	900	13,8	Continue straight ahead	VF sign	S	137
80.022	1700	15,5	At the T-junction, turn left between two houses	VF sign	SE	108
80.023	210	15,7	At the T-junction, turn left onto the road	VF sign	NE	104
80.024	140	15,8	Turn sharp right onto the track	VF sign	SE	105
80.025	1000	16,8	After passing a house continue straight ahead onto the grass track	VF sign	S	116

San-Miniato to Gambassi-Terme 23.7km

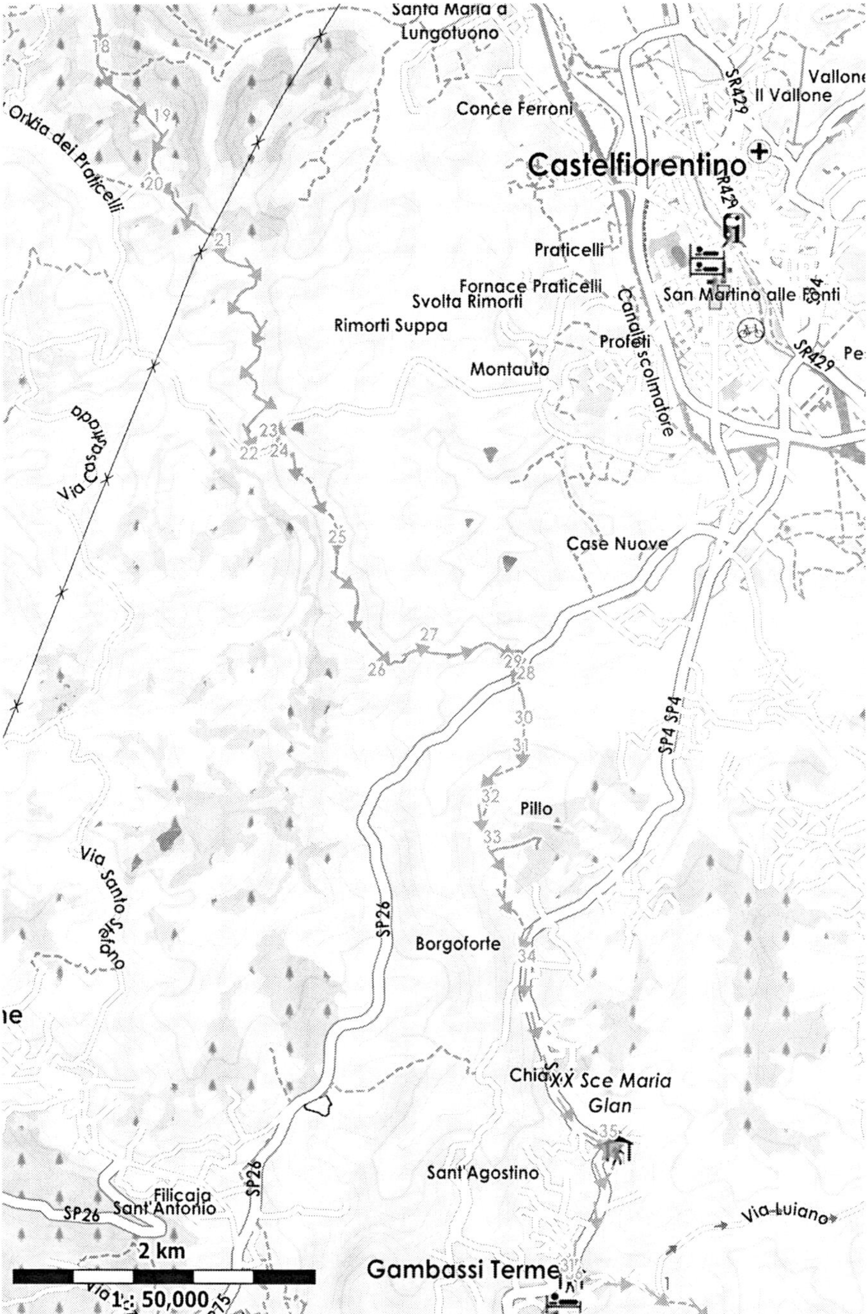
Santa Maria a Lungotuono
Vallone
Il Vallone
Conce Ferroni
Via dei Praticelli
Castelfiorentino
SR429
Praticelli
Fornace Praticelli
Svolta Rimorti
San Martino alle Fonti
Rimorti Suppa
Canali scolmatore
Profeti
SR429
Montauto
Via Casastrada
Case Nuove
SP4 SP4
Pillo
Via Santo Stefano
SP26
Borgoforte
Sce Maria Glan
Sant'Agostino
Via Luiano
Filicaja
SP26
Sant'Antonio
SP26
SP75
Gambassi Terme
2 km
1 : 50,000

Waypoint	Distance Between Waypoints (m)	Total (km)	Directions	Verification Point	Compass	Altitude (m)
80.026	800	17,6	At the T-junction turn left	VF sign	E	127
80.027	400	18,0	Keep right	VF sign	E	117
80.028	700	18,7	Turn right at an elevated T-junction, descend the ramp and join the main road	VF sign	SW	92
80.029	210	18,9	Turn left onto an unmade road	VF sign	SE	82
80.030	160	19,1	Bear right after passing the house on the right	VF sign	S	78
80.031	500	19,6	At the T-junction, turn right with house on left	VF sign	SW	111
80.032	220	19,8	Fork left up the hill	Red and white sign	S	122
80.033	600	20,3	Keep left, uphill on the gravel road	VF sign, pass hedged garden on your right	SE	151
80.034	700	21,0	At the T-junction, turn right onto the SP4	VF sign, shrine just before the junction on the left	S	183
80.035	1600	22,6	Santa Maria a Chianni (XX) is to the left. To follow the route to Gambassi-Terme, continue uphill on the main road	VF sign	S	247
80.036	800	23,4	At the traffic lights, fork left direction Gambassi	VF sign	S	293
80.037	260	23,7	Arrive at Gambassi-Terme	Beside the church of Cristo Re in Santi Jacopo e Stefano		297

San-Miniato to Gambassi-Terme 23.7km

Religious Hostel

Ostello Sigerico - Pieve di Santa Maria Assunta,(Anna Giubbolini),Chiani,50050 Gambassi-Terme(FI),Italy Tel:+39 3397 832270,parrocchia.gambassi@libero.it,Price:C,

Parrocchia Ss.Jacopo e Stefano,Via Volterrana Nord, 59,50050 Gambassi-Terme(FI),Italy Tel:+39 0571 638208,parrocchiagambassi@libero.it,

Commercial Hostel

Osteria Matta Gatta,Viale Franklin Delano Roosevelt, 26,50051 Castelfiorentino(FI),Italy Tel:+39 0571 633256,
info@ostellocastelfiorentino.com,www.ostellocastelfiorentino.com,Price:C,

B&B, Hotel, Gite d'Etape

Albergo Osteria Pinchorba,Route d, 26,50050 Gambassi-Terme(FI),Italy Tel:+39 0571 638188,Price:B,

Tourist Information

Ufficio Turistico,Via Cosimo Ridolfi,50051 Castelfiorentino(FI),Italy Tel:+39 0571 629049,

Comune di Gambassi Terme,Via Giuseppe Garibaldi, 7,50050 Gambassi-Terme(FI),Italy Tel:+39 0571 638224,

Banks and ATMs

Banca di Credito Cooperativo,Via Giuseppe Garibaldi, 14,50050 Gambassi-Terme(FI),Italy Tel:+39 0571 638644,

Cassa di Risparmio di San Miniato,Via Vittorio Veneto, 70,50050 Gambassi-Terme(FI),Italy Tel:+39 0571 638000,

Travel

Peretola Airport,Via del Termine, 11,50127 Firenze(FI),Italy Tel:+39 0553 0615,www.aeroporto.firenze.it,

Hospital

Ospedale Santa Verdiana,Via dei Mille,50051 Castelfiorentino(FI),Italy Tel:+39 0571 6831,

Veterinary

Studio Veterinario,Viale Antonio Gramsci,50050 Gambassi-Terme(FI),Italy Tel:+39 0571 638636,

Bicycle Shop

Ancilotti Bike di Ancilotti Marco,Via Bruno Fanciullacci, 30,50051 Castelfiorentino(FI),Italy Tel:+39 0571 631007,

San-Miniato to Gambassi-Terme 23.7km

Stage Eight-one Summary: the section is undertaken substantially on remote tracks winding over Tuscan hills. Although beautiful, the section can be very tiring in the heat of summer.

Distance from Canterbury: 1726km   Distance to Saint-Peter's-Square: 348km
Stage Ascent: 329m   Stage Descent: 300m

Waypoint	Distance Between Waypoints (m)	Total (km)	Directions	Verification Point	Compass	Altitude (m)
81.001	0	0,0	From the church of Cristo Re in Santi Jacopo e Stefano, take via Icilio Franchi	Direction Certaldo, VF sign	E	296
81.002	700	0,7	On the apex of the bend to the left, bear right onto a small road. Note:- the route ahead is passable and generally pleasant for all groups, however there are sections where cyclists will be challenged by steep off-road climbs. Cyclists may want to remain on the road and bear left to follow the Alternate Route to Pancole via the Elsa valley	Direction Luiano, VF sign	SE	267
81.003	700	1,4	Beside the small chapel, take the left fork	VF sign	SE	210
81.004	1900	3,3	At the junction, keep left down the hill	VF sign	SE	144
81.005	400	3,7	Fork right up the hill	VF sign	SW	115
81.006	50	3,7	Bear left through a gap in the fence and continue with the fence on left	VF sign	SE	115
81.007	120	3,9	Bear left uphill away from the field and into the trees	VF sign	SE	120
81.008	60	3,9	Turn right at the top of the track	VF sign, trees on the right	SE	126
81.009	210	4,1	Track enters another field, bear left	Uphill	SE	152
81.010	80	4,2	Bear left up the hill	VF sign	SE	164

Gambassi-Terme to San-Gimignano 12.7km

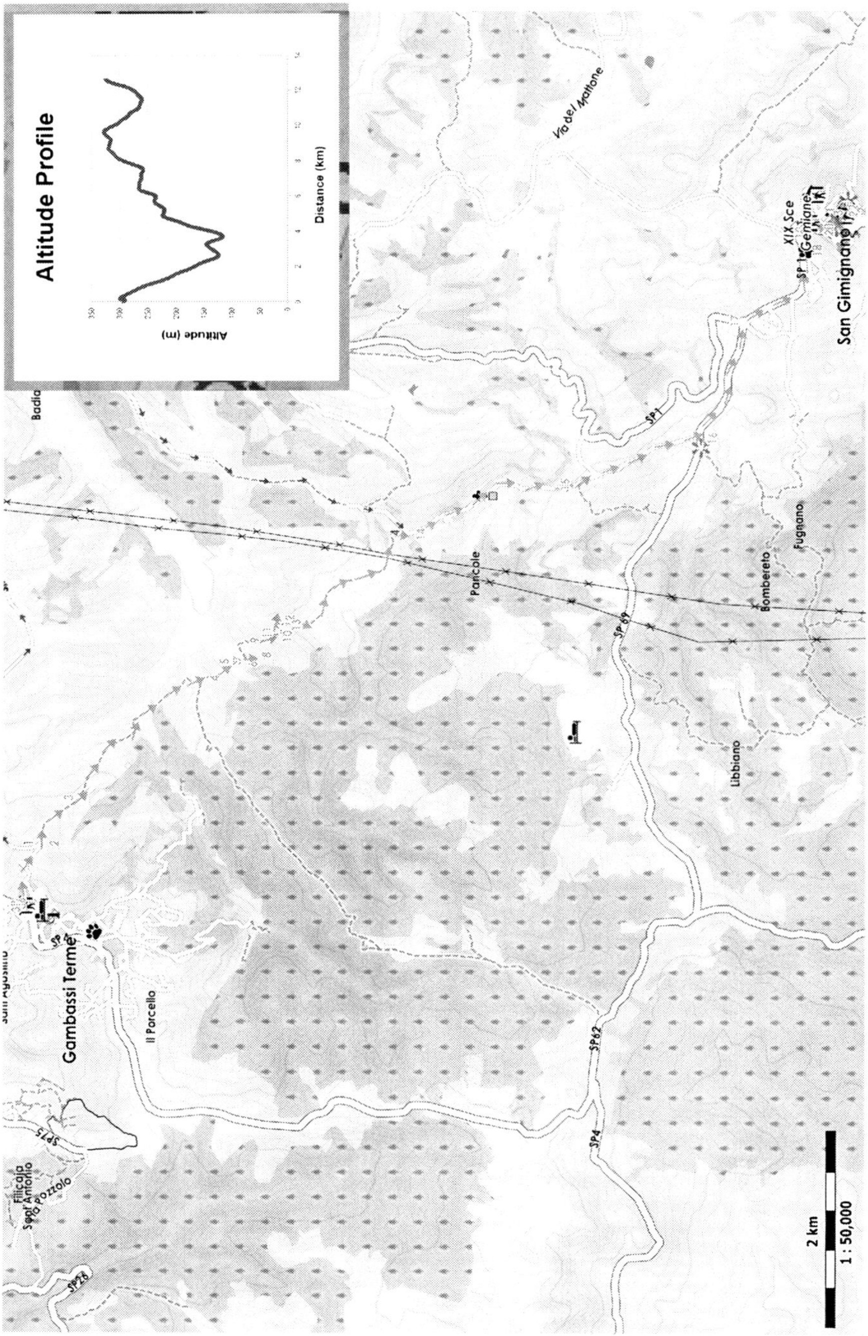
Altitude Profile
Altitude (m)
Distance (km)
Via del Mattone
Badia
Gambassi Terme
Il Porcello
Pancole
Libbiano
Bombereto
Fugnano
San Gimignano
SP1
SP62
SP4
SP75
SP26
Filicaja
2 km
1 : 50,000

Waypoint	Distance Between Waypoints (m)	Total (km)	Directions	Verification Point	Compass	Altitude (m)
81.011	70	4,3	Directly in front of a farmhouse, turn left onto a gravel track	Proceeding up the hill	E	173
81.012	180	4,5	At the T-junction in the track, turn right up the hill	VF sign	S	187
81.013	400	4,8	Fork left	VF sign	SE	219
81.014	1600	6,4	At the T-junction with a tarmac road (SP1), turn right up hill - Alternate Route rejoins on left	VF sign, pass through Pancole	S	263
81.015	1900	8,3	Continue straight ahead on the road. Note:- the Ministry Route turns right on the track and rejoins our route at the next Waypoint. The Ministry Route adds 1km to the section and also increases distance on the busy main road	VF sign to the right	S	305
81.016	1500	9,7	At the Stop sign, turn left, down the hill	Direction San Gimignano	E	327
81.017	1400	11,1	At the roundabout, bear right, direction San Gimignano centre	Via Martiri di Citerna, VF sign	SE	264
81.018	1100	12,1	Fork right up the hill on via Niccolo Cannicci	Pass crucifix on your left, VF sign	SE	279
81.019	210	12,3	At the junction, continue straight ahead	Uphill	SE	298
81.020	50	12,4	At the intersection with the main road, take the underpass to enter San-Gimignano (XIX)	Pass through the arch, porta San Matteo	SE	304
81.021	20	12,4	Continue straight ahead on the paved road	Via San Matteo	SE	307
81.022	300	12,7	Arrive at San-Gimignano (XIX) in piazza Duomo	Tourist offices to the right		324

Alternate Route #81.A1 12.3km

Stage Summary: the Alternate Route allows cyclists to avoid difficult off-road climbs. The route descends to Certaldo before climbing to rejoin the Main Route in Pancole.

Stage Ascent: 290m   Stage Descent: 291m

81A1.001	0	0,0	Continue straight ahead on SP40	Direction Ponte a Elsa	E	266
81A1.002	6800	6,8	Just before the bridge over the river Elsa, turn right	Direction San Gimignano	S	65
81A1.003	500	7,3	Bear right	Direction Pancole	SW	68
81A1.004	5100	12,3	Turn left to rejoin the Main Route	Enter Pancole		266

191

Religious Hostel

Convento Sant'Agostino,(Padre Brian),Piazza Sant'Agostino, 10,53037 San-Gimignano(SI),Italy Tel:+39 0577 907012,sangimignanoconvento@yahoo.it,Price:C,

Foresteria del Monastero di S.Girolamo,Via Folgore, 32,53037 San-Gimignano(SI),Italy
Tel:+39 0577 940573,vallombrosane@virgilio.it,Price:B,

Santa Maria Assunta,Piazza Pecori,53037 San-Gimignano(SI),Italy
Tel:+39 0577 940316,collegiata@cheapnet.it,

B&B, Hotel, Gite d'Etape

Ristoro Poggio a Issi,(Freddi Pierluca),SP69-Km4,53037 San-Gimignano (SI),Italy
Tel:+39 0577 946004,info@poggioaissi.com,poggioaissi.com,Price:C,

Camping

Camping Boschetto di Piemma,Località Santa Lucia,53037 San-Gimignano(SI),Italy
Tel:+39 0577 940352,

Tourist Information

Associazione Turistica Pro Loco,Via G.Boccaccio, 16,50052 Certaldo(FI),Italy
Tel:+39 0571 652730,

Comune San Gimignano,Via San Matteo, 24,53037 San-Gimignano(SI),Italy
Tel:+39 0577 955604,

Banks and ATMs

Banca Toscana,Piazza Martiri della Liberta, 2,53037 San-Gimignano(SI),Italy
Tel:+39 0577 940329,

Banca Monte dei Paschi di Siena,Piazza Cisterna, 9,53037 San-Gimignano(SI),Italy
Tel:+39 0577 941377,

Doctor

Profeti - Medico,Localita' Camporeccia, 2,53037 San-Gimignano(SI),Italy
Tel:+39 0577 941152,

Veterinary

Studio Veterinario,Via Nicola Cannicci, 41,53037 San-Gimignano(SI),Italy
Tel:+39 0577 941179,

Hiking Equipment

Dany Sport,Piazza della Cisterna,53037 San-Gimignano(SI),Italy Tel:+39 0577 941698,

Gambassi-Terme to San-Gimignano 12.7km

Stage Eighty-two Summary: the route leaves San Gimignano on tarmac roads before returning to the tracks through the Tuscan hills. There are limited opportunities to break the journey on the Main Route. An Alternate Route offers the opportunity to divert to the large town of Colle di Val d'Elsa where all facilities are available.

Distance from Canterbury: 1738km   Distance to Saint-Peter's-Square: 335km
Stage Ascent: 390m   Stage Descent: 510m

Waypoint	Distance Between Waypoints (m)	Total (km)	Directions	Verification Point	Compass	Altitude (m)
82.001	0	0,0	From piazza Duomo, continue straight ahead	Duomo and steps to the right	S	324
82.002	60	0,1	In piazza Cisterna, continue straight ahead down a narrow passage way, via San Giovanni	VF sign, pass through arch	SW	322
82.003	40	0,1	Bear left on via San Giovanni	VF sign	S	319
82.004	260	0,4	After passing underneath the last archway, porta San Giovanni, bear left. Note:- cyclists and riders should follow the road ahead - viale Romana - to avoid a flight of steps	Keep small park to your right	S	303
82.005	70	0,5	Turn left and go down the steps. Note:- riders remain on the road and take the first left turn	Towards the stopping place for buses	S	299
82.006	110	0,6	Turn right on via Baccanella	VF sign	SW	293
82.007	150	0,7	At a mini roundabout, take the exit direction Montauto	Red and white VF sign	SW	282
82.008	90	0,8	Turn left direction Santa Lucia	VF sign	SE	274
82.009	1900	2,7	Shortly after passing the sports field on the left, turn right on an unmade road. Note:- for the Alternate Route via Colle di Val d'Elsa continue straight ahead on the road. Cyclists are advised to take this route to avoid a number of water crossings	Pass small shrine and tree lined driveway on your left	SW	266

San-Gimignano to Abbadia-a-Isola 26.3km

193

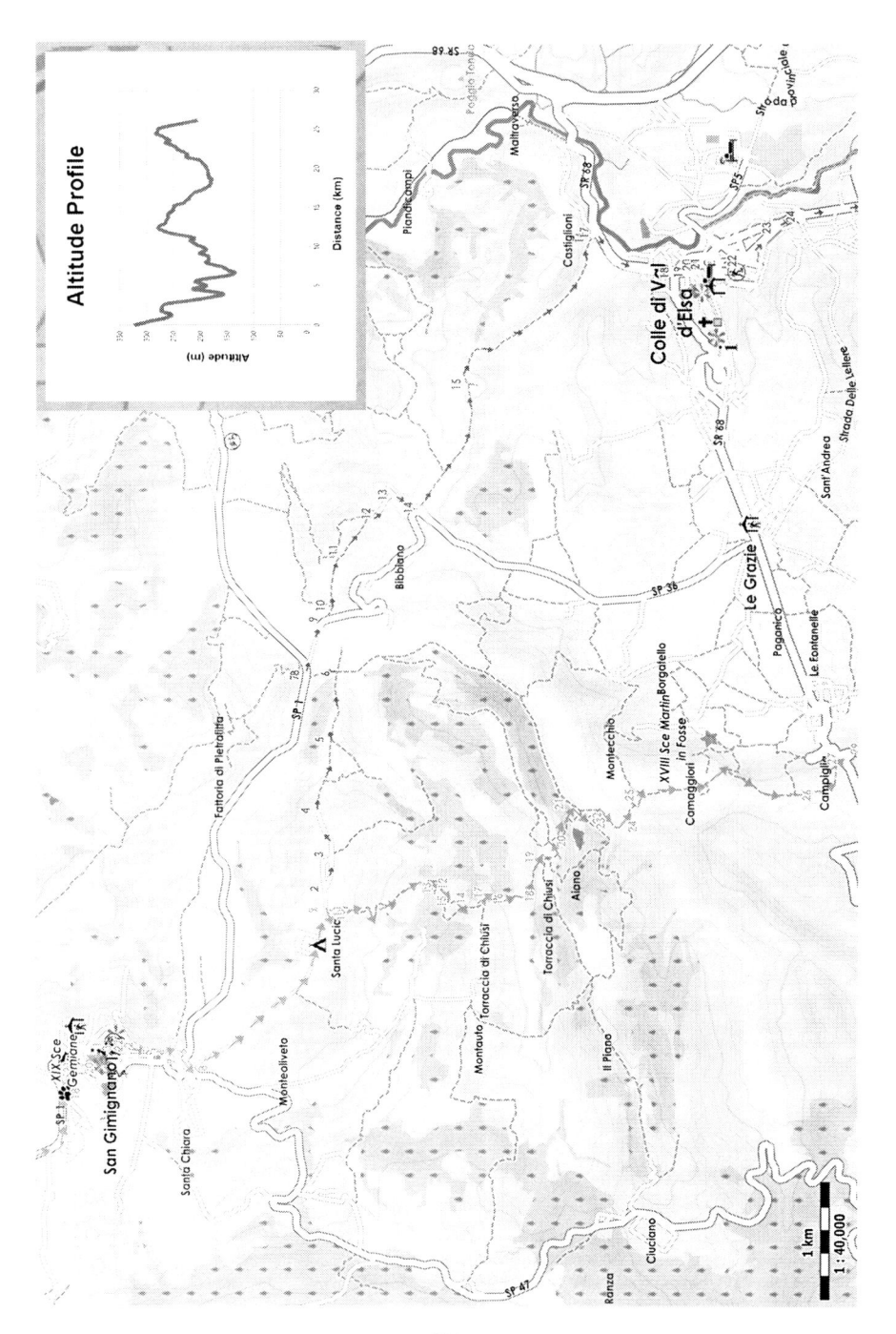
Altitude Profile
Altitude (m)
Distance (km)
San Gimignano
XIX Sce Gemiane
SP 1
Santa Chiara
Monteoliveto
Fattoria di Pietrafitta
Santa Lucia
Montauto
Torraccia di Chiusi
Aiano
Il Piano
Ciuciano
Ranza
SP 47
Bibbiano
Piandicampi
Maltraverso
Castiglioni
SR 68
Colle di Val d'Elsa
SP 36
SP 5
Le Grazie
Paganico
Le Fontanelle
Sant'Andrea
Strada Delle Lellere
Montecchio
XVIII Sce Martin in Fosse
Borgatello
Camaggiori
Campiglia
1 km
1 : 40,000

Waypoint	Distance Between Waypoints (m)	Total (km)	Directions	Verification Point	Compass	Altitude (m)
82.010	50	2,7	Turn right	Near to shed	S	265
82.011	240	2,9	Bear right on the track	Downhill	S	246
82.012	1000	4,0	Beside the house in the valley bottom turn left and ford the stream		SW	155
82.013	150	4,1	Continue straight ahead across the field towards the house		SW	160
82.014	130	4,3	Turn right and skirt the house	House on your left	SW	172
82.015	110	4,4	Turn right on the access road to the house	Leave the house directly behind	S	184
82.016	300	4,7	At the junction at the top of the ridge turn left		SE	213
82.017	70	4,8	Take the track to the right	Downhill between trees	S	209
82.018	270	5,0	At the bottom of the hill, continue straight ahead	Cross the stream	SE	188
82.019	500	5,5	Beside the house turn right and then left to skirt the house	Villa della Torraccia di Chiusi	SE	206
82.020	290	5,8	At the intersection with the entrance to the house, turn right on the road	Downhill	SE	205
82.021	500	6,3	In the hamlet of Aiano turn right	Near to farm building	SW	153
82.022	190	6,4	Take the left fork	Reservoir on the right	S	141
82.023	280	6,7	Continue straight ahead across the ford		S	134
82.024	100	6,8	Take the left fork		SE	136
82.025	300	7,1	Take the right fork		S	149
82.026	1400	8,5	At the road junction, continue straight ahead		SE	183

San-Gimignano to Abbadia-a-Isola 26.3km

Colle di Val
d'Elsa
Staggia Senese
Strada provinciale Castello di Staggia
Fontana
SR 2
Vivaino
Vivaio
Quercia
Cucule
Strada provinciale Colligiana
XVI Burgenove
Abbadia a Isola
Traversa Monteriggioni
Scarna
Acquaviva
Strove
Castel Petraio
SP 541
SP 5
Carpiglioni
Strada di Scorgiano
SR 514
Panette
Gracciano d'Elsa
Pieve a Elsa
Onci
Mensanello
Traversa Montemaggioni- Casole
Strada Delle Lellere
Sant'Andrea
SR 68
Le Grazie
SP 36
Boscona
Paganico
Le Fontanelle
Quartaia
Montecchio
XVIII Sce Martin
in Fosse
Borgatello
Camaggiori
Campiglia
1 km
1 : 40,000

Waypoint	Distance Between Waypoints (m)	Total (km)	Directions	Verification Point	Compass	Altitude (m)
82.027	600	9,1	At the T-junction with the main road, turn left		SE	199
82.028	90	9,2	Immediately after the bend to the left, turn right onto the track	Direction Bagnoli, VF sign	S	200
82.029	140	9,4	Take the next turning to the right		S	197
82.030	900	10,3	After a section of an old paved road bear right		S	206
82.031	100	10,4	Turn right		SW	209
82.032	150	10,6	At the T-junction, turn left	Uphill	S	211
82.033	70	10,6	Cross the road and bear right	Direction Badia a Coneo	S	213
82.034	200	10,8	Continue straight ahead on the unmade road	Abbey on your left	S	218
82.035	50	10,9	Take the old paved road to the right	Downhill	SW	218
82.036	800	11,7	Emerge from the woods and skirt the house before turning left	House on the left	SE	247
82.037	400	12,0	At the T-junction at the end of the field, turn left and then right	Into the woods	SE	266
82.038	170	12,2	Take the right fork		SE	272
82.039	150	12,4	At the crossroads continue straight ahead		SE	277
82.040	240	12,6	At the T-junction, turn left on the unmade road		E	277
82.041	180	12,8	At the crossroads, continue straight ahead		SE	274
82.042	600	13,3	At the T-junction, turn left towards the village	San Donato	E	263
82.043	300	13,6	Take the left fork on the tarmac	Towards the main road	E	260

San-Gimignano to Abbadia-a-Isola 26.3km

Waypoint	Distance Between Waypoints (m)	Total (km)	Directions	Verification Point	Compass	Altitude (m)
82.044	130	13,8	At the T-junction with the main road (SP27), take the pedestrian crossing and turn right on the pavement	Gantry overhead	S	259
82.045	170	13,9	Turn left into Quartaia, on via degli Aragonesi	VF sign, pass Tabacchi on the right	E	258
82.046	150	14,1	Turn right	Via della Concordia	S	260
82.047	130	14,2	At the T-junction, turn left on the unmade road	Exit the village	NE	259
82.048	1100	15,3	Pass through the farm and continue on the unmade road	Road bears right shortly after leaving the farm and passes beside water source	SE	248
82.049	500	15,7	At the T-junction at the foot of the hill, turn left and continue straight ahead	Beside the woods	E	228
82.050	500	16,2	Turn left on the track	Just before reaching the bridge	E	220
82.051	90	16,3	Take the right fork		NE	219
82.052	500	16,8	Take the right fork		NE	214
82.053	260	17,0	Bear right on the white road	Towards Molino le Vene	NE	209
82.054	1000	18,0	Join a tarmac road and bear right	Village of Onci to the left	E	180
82.055	70	18,1	Turn left on the road	Beside the canal	NE	179
82.056	600	18,7	After crossing the waterway, bear right and immediately left	Via Nino Bixio	E	177
82.057	210	18,9	In the centre of Gracciano d'Elsa (XVII), at the crossroads between via Fratelli Bandiera (SP541) and via Nino Bixio, continue straight ahead	Via Pastrengo, red and white sign	E	182

San-Gimignano to Abbadia-a-Isola 26.3km

Waypoint	Distance Between Waypoints (m)	Total (km)	Directions	Verification Point	Compass	Altitude (m)
82.058	140	19,0	After passing house N° 27, turn right	Via Goito, VF sign	S	183
82.059	80	19,1	At the Stop sign turn left	Towards roundabout, VF sign	E	183
82.060	170	19,3	At the roundabout, take the second exit	Pass industrial buildings on the left	E	184
82.061	290	19,5	Take the right fork and keep straight ahead	Into open country	SE	185
82.062	800	20,4	Bear left	Line of trees on the right	E	189
82.063	400	20,7	Continue straight ahead on the path	Beside the fence	E	194
82.064	500	21,2	Take the right fork	Woods on the left	SE	202
82.065	100	21,3	Bear left and continue straight ahead up the hill	Into the woods	NE	208
82.066	400	21,7	At the junction, continue straight ahead on the gravel road	Strada della Cerreta, VF sign	E	223
82.067	140	21,9	Turn right, direction Strove	Strada di Acquaviva	SE	222
82.068	700	22,6	Bear right on the tarmac	Stone wall on the right	SE	242
82.069	800	23,3	In Strove, fork left	Beside brick electricity tower	SE	263
82.070	140	23,5	After passing the basketball court, bear left on strada di Strove	VF sign	E	264

San-Gimignano to Abbadia-a-Isola 26.3km

199

Waypoint	Distance Between Waypoints (m)	Total (km)	Directions	Verification Point	Compass	Altitude (m)
82.071	130	23,6	At the T-junction with the main road, turn left	Gravel path beside main road	E	259
82.072	180	23,8	Take the pedestrian crossing and turn right	Towards Castel Pietraia	E	256
82.073	170	24,0	On the apex of the bend to right, turn left on the track		NE	263
82.074	250	24,2	Turn right towards woods	After passing between houses	E	269
82.075	300	24,5	Turn right on the path into the woods and then quickly fork to the left	Ignore road on the left – leads into an industrial site	SE	280
82.076	230	24,7	Take the left fork		E	280
82.077	270	25,0	Turn left	Remain in the woods	NE	279
82.078	100	25,1	Continue straight ahead	Exit woods and cross the olive grove	NE	278
82.079	170	25,3	At the T-junction, turn left on the white road, strada di Certino	Between stone walls	N	274
82.080	700	25,9	At the T-junction, turn right	VF sign	NE	227
82.081	90	26,0	Take the left fork	Downhill, between houses	NE	220
82.082	240	26,3	Rejoin the main road and turn right	Towards bar	NE	205
82.083	40	26,3	Arrive at Abbadia-a-Isola (XVI)	Ancient church on the right		203

San-Gimignano to Abbadia-a-Isola 26.3km

Stage Summary: the Alternate Route provides the opportunity to find accommodation in Colle di Val d'Elsa. It progresses to the town on minor roads and tracks, but returns to the Main Route on more major roads.

Stage Ascent: 247m   Stage Descent: 335m

Waypoint	Distance Between Waypoints (m)	Total (km)	Directions	Verification Point	Compass	Altitude (m)
82A1.001	0	0,0	Continue straight ahead on the road	Pass small shrine on your right	E	268
82A1.002	170	0,2	Take right fork	VF sign, pass park on the left	E	266
82A1.003	300	0,5	At the junction, continue straight ahead on a small unmade road	VF sign and shrine on the corner	E	261
82A1.004	400	0,9	After passing two houses, on the left and right, continue straight ahead	Down the hill	E	237
82A1.005	700	1,5	At the T-junction in the track, turn left	VF arrow on a tree	E	177
82A1.006	600	2,1	At a T-junction with a small tarmac road, turn left on the road	Pass gated driveway on your right	N	115
82A1.007	280	2,4	At the T-junction with a major road (SP1), turn right	VF sign, towards bar	E	119
82A1.008	30	2,4	Take the right fork	Direction Volterra, SP36	E	119
82A1.009	500	2,9	Immediately after first right hand bend, turn left onto a track		SE	106
82A1.010	140	3,1	At a junction with a number of tracks continue straight ahead on the narrowest	The third track from the left	E	113
82A1.011	500	3,6	The small track joins a larger track, bear right towards the crest of the hill	Between vines	SE	150
82A1.012	500	4,0	Bear right	Up the hill	SE	184
82A1.013	230	4,2	At the T-junction, turn right on the road	Podere Bibbiano on the left	SW	204

Alternate Route #82.A1 11.7km

Waypoint	Distance Between Waypoints (m)	Total (km)	Directions	Verification Point	Compass	Altitude (m)
82A1.014	250	4,5	Turn left onto the gravel track	VF sign	E	213
82A1.015	1200	5,7	At the T-junction at the top of the hill, turn left downhill	Away from the house	SE	208
82A1.016	1900	7,5	Track joins a tarmac road, bear right	Main road directly ahead	SE	147
82A1.017	70	7,6	At the T-junction with main road, turn right, SS68	VF sign, enter Colle di Val d'Elsa	SW	133
82A1.018	800	8,4	At the roundabout, continue straight ahead	Towards the centro historico	S	142
82A1.019	120	8,5	Turn left direction Siena	VF sign	SE	143
82A1.020	100	8,6	At the crossroads, continue straight ahead	Direction piazza Arnolfo	S	141
82A1.021	70	8,7	Arrive in the centre of Colle di Val d'Elsa, continue straight ahead across the square	Piazza Arnolfo di Cambio	S	142
82A1.022	300	9,0	At the end of the road bear left	Via Armando Diaz, pass bank on the left	SE	151
82A1.023	400	9,4	At the roundabout, go straight ahead	SS541, direction Grosseto	SE	169
82A1.024	220	9,7	At the next roundabout continue straight ahead	SS541, direction Grosseto	S	165
82A1.025	1400	11,1	At the roundabout, after crossing the river Elsa, bear right	SS541, direction Grosseto	S	175
82A1.026	700	11,7	Arrive in Gracciano d'Elsa and turn left to rejoin the Main Route	Via Pastrengo		180

Alternate Route #82.A1 11,7km

Pilgrim Hostel

Casa Per Ferie Santa Maria Assunta Ospitalita Pellegrini,Piazza Roma, 23,53035 Monteriggioni(SI),Italy Tel:+39 0577 304066,Mobile:+39 3356 651581, dondoriano@interfree.it casaferiesma@yahoo.it,Price:D,

Religious Hostel

Parrocchia,Piazza Cristo Re, 1,53035 Castellina-Scalo-Abate(SI),Italy Tel:+39 0577 307628,dondoriano@interfree.it,Price:D,

Parrocchia di Santa Maria a le Grazie,(Don Luigi Colleoni),Via Volterrana, 49,53034 Colle-di-Val-d'Elsa(SI),Italy Tel:+39 0577 959068,gigicol64@libero.it,Price:D,

Abbazia dei Santi Salvatore e Cirino,Località Abdadia d'Isola,53035 Monteriggioni(SI),Italy Tel:+39 0577 304214,dondoriano@interfree.it,Price:D,

Church or Religious Organisation

Comunità Salesiana Sant'Agostino,Piazza Sant'Agostino,53034 Colle-di-Val-d'Elsa(SI),Italy Tel:+39 0577 920195,sdbcolle@tin.it,Price:D,

B&B, Hotel, Gite d'Etape

Il Nazionale B&B,Via Giuseppe Garibaldi, 20,53034 Colle-di-Val-d'Elsa(SI),Italy Tel:+39 0577 920039,Price:B,

Hotel Villa Belvedere,SP5 Colligiana,53034 Colle-di-Val-d'Elsa(SI),Italy Tel:+39 0577 920966,Price:B,

Hotel Cristall,Via Liguria, 1,53034 Colle-di-Val-d'Elsa(SI),Italy Tel:+39 0577 920361,Price:B,

Tourist Information

Pro Loco,Via Francesco Campana, 43,53034 Colle-di-Val-d'Elsa(SI),Italy Tel:+39 0577 922621,

Ufficio Turistico,Piazza Roma,53035 Monteriggioni(SI),Italy Tel:+39 0577 304834,

Banks and ATMs

Chiantibanca Credito Cooperativo,Via Fratelli Bandiera, 67,53034 Colle-di-Val-d'Elsa(SI),Italy Tel:+39 0577 908080,www.chiantibanca.it,

Cassa di Risparmio di Volterra,Via Guglielmo Oberdan, 33,53034 Colle-di-Val-d'Elsa(SI),Italy Tel:+39 0577 923781,www.crvolterra.it,

Hospital

Ospedale Dell'Alta Val d'Elsa,Campostaggia,53036 Poggibonsi(SI),Italy Tel:+39 0577 9941,

Doctor

Berti,Via Fratelli Bandiera, 118,53034 Colle-di-Val-d'Elsa(SI),Italy Tel:+39 0577 928703,

Azienda Speciale Multiservizi,Via Liguria,53034 Colle-di-Val-d'Elsa(SI),Italy Tel:+39 0577 922569,

Veterinary

Dr Francesca Messeri,Via Teano, 7,53034 Colle-di-Val-d'Elsa(SI),Italy Tel:+39 0577 908145,

Hiking Equipment

Idea Sport,Via Guglielmo Oberdan, 27,53034 Colle-di-Val-d'Elsa(SI),Italy Tel:+39 0577 921993,

Bicycle Shop

Ciclosport di Porciatti Fabio,Via Lazio, 19,53036 Poggibonsi(SI),Italy Tel:+39 0577 938507,

Farrier

Podere Tremulini Centro di Equitazione Toscana,Loc.Tremulini,53031 Casole-d'Elsa(SI),Italy Tel:+39 0577 963910,

Stage Eight-three Summary: the route largely follows tracks and small roads to the edge of Siena. The Main Route adds a little distance to visit the unmissable Monteriggioni.

Distance from Canterbury: 1765km   Distance to Saint-Peter's-Square: 309km

Stage Ascent: 448m   Stage Descent: 300m

Waypoint	Distance Between Waypoints (m)	Total (km)	Directions	Verification Point	Compass	Altitude (m)
83.001	0	0,0	With the church on the right, continue straight ahead beside the main road	Monteriggioni on hill-top to the right	NE	203
83.002	220	0,2	At the crossroads, turn right and then bear left on the track	VF sign, strada di Valmaggiore	SE	199
83.003	1500	1,7	At the end of the road, turn left. Note:- the turning to the right reduces the distance, but bypasses Monteriggioni and involves a steep climb	Woods close on the right	NE	200
83.004	1300	3,0	At the T-junction with the SP5, turn right and right again – keep to the grass verge on the right	SR2 towards Monteriggioni, café on the left at the junction	SE	206
83.005	250	3,3	Carefully cross the main road and turn left onto the unmade road	Uphill, towards the entrance to the walled town, VF sign	E	216
83.006	290	3,6	Pass through the arched Porta Fiorentina and continue straight ahead	Via Primo Maggio	SE	248
83.007	240	3,8	On leaving the town, turn right and then left on the tarmac road, towards the main road	Porta Senese	S	260
83.008	500	4,4	At the Stop sign, cross over the main road, turn left and then right on the unmade road	Strada del Gallinaio, VF sign	S	242
83.009	190	4,5	Take the right fork	VF sign, uphill	SW	245
83.010	300	4,9	Take the next turning to the left	White road, between trees	S	275
83.011	120	5,0	At the crossroads, turn left on the track		SE	279

Abbadia-a-Isola to Siena 24.1km

205

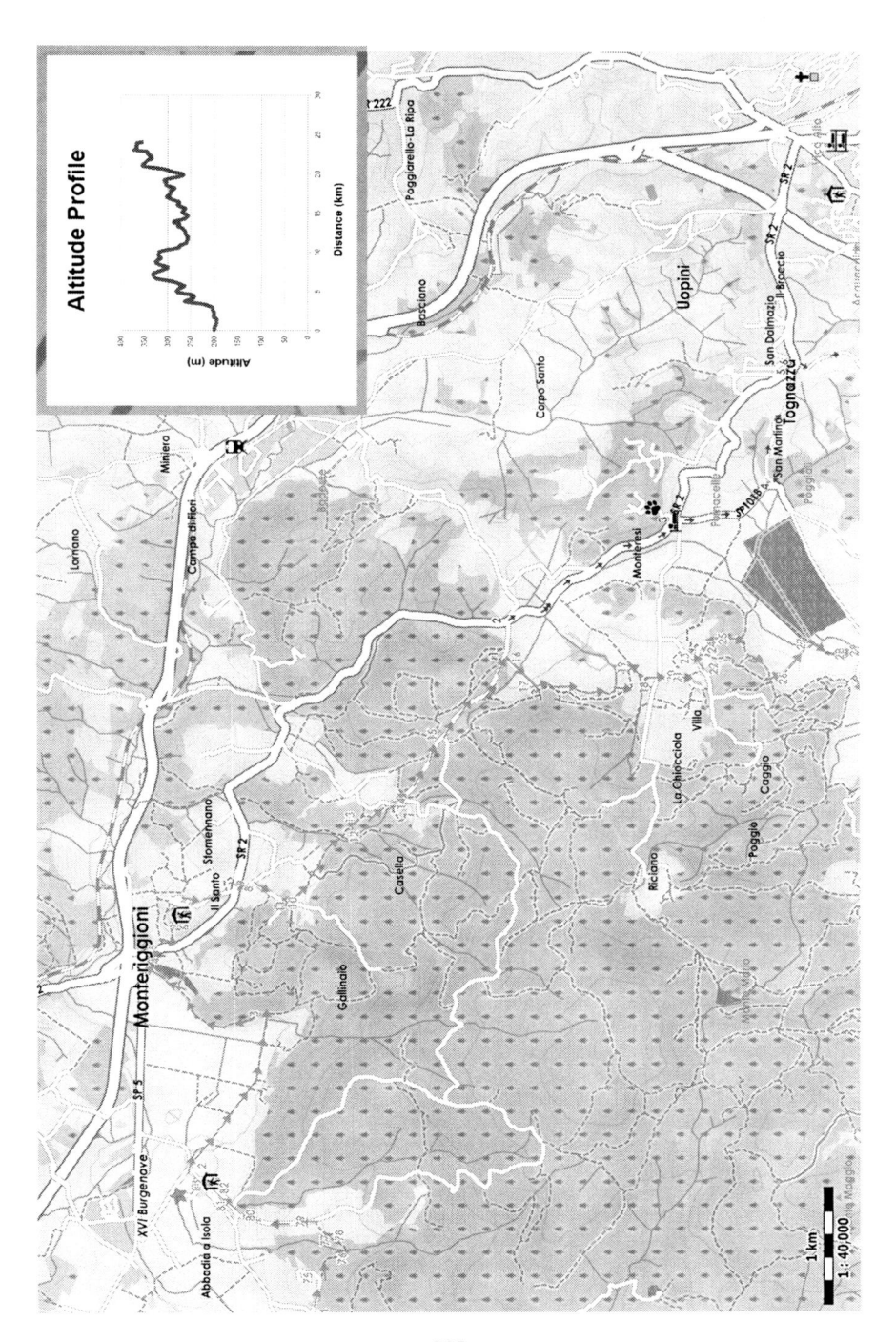

Waypoint	Distance Between Waypoints (m)	Total (km)	Directions	Verification Point	Compass	Altitude (m)
83.012	800	5,7	At the junction, take the second track from the left	Red and white VF sign	SE	263
83.013	250	6,0	Bear right	VF sign	SE	273
83.014	280	6,3	At the T-junction, turn right	VF sign	SE	288
83.015	800	7,0	At the T-junction, turn left	VF sign, large farmhouse on left	SE	329
83.016	900	7,9	Turn right on the track. Note:- to avoid broken ground and reduce distance by 5.5km continue ahead on the Alternate Route	Across the fields towards woods	SW	303
83.017	400	8,3	On the apex of the bend to the right, take the pathway to the left	Field to the left, woods to the right	S	305
83.018	900	9,1	Turn left on the access road to the farm		E	317
83.019	200	9,3	At the T-junction, turn right		S	313
83.020	250	9,6	Cross the tarmac road and take the unmade road straight ahead	Pass the castello on the hill to the right	S	318
83.021	270	9,8	Bear left on the track		SE	318
83.022	130	10,0	At the T-junction, turn left on the tarmac road	Towards castellated tower	NE	317
83.023	100	10,1	Take the right fork	Towards the Villa castello	E	317
83.024	100	10,1	Bear right on the track	Pass circular tower on the left	S	315
83.025	400	10,5	Take the right fork	Downhill and with fields on the left	SW	286

Abbadia-a-Isola to Siena 24.1km

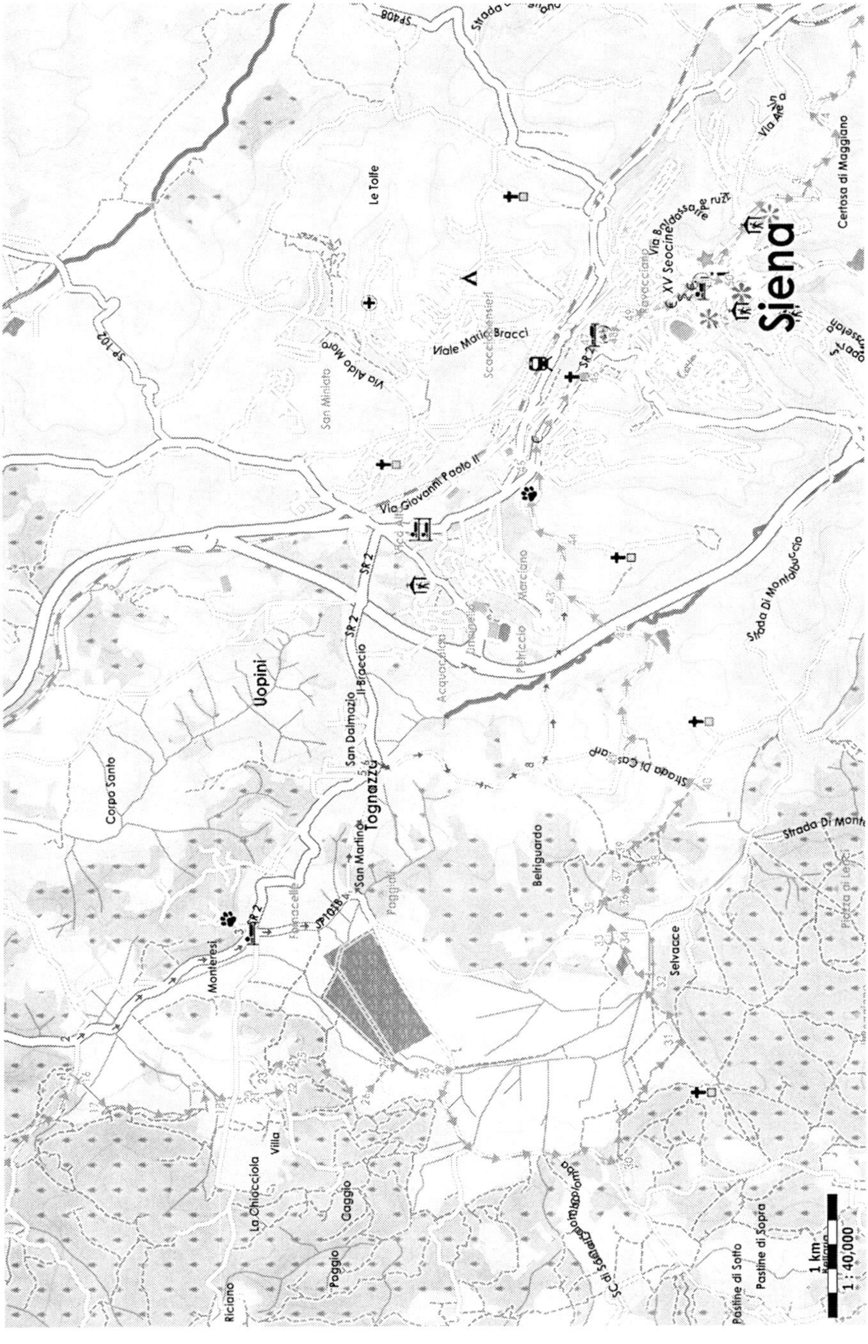
Siena
Tognazzo
Uopini
Corpo Santo
Monteresi
San Dalmazio
Il Braccio
San Martino
Belriguardo
Selvacce
Le Tolfe
San Miniato
Viale Mario Bracci
Via Aldo Moro
Via Giovanni Paolo II
Strada Di Montalbuccio
Certosa di Maggiano
Pastine di Sotto
Pastine di Sopra
Riciano
La Chiocciola
Villa
Poggio
Caggio
Marciano
Acquacalda
Petriccio
Ravacciano
SR 2
SP 102
SP408
1 km
1 : 40,000

Waypoint	Distance Between Waypoints (m)	Total (km)	Directions	Verification Point	Compass	Altitude (m)
83.026	500	11,0	Turn left on the track between fields	Line of trees on the left of the track	SE	270
83.027	500	11,4	Turn right on the track	Continue with stream on your left in the trees	SW	258
83.028	150	11,6	At the junction, bear left	Remain beside the trees	S	257
83.029	300	11,9	At the T-junction with the tarmac road, SP101, turn right	Small bridge on the left at the junction	SW	256
83.030	2000	13,9	At the junction in the woods, turn left on the gravel road	Via dell'Osteriaccia, direction Montalbuccio	SE	285
83.031	1200	15,1	Bear left on the road and quickly take the pathway to the left	Beside house on the edge of the woods	NE	265
83.032	600	15,7	Bear right and then left on the track	Beside monument	NE	262
83.033	500	16,2	At the T-junction beside the house, turn right	Towards the main road	E	278
83.034	30	16,2	Take the pedestrian crossing over the main road and continue on the track straight ahead	VF signs	E	277
83.035	260	16,5	Take the track to the right uphill	Into the woods	SE	276
83.036	140	16,6	At the crossroads, turn left and then right		SE	281
83.037	280	16,9	Turn right on the track		SE	295
83.038	170	17,1	Turn left on the track		NE	301

Abbadia-a-Isola to Siena 24.1km

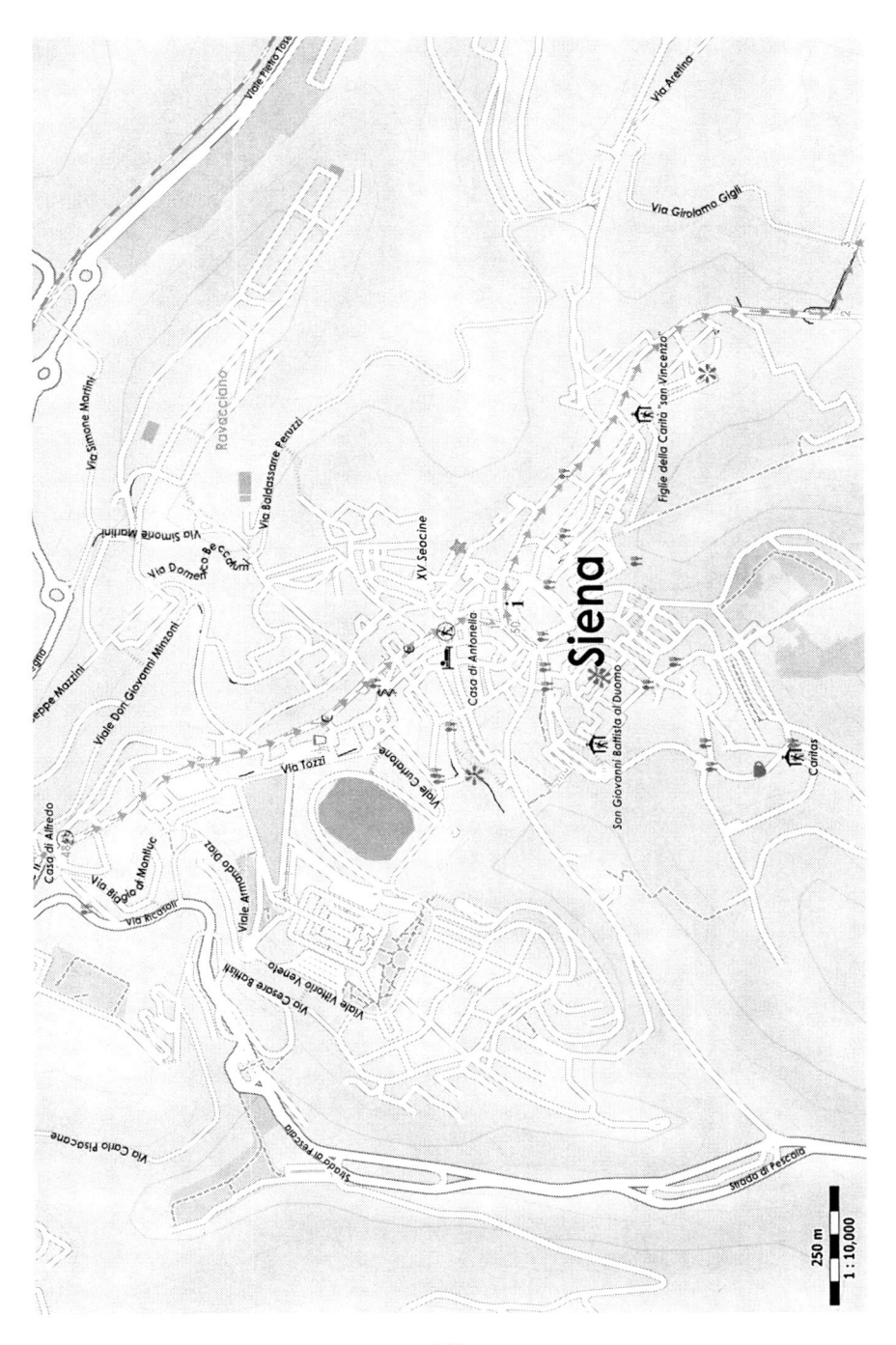
Siena
Via Aretina
Via Girolamo Gigli
Figlie della Carità "san Vincenzo"
San Giovanni Battista al Duomo
Caritas
Casa di Antonella
Ravacciano
Via Baldassarre Peruzzi
Via Simone Martini
Viale Don Giovanni Minzoni
Via Tozzi
Viale Curtatone
Casa di Alfredo
Via Biagio di Montluc
Via Ricasoli
Viale Armando Diaz
Viale Vittorio Veneto
Via Cesare Battisti
Via Carlo Pisacane
Strada di Pescaia
250 m
1 : 10,000

Waypoint	Distance Between Waypoints (m)	Total (km)	Directions	Verification Point	Compass	Altitude (m)
83.039	150	17,2	At the T-junction, turn right		SE	299
83.040	700	17,9	At the junction with the tarmac road, turn left	Cemetery on your left	N	291
83.041	600	18,5	At the top of the hill, turn right	Strada delle Coste	E	300
83.042	1500	20,0	Continue straight ahead	Under the highway and then up the hill	NE	266
83.043	500	20,5	At the crossroads, turn right. Note:- the Alternate Route rejoins from the left	Via Gaetano Milanesi	E	298
83.044	500	21,0	At the T-junction, turn left on strada di Marciano	Between stone walls	E	349
83.045	800	21,8	At the roundabout, turn right direction Centro	Viale Camillo Benso Conte di Cavour	SE	341
83.046	900	22,6	Go straight ahead under the archway - Antiporto di Camollia	Direction centro	SE	341
83.047	400	23,0	At the traffic lights, continue straight ahead	Pass through porta Camollia	SE	358
83.048	20	23,0	Cross the piazza and take via Camollia straight ahead	Pass bike shop on the left	SE	361
83.049	400	23,4	At the crossroads, continue straight ahead on via Camollia	Direction Porta Romana	SE	366
83.050	700	24,1	Arrive at Siena (XV) centre	Piazza del Campo directly ahead		352

Abbadia-a-Isola to Siena 24.1km

Stage Summary: the Alternate Route allows cyclists to bypass broken ground on the woodland and horse tracks. Initially the route follows the via Cassia (SR2) before continuing on quieter country roads and reduces the length of the section by 5.5km

Stage Ascent: 121m   Stage Descent: 124m

Waypoint	Distance Between Waypoints (m)	Total (km)	Directions	Verification Point	Compass	Altitude (m)
83A1.001	0	0,0	Continue straight ahead	Towards the main road	E	302
83A1.002	290	0,3	At the crossroads, turn right down the hill towards Siena on the SR2. Keep to the grass verge	Brown signpost ahead for Poggiolo	SE	291
83A1.003	1800	2,0	Turn right on strada del Pecorile direction Sovicille	Bar on the right at the junction	S	275
83A1.004	1000	3,0	Turn left and then left again on strada del Pian del Lago	Direction Siena	E	278
83A1.005	1100	4,1	At the T-junction, turn right direction Siena, SR2	VF sign	E	335
83A1.006	100	4,2	Turn right direction Montalbuccio	Strada del Petriccio e Belriguardo	S	336
83A1.007	1200	5,4	Bear left at the fork in road	Strada del Petriccio e Belriguardo	SE	323
83A1.008	400	5,8	Take the left fork	Towards Petriccio	E	326
83A1.009	1400	7,2	At the crossroads, continue straight ahead and rejoin the Main Route	Via G. Milanese		299

Alternate Route #83.A1 7.2km

Religious Hostel

Figlie della Carità "san Vincenzo",(Suor Ginetta),Via di San Girolamo, 8,53100 Siena(SI),Italy Tel:+39 0577 21271,Mobile:+39 3408 721787, casaprovinciale@yahoo.it,Price:D,

Caritas,Via della Diana, 4,53100 Siena(SI),Italy Tel:+39 0577 280643, www.caritas-siena.org,Price:D,

Casa Ritiri Santa Regina,(Maria Gasperini),Via Bianca Piccolomini Clementini,53100 Siena(SI),Italy Tel:+39 0577 221206,Price:C,

Parrocchia S.Michele,Località Rencine, 9,53011 Castellina-In-Chianti(SI),Italy Tel:+39 0577 304214,Mobile:+39 3356 651581,dondorian@interfree.it,

Religious Hostel
Santa Caterina Dottore della Chiesa All'Acquacalda,Via Bologna, 4,53100 Siena(SI),Italy
Tel:+39 0577 52095,donenricosiena@alice.it,

San Giovanni Battista al Duomo,Piazza Duomo, 7,53100 Siena(SI),Italy
Tel:+39 0577 289178,domenico.poeta@arcidiocesi.siena.it,www.arcidiocesi.siena.it,

Commercial Hostel
Ostello della Gioventù Guidoriccio,Via Fiorentina, 89,53100 Siena(SI),Italy
Tel:+39 0577 601282,info@ostellosiena.it,www.ostellosiena.it,Price:C,

B&B, Hotel, Gîte d'Etape
Casa di Antonella,Via delle Terme, 72,53100 Siena(SI),Italy
Mobile:+39 3393 004883,Price:B,

Casa di Alfredo,Via Lelio e Fausto Socino, 4,53100 Siena(SI),Italy
Tel:+39 0577 47628,Price:B,

Bed and Brekfast il Ceppo,Via Cassia Nord, 3,53035 Monteriggioni(SI),Italy
Tel:+39 0577 593387,Price:B,

Camping
Camping Siena Colleverde,Via Scaccapensieri, 47,53100 Siena(SI),Italy
Tel:+39 0577 334080,

Tourist Information
Agenzia Per il Turismo,Piazza il Campo, 56,53100 Siena(SI),Italy Tel:+39 0577 280551,

Banks and ATMs
Banca Monteriggioni,Via dei Montanini,53100 Siena(SI),Italy
Tel:+39 0577 41113,www.chiantibanca.it,

Banca Monte dei Paschi di Siena,Via Banchi di Sopra, 84,53100 Siena(SI),Italy
Tel:+39 0577 294111,www.mps.it/default.htm,

Bancaetruria,Viale Camillo Benso Conte di Cavour, 202,53100 Siena(SI),Italy
Tel:+39 0577 49590,www.bancaetruria.it,

Travel
Ampugnano Airport,53018 Ampugnano,53018 Sovicille(SI),Italy
Tel:+39 0577 392226,www.aeroportosiena.it,

Stazione Ferrovie,Piazza Carlo Rosselli, 7,53100 Siena(SI),Italy
Tel:+39 06 6847 5475,www.renitalia.it,

Hospital
Policlinico,Viale Bracci, 16,53100 Siena(SI),Italy Tel:+39 0577 586111,

Doctor
Bausani - Studio Medico,Piazza Giacomo Matteotti, 3,53100 Siena(SI),Italy
Tel:+39 0577 285508,

Veterinary
Ciampoli - Medico Veterinario,Strada di Monteresi,53035 Monteriggioni(SI),Italy
Tel:+39 0577 319949,

Clinica Veterinaria,Via Piero Strozzi,53100 Siena(SI),Italy Tel:+39 0577 289103,

Hiking Equipment
In Voga,Via dei Pontani,53100 Siena(SI),Italy Tel:+39 0577 236338,

Bicycle Shop
Rossi Martino di Rossi Luca & C.S.A.S.- Cicli e Ricambi Noleggio,Via Camollia, 204,53100 Siena(SI),Italy Tel:+39 0577 249161,

Farrier
Ido Fantin,Via Arturo Toscanini, 19,53018 Sovicille(SI),Italy
Tel:+39 0577 345285,Mobile:+39 3358 070224,

Stage Eighty-four Summary: the route quickly leaves the centre of Siena on a small tarmac road. After a short section on a busy road, the route returns to the tracks over the beautiful, but exposed Tuscan hills. The route passes close to, but not through, a number of intermediate villages with a range of facilities.

Distance from Canterbury: 1789km Distance to Saint-Peter's-Square: 285km

Stage Ascent: 242m Stage Descent: 446m

Waypoint	Distance Between Waypoints (m)	Total (km)	Directions	Verification Point	Compass	Altitude (m)
84.001	0	0,0	In via di Citta with piazza del Campo on your right, go straight ahead	Direction Porta Romana	SE	350
84.002	1100	1,1	After passing through the Porta Romana, immediately turn left through the archway and take the narrow road downhill	VF sign	E	298
84.003	160	1,3	Cross the main road (SR2) and go straight ahead	VF sign, strada di Certosa	E	280
84.004	700	2,0	Turn right, remain on strada di Certosa	VF sign, direction Renaccio	SE	267
84.005	3600	5,5	Road becomes a gravel track, continue straight ahead	VF sign, pass house on your right	E	219
84.006	800	6,3	At the T-junction with a major road, turn right and proceed with care	Direction strada Cassia, VF sign	SW	197
84.007	1200	7,4	After a long bend to the right, turn left towards the Fattoria	Equestrian centre	S	192
84.008	120	7,5	Bear right though the Fattoria		S	195
84.009	290	7,8	At the crossroads go straight ahead and then right down a small slope over a stream	Houses on your left, continue towards trees	S	194
84.010	400	8,3	At the T-junction in the tracks, turn left	Red and white VF sign and arrow	E	197
84.011	210	8,5	Fork right	Metal gate on the left	S	197
84.012	400	8,8	At the T-junction, turn right on strada di Borgo Vecchia	Line of conifers on your left at the junction	W	193

Siena to Ponte-d'Arbia 28.2km

213

214

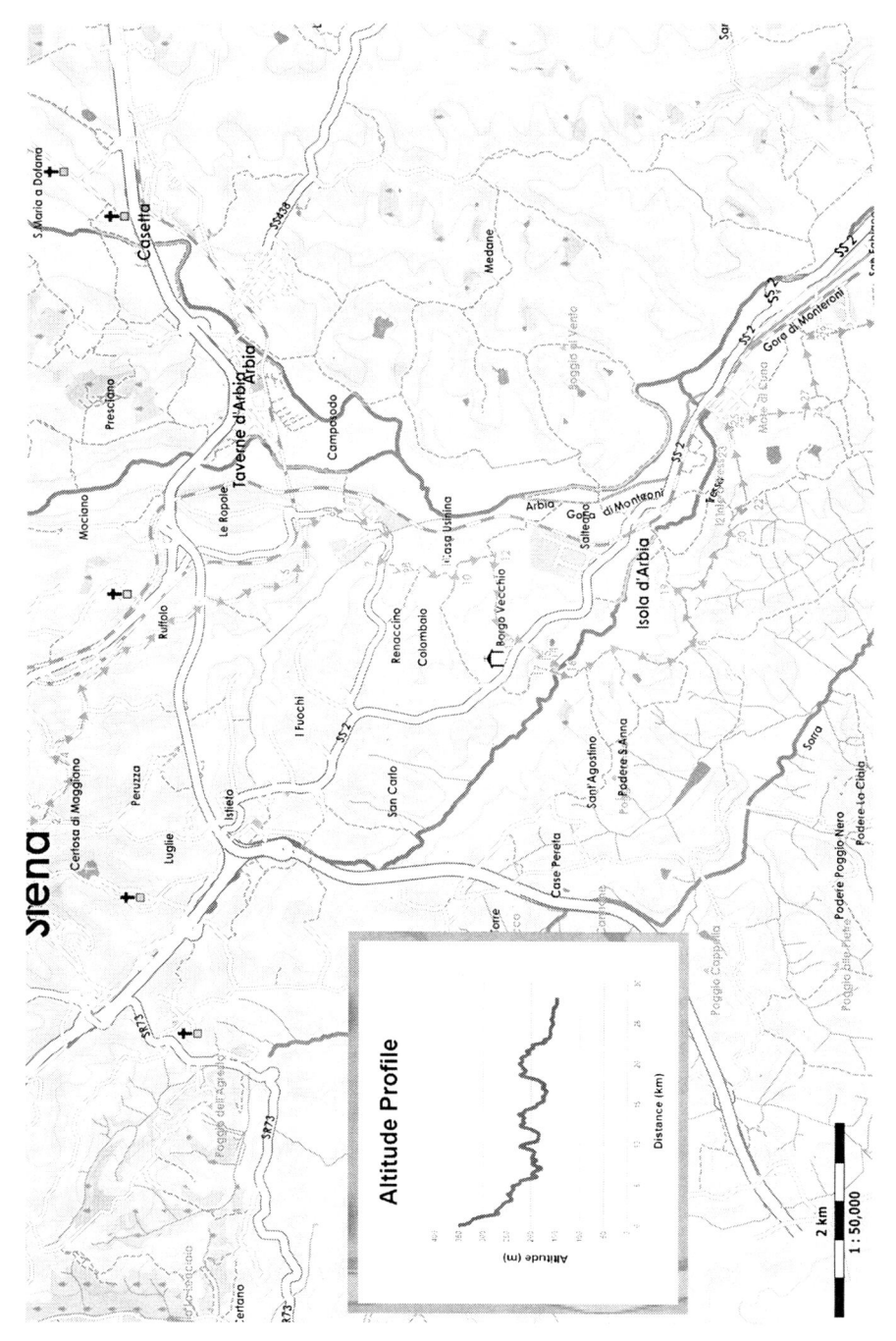

Waypoint	Distance Between Waypoints (m)	Total (km)	Directions	Verification Point	Compass	Altitude (m)
84.013	1100	9,9	Cross the main road (SR2) and continue straight ahead on the gravel road	VF sign, downhill	SW	220
84.014	240	10,1	Bear left in front of the house	Pass pond on your left	S	207
84.015	220	10,3	Turn right on the track	Beside greenhouses	W	190
84.016	150	10,5	Shortly after a bend to the left in the track, turn right	Over the bridge	NW	185
84.017	100	10,6	At the T-junction, turn left on the road	Strada di Murlo	S	185
84.018	1600	12,2	Shortly before reaching a farmhouse surrounded by trees, turn left on the track	Track passes between fields	E	219
84.019	700	12,9	At the end of the field, turn right on the track	Track continues between fields	SE	216
84.020	900	13,8	Bear left on the track		E	223
84.021	230	14,0	Take the right fork towards Ponte a Tressa	VF sign	SE	213
84.022	200	14,2	At the top of the ridge fork left down the hill and away from the crucifix	VF sign, via del Poggio	E	212
84.023	600	14,7	Continue straight ahead	Pass equestrian centre	E	189
84.024	300	15,1	In Ponte a Tressa turn right	Via di Villa Canina	S	185
84.025	210	15,3	At the end of the housing development, fork right onto a less well-defined track	Direction Il Canto del Sole	S	176

Siena to Ponte-d'Arbia 28.2km

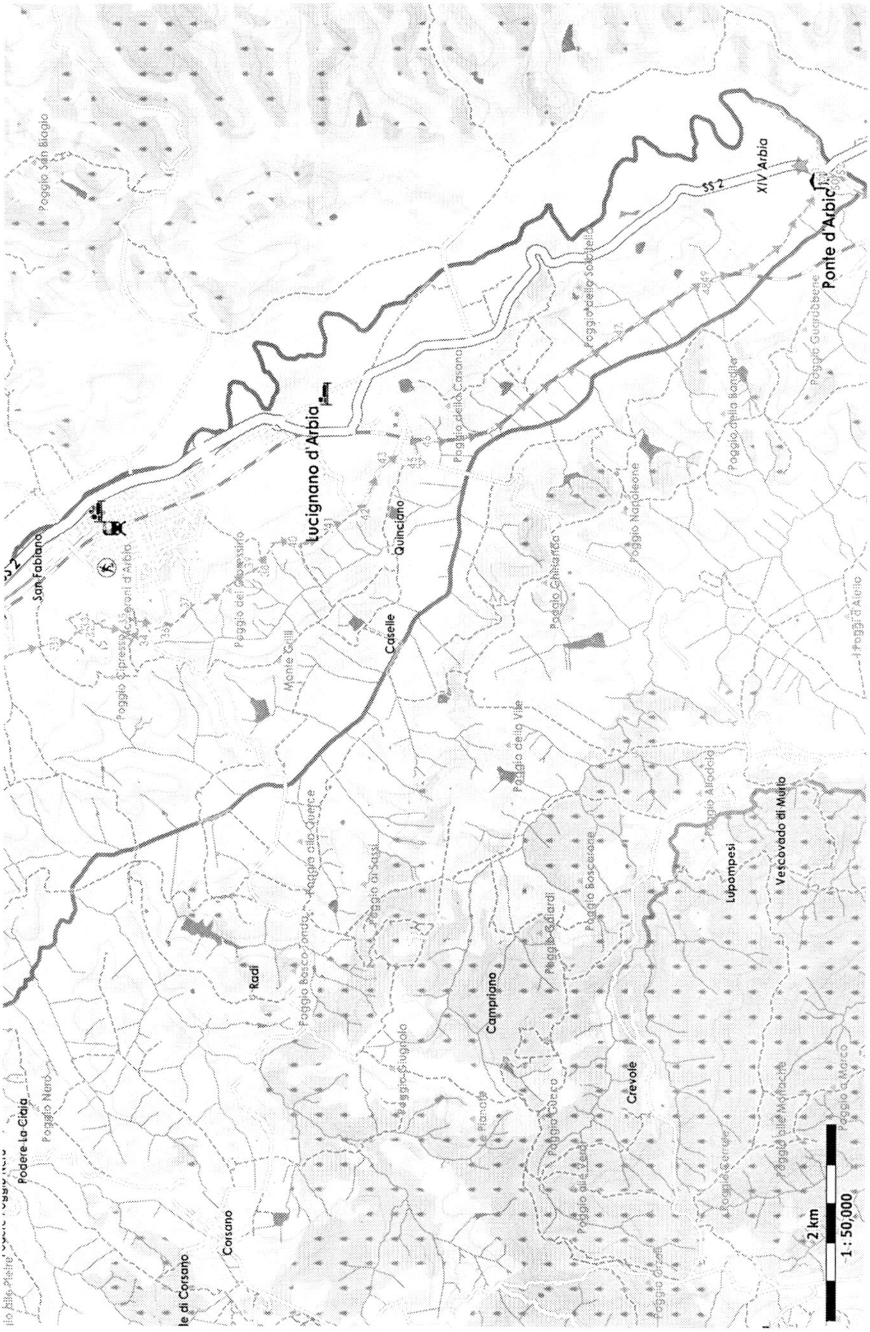
Podere la Ciaia
Poggio Nero
Corsano
Radi
Campriano
Crevole
Lupompesi
Vescovado di Murlo
Caselle
Quinciano
Lucignano d'Arbia
San Fabiano
SS 2
Ponte d'Arbia
XIV Arbia
Poggio San Biagio
Poggio Napoleone
Poggio delle Vite
Poggio di Sassi
Poggio alle Querce
2 km
1 : 50,000

Waypoint	Distance Between Waypoints (m)	Total (km)	Directions	Verification Point	Compass	Altitude (m)
84.026	600	15,9	At the T-junction on the top of the ridge, turn left on via di Villa Canina	VF sign	SE	175
84.027	230	16,1	Turn left	Towards Cuna	E	171
84.028	700	16,8	At the entrance to Cuna turn right on the track	Beside the wall	S	170
84.029	300	17,1	At the crossroads in the tracks, continue straight ahead	VF sign and metal cross	S	175
84.030	500	17,6	Fork right up the hill	VF sign	S	173
84.031	250	17,8	Fork left	Avoiding strada della Fornacina	SE	180
84.032	140	17,9	Track forks in three directions take middle track straight up the hill	VF sign	SE	183
84.033	230	18,2	Just before reaching the top of the hill, fork right	VF sign	SW	196
84.034	400	18,6	Turn sharp left onto the ridge	VF sign	E	221
84.035	260	18,9	At the T-junction, turn right up the hill	VF sign, farm on the left	SW	215
84.036	250	19,1	At the T-junction with a minor road, cross straight over and turn immediately left and follow the gravel track. Cyclists should turn left on the road and then bear right on the track in 70 metres	Gravel track initially parallel to the road	SE	210
84.037	600	19,7	Fork right up the hill	VF sign	SE	218
84.038	700	20,3	Fork left	Pass farm on the right	SE	217
84.039	150	20,5	Continue straight ahead	Towards the top of the ridge	SE	217

Siena to Ponte-d'Arbia 28.2km

Waypoint	Distance Between Waypoints (m)	Total (km)	Directions	Verification Point	Compass	Altitude (m)
84.040	280	20,7	Fork right	Towards the farm on the ridge	S	220
84.041	700	21,5	Continue on the tarmac section and pass between two houses	White arrow	SE	207
84.042	100	21,6	Fork right	Direction Quinciano, VF sign	SE	209
84.043	800	22,3	After entering Quinciano on a tarmac road, turn right onto a gravel track	Via delle Caselle	SW	195
84.044	110	22,5	Fork left down the hill	VF sign	S	187
84.045	220	22,7	At the T-junction with the main road, turn left uphill	VF sign	NE	169
84.046	270	22,9	Turn sharp right down a gravel track	VF sign, continue beside railway track	SE	173
84.047	2600	25,5	Continue straight over the crossroads	VF sign, bridge on left	SE	158
84.048	800	26,3	Turn left over the level crossing and bear right parallel and close to the railway track - metal barrier but passable with care	VF sign	SE	154
84.049	290	26,5	After crossing small ditch, continue straight ahead on the track	Railway on the right	SE	153
84.050	1500	28,0	At the junction with a tarmac road on the edge of Ponte d'Arbia, fork right on via degli Stagni towards river	VF sign, direction Piana	SE	146
84.051	130	28,2	At the T-junction turn left	VF sign, river on right	NE	146
84.052	90	28,2	Arrive at Ponte-d'Arbia (XIV) at the T-junction with the SR2	Beside the bridge over the Arbia		146

Siena to Ponte-d'Arbia 28.2km

Pilgrim Hostel

Centro Cresti,Località Ponte d'Arbia ,53014 Monteroni-d'Arbia(SI),Italy
Tel:+39 0577 370096,Mobile:+39 3277 197439,

Church or Religious Organisation

Parrocchia Santi Pietro e Paolo,Via del Sole, 13,53022 Buonconvento(SI),Italy
Tel:+39 0577 806089,Mobile:+39 3333 097138,donclaudiorosi@libero.it,Price:D,

Santi Simone e Giuda,Locailità,Colle Malamerenda,53100 Siena(SI),Italy
Tel:+39 0577 282182,

B&B, Hotel, Gite d'Etape

Hotel Bella Napoli,Via Roma, 55,53014 Monteroni-d'Arbia(SI),Italy
Tel:+39 0577 375255,Price:B,

Albergo Roma,Via Soccini, 14,53022 Buonconvento(SI),Italy Tel:+39 0577 807284,Price:B,

Hotel Borgo Antico,Via di Lucignano, 405,53014 Monteroni-d'Arbia(SI),Italy
Tel:+39 0577 374688,Price:A,

Tourist Information

Comune di Buonconvento,Via Soccini, 32,53022 Buonconvento(SI),Italy
Tel:+39 0577 80971,

Banks and ATMs

Banca Monte dei Paschi di Siena,Piazza Matteotti, 19,53022 Buonconvento(SI),Italy
Tel:+39 0577 809041,

Cassa di Risparmio di Firenze,Via Roma, 134,53014 Monteroni-d'Arbia(SI),Italy
Tel:+39 0577 375411,

Doctor

Cerruto - Studio Medico,Via del Sole, 46,53022 Buonconvento(SI),Italy
Tel:+39 0577 806070,

Veterinary

Vittoria - Ambulatorio Veterinario,Via Siena, 23,53014 Monteroni-d'Arbia(SI),Italy
Tel:+39 0577 374723,

Hiking Equipment

Linea Sport,Circonvallazione John Kennedy,53014 Monteroni-d'Arbia(SI),Italy
Tel:+39 0577 374000,

Stage Eighty-five Summary: the route continues over the Tuscan hills interleaving long stretches on gravel and tarmac roads. Aa Alternate Route reduces the total distance by 2.5km, but at the expense of using more tarmac.

Distance from Canterbury: 1817km   Distance to Saint-Peter's-Square: 257km

Stage Ascent: 610m   Stage Descent: 350m

Waypoint	Distance Between Waypoints (m)	Total (km)	Directions	Verification Point	Compass	Altitude (m)
85.001	0	0,0	From the junction beside the bridge in Ponte d'Arbia return along via del Magistrato beside the river	River on the left	SW	146
85.002	1000	1,0	After crossing the railway bridge, turn left onto a gravel track	Avoid turning to Saltemmano	S	147
85.003	2000	3,0	Take left fork	VF sign, large farm on left	SE	160
85.004	1500	4,5	At the T-junction with major road, turn left	VF sign, via di Bibbiano	E	139
85.005	900	5,4	At the crossroads in Buonconvento, turn left on via Roma. Note:- cyclists may reduce the total distance by 2km by turning right and following the busy via Cassia to the Montalcino junction	Pass café terrace on the right, No Entry	N	145
85.006	100	5,5	Take the first turning to the right, on the small road - via di Tercena	Sign Roma 201km, VF sign	E	146
85.007	130	5,6	Cross the main road (SR2) and continue straight ahead	Over the level crossing	E	146
85.008	600	6,2	At the top of the hill, turn right on the track	Continue uphill	S	179
85.009	300	6,5	Bear left along the ridge	Pass industrial zone below on the right	S	198
85.010	1600	8,1	At the end of the ridge bear right down the hill	Pass farm on the left	SW	179
85.011	240	8,4	Bear right towards the main road	House on the left, row of conifers to the right	W	159

Ponte-d'Arbia to San-Quirico-d'Orcia 29,7km

221

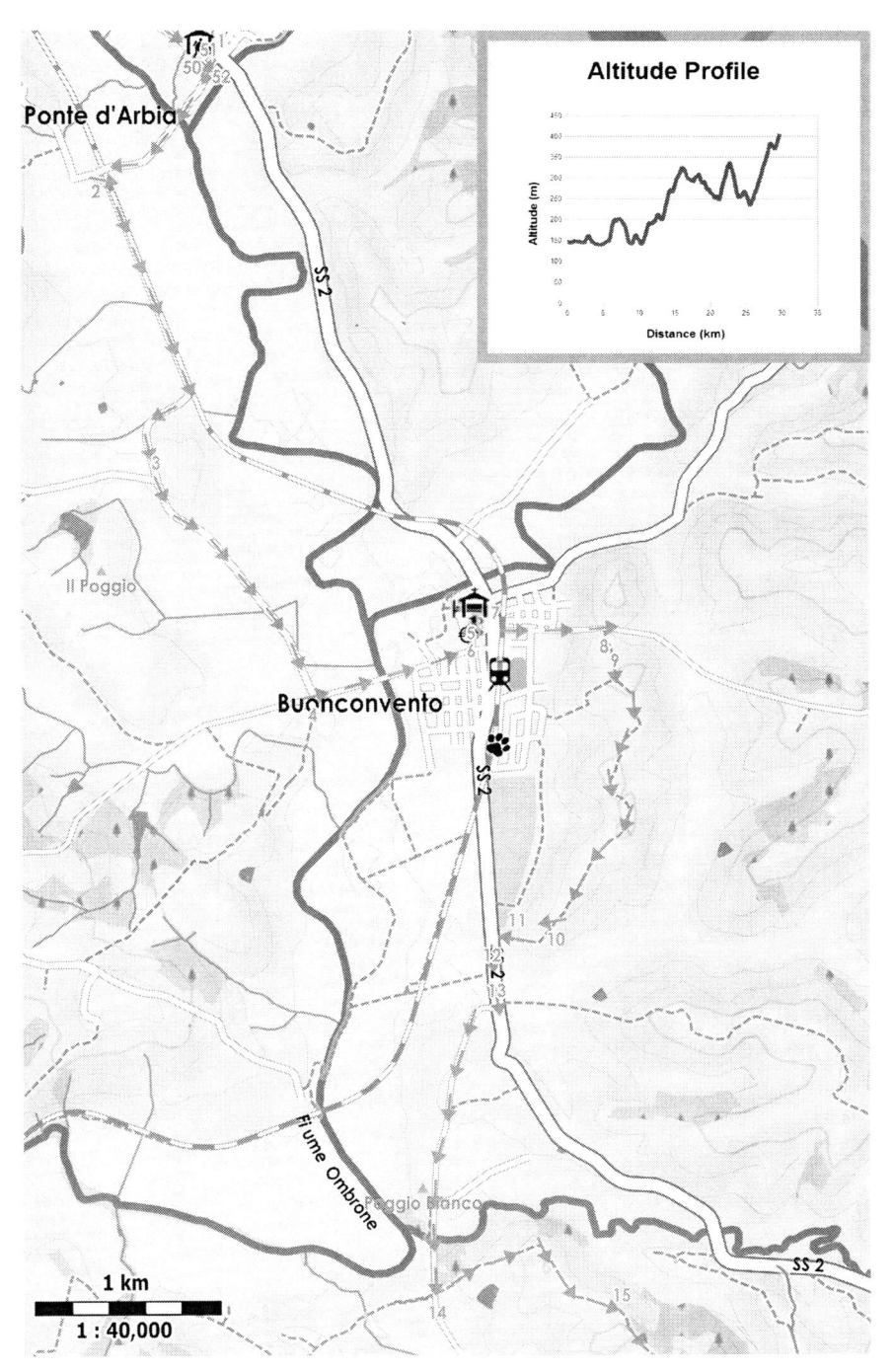

Waypoint	Distance Between Waypoints (m)	Total (km)	Directions	Verification Point	Compass	Altitude (m)
85.012	140	8,5	At the T-junction with the busy main road, cross over and turn left on the grass verge	Via Cassia – SR2	S	148
85.013	400	9,0	Turn right on the road	Direction Montalcino	S	142
85.014	1700	10,7	Just before the road bends to the left, turn sharp left	Direction Castello Altesi	E	150
85.015	1300	11,9	After passing the castello take the left fork	Follow ridge	SE	191
85.016	1100	13,0	Bear left to skirt the buildings on the right	Tree lined road	S	202
85.017	1200	14,2	Keep left on the white road		SW	263
85.018	600	14,7	Just before reaching a large farm on the right, turn left	Follow the road to Torrenieri	E	266
85.019	5100	19,8	At the T-junction in Torrenieri (XIII), turn right on the main street	Via Romana	E	272
85.020	400	20,2	At the crossroads in the centre of Torrenieri (XIII), continue straight ahead	VF sign, church directly in front	SE	261
85.021	600	20,8	Immediately after passing the cemetery on your right, turn right on the track. Note:- to reduce the section by 2.5km continue straight ahead on the Alternate Route	Pass pond on the left	S	251
85.022	160	21,0	At the crossroads, continue straight ahead	Cypress lined track	S	254
85.023	600	21,5	Bear left and continue uphill	Pass house on your right	E	265
85.024	900	22,5	In front of the house, bear left	Pass pond on your right	E	327

Ponte-d'Arbia to San-Quirico-d'Orcia 29,7km

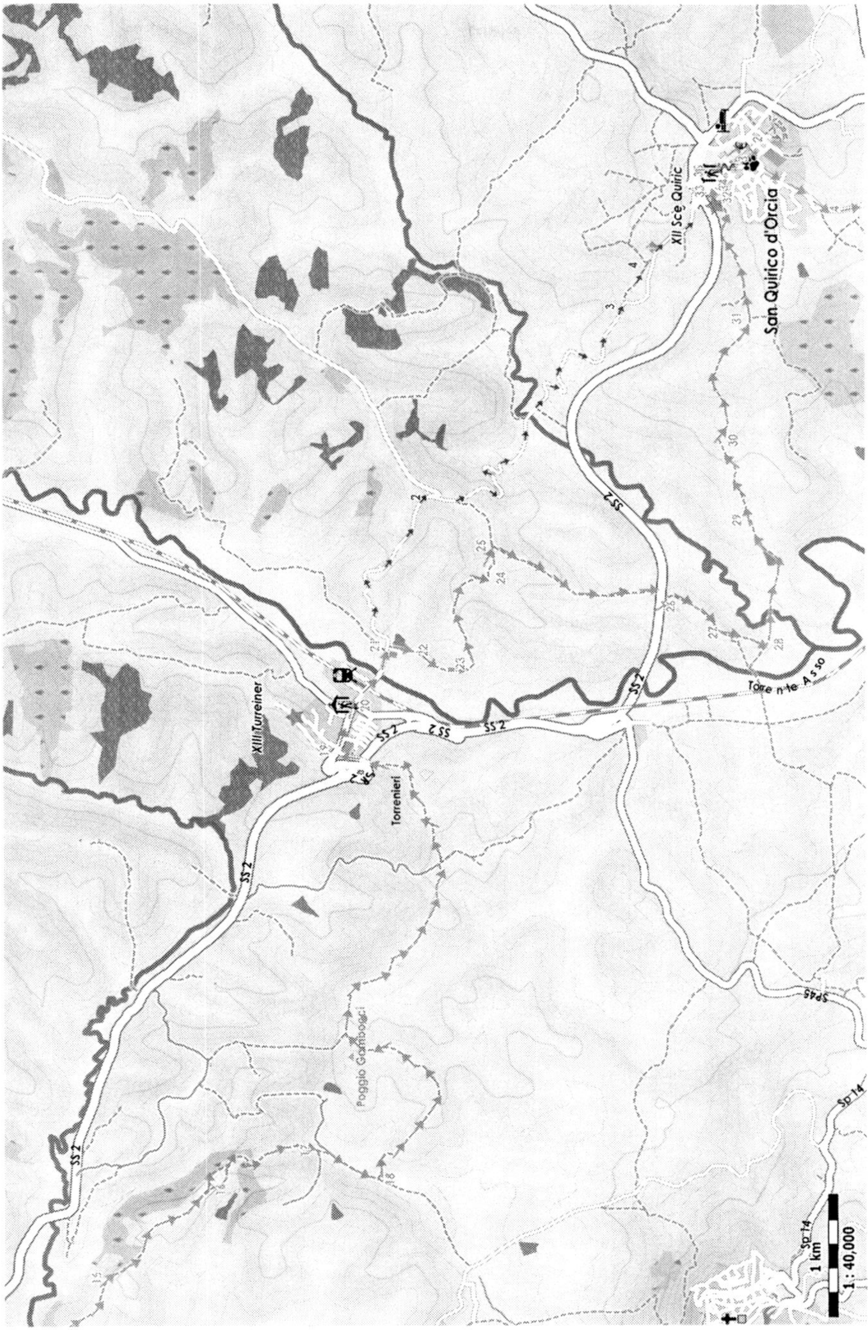
San Quirico d'Orcia
XII Sce Quiric
XIII Turreiner
Torrenieri
SS 2
SP45
Sp 14
1 km
1: 40,000

Ponte-d'Arbia to San-Quirico-d'Orcia ≥9.7km

Waypoint	Distance Between Waypoints (m)	Total (km)	Directions	Verification Point	Compass	Altitude (m)
85.025	280	22,7	At the crossroads, turn right	Along ridge	S	335
85.026	1600	24,3	Continue straight ahead	Under the main road bridge	S	257
85.027	800	25,0	Continue straight ahead	Pass farm on your right	S	260
85.028	400	25,4	Bear left on the track		E	242
85.029	1100	26,5	At the crossroads, continue straight ahead		E	273
85.030	700	27,2	Bear right on the track	Continue uphill	E	314
85.031	1200	28,4	Keep left on the track	Towards the town	E	382
85.032	1100	29,5	Continue straight ahead	Under arch	E	391
85.033	70	29,5	Continue straight ahead, Alternate Route rejoins from the left. Note:- to avoid the steps, turn left and then take the second left over the bridge to the town centre	Climb steps	E	395
85.034	50	29,6	At the top of the steps, continue straight ahead on via Dante Alighieri	Towards the church	E	397
85.035	120	29,7	Arrive at San-Quirico-d'Orcia (XII) beside the church	Piazza Chigi		406

Stage Summary: the Alternate Route remains on the tarmac to reduce the section by 2.5km

Stage Ascent: 228m   Stage Descent: 81m

Waypoint	Distance Between Waypoints (m)	Total (km)	Directions	Verification Point	Compass	Altitude (m)
85A1.001	0	0,0	Continue straight ahead on the road		E	249
85A1.002	1600	1,6	Fork right and continue on the main road	VF sign	SE	333
85A1.003	3400	5,0	For some relief from the road it is possible to fork left on the clay track. Note:- in wet weather the clay makes for impossible going on bikes and difficulties for all	Towards cemetery	SE	327
85A1.004	400	5,3	Take the right fork and rejoin the main road	Pass cemetery on your left	SE	360
85A1.005	600	6,0	Turn right over the road bridge. Caution, crash barriers and no pavement on the roadside	VF sign	SE	383
85A1.006	210	6,2	After crossing the bridge, turn right at the T-junction	Direction San Quirico centre	SW	392
85A1.007	30	6,2	Bear left. Note:- there are steps ahead, riders should bear right onto the ramp of the bridge	Towards the arches	S	393
85A1.008	20	6,2	Turn left and rejoin the the Main Route	Climb steps		395

Alternate Route #85-A1 6.2km

Religious Hostel

Abbazia di S.Antimo,Localita' S.Antimo, 222,53024 Castelnuovo-Dell'Abate(SI),Italy Tel:+39 0577 835659,foresterie@antimo.it,Price:C,

Collegiata dei Santi Quirico e Giulitta,(Signora Maramai Lucrezia),Via delle Carbonaie, 1,53027 San-Quirico-d'Orcia(SI),Italy Tel:+39 0577 897278, Mobile:+39 3477 748732,giorgio.maramai@tele3.it,Price:C,

Parrocchia S.Maria Maddalena,Via San Giovanni, 24,53024 Montalcino(SI),Italy Tel:+39 0577 834138,Price:B,

B&B, Hotel, Gite d'Etape

Hotel il Garibaldi,Via Cassia, 17,53027 San-Quirico-d'Orcia(SI),Italy Tel:+39 0577 898315,Price:B,

Equestrian

Fattoria Pieve a Salti Bio,Strada Provinciale Pieve a Salti,53022 Buonconvento(SI),Italy Tel:+39 0577 807244,info@pieveasaltibio.it,pieveasaltibio.it,

Tourist Information

Ufficio Turistico,Piazza Chigi, 33,53027 San-Quirico-d'Orcia(SI),Italy Tel:+39 0577 897211,

Banks and ATMs

Banca Monte dei Paschi di Siena,Via Dante Alighieri, 32,53027 San-Quirico-d'Orcia(SI),Italy Tel:+39 0577 897507,

Doctor

Bani Antonio,Via dei Canneti, 37B,53027 San-Quirico-d'Orcia(SI),Italy Tel:+39 0577 897262,

Veterinary

Ambulatorio Veterinario Cereda Mulinari Dott.Vanni - Veterinari,Via Oreste Lizzadri, 27,53022 Buonconvento(SI),Italy Tel:+39 0577 807066,

Ambulatorio Veterinario,Via dei Canneti, 45/a,53027 San-Quirico-d'Orcia(SI),Italy Mobile:+39 3393 282810,

Stage Eighty-six Summary: a very strenuous and long uphill stage with few en route opportunities to break the journey. The route is generally undertaken on quiet roads and tracks, however there are 2 brief sections on the potentially dangerous via Cassia.

Distance from Canterbury: 1847km Distance to Saint-Peter's-Square: 227km

Stage Ascent: 959m Stage Descent: 575m

Waypoint	Distance Between Waypoints (m)	Total (km)	Directions	Verification Point	Compass	Altitude (m)
86.001	0	0,0	From the church in San-Quirico-d'Orcia on piazza Chigi continue ahead on via Dante Alighieri	Pass through piazza della Libertà	SE	407
86.002	400	0,4	Turn right at the crossroads on the edge of the old town	VF sign, via Giacomo Matteotti	SW	412
86.003	190	0,6	At the crossroads, continue straight ahead on via Giuseppe Garibaldi	VF sign, direction Vignoni	SW	417
86.004	700	1,2	Take the left fork, towards Vignoni	VF sign	S	425
86.005	1300	2,5	Take the left fork	Towards Vignoni	SE	495
86.006	900	3,4	Continue straight ahead	Pass tower in Vignoni Alto on your left	SE	486
86.007	500	3,9	Take the left fork		SE	443
86.008	1300	5,2	At the T-junction in Bagno Vignoni, turn left	VF sign	E	299
86.009	400	5,5	Turn sharp right on the gravel track	VF sign	SW	268
86.010	120	5,7	Continue straight ahead	Cross bridge	SE	267
86.011	400	6,0	At the T-junction with the road, turn left	Road sign for Roma ahead	SE	276
86.012	120	6,2	At the Stop sign, continue straight ahead. Note:- to escape the busy road cross onto the track in the field, parallel to the road	Via Cassia	SE	275
86.013	240	6,4	Just before the road bends to the left, bear right on the track, cross the stream and turn right	Proceed with the stream on the right and fields on the left	S	266

San-Quirico-d'Orcia to Radicofani 32.8km

227

228

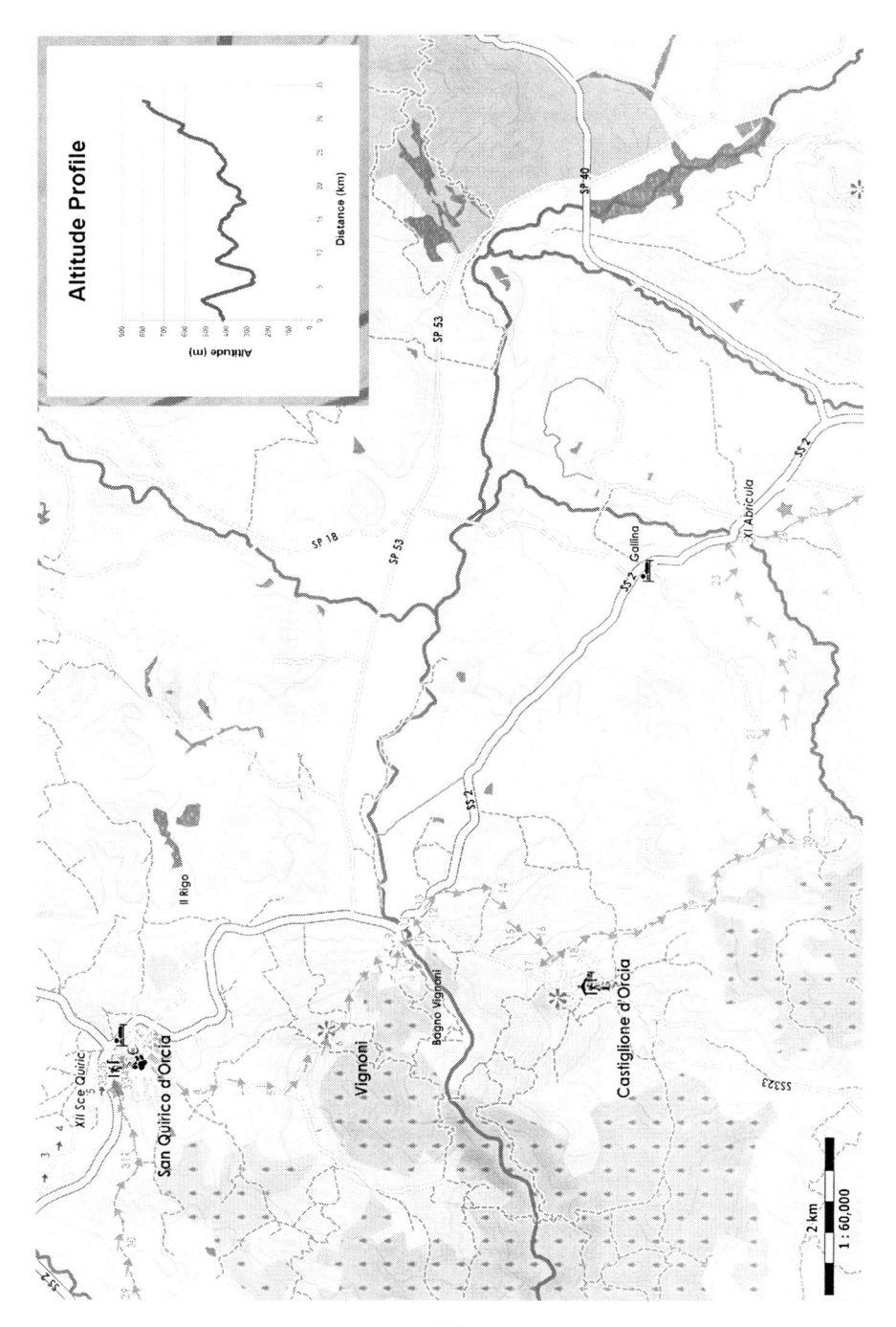

Waypoint	Distance Between Waypoints (m)	Total (km)	Directions	Verification Point	Compass	Altitude (m)
86.014	800	7,2	At the junction in tracks, turn right and then take the second turning to the left	Across the stream	SW	276
86.015	800	7,9	Take the left fork	Beside farmhouse, towards another farm	SE	358
86.016	90	8,0	Turn right	Beside farmhouse	W	369
86.017	600	8,6	At the T-junction with the road, turn sharp left onto the road	Hairpin bend to the right at the junction	SE	434
86.018	300	9,0	At the next junction, bear left	Strada del Pozzo, VF sign	S	445
86.019	2100	11,0	In the valley bottom, continue straight ahead	Cross the bridge	SE	346
86.020	1800	12,8	At the junction, after passing woods on the right, turn sharp left along the ridge	Via delle Querciole	E	414
86.021	1600	14,4	On the crown of the bend to the left, turn right on the track	Pass farm on the left	E	426
86.022	1300	15,6	Continue straight ahead on the white road	Farmhouse on the left	NE	383
86.023	1300	16,9	Turn right, downhill on the track	Pass Agriturismo on the left	E	365
86.024	600	17,5	Bear right on the track and cross the stream	Main road close on the left	S	313
86.025	400	17,9	At the junction with the white road, bear right	Uphill	S	322
86.026	90	18,0	Take the left fork, towards Briccole (XI)	Pass farm on the left	SE	329
86.027	800	18,8	Cross the main road and continue straight ahead on the track	Across the stream	SE	338

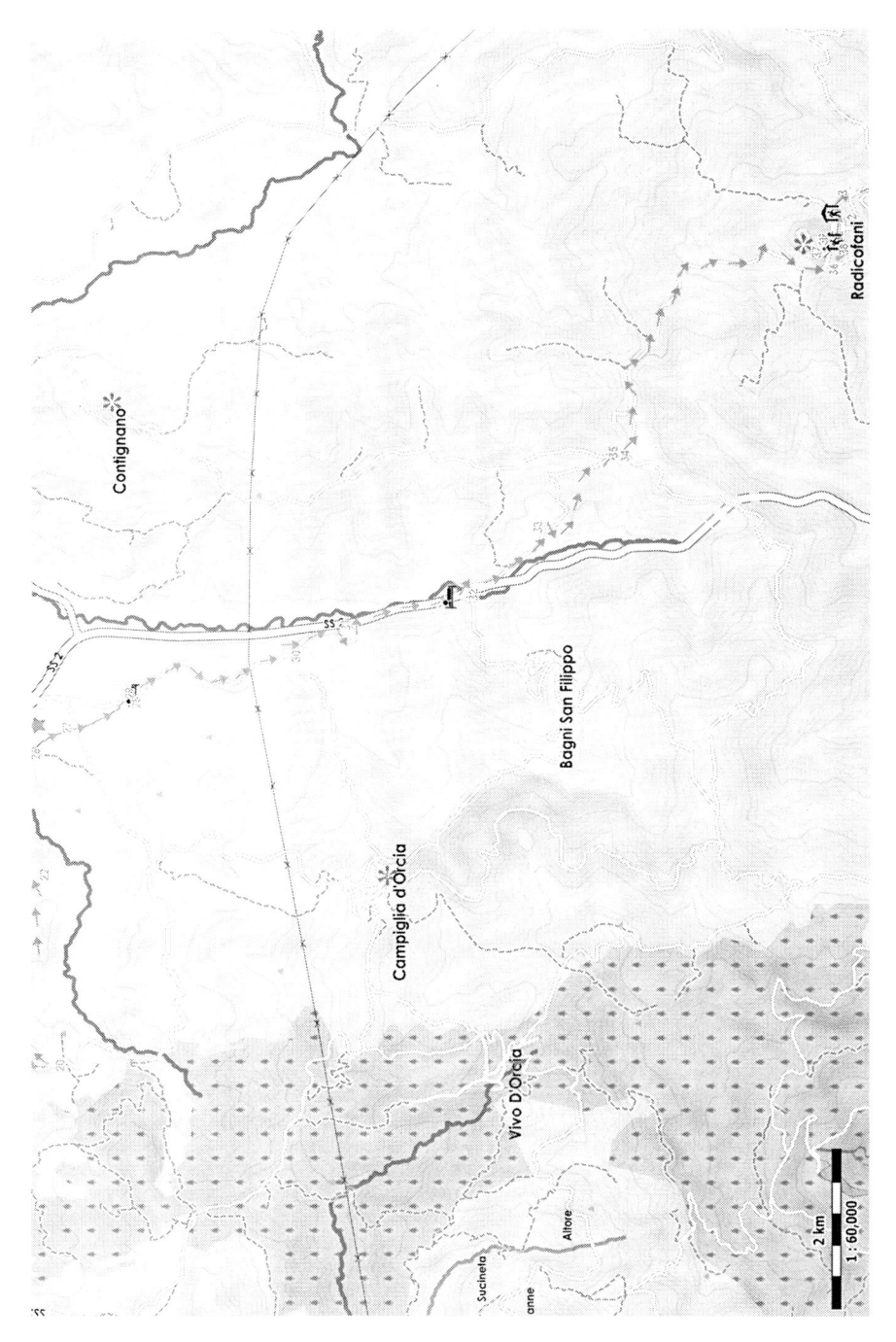

Waypoint	Distance Between Waypoints (m)	Total (km)	Directions	Verification Point	Compass	Altitude (m)
86.028	700	19,5	At the intersection with the old via Cassia, turn right on the road	Pass agriturismo	SE	337
86.029	250	19,7	Take the left fork	Tarmac road, uphill	S	345
86.030	2200	21,9	Take the left fork	Towards the via Cassia	SE	437
86.031	1300	23,2	At the T-junction with the via Cassia (SR2), turn right and proceed with care on the main road	Concrete wall on the right	S	401
86.032	1400	24,5	Turn left on the road across the river	Towards Radicofani, VF sign	SE	421
86.033	1500	26,0	Shortly after sign 32	Pass farm buildings on your left	SE	464
86.034	1600	27,6	At the T-junction with the road, turn right	Direction Radicofani	S	586
86.035	170	27,8	Bear left on the road	Direction Radicofani	SE	596
86.036	4600	32,4	Turn left towards the centre of Radicofani	Viale Odoardo Lucchini	SE	768
86.037	260	32,7	At the crossroads, go straight ahead and then bear right on the ramp	Towards centre, VF signs	SE	789
86.038	40	32,7	Fork left, uphill	No Entry	SE	792
86.039	140	32,8	Arrive at Radicofani centre	Church of San Pietro to the right		791

San-Quirico-d'Orcia to Radicofani 32.8km

Pilgrim Hostel

Casa d'Accoglienza San Jacopo di Compostela,Via Renato Magi,53040 Radicofani(SI),Italy
Tel:+39 0578 55614,Mobile:+39 3389 240307,doneliasantori@libero.it,Price:D,

Ospitale del Comune,Via Fonte Antese,53040 Radicofani(SI),Italy
Tel:+39 3293 812742,comunediradicofani@inwind.it,Price:C,

Religious Hostel

Parrocchia Ss.Quirico e Giulitta,Via Roma, 22,53023 Castiglione-d'Orcia(SI),Italy
Tel:+39 0577 897278,

B&B, Hotel, Gite d'Etape

Le Rocche,Via Senese, 10,53023 Castiglione-d'Orcia(SI),Italy Tel:+39 0577 887031,Price:B,

Hotel Beyfin - Bisarca,Via Cassia, 161,53023 Castiglione-d'Orcia(SI),Italy
Tel:+39 0577 872877,Price:B,

Osteria Gallina,Via Cassia, 5,53023 Castiglione-d'Orcia(SI),Italy Tel:+39 0577 880130,Price:B,

Agriturismo - Sant'Alberto,Via Vecchia Cassia,53023 Castiglione-d'Orcia(SI),Italy
Tel:+39 0577 897227,Mobile:+39 3382 988959,Price:A,

Tourist Information

Comune di Radicofani,Via Renato Magi, 59,53040 Radicofani(SI),Italy Tel:+39 0578 55878,

Comune di Castiglione d'Orcia,Via Aldobrandeschi, 13,53023 Castiglione-d'Orcia(SI),Italy
Tel:+39 0577 88401,

Banks and ATMs

Banca Monte dei Paschi di Siena,Piazza Tassi, 8,53040 Radicofani(SI),Italy
Tel:+39 0578 55907,

Hospital

Presidio Ospedaliero Amiata Senese,Via Trento,53021 Abbadia-San-Salvatore(SI),Italy
Tel:+39 0577 7731,

Doctor

Mengano - Studio Medico,Via Sandro Pertini, 3,53023 Castiglione-d'Orcia(SI),Italy
Tel:+39 0577 887455,

San-Quirico-d'Orcia to Radicofani 32.8km

Stage Eighty-seven Summary: this is another long section with few opportunities for intermediate stops. The descent from Radicofani is followed by a dangerous section on the main roads before another exposed stretch over the the hills on broad country tracks. With the exception of the main road the section is easy going for cyclists and riders.

Distance from Canterbury: 1880km Distance to Saint-Peter's-Square: 194km
Stage Ascent: 453m Stage Descent: 854m

Waypoint	Distance Between Waypoints (m)	Total (km)	Directions	Verification Point	Compass	Altitude (m)
87.001	0	0,0	From the church of San Pietro turn right and continue along street	Via Roma	E	791
87.002	280	0,3	Pass through the archway and leave the historic centre. Continue with care straight ahead on the road downhill - no pavement and road bounded with crash barriers	Viale Giacomo Matteotti	SE	765
87.003	500	0,8	At the crossroads, continue straight ahead	Direction Roma	S	719
87.004	200	1,0	On the apex of the bend to the right, continue straight ahead on the unmade road	Old via Cassia, VF sign	S	699
87.005	2000	2,9	Take the right fork	Uphill	S	563
87.006	900	3,8	Take the left fork	Towards the "Pantano" agriturismo	SE	586
87.007	1500	5,3	Take the right fork	Pass farm on your left	S	521
87.008	3000	8,2	Take the right fork, remaining between the trees	Keep river Rigo to the left	SW	311
87.009	2300	10,5	At the T-junction with the main road, turn right, cross the road and continue to the right on the track parallel to the road	SR2, pass bar on the right	SW	296
87.010	500	10,9	Leave Ponte a Rigo, and keep left on the track. In the event the track is overgrown or has been ploughed in proceed on the grass beside the road to the Sovana junction	SR2, pass bar on the right	SW	295

Radicofani to Aquapendente 31.8km

233

Radicofani

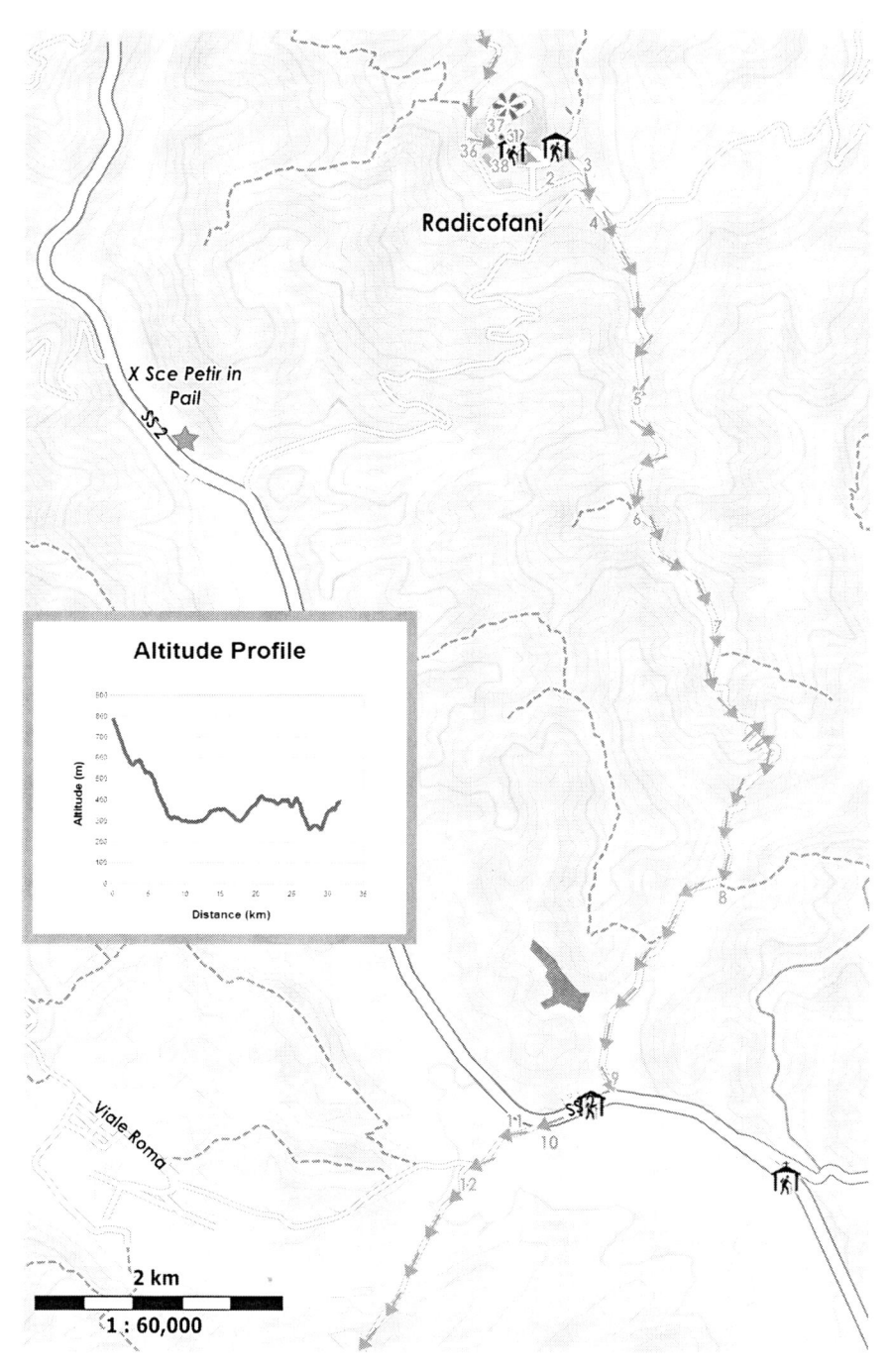

X Sce Petir in Pail

Altitude Profile

2 km
1 : 60,000

Waypoint	Distance Between Waypoints (m)	Total (km)	Directions	Verification Point	Compass	Altitude (m)
87.011	500	11,4	At the end of the track turn right and then left to follow the road with care - crash barriers bound the road ahead	The road crosses the river	SW	294
87.012	500	11,9	Take the next road to the left	Direction Sovana	S	298
87.013	3700	15,6	Turn left onto a gravel track, direction la Valle	VF sign	SE	357
87.014	700	16,4	Fork right down the hill	VF sign at end of farmyard	E	336
87.015	700	17,1	Continue straight ahead, over the crossroads in the track	VF sign on telegraph pole	E	313
87.016	900	17,9	At the T-junction in the track, shortly after crossing the river, turn right	VF sign	S	300
87.017	1200	19,2	Take the left fork		E	356
87.018	1300	20,5	Continue straight ahead	Towards la Casina	NE	407
87.019	1000	21,5	At the T-junction, turn right	VF sign	SE	400
87.020	3400	24,9	At the T-junction, turn left up the hil,l on the road	Direction Proceno	SE	368
87.021	150	25,1	Take the right fork	VF sign, towards the castello in Proceno	SE	371
87.022	600	25,7	In the piazza in Proceno, bear left on viale Marconi	Pass palazzo Sforza on your left	NE	407
87.023	90	25,7	At the T-junction, turn left and continue downhill on the winding road	Skirting the village on via Belvedere	NE	402
87.024	400	26,1	On the crown of the sharp bend to the left, continue straight ahead	Via della Pace	NE	380
87.025	400	26,5	Take right fork	Downhill	NE	334

Radicofani to Aquapendente 31.8km

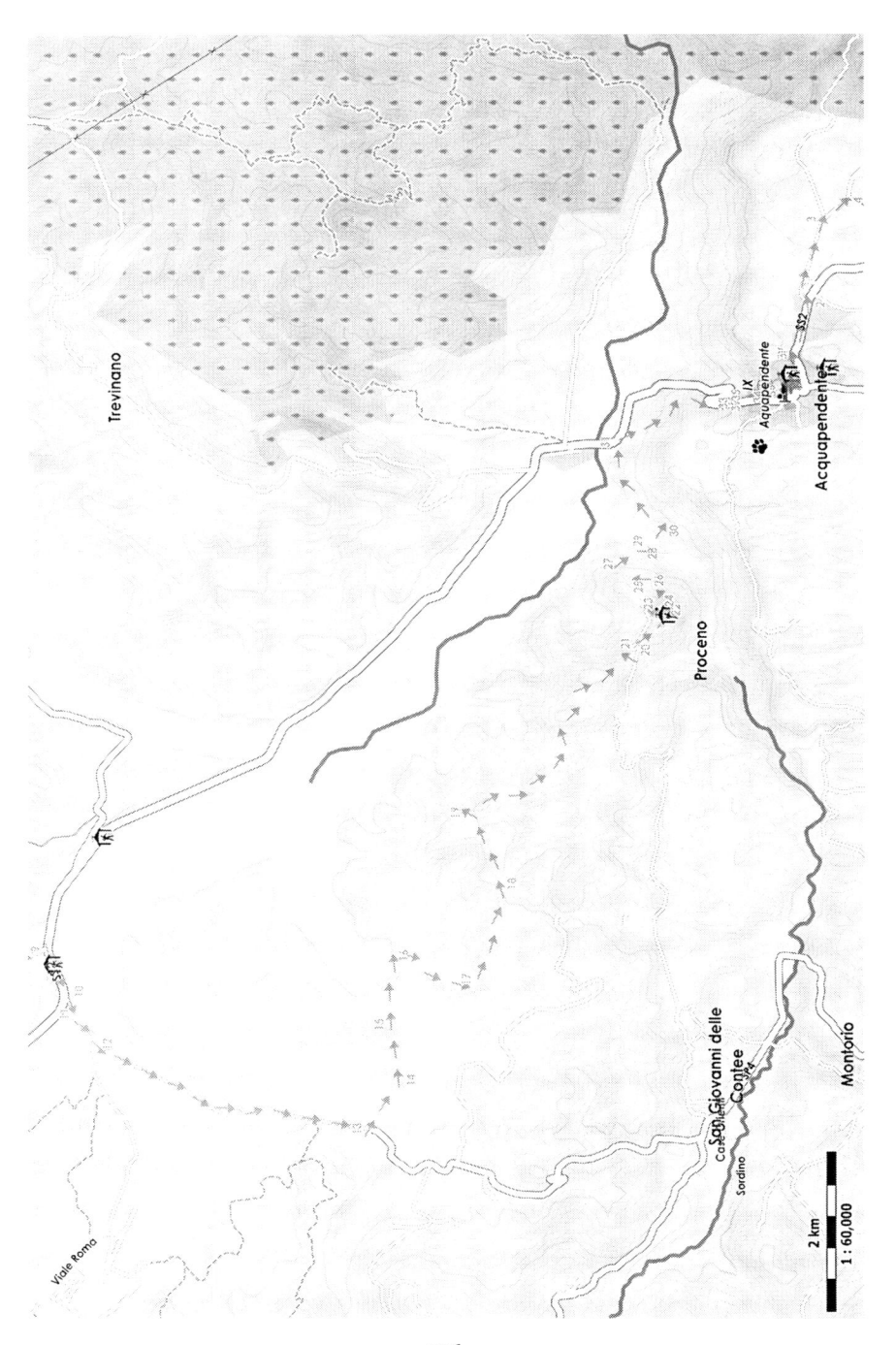

Waypoint	Distance Between Waypoints (m)	Total (km)	Directions	Verification Point	Compass	Altitude (m)
87.026	110	26,6	At the T-junction, turn left	Downhill	NE	324
87.027	400	27,0	At the T-junction, turn right on the Strada Provinciale	Beside sports ground	SE	296
87.028	270	27,2	Bear right on the disused road		SE	273
87.029	290	27,5	Return to the strada Provinciale and bear right		SE	260
87.030	200	27,7	Bear left on the strada Provinciale	After river bridge	NE	266
87.031	1300	29,0	At the bottom of the hill, shortly before the T-junction with the via Cassia, turn right on the small road	Strada Viccinale di San Giglio, VF sign	S	258
87.032	1600	30,6	At the T-junction with the via Cassia, turn right	Enter Aquapendente	S	357
87.033	160	30,7	Turn left, across the car park, and take the track to the left of the Albergo	"Aquila d'Oro"	SE	361
87.034	160	30,9	Cross the orchard and take the footpath downhill and to the left		SE	353
87.035	40	30,9	Turn right on the track		SE	352
87.036	160	31,1	In front of the albergo "la Ripa" turn left and then bear right	Continue along via Cesare Battisti and via Roma	SE	361
87.037	800	31,8	Arrive at Aquapendente (IX), beside the church of Santo Sepulcro	Piazza del Duomo		390

Radicofani to Aquapendente 31.8km

Pilgrim Hostel

La Casa del Pellegrino via Cassia,Località Ponte a Rigo,53040 San-Casciano-dei-Bagni(SI),Italy Tel:+39 0578 53628,Mobile:+39 3398 999610,Price:D,

La Casa del Pellegrino,(Leonello Toccaceli),Via Cassia (Km146),01021 Aquapendente(VT),Italy Tel:+39 0578 53628,Mobile:+39 3398 999610,Price:D,

Religious Hostel

Convento Cappuccini-Casa Sanlazzaro,(Suor Amelia),Via dei Cappuccini, 21,01021 Acquapendente(VT),Italy Tel:+39 0763 730177,
Mobile:+39 3394 327383,cercam@libero.it,www.casadilazzaro.org,Price:D,

Villa San Ermanno,Via Cassia Km,01021 Aquapendente(VT),Italy Tel:+39 3291 644501,gerokhappa@libero.it ,Price:D,

Casa del Pellegrino San Rocco,(Don Erico Castauro),Via Roma, 51,01021 Acquapendente(VT),Italy Tel:+39 0763 733958,Mobile:+39 3454 452534,

Parrocchia Ss.Salvatore,Via Sant'Agnese,01020 Proceno(VT),Italy Tel:+39 3402 265595,

B&B, Hotel, Gite d'Etape

Albergo "il Borgo",Via Porta Sant'Angelo, 3,01021 Acquapendente(VT),Italy Tel:+39 0763 711264,Price:B,

Equestrian

Agriturismo - Maneggio San Filippo,Strada della Falconiera,02043 San-Filippo(RI),Italy Mobile:+39 3387 524339,

Tourist Information

Comune di Acquapendente,Piazza Girolamo Fabrizio, 17,01021 Acquapendente(VT),Italy Tel:+39 0763 711215,

Comune di Proceno,Piazza della Libertà, 12,01020 Proceno(VT),Italy Tel:+39 0763 710092,

Banks and ATMs

Banco di Brescia,Via del Rivo, 34,01021 Acquapendente(VT),Italy Tel:+39 0763 711179,

Cassa di Risparmio di Viterbo,Piazza Nazario Sauro, 6,01021 Acquapendente(VT),Italy Tel:+39 0763 711223,

Hospital

Ospedale Civile,Via Cesare Battisti, 68,01021 Acquapendente(VT),Italy Tel:+39 0763 731455,

Doctor

Menchinelli - Studio Medico,Via del Teatro, 14,01021 Acquapendente(VT),Italy Tel:+39 0763 733337,

Veterinary

Fratangeli - Medico Veterinario,Località Villa le Grazie, 79C,01021 Acquapendente(VT),Italy Tel:+39 0763 733032,

Stage Eighty-eight Summary: initially the route meanders on farm and sheep tracks to avoid the via Cassia, then it proceeds in the lower slopes of the hills overlooking lake Bolsena. The latter half includes paths over broken ground with some short steep ascents making for difficult progress for cyclists.

Distance from Canterbury: 1911km   Distance to Saint-Peter's-Square: 162km

Stage Ascent: 235m   Stage Descent: 301m

Waypoint	Distance Between Waypoints (m)	Total (km)	Directions	Verification Point	Compass	Altitude (m)
88.001	0	0,0	From the Basilica del Santo Sepolcro, turn left on the main road	Pass Torre Giulia de Jacopo on your right	E	389
88.002	600	0,6	Turn left, direction Torre Alfina	VF sign, shrine on the apex of the bend	E	408
88.003	1200	1,8	After a large factory building, bear right onto the gravel track	VF sign, pass silos on your right	SE	437
88.004	400	2,2	At the fork, bear right on the gravel track	VF sign, line of trees to your left	SW	435
88.005	1300	3,5	At the junction with the via Cassia, cross straight over onto the small road	VF sign	S	435
88.006	1800	5,3	At the T-junction with a minor road, turn left and then immediately right	VF sign, farmhouse on your left	SE	445
88.007	700	6,0	Take the right fork	Strada del Podere del Vescovo	S	445
88.008	1900	7,9	At the T-junction, turn left		E	461
88.009	60	8,0	At the next T-junction, turn left	VF sign on small building ahead	NE	461
88.010	130	8,1	Fork right on the track		NE	461
88.011	900	9,0	At the T-junction, turn sharp right	Track quickly bends to the left	E	461
88.012	600	9,5	At the T-junction with the main road, turn right on the via Cassia	Towards San Lorenzo Nuovo	S	466
88.013	1100	10,6	At the traffic lights, in the centre of San Lorenzo Nuovo, continue straight ahead	Direction Bolsena, Roma 124	SE	493

Aquapendente to Bolsena 22.1km

Acquapendente

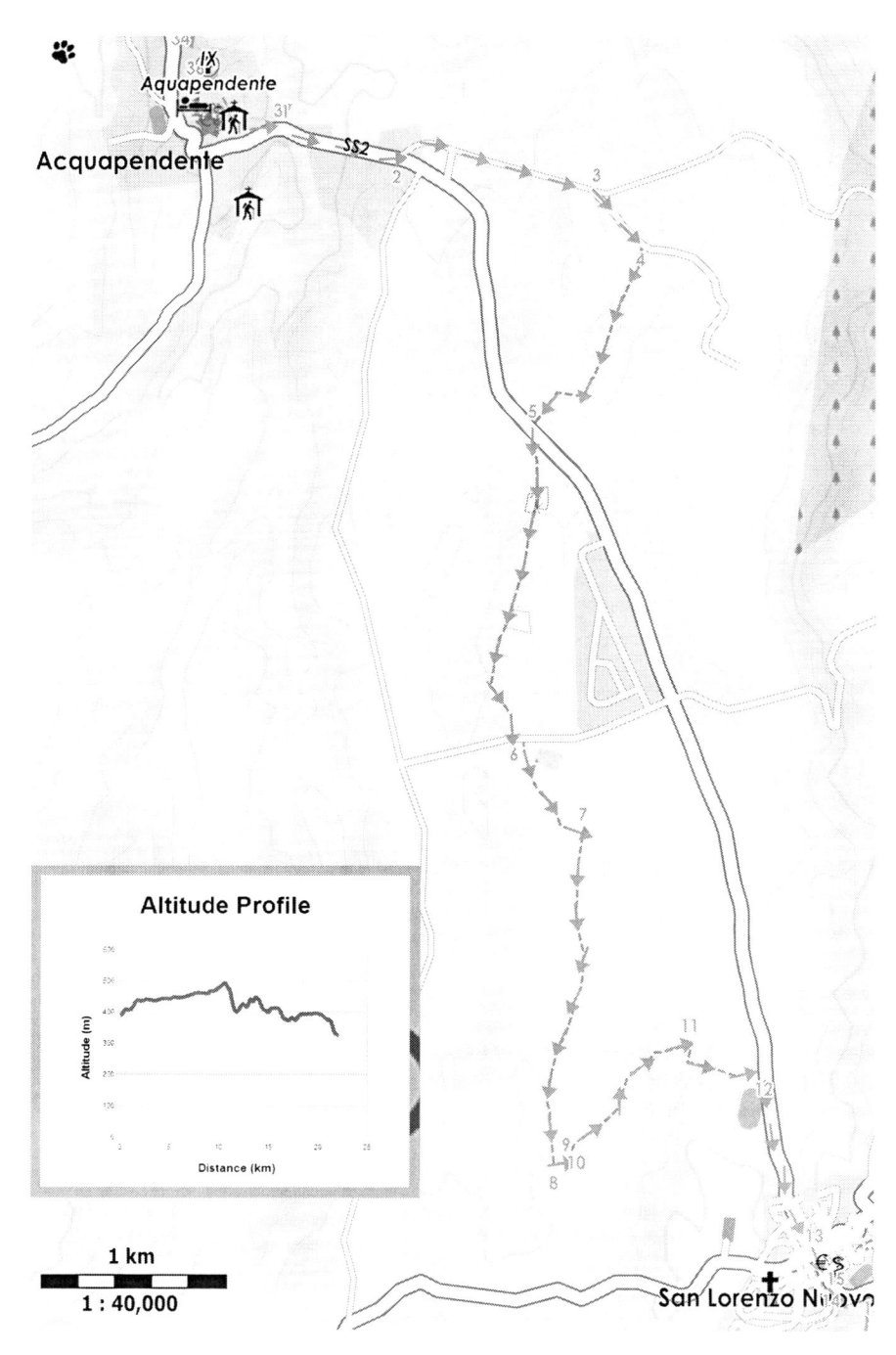

Altitude Profile

1 km
1 : 40,000

San Lorenzo Nuovo

Waypoint	Distance Between Waypoints (m)	Total (km)	Directions	Verification Point	Compass	Altitude (m)
88.014	210	10,8	Take the right fork down the hill, parallel to main road	VF sign	S	486
88.015	60	10,9	At the next junction bear left	Returning towards the main road	E	482
88.016	220	11,1	Bear right, parallel to the main road, and then right again on the concrete road. **Note:** there have been reports of the track ahead being blocked by a farmer. If in doubt, remain on the main road and proceed with care for 1200m to Waypoint 88.020	Steeply downhill, house on the right	S	473
88.017	500	11,6	Continue straight ahead across the clearing and then turn left to follow the track		E	407
88.018	150	11,7	Skirt the house and bear left on the white road	House on your left	E	400
88.019	700	12,4	At the T-junction cross the road with great care and turn right	Via Cassia, stone wall on your left	SE	425
88.020	160	12,6	Turn left onto a gravel track. Note:- the route ahead is generally off-road and while the conditions for walkers and horse-riders are good it is strenuous for bike riders, who can remain on the via Cassia rejoining the Main Route in Bolsena	VF sign, km 122,7, direction agriturismo "Pomele"	SE	422
88.021	1400	14,0	At the fork in the track, continue straight ahead down the hill	VF sign	SE	443
88.022	270	14,2	Bear right and then fork left parallel to lake-shore	VF sign, "vocabolo Pomele"	E	427
88.023	600	14,8	Fork right down the hill	Quarry on left	SE	404
88.024	900	15,7	At the fork, keep right	VF sign	E	412
88.025	500	16,1	At the T-junction, turn right	VF sign	S	408

Aquapendente to Bolsena 22.1km

San Lorenzo Nuovo
Strada Vecchia
SS2
Vill Sca Cristina
SP 53
Bolsena
1 km
1 : 40,000

Waypoint	Distance Between Waypoints (m)	Total (km)	Directions	Verification Point	Compass	Altitude (m)
88.026	400	16,5	Turn left	VF sign, strada della Roccaccia	E	379
88.027	700	17,3	Fork left up the hill	Line of posts directly on right	SE	378
88.028	300	17,6	At T-junction with another track, turn right down the hill	Entrance to large house on left	SE	376
88.029	140	17,7	Take the left fork	VF sign	NE	373
88.030	600	18,3	Fork right onto a smaller track	VF sign	SE	390
88.031	600	18,9	Bear right	Parallel to lake-shore	E	392
88.032	400	19,2	Fork left	Between a line of trees	SE	392
88.033	1100	20,3	Fork left on the track		SE	390
88.034	250	20,6	Continue straight ahead onto a minor tarmac road	Pass house and parking area on your right	SE	385
88.035	210	20,8	At the T-junction, turn left	VF sign	E	379
88.036	20	20,8	Continue straight ahead at the junction. Ignore VF sign to the left	Shrine on the corner	S	379
88.037	290	21,1	At the Stop sign turn right down the hill	VF sign	S	373
88.038	500	21,6	Bear right on the small road	Pass castello close on your left	SW	346
88.039	40	21,6	At the T-junction, turn left	Under the arch	S	341
88.040	30	21,6	Turn right	Via delle Piagge	SW	338
88.041	70	21,7	At the end of the road, in piazza Primo Maggio, turn left	Corso Cavour	SE	333
88.042	260	22,0	Pass under the archway, cross piazza Guglielmo Matteotti and continue straight ahead on Corso della Repubblica	Pedestrian zone	SE	326
88.043	140	22,1	Arrive at Bolsena (VIII) centre in piazza Santa Cristina	The Basilica of Santa Cristina ahead		324

Aquapendente to Bolsena 22.1km

243

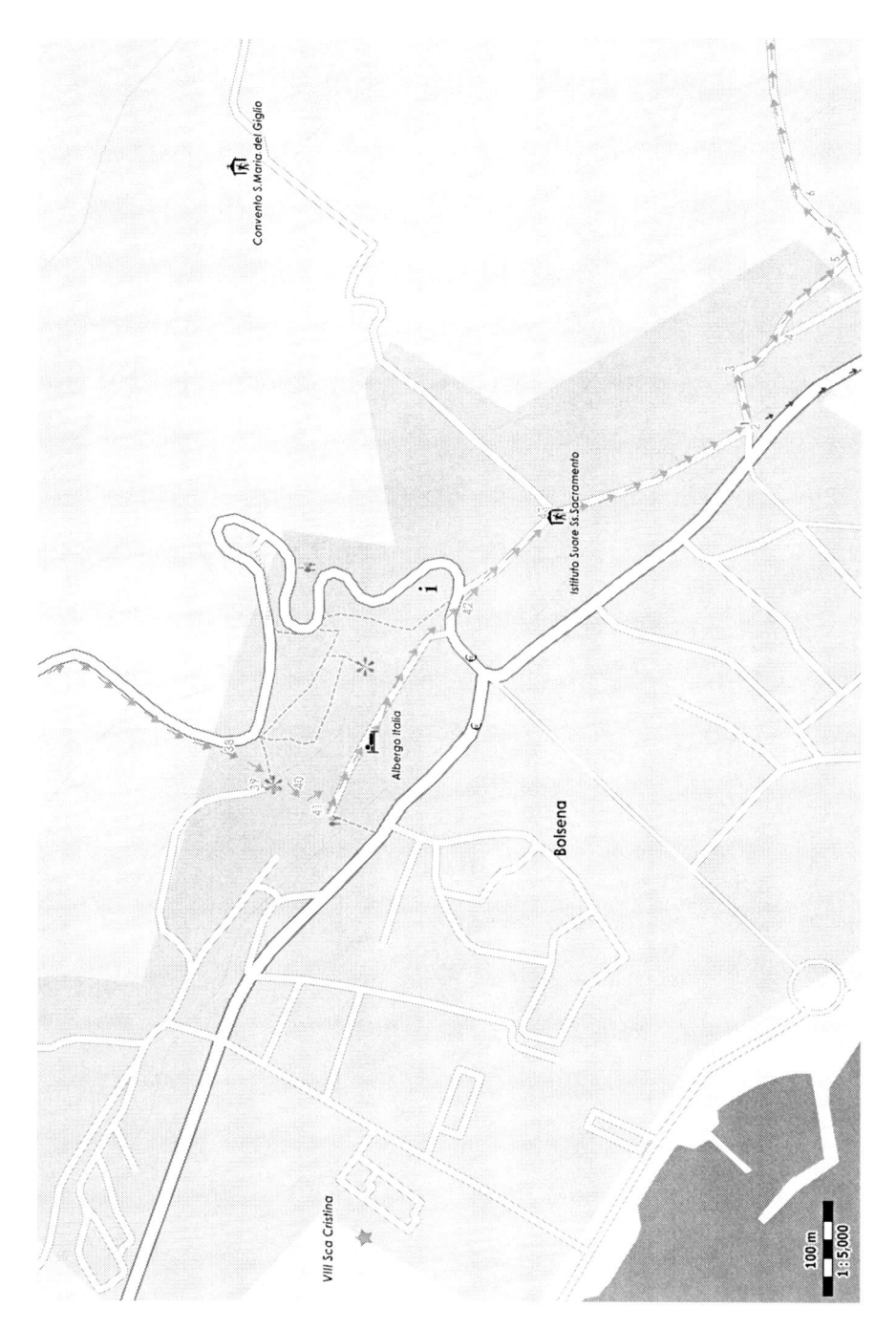
Convento S.Maria del Giglio
Istituto Suore Ss.Sacramento
Albergo Italia
Bolsena
VIII Sca Cristina
100 m
1:5,000

Pilgrim Hostel

Ostello Ristoro Gazzetta,(Mauro),Strada di Gazzetta le Valli,01023 Bolsena(VT),Italy
Tel:+39 0761 798753,Mobile:+39 3357 383702,

Religious Hostel

Convento S.Maria del Giglio,Via Madonna del Giglio,01023 Bolsena(VT),Italy
Tel:+39 0761 799066,Mobile:+39 3286 027357,puntidivista@pelagus.it,Price:C,

Istituto Suore Ss.Sacramento,Piazza Santa Cristina,01023 Bolsena(VT),Italy
Tel:+39 0761 799058,Price:B,

B&B, Hotel, Gite d'Etape

Albergo Italia,Corso Cavour, 53,01023 Bolsena(VT),Italy Tel:+39 0761 799193,Price:B,

Camping

Camping la Cappelletta di Stella P.Luigi,Via Cassia Nord,01023 Bolsena(VT),Italy
Tel:+39 0761 799543,

Camping Pineta di Leoncini Massimo,Viale Diaz,01023 Bolsena(VT),Italy
Tel:+39 0761 796905,

Tourist Information

Comune di Bolsena,Via Guglielmo Marconi,01023 Bolsena(VT),Italy Tel:+39 0761 799601,

Banks and ATMs

Banca di Roma,Piazza Europa, 1,01020 San-Lorenzo-Nuovo(VT),Italy Tel:+39 0763 727014,

Cassa di Risparmio di Orvieto,Piazza Guglielmo Matteotti, 22,01023 Bolsena(VT),Italy
Tel:+39 0761 799004,

Banco di Brescia,Via A.Gramsci, 28,01023 Bolsena(VT),Italy Tel:+39 0761 799014,

Doctor

Zanoni - Studio Medico,Via Dell'Ospedale, 17,01020 San-Lorenzo-Nuovo(VT),Italy
Tel:+39 0763 727774,

Veterinary

Studio Medico Veterinario,Viale Santa Maria,01023 Bolsena(VT),Italy
Mobile:+39 3386 116903,

Stage Eighty-nine Summary: the route climbs back into the hills overlooking the lake. The Aternate Route allows cyclists to bypass difficult hillside tracks and avoid a number of barriers. Main Route progresses on farm and forest tracks to approach the hilltop town of Montefiscone on a minor road.

Distance from Canterbury: 1934km   Distance to Saint-Peter's-Square: 140km
Stage Ascent: 479m   Stage Descent: 199m

Waypoint	Distance Between Waypoints (m)	Total (km)	Directions	Verification Point	Compass	Altitude (m)
89.001	0	0,0	Leave piazza Santa Cristina by Porta Romana	Basilica and café on the left	SE	323
89.002	210	0,2	At the crossroads with trees in the traffic island ahead, turn right. Note: - the Main Route returns quickly to the hills overlooking the lake. Unfortunately there are a number of barriers on the route, to avoid these carefully follow the Alternate Route straight ahead following the potentially busy via Cassia	Via Acqua della Croce, pass water trough on the right	E	321
89.003	70	0,3	Take the first turning to the right	Pass building supplies yard on your left	SE	322
89.004	50	0,3	Take the left fork	No Entry	SE	323
89.005	110	0,5	At the T-junction, turn left, uphill on località Vigna	House N° 15 on the left	NE	326
89.006	80	0,5	Continue straight ahead on the track		E	331
89.007	190	0,7	Bear right on the track		E	352
89.008	160	0,9	Turn sharp right over the stream		SW	360
89.009	300	1,2	At the T-junction, turn right and immediately left	Parallel to the lake-shore	SE	354
89.010	600	1,8	Turn right		S	352
89.011	120	1,9	At the T-junction, turn right		W	352
89.012	110	2,0	Turn left	On the straight tarmac road	SE	350

Bolsena to Montefiascone 17.4km

247

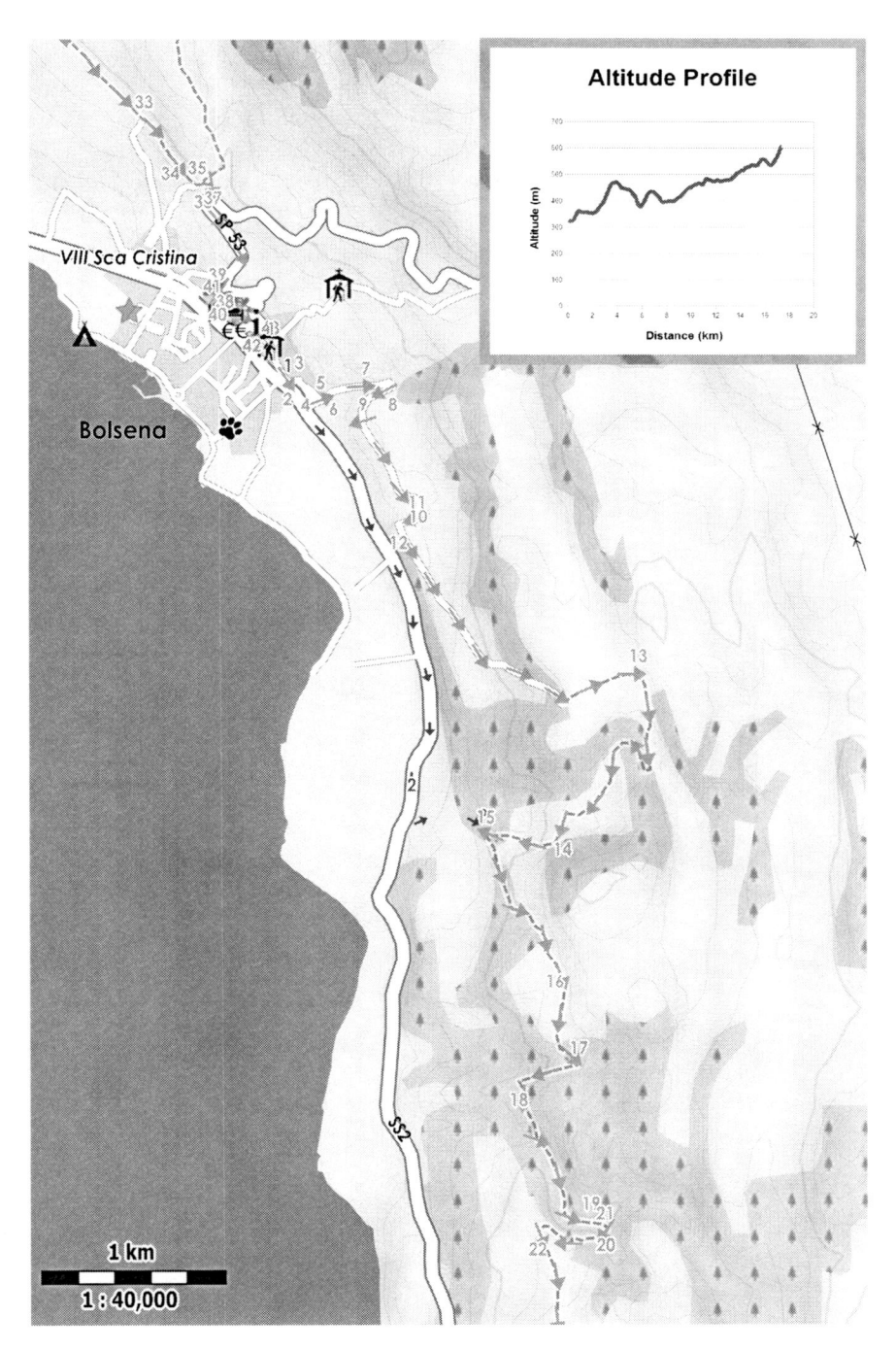

Waypoint	Distance Between Waypoints (m)	Total (km)	Directions	Verification Point	Compass	Altitude (m)
89.013	1900	3,9	Beside two pine trees, turn right onto a track	Downhill between fields	SW	470
89.014	1500	5,4	Continue straight ahead	Across barrier	W	417
89.015	500	5,9	At the T-junction with the tarmac road turn left – Alternate Route rejoins from the right	Parallel to the lake-shore	SE	376
89.016	900	6,7	Fork right onto the gravel track, direction Parco di Turona	VF sign	S	433
89.017	600	7,4	Fork right, down the hill	VF sign	W	414
89.018	300	7,7	Turn left on a gravel track, just before a small white chapel	VF sign	SE	393
89.019	1000	8,6	Fork right through a thin band of trees	Proceed into clearing	E	398
89.020	90	8,7	After crossing the stream bear right	Derelict house to your left	S	400
89.021	20	8,8	At a junction of three tracks take the furthest right up the hill	Towards the house on the ridge	W	400
89.022	500	9,2	Turn left on to a paved road	The old via Cassia	S	417
89.023	800	10,0	Fork left	VF milestone	SE	450
89.024	700	10,7	Proceed straight ahead at the crossroads	VF sign	SE	465

Bolsena to Montefiascone 17.4km

VII Sce Flaviane

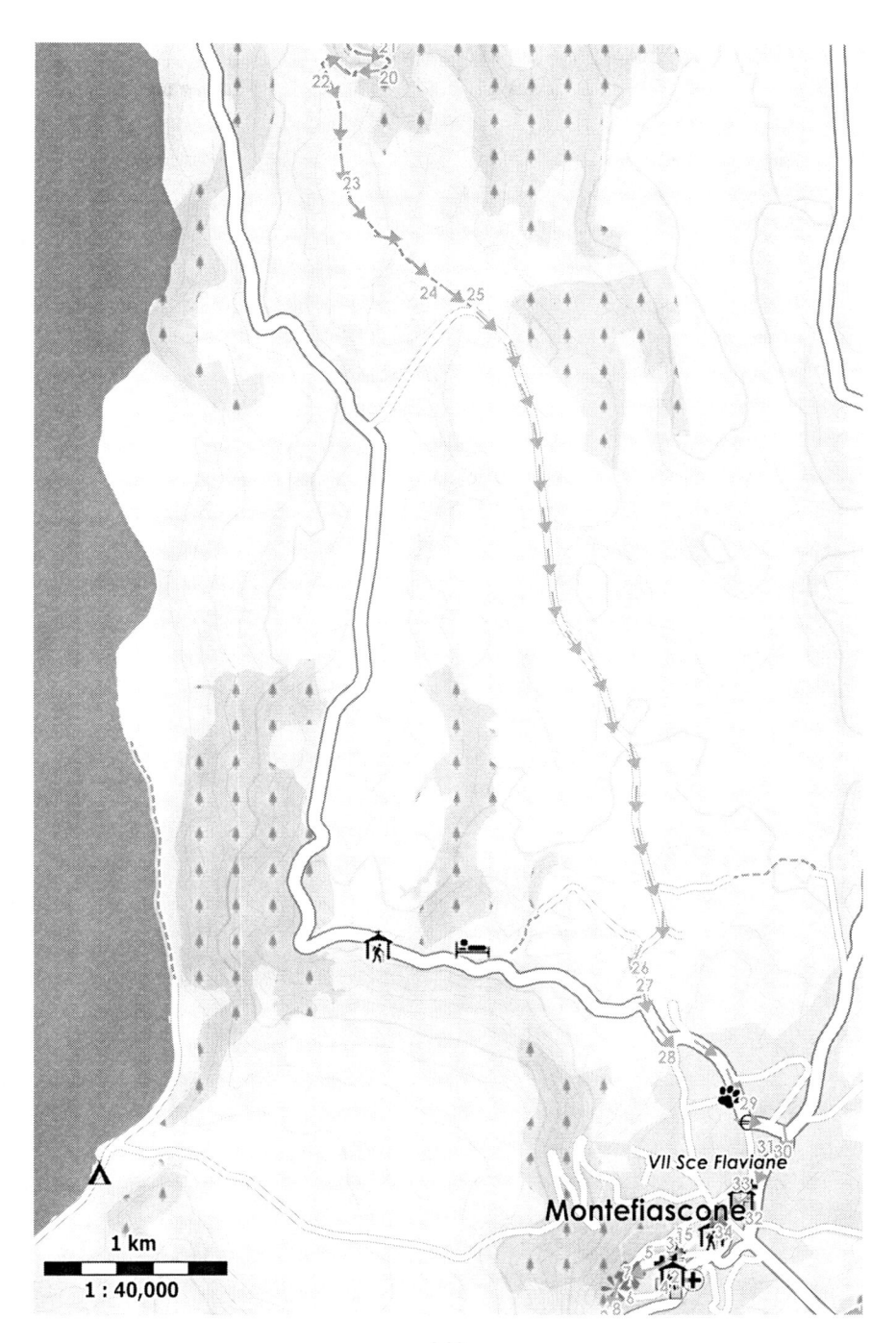

Montefiascone

1 km
1 : 40,000

Waypoint	Distance Between Waypoints (m)	Total (km)	Directions	Verification Point	Compass	Altitude (m)
89.025	300	11,0	At the junction with the road, continue straight ahead. Note:- the Ministry Route turns right to temporarily rejoin the busy via Cassia and add 1km to the section	Pilgrim milestone	S	461
89.026	3900	14,9	Keep left at the junction. Note:- the Ministry Route joins from the right	Stone VF sign	S	534
89.027	400	15,3	Turn left at the T-junction with the major road, direction Viterbo	Via Cassia, hotel on the left at the junction	SE	532
89.028	220	15,5	Turn left beside the modern office building	Towards Orvieto on via Cardinal Salotti	SE	536
89.029	700	16,2	Bear left	Towards Orvieto on via Santa Maria delle Grazie	E	546
89.030	230	16,4	At the junction with the SS71, turn right	Direction Viterbo	SW	533
89.031	210	16,6	Take the left fork	Trees lining the left side of the road	S	537
89.032	230	16,9	Turn right, uphill onto via San Flaviano	Keep church on your right	W	552
89.033	60	16,9	Bear left continuing uphill	High stone wall on your right	SW	558
89.034	130	17,0	Continue straight ahead across the road and up the ramp to enter the historic centre	Corso Cavour, pass through archway	SW	569
89.035	300	17,4	Arrive at Montefiascone (VII) centre	In piazza Vittorio Emanuele		603

Bolsena to Montefiascone 17.4km

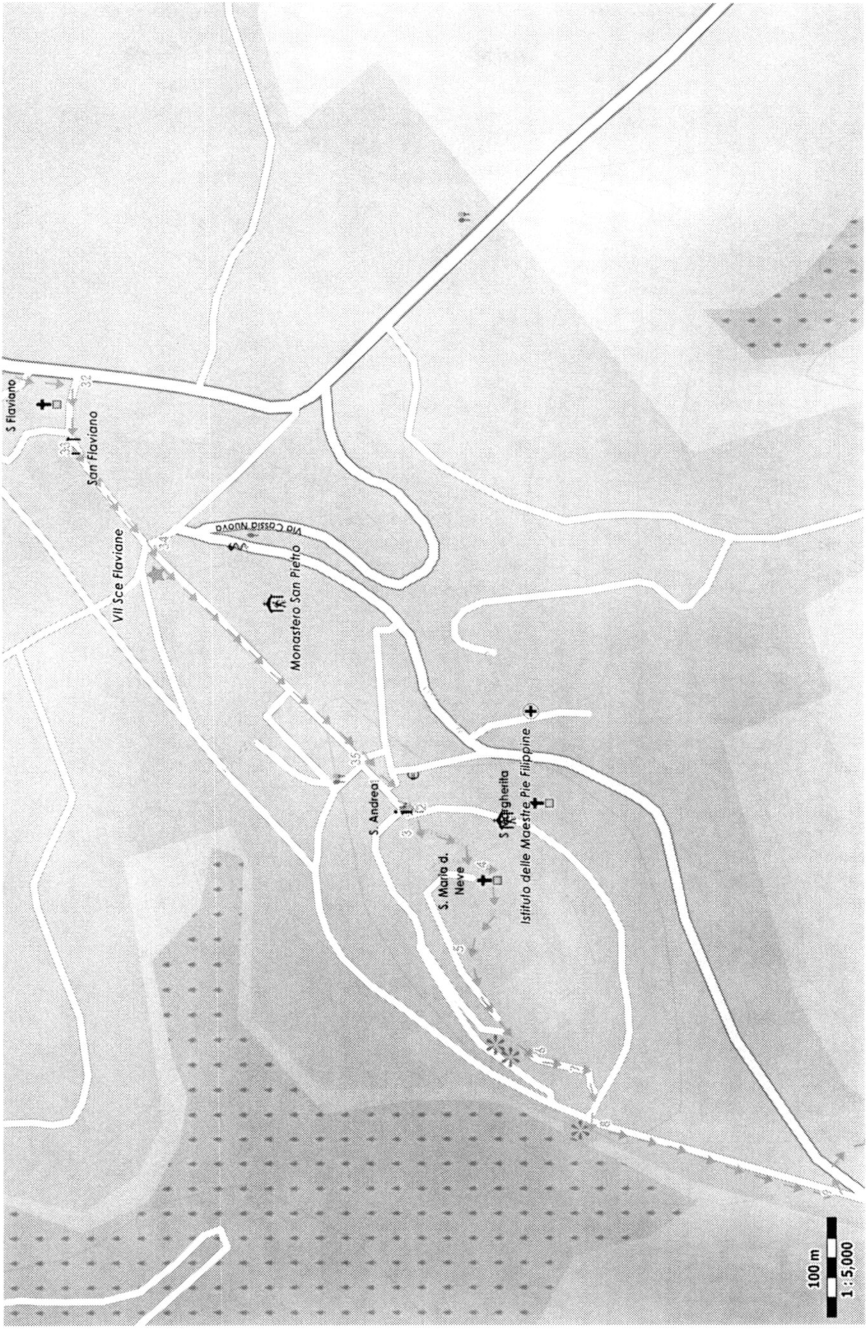
S Flaviano
San Flaviano
VII Sce Flaviane
Via Cassia Nuova
Monastero San Pietro
S. Andrea
S Margherita
Istituto delle Maestre Pie Filippine
S. Maria d. Neve
100 m
1 : 5,000

Stage Summary: the Alternate Route allows cyclists, riders and those not wishing to deal with additional hillside tracks to proceed on the generally level main road. The Alternate Route reduces total distance by 2.5km.

Stage Ascent: 90mStage Descent: 41m

Waypoint	Distance Between Waypoints (m)	Total (km)	Directions	Verification Point	Compass	Altitude (m)
89A1.001	0	0,0	Continue straight ahead and at the T-junction turn left onto the via Cassia. Note:- the via Cassia can be very busy, without pavements in some sections. Proceed with caution	Piazza Vittorio Emanuele	S	320
89A1.002	2600	2,6	Shortly after passing strada di Melona on the right, turn left onto the small tarmac road, uphill	VF sign	SE	319
89A1.003	600	3,2	After a long curve to the right the Main Route rejoins from the left and continues straight ahead	VF sign		367

Religious Hostel

Istituto delle Maestre Pie Filippine,Via Santa Lucia Filippini, 34,01027 Montefiascone(VT),Italy Tel:+39 0761 826088,Price:D,

Parrocchia Corpus Domini,(Don Giuseppe Fucili),Coste,01027 Montefiascone(VT),Italy Tel:+39 0761 826567,Price:D,

Convento dei Cappuccini,via San Francesco,3,Montefiascone Vt,Italy,(Padre Gianfranco),Via Cassia Nuova,01027 Montefiascone(VT),Italy Tel:+39 0761 820340,
Mobile:+39 0335 354799,
g.palmisani@tin.it,www.cappuccinilazio.com/viterbo/conventodimontefiascone,Price:C,

Monastero San Pietro,(Suor Clara),Via Garibaldi, 31,01027 Montefiascone(VT),Italy Tel:+39 0761 826066,Price:C,

Church or Religious Organisation

San Flaviano,(Don Luciano Trapè),01027 Montefiascone(VT),Italy Tel:+39 0761 826198,sanflavianom.mf@alice.it,

B&B, Hotel, Gite d'Etape

B&B Cassia Antica,Via Paoletti, 12,01027 Montefiascone(VT),Italy Mobile:+39 3493 408642,Price:B,

Francigena Arcobaleno,Via Pelucche, 10,01027 Montefiascone(VT),Italy Mobile:+39 3388 125427,Price:B,

Camping

Amalasunta,Via del Lago, 77,01027 Montefiascone(VT),Italy Tel:+39 0761 825294,

Tourist Information

Ufficio Turistico,Largo Plebiscito,01027 Montefiascone(VT),Italy Tel:+39 0761 820884,

Banks and ATMs

Banca Cooperativa Cattolica,Via Indipendenza, 4,01027 Montefiascone(VT),Italy Tel:+39 0761 824524,

Banca di Roma,Via Cardinal Salotti, 76,01027 Montefiascone(VT),Italy Tel:+39 0761 825798,

Hospital

Ospedale di Montefiascone,Via Donatori di Sangue,01027 Montefiascone(VT),Italy Tel:+39 0761 8331,

Doctor

Minciotti - Studio Medico,Via Verentana,01027 Montefiascone(VT),Italy Tel:+39 0761 824167,

Veterinary

Roncella - Medico Veterinario,Via Aldo Moro, 28,01027 Montefiascone(VT),Italy Tel:+39 0761 823056,

Stage Ninety Summary: the route descends and becomes easier on farm tracks and ancient roads. The Main Route passes thermal springs before entering the large town of Viterbo on very busy roads.
Distance from Canterbury: 1951km   Distance to Saint-Peter's-Square: 123km
Stage Ascent: 141m   Stage Descent: 392m

Waypoint	Distance Between Waypoints (m)	Total (km)	Directions	Verification Point	Compass	Altitude (m)
90.001	0	0,0	In piazza Vittorio Emanuele, continue straight ahead through the arch	Uphill, clock tower on the left	SW	606
90.002	30	0,1	Continue straight ahead up the steps - to avoid the steps, take via 24 Maggio to the left and rejoin the Main Route just before exiting the old town	Direction Rocca dei Papi	W	608
90.003	40	0,1	Turn left into the alley	Beside Tourist Office	SW	611
90.004	70	0,2	Enter the gardens and go straight ahead		W	616
90.005	120	0,3	Continue straight ahead through the gardens of Rocca dei Papi and descend on the steps before turning left	Pass beside the Torre del Pellegrino	SW	619
90.006	100	0,4	From the parking area behind la Rocca, keep right in the narrow street - via della Rocca	View of lake Bolsena to your right	S	614
90.007	80	0,5	At the T-junction, turn right	Towards the archway	W	608
90.008	60	0,5	Pass through the arch and turn left downhill	Town walls on your left	S	603
90.009	260	0,8	At the intersection with the busy SP8, turn left and immediately right, downhill on the unmade road	VF map and sign	SE	580
90.010	110	0,9	Take the left fork on the unmade road	Downhill	SE	571
90.011	800	1,7	At the crossroads, continue straight ahead, direction Viterbo	VF sign, towards pylons	SE	487

Montefiascone to Viterbo 18.1km

VII Sce Flaviane

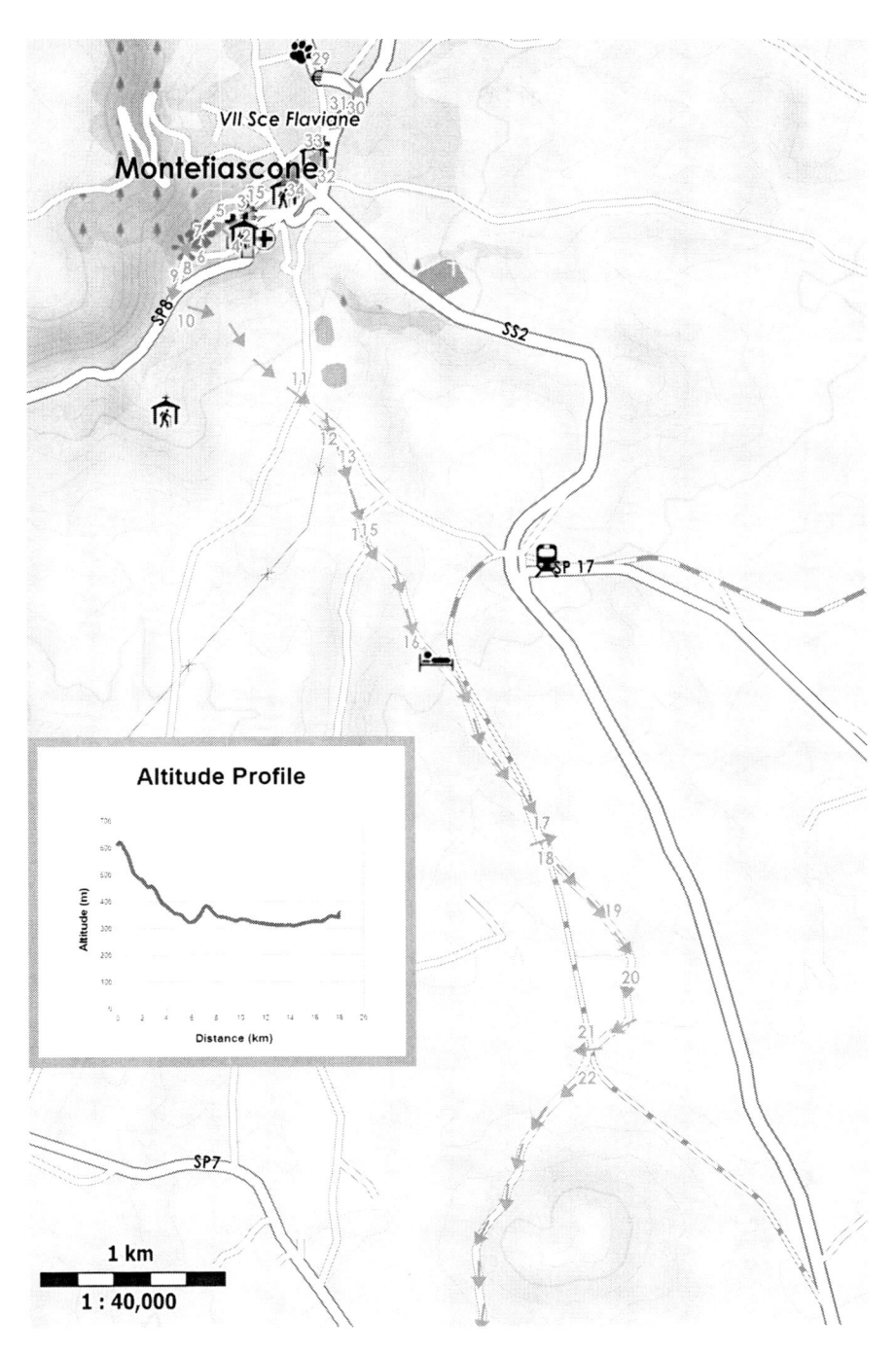

Montefiascone

Altitude Profile

1 km
1 : 40,000

Montefiascone to Viterbo 18.1km

Waypoint	Distance Between Waypoints (m)	Total (km)	Directions	Verification Point	Compass	Altitude (m)
90.012	210	1,9	Just after power substation, fork right onto a dirt track	VF milestone and VF sign	S	482
90.013	300	2,3	Bear left on the paved section	VF sign	S	467
90.014	240	2,5	Bear right	VF sign, olive grove on the left	S	454
90.015	200	2,7	Bear left onto the ancient paved road with a shrine directly to your right	VF sign	SE	453
90.016	500	3,2	Fork left down the hill	VF sign, via Paoletti	SE	436
90.017	1500	4,6	Turn left under the railway	VF sign	E	356
90.018	20	4,7	At the exit from the tunnel, turn right	Between the trees	SE	355
90.019	600	5,3	At the junction, continue straight ahead	VF signs	SE	346
90.020	190	5,5	Bear right to continue on the main track	VF signs	SW	337
90.021	700	6,1	Turn left after going under second railway tunnel	VF sign	S	321
90.022	40	6,2	Fork right remaining on the main track	VF sign painted on the electricity pole	S	321
90.023	2100	8,3	At crossroads with the major road (SP7), go straight ahead	VF sign, strada Casetta	S	341
90.024	500	8,8	At the crossroads in the track, continue straight ahead with farms on either side	VF sign	S	339
90.025	400	9,2	Fork left after passing the house on the right	VF sign	SE	332

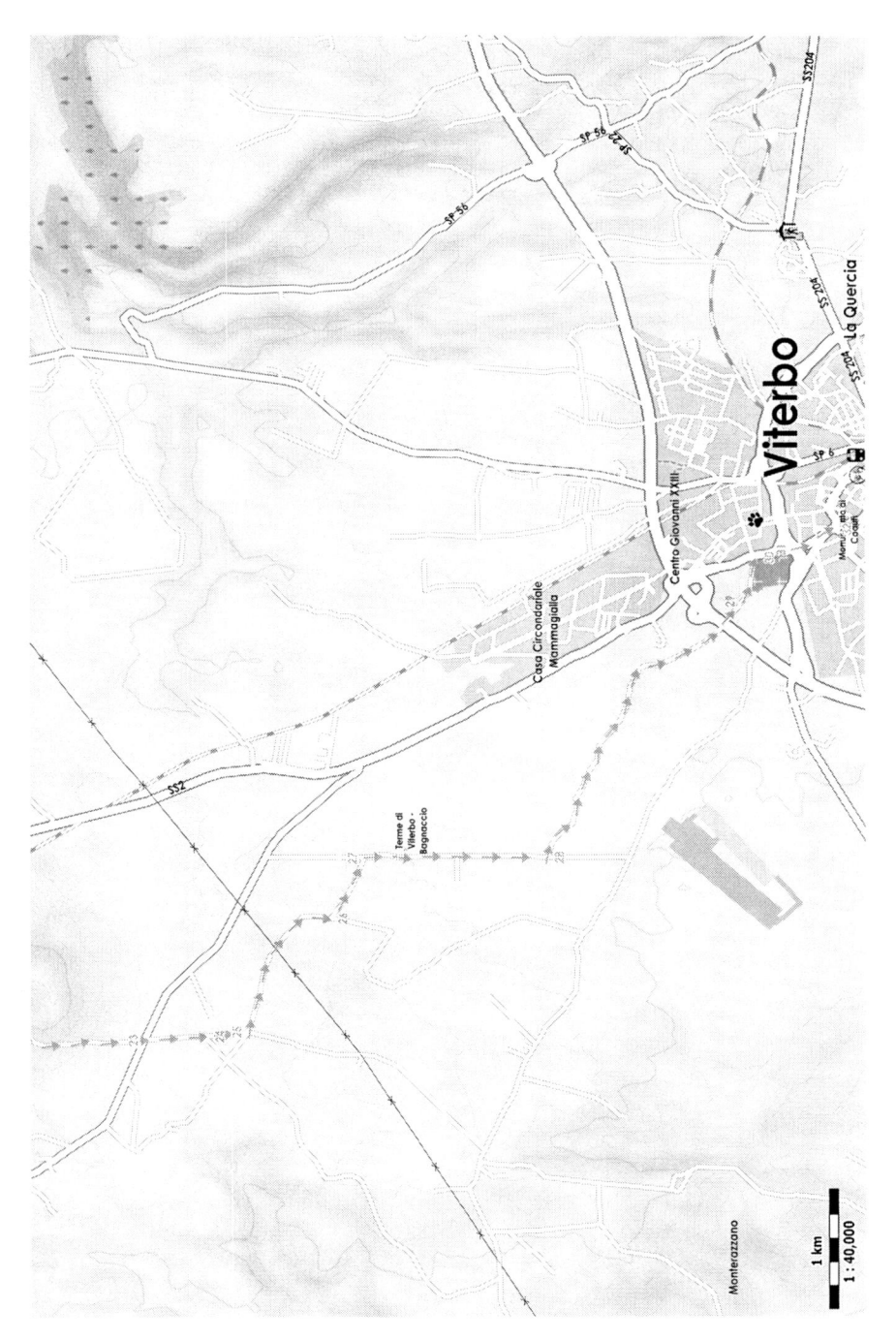

Waypoint	Distance Between Waypoints (m)	Total (km)	Directions	Verification Point	Compass	Altitude (m)
90.026	1300	10,5	Fork left beside a fence and a line of trees	VF sign	SE	330
90.027	600	11,1	At the T-junction in the tracks, turn right towards the thermal ponds	VF sign	S	320
90.028	1500	12,6	With metal gates to your right, turn left	VF sign	SE	311
90.029	2900	15,5	Track joins a tarmac road, continue straight ahead	VF sign, factory buildings on your right	E	319
90.030	400	15,9	At the T-junction, turn right onto strada Cassia Nord	VF sign and large cemetery on your right	S	323
90.031	400	16,2	Pass under the fly-over and continue straight ahead	No Entry, towards petrol station	SE	324
90.032	400	16,6	At the roundabout, continue straight ahead, towards Viterbo centre	Via della Palazzina, pass bank offices on the left	SE	322
90.033	800	17,3	Pass through the arched Porta Fiorentina into the old town of Viterbo and continue straight ahead	Via Matteotti, pass piazza della Rocca on the right	SE	342
90.034	400	17,7	Cross piazza Verdi and take the second right	Corso Italia, pass Banca di Roma on the right	SW	339
90.035	300	18,0	In piazza delle Erbe continue straight ahead	Via Roma, pass fountain on your left	SW	337
90.036	120	18,1	Arrive at Viterbo (VI) centre	Piazza del Plebiscito, beneath bell tower		354

Montefiascone to Viterbo 18.1km

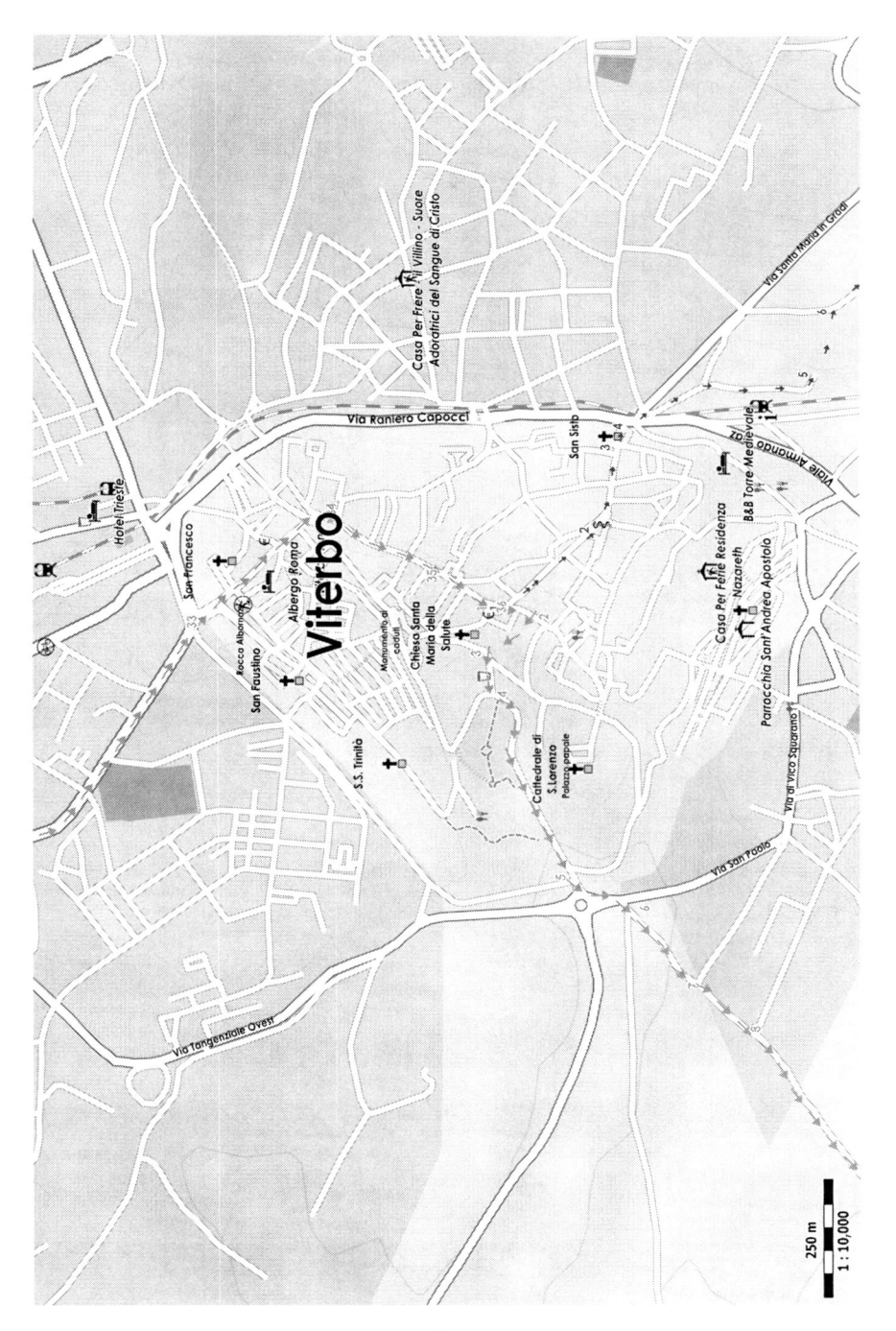
Viterbo
Via Raniero Capocci
Casa Per Ferie Il Villino - Suore Adoratrici del Sangue di Cristo
San Sisto
Viale Armando Diaz
B&B Torre Medievale
Casa Per Ferie Residenza Nazareth
Parrocchia Sant'Andrea Apostolo
Via Santa Maria in Gradi
Via di Vico Squarano
Via San Paolo
Cattedrale di S.Lorenzo
Palazzo papale
S.S. Trinità
Chiesa Santa Maria della Salute
Monumento ai caduti
Albergo Roma
Rocca Albornoz
San Faustino
San Francesco
Hotel Trieste
Via Tangenziale Ovest
250 m
1 : 10,000

Religious Hostel

Complesso Santa Maria della Quercia,Viale Fiume, 112,01100 Viterbo(VT),Italy Tel:+39 0761 321322,Price:B,

Casa Per Ferie Residenza Nazareth,Via San Tommaso, 26,01100 Viterbo(VT),Italy Tel:+39 76 1132 1525,info@residenzanazareth.it,www.residenzanazareth.it,Price:B,

Casa Per Frere - il Villino - Suore Adoratrici del Sangue di Cristo,Viale 4 Novembre, 25,01100 Viterbo(VT),Italy Tel:+39 0761 341900,Mobile:+39 3395 687389, www.ilvillinodiviterbo.it,Price:B,

Church or Religious Organisation

Parrocchia Sant'Andrea Apostolo,Via della Fontana,01100 Viterbo(VT),Italy Tel:+39 0761 347334,Mobile:+39 3398 783818,Price:D,

B&B, Hotel, Gite d'Etape

B&B Torre Medievale,Via delle Fortezze, 27,01100 Viterbo(VT),Italy Mobile:+39 3388 358534,Price:B,

Hotel Trieste,Via Nazario Sauro, 32,01100 Viterbo(VT),Italy Tel:+39 0761 341882,Price:B,

Albergo Roma,Via della Cava, 26,01100 Viterbo(VT),Italy Tel:+39 0761 227274,Price:B,

Viterbo Inn,Via San Luca, 17,01100 Viterbo(VT),Italy Tel:+39 0761 326643,Price:B,

Tourist Information

Azienda di Promozione Turistica,Via Maresciallo Mariano Romiti,01100 Viterbo(VT),Italy Tel:+39 0761 304795,

Banks and ATMs

Cassa di Risparmio di Viterbo,Piazza del Plebiscito, 1,01100 Viterbo(VT),Italy Tel:+39 0761 324848,

Cassa Risparmio di Civitavecchia,Via S.Bonaventura, 4,01100 Viterbo(VT),Italy Tel:+39 0761 30391,

Travel

Stazione Ferrovie,Viale Trieste,01100 Viterbo(VT),Italy Tel:+39 06 6847 5475,www.renitalia.it,

Hospital

Ospedale di Belcolle,Strada Sammartinese,01100 Viterbo(VT),Italy Tel:+39 0761 3391,

Doctor

Meschini - Studio Medico,Via delle Fabbriche,01100 Viterbo(VT),Italy Tel:+39 0761 223449,

Veterinary

Ambulatorio Veterinario,Via Igino Garbini, 81,01100 Viterbo(VT),Italy Tel:+39 0761 354581,

Hiking Equipment

Di Marco Sport,Piazza della Rocca,01100 Viterbo(VT),Italy Tel:+39 0761 220197,

Bicycle Shop

Ranaldi Moto e Cicli,Via Igino Garbini, 66,01100 Viterbo(VT),Italy Tel:+39 0761 340865,

Stage Ninety-one Summary: the Main Route route quickly leaves Viterbo and takes again to the country lanes avoiding the main roads. There is the opportunity to break the journey at Vetralla. The latter stages involve woodland tracks, before winding through hazel groves to the outskirts of Capranica. The Alternate Route, also chosen by pilgrims in the middle ages, is more direct (8km shorter) and passes the Cistercian Abbazia di San Martino al Cimino before following the rim of the volcano surrounding Lago di Vico.

Distance from Canterbury: 1969km   Distance to Saint-Peter's-Square: 105km

Stage Ascent: 419m   Stage Descent: 405m

Waypoint	Distance Between Waypoints (m)	Total (km)	Directions	Verification Point	Compass	Altitude (m)
91.001	0	0,0	From the piazza del Plebiscito bear left and leave the square on via San Lorenzo	Pass Tabacchi on your left	S	354
91.002	80	0,1	Turn right on the narrow street. Note:- to avoid a flight of steps, riders should continue to the next right turn, via Chigi, and then turn right again on via Sant'Antonio to rejoin the Main Route on via Faul	Via del Ganfione	NW	353
91.003	130	0,2	At the foot of the steps, turn left and immediately right	Via Faul	W	323
91.004	90	0,3	Bear left, remain on via Faul	Pass Palazzo dei Papi on the left	SW	315
91.005	500	0,8	Exit the old town by Porta Faul, turn left at the roundabout and take the first road to the right direction Podere dell' Arco	Strada Signorino, red and white VF sign	SW	296
91.006	140	0,9	Continue straight ahead on the road. Note:- the Ministry Route bears right and adds 1.5km to the journey, before returning to our Main Route	Stone wall on your left	SW	294
91.007	230	1,1	At the fork in the road keep to the right	VF sign, road continues between rock faces	SW	308
91.008	140	1,3	Take right fork	Strada Signorino	SW	312

Viterbo to Capranica 32.4km

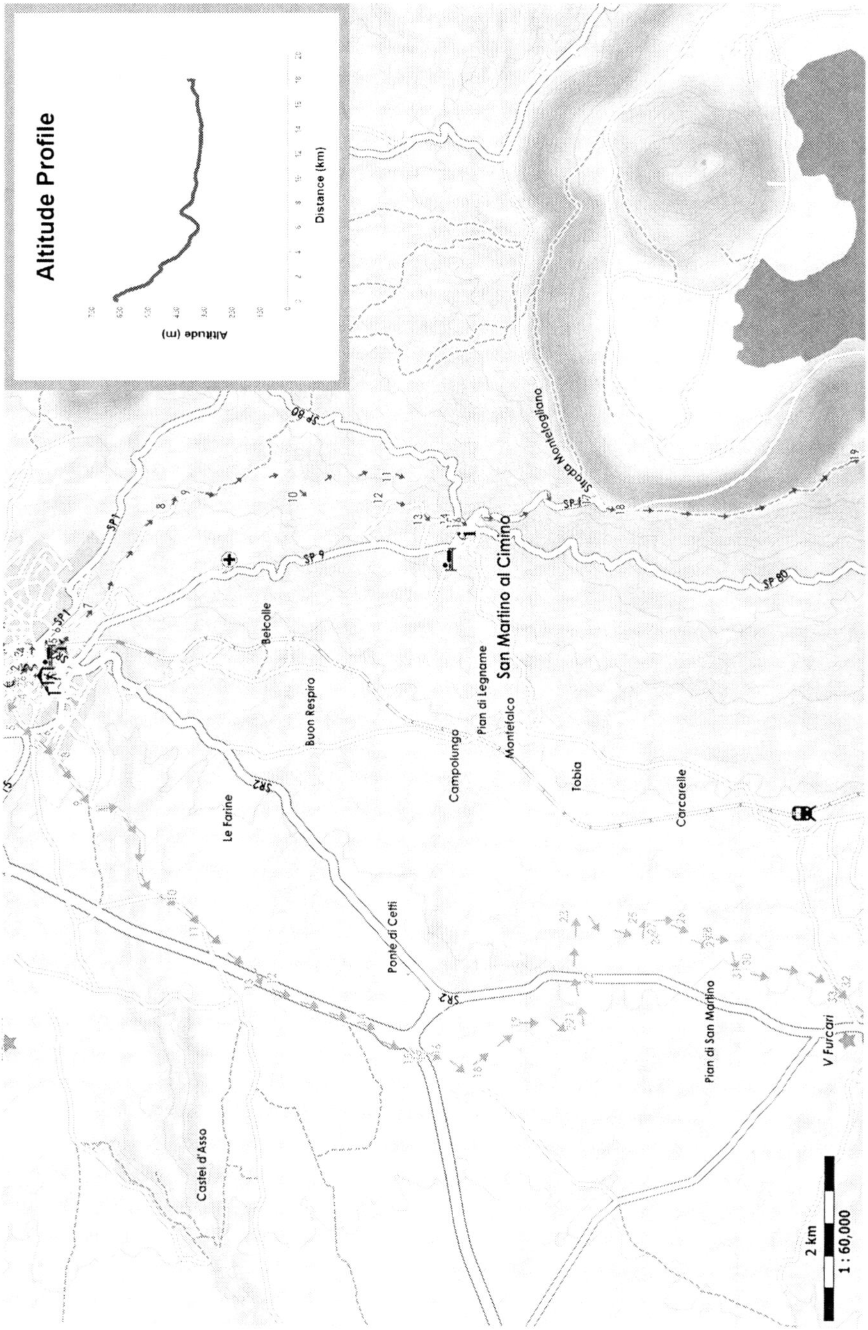
Altitude Profile
Altitude (m)
Distance (km)
San Martino al Cimino
Strada Montefogliano
SP 80
SP 9
SP1
SR2
Belcolle
Buon Respiro
Pian di Legname
Montefalco
Campolungo
Tobia
Carcarelle
Le Farine
Ponte di Cetti
Pian di San Martino
V Furcari
Castel d'Asso
2 km
1 : 60,000

Waypoint	Distance Between Waypoints (m)	Total (km)	Directions	Verification Point	Compass	Altitude (m)
91.009	800	2,0	At the crossroads, continue straight ahead	Between rock faces	SW	294
91.010	1600	3,6	Continue straight ahead	VF sign on the crash barrier	SW	263
91.011	700	4,3	Fork left onto the gravel track, strada Risiere	VF sign, shrine on the corner	SW	259
91.012	900	5,2	Take the right fork under the highway	VF sign painted on the concrete	W	244
91.013	80	5,3	Take the left fork	Track close and parallel to the main road	S	242
91.014	1100	6,4	At crossroads in track continue straight ahead with the main road remaining on your left. Note:- there are red and white signs that lead under the road and on towards the thermal ponds of Paliano. However, the signs quickly peter out. We advise those visiting the ponds to return here	Track close and parallel to the main road	SW	239
91.015	1100	7,5	After skirting the loop of the main road intersection, turn left to go under the road	Red and white VF sign painted on wall	E	228
91.016	140	7,6	At the T-junction in track, turn right	Strada Primomo	SW	230
91.017	140	7,7	At the junction, continue straight ahead on the tarmac	Multiple VF signs	SW	231
91.018	500	8,2	Turn left on the grassy track	VF sign	SE	233
91.019	1000	9,2	Bear right on the track	Uphill	S	276
91.020	400	9,6	Bear right	Pass trees on your left	S	294

Viterbo to Capranica 32.4km

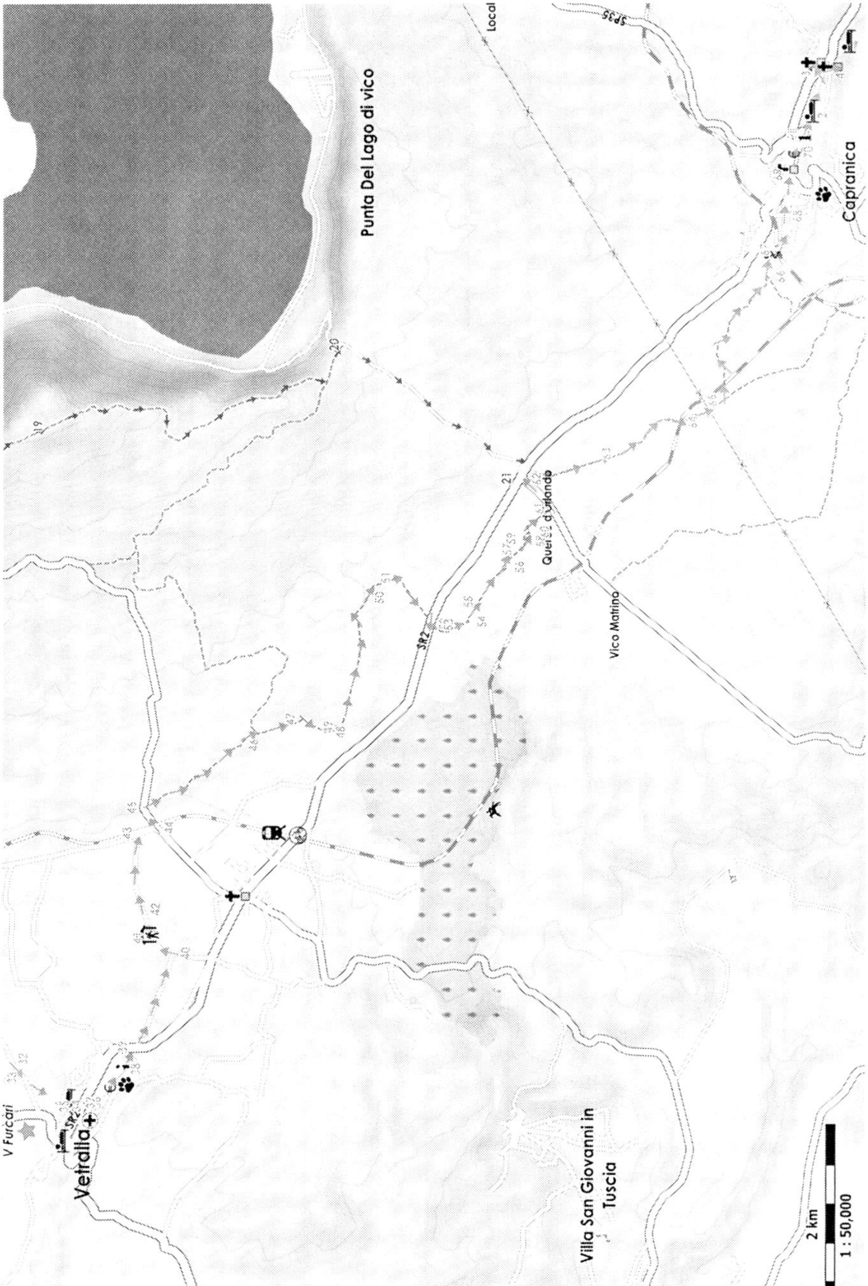
Punta Del Lago di vico
Vetralla
V Furcari
Villa San Giovanni in Tuscia
Capranica
Vico Mattina
SR2
SP35
Local
2 km
1 : 50,000

Waypoint	Distance Between Waypoints (m)	Total (km)	Directions	Verification Point	Compass	Altitude (m)
91.021	400	9,9	At the T-junction, turn left	Strada Quartuccio	E	300
91.022	500	10,4	At the junction, take the road bridge over the via Cassia and continue straight ahead	Strada Sasso San Pellegrino	E	313
91.023	800	11,2	Take the next turning to the right		S	340
91.024	900	12,0	At the T-junction, turn left on the road	Tree lined driveway ahead at the junction	E	325
91.025	260	12,3	Turn right on the track	Beside olive grove	S	333
91.026	270	12,5	Shortly after the track bends to the left turn sharp right on the path	Into the trees	W	328
91.027	130	12,7	Turn left on the track	Uphill	S	327
91.028	400	13,1	At the T-junction, turn right	Via Doganella	S	331
91.029	600	13,7	At the T-junction, turn right on the white road	Via Doganella	SW	315
91.030	280	13,9	At the junction, bear right	Via Doganella	SW	305
91.031	260	14,2	At the junction bear left on the road	Walled gardens on both sides at the junction	S	299
91.032	1100	15,3	At the T-junction, turn right on the pavement beside the road	Orchard on the right	SW	304
91.033	240	15,5	Take the left fork	Lower road between the trees	SW	300
91.034	500	16,0	At the crossroads, continue straight ahead into Vetralla (V)	Pass elevated road on your left	S	293
91.035	130	16,1	Bear left and then right	Cross piazza del Mattatoio	SE	298

Viterbo to Capranica 32.4km

Waypoint	Distance Between Waypoints (m)	Total (km)	Directions	Verification Point	Compass	Altitude (m)
91.036	50	16,2	At the traffic lights, continue straight ahead	Via della Pietà, town walls to the right	S	299
91.037	230	16,4	At the T-junction, turn left	Via Roma, cobbled street	SE	306
91.038	400	16,8	Shortly after the road bears right through piazza Marconi, take the left fork on the narrow road	Via San Michele, crucifix at the junction	SE	318
91.039	250	17,1	Take the subway to cross the via Cassia and continue straight ahead. Note:- to avoid the steps, turn right and then take the first turning to the left, via Dante Alighieri. Rejoin the Main Route by turning right at the crossroads	Via dei Cappuccini	E	322
91.040	1100	18,1	At the T-junction, turn left on via del Giardino	VF signs, Benedictine Monastery	NE	379
91.041	290	18,4	Bear right on the road	Pass olive grove on the left	E	381
91.042	300	18,7	At the junction, continue straight ahead on strada del Giardino	VF sign	E	385
91.043	800	19,5	At the T-junction turn right on the road	Railway track on your left	S	390
91.044	170	19,6	At the T-junction, turn left	Over railway crossing	NE	392
91.045	230	19,9	At the crossroads turn right across the car park onto the track towards the woods	Follow the edge of the woods with fields on the right	SE	398
91.046	1200	21,1	At the crossroads, continue straight ahead		SE	439
91.047	700	21,8	Turn right on the track towards Botte	Strada Pian della Botte	SW	437

Viterbo to Capranica 32.4km

Waypoint	Distance Between Waypoints (m)	Total (km)	Directions	Verification Point	Compass	Altitude (m)
91.048	270	22,0	Turn left uphill on the road	VF sign	S	433
91.049	160	22,2	At the top of the hill and before entering Botte, turn left onto a gravelled track into the woods	White arrow on a tree further along the track	E	440
91.050	1400	23,6	take the right fork, down the hill	VF sign on tree	SE	494
91.051	400	24,0	At the T-junction turn right	VF sign	SW	484
91.052	600	24,6	At the intersection with the via Cassia, turn right and immediately left down a small track. Note:- the path ahead crosses cultivated hazel nut groves and may make for difficult going for cyclists who can turn left on the via Cassia to rejoin the Main Route at the Vico Marino junction	VF signs, pass disused chapel on your left	S	468
91.053	400	24,9	At a large stone go straight ahead between the trees	Broken fence to the right	S	463
91.054	100	25,0	At the end of the fence, turn left and immediately right	Parallel to the via Cassia	SE	464
91.055	270	25,3	At the T-junction turn left on the unmade road and immediately right through the gate	Continue across the fields parallel to the main road	SE	469
91.056	500	25,7	Turn left on the track and then immediately right	Beside hazel grove	SE	470
91.057	240	26,0	Continue straight ahead across the track		SE	470

Viterbo to Capranica 32.4km

267

Viterbo to Capranica 32.4km

Waypoint	Distance Between Waypoints (m)	Total (km)	Directions	Verification Point	Compass	Altitude (m)
91.058	120	26,1	Turn left	Beside the hazel grove	NE	468
91.059	50	26,1	Turn right		SE	468
91.060	110	26,2	Turn sharp left and then right and right again beside the earthworks	Continue parallel to the main road	SE	469
91.061	400	26,6	At the T-junction with a broad tarmac, road turn left	Open field on your right	NE	477
91.062	400	27,1	Just before reaching the via Cassia turn sharp right onto the unmade road. Note:- Alternate Route rejoins from the via Cassia ahead	Carved wooden VF sign	S	482
91.063	1000	28,1	At the crossroads in track continue straight ahead on strada Doganale Oriolese		SE	466
91.064	800	28,8	Cross over railway and continue straight ahead	VF sign and hazelnut grove on the left	SE	451
91.065	600	29,4	Turn left to pass through the tunnel under railway track		E	445
91.066	1500	30,9	At the T-junction in the tracks, turn left	VF sign and crash barriers to your right	E	405
91.067	300	31,2	After passing through a tunnel under the railway, continue straight ahead	Enter Capranica, via Valle Santi	E	400
91.068	400	31,5	At the crossroads, continue straight over on the Antica strada della Valle Santi	VF sign	E	391
91.069	400	32,0	At the Stop sign, turn left down the hill	High wall to the left	E	382
91.070	250	32,2	At the T-junction, turn right on via Nardini	Elevated road on the left	SE	381
91.071	220	32,4	Arrive at Capranica	Archway ahead		369

Stage Summary: the Alternate Route via San Martino al Cimino and Lago di Vico follows minor roads and woodland tracks to reach the rim of the volcano, before returning to the Main Route on a quiet minor road.

Stage Ascent: 656m   Stage Descent: 507m

Waypoint	Distance Between Waypoints (m)	Total (km)	Directions	Verification Point	Compass	Altitude (m)
91A1.001	0	0,0	From the piazza del Plebiscito take via Cavour	No Entry	SE	336
91A1.002	250	0,3	In piazza Fontana Grande, bear left on via Garibaldi	Pass to the left of the fountain	E	348
91A1.003	190	0,4	Cross piazza S. Sisto and exit the old town through the archway	Porta Romana	SE	357
91A1.004	50	0,5	At the traffic lights cross the main road and then bear right on the small road, via San Biele	Railway on your right	S	357
91A1.005	500	0,9	Continue straight ahead up the hill	Pass through the archway of Torre di S. Biele	E	359
91A1.006	150	1,1	At the Stop sign, take the pedestrian crossing, turn right and follow the pavement beside the main road	Tree lined road	SE	369
91A1.007	500	1,6	As the main road bears right, keep left on strada Roncone	Map on the left	SE	383
91A1.008	1600	3,2	Continue straight ahead, avoid left fork	Fence and metal gate on the right	SE	470
91A1.009	400	3,5	At the end of the road, bear right on the pathway into the woods	VF sign	S	491
91A1.010	1600	5,1	At the crossroads, turn left	Clearing on the right	S	540
91A1.011	1300	6,4	Bear right on the track		W	612
91A1.012	300	6,8	At the junction with the tarmac road, take the middle road, straight ahead	Yellow arrow on electricity pole to the right	SW	584
91A1.013	700	7,4	At the T-junction, turn left	Uphill into San Martino al Cimino	S	575

Alternate Route #91.A1 19.7km

269

Alternate Route #91.A1 19.7km

Waypoint	Distance Between Waypoints (m)	Total (km)	Directions	Verification Point	Compass	Altitude (m)
91A1.014	300	7,7	Take the right fork	Strada Montagna on the left	SW	583
91A1.015	100	7,8	Bear left	Direction Roma	S	579
91A1.016	80	7,9	Turn left. Note:- archway to Abbazia di San Martino al Cimino on the right	Direction Riserva Naturale Lago di Vico	S	580
91A1.017	2000	9,9	At the T-junction, turn right	Direction Ronciglione, shrine on the left	S	740
91A1.018	500	10,4	As the road bends to the left, bear right on the unmade road	Milestone at the junction	S	742
91A1.019	3100	13,5	At the crossroads, continue straight ahead	Continue through woodland on volcano rim	S	908
91A1.020	3900	17,3	At the junction with the tarmac road, turn right	Farm ahead	SW	623
91A1.021	2400	19,7	At the T-junction with the via Cassia, turn left and immediately right, then bear left on the unmade road. Rejoin Main Route	Signpost Vico Matrino, VF signs		484

Religious Hostel

Suore Francescane "oasi di Pace",Via delle Viole, 15,01015 Sutri(VT),Italy
Tel:+39 0761 659175,info@oasidipace.it,www.oasidipace.it,Price:B,

Monastero delle Benedettine Regina Pacis,Via del Giardino,01019 Vetralla(VT),Italy
Tel:+39 0761 481519,accoglienza@casareginapacis.com,Price:B,

Monastero Santissima Concezione,Via Garibaldi, 1,01015 Sutri(VT),Italy
Tel:+39 0761 609082,carmelo.s.concezione@libero.it,Price:B,

B&B, Hotel, Gite d'Etape

Sala Nardini,Piazza Corte Degli Anguillara,01012 Capranica(VT),Italy
Tel:+39 76 1667 9171,capranicasegreteria@hotmail.com,Price:D,

Hotel Alpino Solitario,Via Cassia, 299,01019 Vetralla(VT),Italy Tel:+39 0761 481045,Price:B,

Albergol Doria,Via Abate Lamberto, 4,01100 Viterbo(VT),Italy Tel:+39 0761 379924,Price:B,

Da Benedetta,Via Francesco Petrarca, 3,01019 Vetralla(VT),Italy
Tel:+39 0761 460093,Price:B,

B&B, Hotel, Gite d'Etape

B&B Monticelli,Località Monticelli, 1,01012 Capranica(VT),Italy Tel:+39 0761 678270,Price:B,

Hotel Sutrium,Piazza San Francesco, 1,01015 Sutri(VT),Italy Tel:+39 0761 600468,Price:B,

Equestrian

Centro Equitazione di Campagna le Valli,Strada Orto Rosato,01019 Vetralla(VT),Italy Mobile:+39 3313 685178,

Tourist Information

Comune di Sutri,Piazza del Comune, 34,01015 Sutri(VT),Italy Tel:+39 0761 609368,

Ufficio Turistico,Piazzale delle Rimembranze, 1,01012 Capranica(VT),Italy Tel:+39 0761 669364,

Ufficio Turistico,Via Cassia Sutrina,01019 Vetralla(VT),Italy Tel:+39 0761 460475,

Azienda di Promozione Turistica,Piazza Dell'Oratorio,01100 Viterbo(VT),Italy Tel:+39 0761 379233,

Banks and ATMs

Cassa di Risparmio di Viterbo,San Martino al Cimino,01100 Viterbo(VT),Italy Tel:+39 0761 379911,

Banco di Brescia,Via Roma, 21,01019 Vetralla(VT),Italy Tel:+39 0761 477025,www.bancodibrescia.it,

Cassa di Risparmio di Viterbo,Viale Nardini,01012 Capranica(VT),Italy Tel:+39 0761 669004,

Cassa di Risparmio di Viterbo,Piazza del Comune, 8,01015 Sutri(VT),Italy Tel:+39 0761 600014,

Hospital

Guardia Medica,Via Cassia Interna, 153,01019 Vetralla(VT),Italy Tel:+39 0761 461242,www.asl.vt.it,

Doctor

Fontana - Studio Medico,Via Orazio Morone,01015 Sutri(VT),Italy Tel:+39 0761 608616,

Salza - Studio Medico,Via Cassia,01012 Capranica(VT),Italy Tel:+39 0761 669083,

Veterinary

Piferi - Studio Veterinario,Viale Laura, 75,01012 Capranica(VT),Italy Tel:+39 0761 669922,

Servizio Veterinario,Via Etruria, 2,01019 Vetralla(VT),Italy Tel:+39 0761 477742,

Ambulatorio Veterinario,Via di Ronciglione, 23,01015 Sutri(VT),Italy Mobile:+39 3394 632429,

Bicycle Shop

Vittorio Bike di Principi Vittorio,Via Cassia In frazione la Botte,01019 Vetralla(VT),Italy Tel:+39 0761 480002,

Stage Summary: the route proceeds generally on farm tracks and minor roads with short sections on the via Cassia and strade provinciali. The route passes through the park surrounding the archaeological site at Sutri.

Distance from Canterbury: 2002km   Distance to Saint-Peter's-Square: 72km

Stage Ascent: 300m   Stage Descent: 394m

Waypoint	Distance Between Waypoints (m)	Total (km)	Directions	Verification Point	Compass	Altitude (m)
92.001	0	0,0	Go straight ahead through the archway into the old town	Towards clock tower	E	368
92.002	200	0,2	Continue straight ahead. Note:- the route ahead involves a flight of steps, cyclists and riders should turn left and follow via Romana to just before the T-junction	Ponte dell'Orolgio	E	364
92.003	500	0,7	After passing through the centro historico, descend on the steps and turn right	Beside the town wall	S	332
92.004	130	0,8	At the junction with the via Romana turn left and immediately right onto a track, strade Pogliere	VF sign, factory on your left as you turn right	S	329
92.005	1000	1,8	Bear right remaining on the main track		SW	358
92.006	300	2,1	At the T-junction with a tarmac road, turn left onto strade Capranichese	Hazel grove on the left	E	364
92.007	1700	3,8	At fork, bear right remaining on the main road	VF sign	E	332
92.008	1400	5,2	Shortly before reaching the via Cassia on the approach to Sutri take the footpath to the right	Bridge over stream on the left	SE	282
92.009	400	5,5	Pass a gate and turn left on the road	Strada Capo Ripa	NE	270
92.010	250	5,8	At the T-junction, turn right to skirt Sutri (IV) on the via Cassia	Pass town walls on your left	E	275
92.011	200	6,0	Beside the park, turn right	Towards the Mithraeum	S	278

Capranica - Campagno-di-Roma 29.7km

273

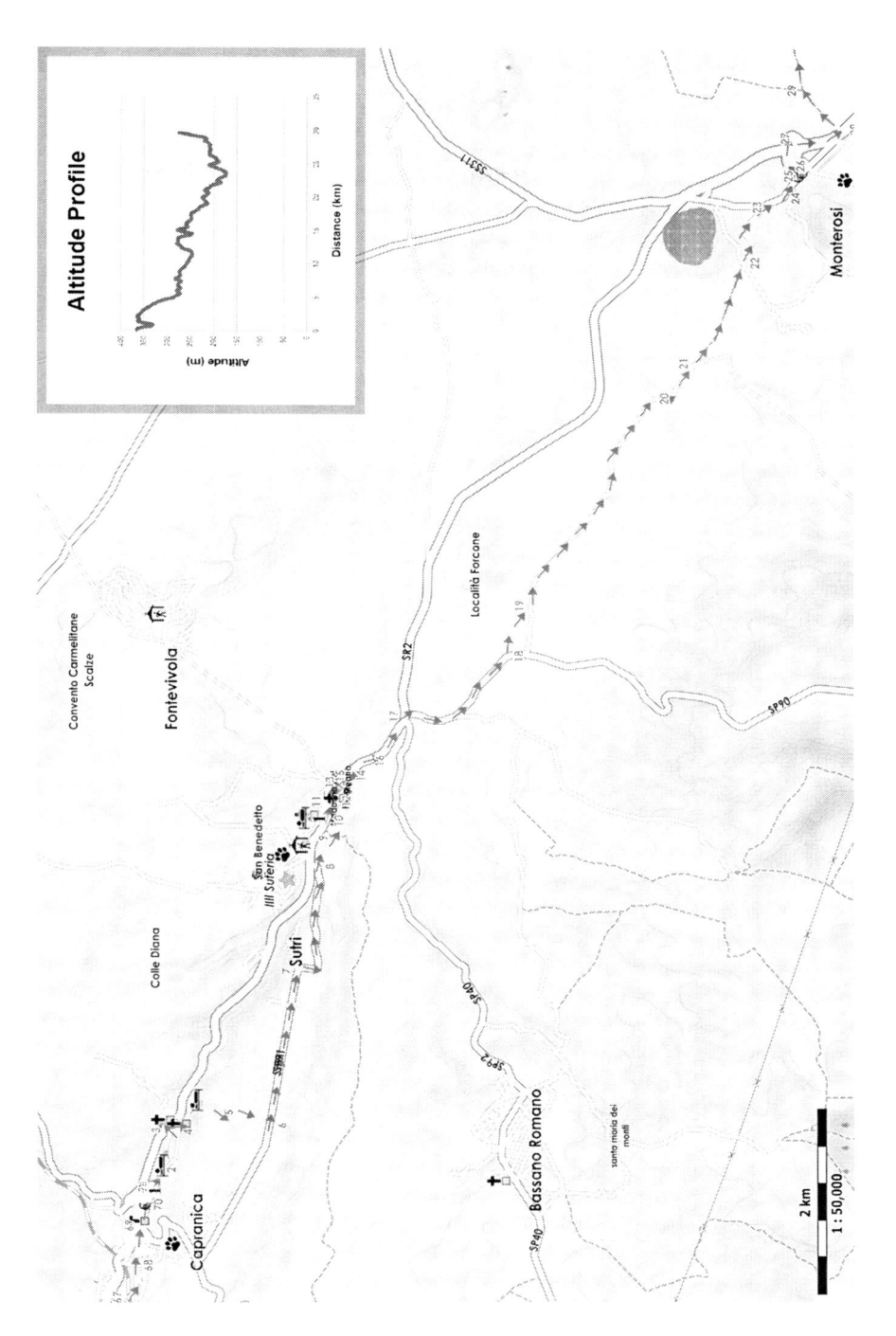

Waypoint	Distance Between Waypoints (m)	Total (km)	Directions	Verification Point	Compass	Altitude (m)
92.012	70	6,0	In front of the Mithraeum turn left on the footpath	Pass beside the excavations in the volcanic rock	E	278
92.013	240	6,3	Continue straight ahead on the footpath	Amphitheatre on the right	SE	271
92.014	120	6,4	Turn right	Over the bridge	S	270
92.015	40	6,4	Turn left, downhill through the trees	Towards the via Cassia	SE	270
92.016	240	6,7	At the junction with the via Cassia, bear right and proceed straight ahead with care	Pass cemetery sign on the left	SE	275
92.017	700	7,3	Take the second turning to the right	SP90, direction Bracciano	SE	269
92.018	1400	8,7	On the apex of a bend to the right, turn left on the broad track	Strada Campo la Pera	SE	273
92.019	700	9,4	At the T-junction, turn left		SE	265
92.020	2700	12,0	At the T-junction, turn right to skirt the golf course on strada per Monterosi	Pass golf academy entrance on your left	SE	250
92.021	700	12,7	At the fork, bear left on the unmade road, remain beside the golf course	VF sign	SE	270
92.022	1200	13,9	At the crossroads, continue straight ahead	Via strada Sutri Vecchia	SE	274
92.023	800	14,7	Continue straight ahead through the car park and up the hill	Elevated road on the left	SE	253
92.024	170	14,9	Continue straight ahead on the main road, via XIII Settembre	Towards the centre of Monterosi	SE	265
92.025	300	15,2	In piazza Garibaldi, turn left	Pass fountain on your right	NE	275

Capranica - Campagno-di-Roma 29.7km

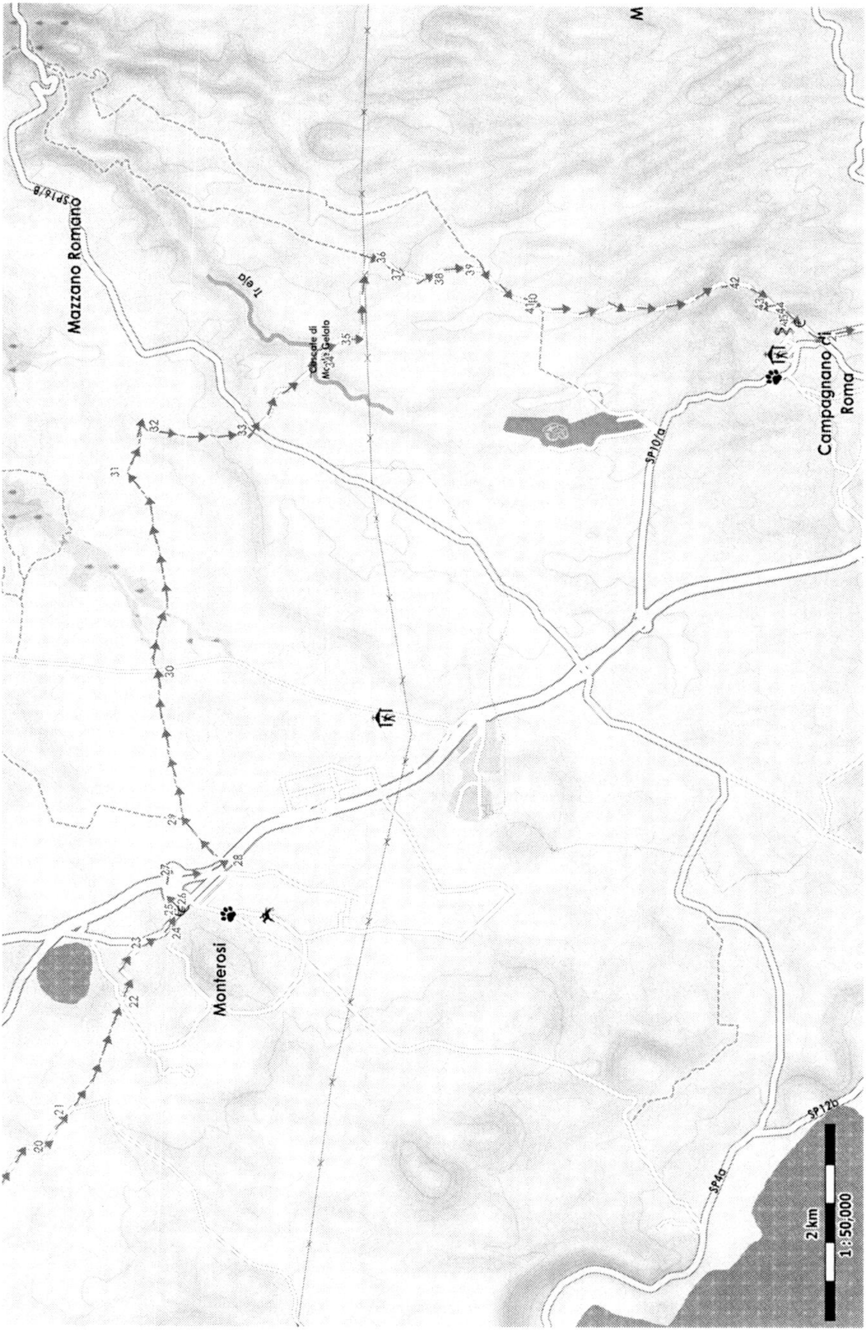
Mazzano Romano
SP16/B
Cascate di Monte Gelato
Monterosi
Campagnano di Roma
SP10/a
SP12b
SP4a
2 km
1 : 50,000

Waypoint	Distance Between Waypoints (m)	Total (km)	Directions	Verification Point	Compass	Altitude (m)
92.026	170	15,4	Bear right with care on the main road	Bridge over dual-carriageway	E	265
92.027	400	15,8	Bear left on the footpath	dual carriageway	S	256
92.028	500	16,3	Turn left on the small road		NE	255
92.029	600	16,9	Take the right fork	House driveway on the right	E	246
92.030	1600	18,4	Cross over the road (SP38) and continue straight ahead	Pass wire fence on the left	E	230
92.031	2200	20,6	At the T-junction turn right		E	210
92.032	500	21,1	At the T-junction, turn sharp right	Signpost via Ronci on the left	S	218
92.033	1200	22,3	At the crossroads with the SP37, continue straight ahead into Parco Regionale Valle del Treja	Strada Monte Gelato, sign Cascate Monte Gelato	SE	185
92.034	1100	23,3	Shortly after crossing the bridge turn left on strada Monte Gelato	Pass Cascate Monte Gelato on the left	SE	172
92.035	600	23,9	Take the left fork on strada Monte Gelato	Exposed rock face on the left	E	176
92.036	900	24,7	At the T-junction, turn right	Direction strada vicinale Bottagone	SW	208
92.037	500	25,2	Take the right fork	Strada vicinale Bottagone	S	191
92.038	170	25,4	Take the left fork	Towards the houses	S	188
92.039	600	26,0	At the T-junction, turn right		SW	196
92.040	500	26,5	Take the right fork	Beside farm building	S	208
92.041	220	26,7	Bear left and continue straight ahead	Towards Parci di Veio	S	208
92.042	1900	28,6	Bear right towards the town	Via Santa Lucia	SW	218
92.043	600	29,2	Bear right onto the ramp leading up to the town		NW	238
92.044	150	29,4	At the T-junction, turn left on the main street through the high town - via Sant'Andrea	Pass bell tower on the left	SW	248
92.045	300	29,7	Arrive at Campagno-di-Roma	Beside the church, piazza Cesare Leonelli		273

Capranica - Campagno-di-Roma 29.7km

Religious Hostel

Parrocchia San Giovanni Battista,Via Dante Alighieri, 7,00063 Campagnano-di-Roma(RM),Italy Tel:+39 06 9015 4333,
Mobile:+39 3339 381576,donrenzotanturli@virgilio.it,Price:D,

Convento Suore Missionarie della Consolata - Sette Vene,Via Cassia Km.37 Località Settevene,01036 Nepi(VT),Italy Tel:+39 0761 527253,fulviarob@tiscali.it
,www.consolazione.org,Price:C,

Suore Francescane "oasi di Pace",Via delle Viole, 15,01015 Sutri(VT),Italy
Tel:+39 0761 659175,info@oasidipace.it,www.oasidipace.it,Price:B,

B&B, Hotel, Gite d'Etape

Hotel Sutrium,Piazza San Francesco, 1,01015 Sutri(VT),Italy Tel:+39 0761 600468,Price:B,

Equestrian

Poscolieri - Agriturismo Centro Ippico,Via del Fontanile,01030 Monterosi(VT),Italy
Tel:+39 0761 699431,

Tourist Information

Comune di Sutri,Piazza del Comune, 34,01015 Sutri(VT),Italy Tel:+39 0761 609368,

Banks and ATMs

Cassa di Risparmio di Viterbo,Piazza del Comune, 8,01015 Sutri(VT),Italy
Tel:+39 0761 600014,

Banca di Formello,Via Roma, 50,01030 Monterosi(VT),Italy Tel:+39 0761 698012,

Banco di Brescia,Via Roma, 36,01030 Monterosi(VT),Italy Tel:+39 0761 699007,

Banca di Roma,Via Roma, 23,00063 Campagnano-di-Roma(RM),Italy Tel:+39 06 9015 1147,

Doctor

Picalarga - Studio Medico,Via Salvo d'Acquisto, 3,00063 Campagnano-di-Roma(RM),Italy
Tel:+39 06 9042 281,

Veterinary

Clinica Veterinaria Cavalli,Strada Valle di Baccano, 80,00063 Campagnano-di-Roma(RM),Italy Tel:+39 06 9015 4681,

Limonta Fabio,Via strada Nuova, 2,01030 Monterosi(VT),Italy Tel:+39 0761 699703,

Nori - Ambulatorio Veterinario,Via del Pavone, 139a,00063 Campagnano-di-Roma(RM),Italy
Tel:+39 06 9042 867,

Stage Ninety-three Summary: despite the proximity to Rome this section remains surprisingly rural on farm and woodland tracks and small roads. There are some tricky descents and climbs between Monte Michele and Isola Farnese with a potentially dangerous river crossing.

Distance from Canterbury: 2031km   Distance to Saint-Peter's-Square: 43km

Stage Ascent: 374m   Stage Descent: 482m

Waypoint	Distance Between Waypoints (m)	Total (km)	Directions	Verification Point	Compass	Altitude (m)
93.001	0	0,0	From the church in piazza Cesare Leonelli, continue straight ahead on the main street	Towards the arch, Corso Vittorio Emanuele, No Entry	SW	274
93.002	290	0,3	Pass through the arch and turn left in piazza Regina Elena	Towards Formello, via San Sebastiano	S	284
93.003	900	1,2	On the Apex of a sharp bend to the left, continue straight ahead on the more minor road - via di Maria Bona	Pass sports ground on the right	SE	318
93.004	300	1,5	Turn right up the hill on strada di Follettino	Painted sign on kerb	SE	352
93.005	180	1,7	Turn sharp right up the hill on via di Monte Razzano	Woodland on the right	SW	363
93.006	240	2,0	Take the left fork - strada delle Piane	House with roof terrace on the left at the junction	S	376
93.007	230	2,2	Take the right fork on the unmade road - strada delle Piane	VF sign	S	378
93.008	1100	3,3	At the T-junction, turn left - strada delle Pastine	VF sign	SE	281
93.009	500	3,8	Take the left fork on the tarmac road - strada del Sorbo	VF sign painted on electricity pole	SE	266
93.010	1600	5,4	Continue straight ahead on the road into the Valle del Sorbo	Pass the Santuario della Madonna del Sorbo on the left	S	210
93.011	1100	6,5	Cross the bridge and continue straight ahead	Uphill, towards the trees	S	188
93.012	1300	7,8	On entering Formello, bear right and right again	VF sign, via Antonio Angelozzi	S	269

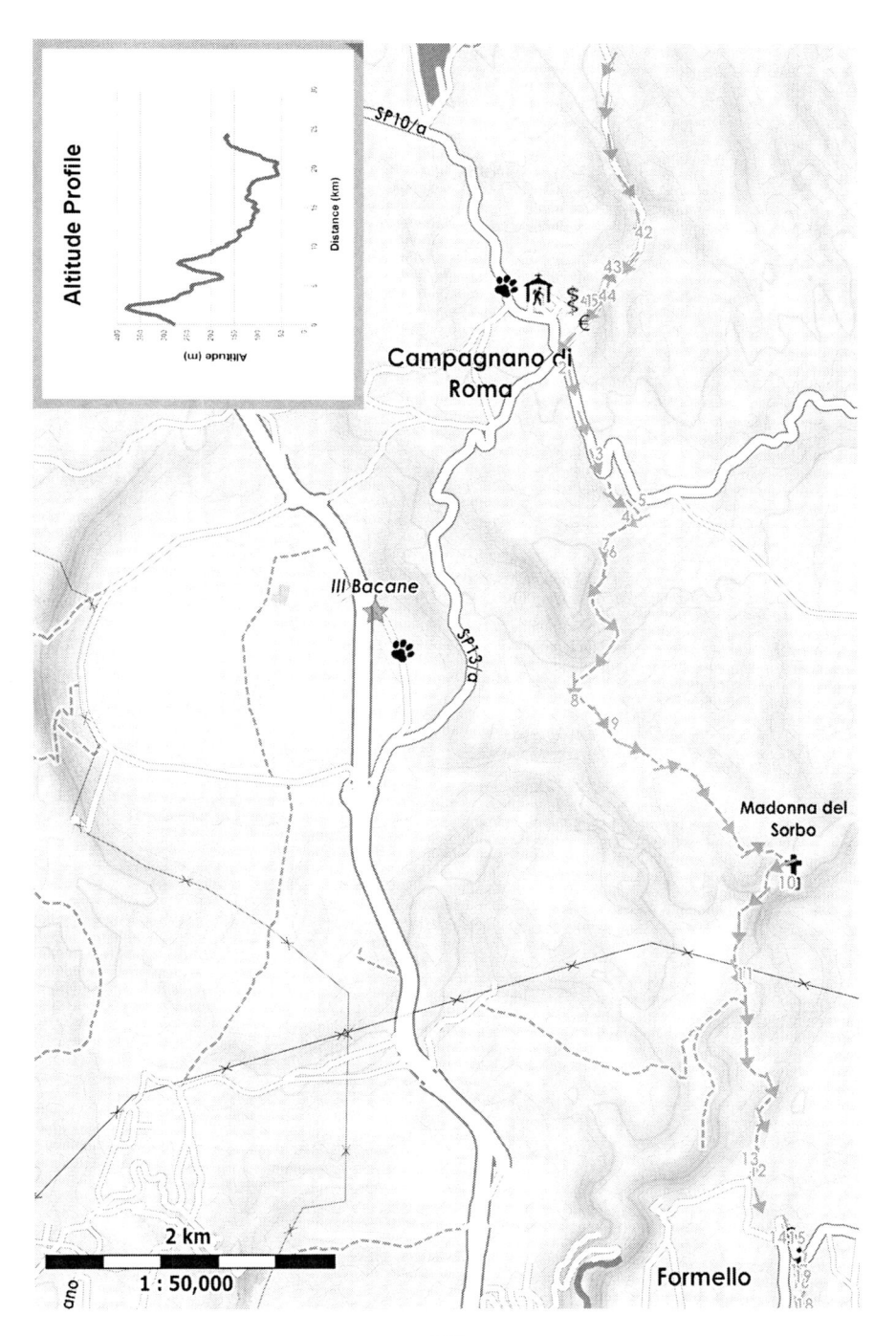

Waypoint	Distance Between Waypoints (m)	Total (km)	Directions	Verification Point	Compass	Altitude (m)
93.013	190	8,0	Take the left fork on the narrow road - via Enrico Bellomi	Downhill, No Entry	SE	265
93.014	400	8,4	At the crossroads, continue straight ahead	Pass house N°132 on the left	SE	239
93.015	300	8,7	In the centre of Formello, bear right across the piazza	Pass through archway	SE	222
93.016	70	8,8	On entering the historical centre of Formello, bear left and then turn right on via 20 Settembre	Pass church of San Lorenzo on your left	S	218
93.017	190	9,0	At the end of the road, bear left down the cobbled street		E	205
93.018	60	9,0	At the T-junction with the main road, turn right downhill	Viale Regina Elena	S	202
93.019	70	9,1	At the foot of the hill, bear left on the small road	Pass car park on your right	S	199
93.020	400	9,5	Take the right fork on the unmade road	Follow valley	S	193
93.021	600	10,1	Turn left, through trees	Pass open field on the right	S	163
93.022	1200	11,3	Turn left		E	137
93.023	700	12,0	At the crossroads, turn right		S	140
93.024	1100	13,1	At the T-junction, turn sharp right	VF sign	NW	112
93.025	170	13,3	Turn left	Via del Selvotta	S	112
93.026	800	14,1	After crossing the bridge over the highway, keep right	Via del Selvotta, VF sign	S	108

Campagno-di-Roma to La-Storta 24.4km

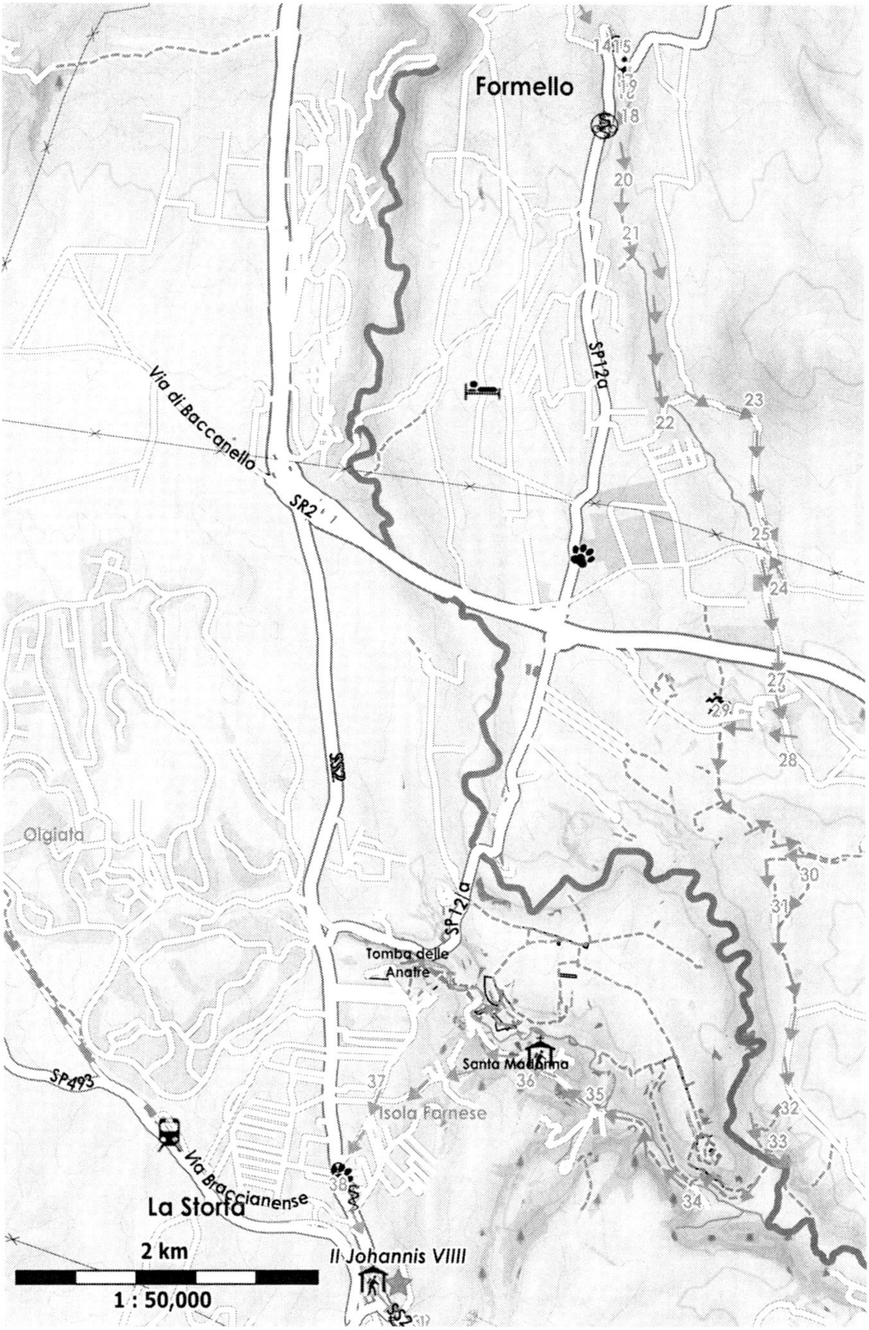
Formello
SP12a
Via di Baccanello
SR2
SS2
Olgiata
SP12/a
Tomba delle Anatre
Santa Maddalena
Isola Farnese
SP493
Via Braccianense
La Storta
Il Johannis VIIII
2 km
1 : 50,000
18
20
21
22
23
24
25
27
28
29
30
31
32
33
34
35
36
37
38

Waypoint	Distance Between Waypoints (m)	Total (km)	Directions	Verification Point	Compass	Altitude (m)
93.027	210	14,3	Keep left on the road		S	106
93.028	300	14,6	Turn sharp right		W	99
93.029	500	15,0	At the crossroads, turn left	Between fields on via Monte Michele	SE	110
93.030	1400	16,4	Turn right and right again to pass through a gap in the line of trees and continue with the trees on the right		S	124
93.031	900	17,3	Pass through the gate and bear left on via del Prato delle Cotte	Hamlet on the right	S	119
93.032	1200	18,4	Take the right fork on the track through gate. The track winds downhill between trees	VF sign on tree	S	105
93.033	800	19,2	Bear right to ford the river with care and bear right again on the far side	Torrente Valchetta	W	56
93.034	800	20,0	Cross the bridge and turn right	Via del Prato della Corte	NW	59
93.035	900	20,9	At the junction bear right up the hill	Football field on the left before the junction	NW	61
93.036	600	21,5	At the T-junction, bear left on the road	Enter Isola Farnese	W	91
93.037	1100	22,5	At the junction, bear left up the hill	VF sign, via dell'Isola Farnese	SW	143
93.038	500	23,1	At the T-junction on the brow of the hill, turn left on the via Cassia	Roma – 17	SE	160
93.039	1400	24,4	Arrive at La-Storta (II) centre	Beside the elevated church on the right		167

Campagno-di-Roma to La-Storta 24.4km

Religious Hostel

Parrocchia San Pancrazio,Piazza della Colonnetta, 8,00123 Isola-Farnese(RM),Italy Tel:+39 06 9171 2163,Price:C,

Convento Suore Missionarie della Consolata - Sette Vene,Via Cassia Km.37 Località Settevene,01036 Nepi(VT),Italy Tel:+39 0761 527253,fulviarob@tiscali.it ,www.consolazione.org,Price:C,

Istituto Palazzo Suore Poverelle,Via Baccarica, 5,00135 Roma(RM),Italy Tel:+39 06 3089 0495,Mobile:+39 3352 74645,lastorta@istitutopalazzolo.it,Price:C,

B&B, Hotel, Gite d'Etape

Da Giovanni,Via delle Rubbia,00060 Formello(RM),Italy Tel:+39 06 9040 0004,Price:B,

Camping

Seven Hills Camping Village,Via Cassia, 1216,00189 Roma(RM),Italy Tel:+39 06 3036 2751,

Equestrian

C.P.R.Quarter Horses Srl,Via della Vaccareccia,00060 Formello(RM),Italy Tel:+39 06 9075 443,

Poscolieri - Agriturismo Centro Ippico,Via del Fontanile,01030 Monterosi(VT),Italy Tel:+39 0761 699431,

Tourist Information

Comune di Roma Municipio Ufficio la Storta,Via Domenico Falcioni, 12,00123 Roma(RM),Italy Tel:+39 06 3089 0461,

Comune di Formello,Piazza San Lorenzo,00060 Formello(RM),Italy Tel:+39 06 9019 41,

Banks and ATMs

Banca di Formello,Via Roma, 50,01030 Monterosi(VT),Italy Tel:+39 0761 698012,

Banco di Brescia,Via Roma, 36,01030 Monterosi(VT),Italy Tel:+39 0761 699007,

Banca di Formello,Viale Umberto Primo, 4,00060 Formello(RM),Italy Tel:+39 06 9014 301,www.bccformello.com,

Banca Nazionale del Lavoro,Via Cassia,00191 La-Storta(RM),Italy Tel:+39 06 3089 6135,

Banca di Roma,Via della Storta, 926,00123 Roma(RM),Italy Tel:+39 06 3386 741,

Travel

Stazione Ferrovie,Via della Storta, 27,00123 Roma(RM),Italy Tel:+39 06 6847 5475,www.renitalia.it,

Doctor

D'Ammando - Studio Medico,Via Valle della Storta, 7,00123 Roma(RM),Italy Tel:+39 06 3089 1543,

Saccomando - Studio Medico,Via Roma,00060 Formello(RM),Italy Tel:+39 06 9088 600,

Veterinary

Dottor Puntieri,Via Cassia, 1819,00123 Roma(RM),Italy Tel:+39 06 3089 1939,

Clinica Veterinaria Parco di Veio,Via Formellese Km,00060 Formello(RM),Italy Tel:+39 06 8982 3139,

Limonta Fabio,Via strada Nuova, 2,01030 Monterosi(VT),Italy Tel:+39 0761 699703,

Bicycle Shop

Cicli Magni di Stefano Magni,Via Roma,00060 Formello(RM),Italy Tel:+39 06 9014 6048,

Stage Summary: the route into Rome initially uses the very busy via Cassia and via Trionfale, there is relief on the pathways and through the Reserva Naturale della Insugherata and the Monte Mario park before returning to the broad city boulevards for the final approach to the Vatican. Parts of the via Trionfale do not have pavements/sidewalks. It is possible to continue on the via Cassia and enter the Reserva Naturale immediately after crossing the bridge over the ring road. However, the gates to the reserve may be locked.

Distance from Canterbury: 2056km　　Distance to Saint-Peter's-Square: 18km
Stage Ascent: 146m　　Stage Descent: 289m

Waypoint	Distance Between Waypoints (m)	Total (km)	Directions	Verification Point	Compass	Altitude (m)
94.001	0	0,0	On the via Cassia, below the church in La-Storta, continue with great care on the road towards Roma	Church on the right and petrol station on the left	SE	167
94.002	2700	2,7	Take the right fork, following the flow of traffic on via Trionfale	Pass motor car sales on the right	S	147
94.003	3200	5,9	Shortly after passing under the flyover, turn left	Via Silvio Antoniano	E	138
94.004	190	6,1	Immediately after passing the garage compound, turn left on the track	Pass apartment block on your right	N	135
94.005	70	6,1	Bear right on the track		E	132
94.006	160	6,3	In the clearing, bear right on the track		S	119
94.007	700	7,0	Turn left on the broad track between the trees		E	89
94.008	700	7,7	Take the right fork		S	78
94.009	160	7,8	Take the left fork	In the valley between the buildings	S	76
94.010	290	8,1	Join the tarmac road and turn right up the hill		SW	99
94.011	200	8,3	Turn left on via della Rimessola. Note:- there are steps on the Main Route ahead, riders should continue straight ahead to the via Trionfale, turn left and rejoin the Main Route at the junction with via Giuseppe Taverna	High walls on the right side of the road	SE	117

La-Storta to Saint-Peter's-Square 18.3km

284

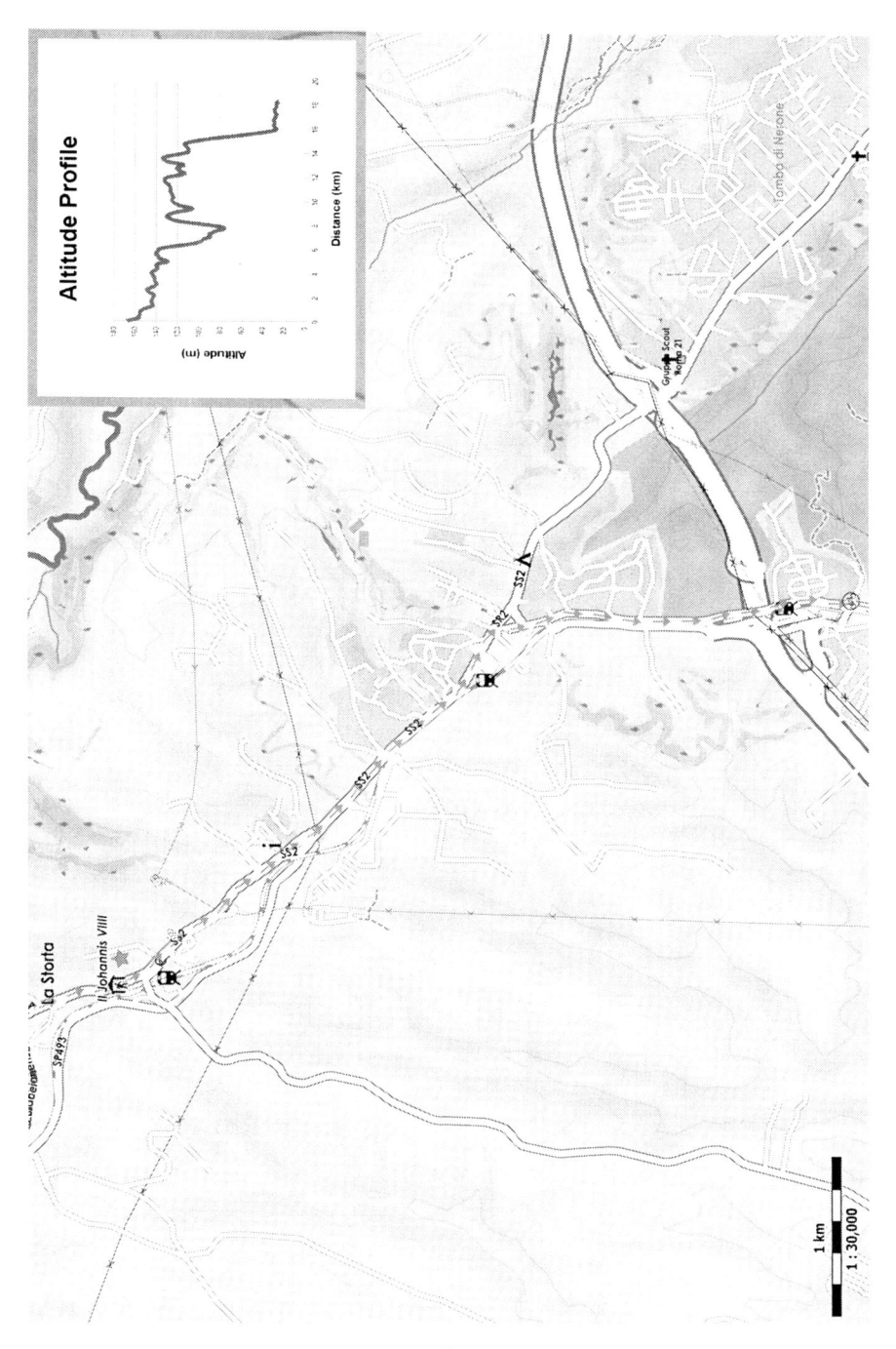

Altitude Profile
Altitude (m)
Distance (km)
La Storta
Il Johannis VIIII
SP493
SS2
SR2
Tomba di Nerone
1 km
1 : 30,000

Waypoint	Distance Between Waypoints (m)	Total (km)	Directions	Verification Point	Compass	Altitude (m)
94.012	400	8,7	At the T-junction, turn right	Pass house N° 7 on the right	SW	129
94.013	50	8,8	At the T-junction, turn left	Hotel ahead at the junction	SE	130
94.014	200	8,9	Turn right	Via Siro Corti	SW	126
94.015	50	9,0	Keep right on via Siro Corti	No Through Road	W	124
94.016	170	9,2	At the foot of the steps, turn left	House N° 56 ahead	S	116
94.017	800	10,0	At the crossroads between via Giuseppe Taverna and via Trionfale, turn left	Against the flow of traffic	E	124
94.018	400	10,4	At the complex intersection, continue to the mini-roundabout and turn right with great care and remain on via Trionfale	Towards the university	SE	123
94.019	1000	11,4	At the traffic lights, turn left on Largo Cervinia	Medical clinic on the right at the junction	E	127
94.020	260	11,6	At the end of the road, cross the small park on the traffic island and turn right	No Entry sign, via della Camilluccia	SE	131
94.021	400	12,0	Turn left, downhill - via Edmondo de Amicis	Chapel on the right at junction	E	129
94.022	240	12,2	Beside the red brick building, turn right onto the pathway through the Monte Mario park	Pass through metal gates	SE	116
94.023	800	13,0	At the T-junction, turn right		S	114

La-Storta to Saint-Peter's-Square 18.3km

Via dei Due Ponti
SR 3
Vigna Clara
Via Flaminia
Via Cassia
Fontana dell'Acqua Acetosa
MAXXI
Tevere
Via Mario Fani
Monte Mario Alto
Via di Valle
Torrevecchia
Torresina
1 km
1 : 30,000

Waypoint	Distance Between Waypoints (m)	Total (km)	Directions	Verification Point	Compass	Altitude (m)
94.024	800	13,9	The path emerges onto a road, continue straight ahead	Municipal building on the left	S	122
94.025	210	14,1	At the traffic lights, turn left	Via Trionfale	S	110
94.026	70	14,1	Turn left up the steps and through the archway to return to the walled Monte Mario park. Note:- to avoid the obstacles in the park remain on via Trionfale to the crossroads with the tree lined via Andrea Doria, where you should bear right on via Leone IV to rejoin the Main Route in piazza del Risorgimento		SE	109
94.027	170	14,3	Cross the road and continue on the path	Pass the observatory on the left, views of the city to the right	E	109
94.028	1500	15,8	At the bottom of the hill pass through the gate and continue straight ahead		SE	38
94.029	150	15,9	After leaving the park, take the pedestrian crossing over the road and continue straight ahead	Via Novenio Bucchi	E	29
94.030	80	16,0	At the T-junction, cross the broad road and go straight ahead through the gardens in piazza Maresciallo and turn right	Viale Angelico	S	26
94.031	1900	17,9	Continue straight ahead across piazza Risorgimento towards the Vatican on via di Porta Angelica	Dome of St Peter's to the right	S	26
94.032	500	18,3	Arrive at Saint-Peter's-Square (I)			24

La-Storta to Saint-Peter's-Square 18.3km

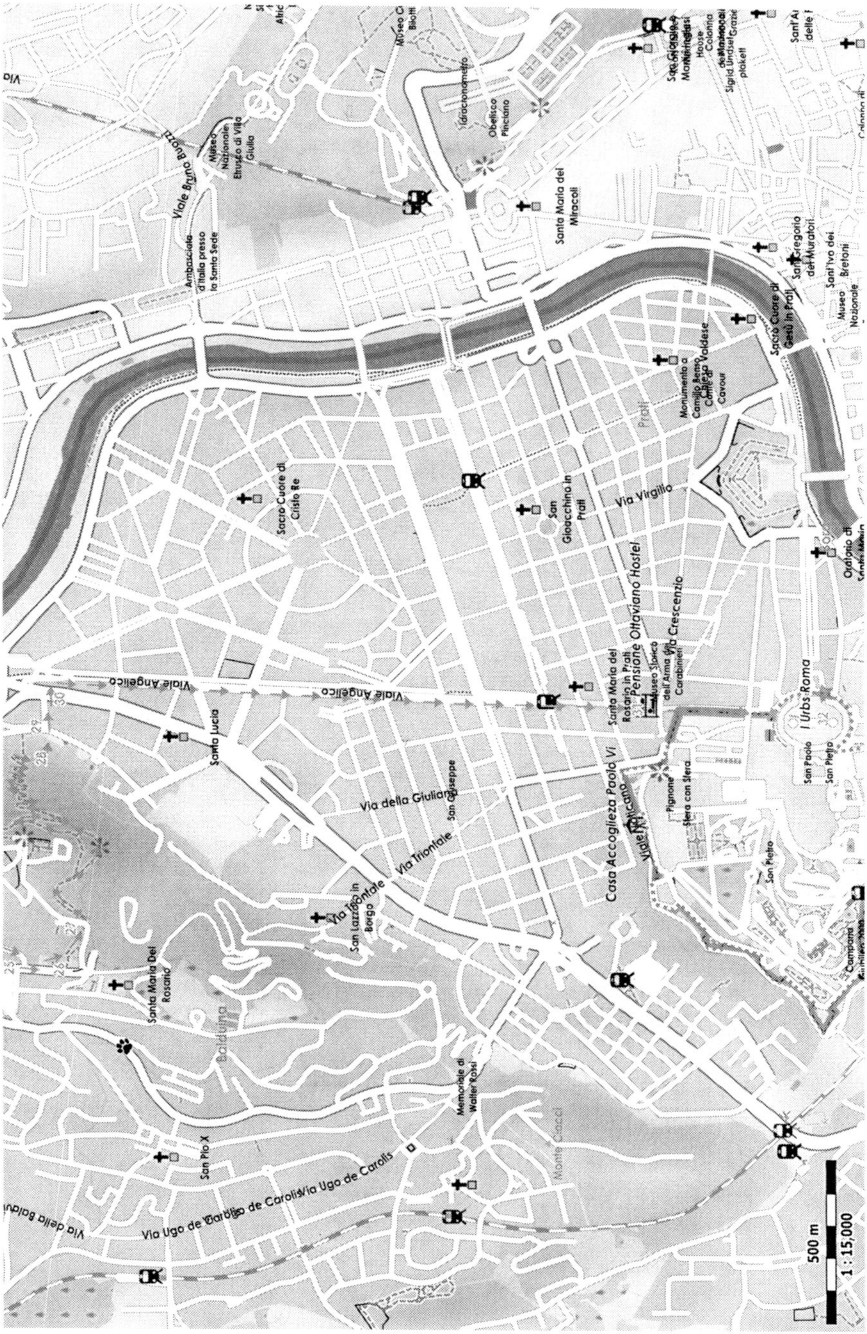
Viale Angelico
Santa Lucia
Via della Giuliana
San Giuseppe
Via Trionfale
San Lazzaro in Borgo
Santa Maria Del Rosario
Balduina
San Pio X
Via Ugo de Carolis
Memoriale di Walter Rossi
Monte Ciocci
Casa Accoglieza Paolo VI
Pensione Ottaviano Hostel
Via Crescenzio
Santa Maria del Rosario in Prati
Museo Storico dell'Arma dei Carabinieri
I Urbs Roma
San Paolo
San Pietro
Pignone
Sfera con Sfera
Via Virgilio
San Gioacchino in Prati
Prati
Monumento a Camillo Benso Conte di Cavour
Chiesa Valdese
Sacro Cuore di Gesù in Prati
Sacro Cuore di Cristo Re
Viale Bruno Buozzi
Ambasciata d'Italia presso la Santa Sede
Museo Nazionale Etrusco di Villa Giulia
Idrocronometro
Obelisco Pinciano
Santa Maria dei Miracoli
Sant'Ivo dei Bretoni
Museo Napoleonico
San Gregorio dei Muratori
Oratorio di Santa Maria
500 m
1 : 15,000

Pilgrim Hostel

Spedale della Provvidenza,(Signora Lucia Colarusso),Via Galvani, 51,00153 Roma(RM),Italy
Mobile:+39 3272 319312,www.pellegriniaroma.it,Price:D,

Religious Hostel

Madonna del Cenacolo,Largo Vincenzo Ambrosio, 9,00136 Roma(RM),Italy
Tel:+39 06 3540 1142,cenacolopellegrini@hotmail.com,Price:D,

Suore Oblate al Divino Amore,Via Marruvio, 4,00183 Roma(RM),Italy
Tel:+39 06 7008 040,Price:B,

Suore Marcelline,(Suor Maria Raffaella),Via Dandolo, 59,00153 Roma(RM),Italy
Tel:+39 06 5812 443,Price:B,

Casa Figlie di S.Giuseppe,Vicolo Moroni, 22,00153 Roma(RM),Italy
Tel:+39 06 5833 3896,Price:B,

Casa Accoglieza Paolo Vi,Viale Vaticano, 92,00165 Roma(RM),Italy
Tel:+39 06 3909 141,casapaolosesto@pssf.it,Price:B,

Commercial Hostel

Ostello di Roma,(Hostel may be relocating),Viale delle Olimpiadi, 61,00194 Roma(RM),Italy
Tel:+39 06 3242 613,info@aighostels.com,Price:C,

Downtown Hostel,Via Carlo Cattaneo, 23,00185 Roma(RM),Italy
Tel:+39 06 4434 0147,downtown@hostelsalessandro.com,aighostels.com,Price:B,

Pensione Ottaviano Hostel,Via Ottaviano, 6,00192 Roma(RM),Italy
Tel:+39 06 3973 8138,info@pensioneottaviano.com,Price:B,

B&B, Hotel, Gite d'Etape

Foyer Phat Diem,Via della Pineta Sacchetti, 45,00167 Roma(RM),Italy
Tel:+39 06 6633 636,foyerpdr@gmail.com,Price:B,

Camping

Camping Village Roma,Via Aurelia, 831,00163 Roma(RM),Italy Tel:+39 06 6623 018,

Equestrian

Centro Ippico Montemario,Via della Camilluccia, 120,00135 Roma(RM),Italy
Mobile:+39 3398 144440,

Tourist Information

Ufficio Turistico Polacco,Via Vittorio Veneto, 54,00187 Roma(RM),Italy Tel:+39 06 4827 060,

Banks and ATMs

Unicredit,Via Trionfale, 7110,00135 Roma(RM),Italy
Tel:+39 06 3386 741,www.unicreditbanca.it,

Travel

Fiumicino Airport,Via Portuense, 2365,00054 Fiumicino(RM),Italy
Tel:+39 06 6595 1,www.adr.it,

Roma Ostiense -Stazione Ferrovie,Piazzale dei Partigiani, 34/35,00154 Roma(RM),Italy
Tel:+39 06 6847 5475,www.renitalia.it,

Roma Termini - Stazione Ferrovie,Via Giovanni Giolitti,00185 Roma(RM),Italy
Tel:+39 06 6847 5475,www.renitalia.it,

Hospital

Azienda Ospedaliera Sant'Andrea,Via di Grottarossa, 1035,00189 Roma(RM),Italy Tel:+39 06 3315 109,www.ospedalesantandrea.it,

Ospedale San Carlo,Via Aurelia, 275,00165 Roma(RM),Italy Tel:+39 06 3975 1937,

Veterinary

Veterinaria Medaglie d'Oro,Viale delle Medaglie d'Oro, 374,00136 Roma(RM),Italy Tel:+39 06 3534 7397,

Hiking Equipment

Tutto Sport,10, via G.B.Morgagni 8 /,00161 Roma(RM),Italy Tel:+39 06 4423 0421,

Bicycle Shop

Cicli Rossi,Via Trionfale,00135 Roma(RM),Italy Tel:+39 06 3081 8820,

Cicli Fatato,Via F.Albergotti, 14/e,00167 Roma(RM),Italy Tel:+39 06 6635 440,

Farrier

Mascalcia Congiu,Via Appia Nuova, 1255,00123 Roma(RM),Italy Tel:+39 3382 115741,info@mascalciacongiu.com,

La-Storta to Saint-Peter's-Square 18.3km

ROUTE	Map References	Number	Description
	Carta topografica d'Italia serie 1:50,000	Foglio 136	SANTHIA Edizione/aggiornamento anno 1974
	Carta topografica d'Italia serie 1:50,000	Foglio 137	VERCELLI currently out of print
Vercelli to Mortara	Carta topografica d'Italia serie 1:50,000	Foglio 137	VERCELLI Edizione/aggiornamento anno 1996
	Carta topografica d'Italia serie 1:50,000	Foglio 058	MORTARA Edizione/aggiornamento anno 1996
Mortara to Garlasco	Carta topografica d'Italia serie 1:50,000	Foglio 058	MORTARA Edizione/aggiornamento anno 1996
Garlasco to Pavia	Carta topografica d'Italia serie 1:50,000	Foglio 058	MORTARA Edizione/aggiornamento anno 1996
	Carta topografica d'Italia serie 1:50,000	Foglio 059	PAVIA Edizione/aggiornamento anno 1996
Pavia to Santa Cristina	Carta topografica d'Italia serie 1:50,000	Foglio 059	PAVIA Edizione/aggiornamento anno 1961
Santa Cristina to Piacenza	Carta topografica d'Italia serie 100/V e 100/L	Foglio 059	PAVIA Edizione/aggiornamento anno 1961
Piacenza to Fiorenzuola d'Arda	Carta topografica d'Italia serie 100/V e 100/L:	Foglio 060	PIACENZA Edizione/aggiornamento anno 1959
	Carta topografica d'Italia serie 1:50,000	Foglio 072	FIORENZUOLA D'ARDA Edizione/aggiornamento anno 1961
Fiorenzuola D'Arda to Fidenza	Carta topografica d'Italia serie 1:50,000	Foglio 072	FIORENZUOLA D'ARDA Edizione/aggiornamento anno 1961
	Carta topografica d'Italia serie 1:50,000	Foglio 073	PARMA Edizione/aggiornamento anno 1961

ROUTE	Map References	Number	Description
Fidenza to Fornovo di Taro	Carta topografica d'Italia serie 1:50,000	Foglio 073	PARMA Edizione/aggiornamento anno 1961
Fornovo di Taro to Berceto	Carta topografica d'Italia serie 1:50,000	Foglio 085	CASTELNOVO NE' MONTI Edizione/aggiornamento anno 1951
Berceto to Pontremoli	Carta topografica d'Italia serie 100/V e 100/L	Foglio 085	CASTELNOVO NE' MONTI Edizione/aggiornamento anno 1951
	Carta topografica d'Italia serie 100/V e 100/L	Foglio 073	PONTREMOLI Edizione/aggiornamento anno 1951
Pontremoli to Aulla	Carta topografica d'Italia serie 100/V e 100/L:	Foglio 084	PONTREMOLI Edizione/aggiornamento anno 1951
	Carta topografica d'Italia serie 100/V e 100/L:	Foglio 096	MASSA Edizione/aggiornamento anno 1951
Aulla to Sarzana	Carta topografica d'Italia serie 1:50,000	Foglio 096	MASSA Edizione/aggiornamento anno 1951
Sarzana to Pietrasanta	Carta topografica d'Italia serie 1:50,000	Foglio 096	MASSA Edizione/aggiornamento anno 1951
	Carta topografica d'Italia serie 1:50,000	Foglio 104	PISA Edizione/aggiornamento anno 1952
Pietrasanta to Lucca	Carta topografica d'Italia serie 100/V e 100/L:	Foglio 104	PISA Edizione/aggiornamento anno 1952
	Carta topografica d'Italia serie 100/V e 100/L:	Foglio 105	LUCCA Edizione/aggiornamento anno 1954
Lucca to Ponte a Cappiano	Carta topografica d'Italia serie 100/V e 100/L:	Foglio 105	LUCCA Edizione/aggiornamento anno 1954
Ponte a Cappriano to Gambassi Terme	Carta topografica d'Italia serie 100/V e 100/L:	Foglio 105	LUCCA Edizione/aggiornamento anno 1954
	Carta topografica d'Italia serie 100/V e 100/L:	Foglio 112	VOLTERRA Edizione/aggiornamento anno 1953
	Carta topografica d'Italia serie 100/V e 100/L:	Foglio 113	CASTELFIORENTINO Edizione/aggiornamento anno 1953

ROUTE	Map References	Number	Description
Gambassi Terme to Gracciano d'Elsa	Carta topografica d'Italia serie 100/V e 100/L:	Foglio 113	CASTELFIORENTINO Edizione/aggiornamento anno 1953
Gracciano d'Elsa to Siena	Carta topografica d'Italia serie 100/V e 100/L:	Foglio 113	CASTELFIORENTINO Edizione/aggiornamento anno 1953
	Carta topografica d'Italia serie 100/V e 100/L:	Foglio 120	SIENA Edizione/aggiornamento anno 1953
Siena to Ponte d'Arbia	Carta topografica d'Italia serie 100/V e 100/L:	Foglio 120	SIENA Edizione/aggiornamento anno 1953
	Carta topografica d'Italia serie 100/V e 100/L:	Foglio 121	MONTEPULCIANO Edizione/aggiornamento anno 1953
Ponte d'Arbia to San Quirico d'Orcia	Carta topografica d'Italia serie 100/V e 100/L:	Foglio 121	MONTEPULCIANO Edizione/aggiornamento anno 1953
San Quirico d'Orcia to Radicofani	Carta topografica d'Italia serie 100/V e 100/L:	Foglio 121	MONTEPULCIANO Edizione/aggiornamento anno 1953
	Carta topografica d'Italia serie 100/V e 100/L:	Foglio 129	SANTA FIORA Edizione/aggiornamento anno 1953
San Quirico d'Orcia to Radicofani	Carta topografica d'Italia serie 100/V e 100/L:	Foglio 129	SANTA FIORA Edizione/aggiornamento anno 1953
Acquapendente to Bolsena	Carta topografica d'Italia serie 100/V e 100/L	Foglio 129	SANTA FIORA Edizione/aggiornamento anno 1953
	Carta topografica d'Italia serie 100/V e 100/L	Foglio 137	VITERBO Edizione/aggiornamento anno 1953
Bolsena to Viterbo	Carta topografica d'Italia serie 100/V e 100/L:	Foglio 137	VITERBO Edizione/aggiornamento anno 1953
Viterbo to Capranica	Carta topografica d'Italia serie 100/V e 100/L:	Foglio 137	VITERBO Edizione/aggiornamento anno 1953
	Carta topografica d'Italia serie 100/V e 100/L:	Foglio 143	BRACCIANO Edizione/aggiornamento anno 1953
Capranica to Campagnano di Roma	Carta topografica d'Italia serie 100/V e 100/L:	Foglio 143	PIACENZA Edizione/aggiornamento anno 1953
Campagnano di Roma to La Storta	Carta topografica d'Italia serie 100/V e 100/L	Foglio 143	BRACCIANO Edizione/aggiornamento anno 1953

The list below gives details of the churches and religious organisations either in or near towns along the route. These have not specifically stated that accommodation is provided for pilgrims, but it is likely that a phone call will put you in contact with someone who will be able/willing to help. * indicates that there are more churches than could be listed in this limited space

VERCELLI *	Basilica Di Sant'Andrea, 35, PIAZZA ROMA 13100 Vercelli (VC) Tel: 0039 (0)161 255513
	Chiesa Cattedrale Di S. Eusebio? PIAZZA S. EUSEBIO 13100 Vercelli (VC) Tel: 0039 (0)161 252930
	Parrocchia Dello Spirito Santo, VIA ERITREA 13100 Vercelli (VC) Tel: 0039 (0)161 212041
	Parrocchia Di S. Agnese, 7, VIA BORGOGNA ANTONIO 13100 Vercelli (VC) Tel: 0039 (0)161 252768
MORTARA	Centro Sociale Padre Francesco Pianzola, 2, VIA MAZZA PRIMO 27036 Mortara (PV) Tel: 0039 (0)384 296585
	3 Parrocchia S. Lorenzo Casa Parrocchiale? 1, CONTRADA S. DIONIGI 27036 Mortara (PV) Tel: 0039 (0)384 99772
PAVIA *	Basilica S. Pietro In Ciel D'Oro, 2, PIAZZA S. PIETRO IN CIEL D'ORO 27100 Pavia (PV) Tel: 0039 (0)382 303040
	Basilica S. Pietro In Ciel D'Oro? 2, PIAZZA S. PIETRO IN CIEL D'ORO 27100 Pavia (PV) Tel: 0039 (0)382 303036
	Parrocchia Dei Santi Primo E Feliciano Martiri, 1, PIAZZA S. PRIMO 27100 Pavia (PV) Tel: 0039 (0)382 26677
PIACENZA *	Chiesa Cattolica Parrocchiale Borgotrebbia, 89, VIA TREBBIA 29100 Piacenza (PC) Tel: 0039 (0)523 480298
	Chiesa Cattolica Parrocchiale Corpus Domini, 24 STRADA FARNESIANA 29100 Piacenza (PC) Tel: 0039 (0)523 592321
	Chiesa Cattolica Parrocchiale della Ss. Trinita' Alessandrini Don Riccardo, 30, VIA MANFREDI GIUSEPPE 29100 Piacenza (PC) Tel: 0039 (0)523 458204
Fiorenzuola D'Arda	Parrocchia Di San Fiorenzo Gestione Scuola Infanzia, VIA PELLICO SILVIO 29017 Fiorenzuola D'Arda (PC) Tel: 0039 (0)523 983171
	Parrocchia Di San Fiorenzo Suore Pastorelle, VIA CAVALIERE 29017 Fiorenzuola D'Arda (PC) Tel: 0039 (0)523 241038

List of churches and religious organisations continued.

FORNOVO DI TARO	1 Parrocchia Di S.Margherita Abitazione Del Parroco, 18, localita' SIVIZZANO CENTRO 43045 Fornovo Di Taro (PR) Tel: 0039 (0)525 56258
BERCETO	Santuario Di Berceto, VIA SEMINARIO 43042 Berceto (PR) Tel: 0039 (0)525 60071
PONTREMOLI	Parrocchia Cattedrale, 54027 Pontremoli (MS) Tel: 0039 (0)187 830572
	Parrocchia Ss. Giovanni E Colombano, 3, VIA REISOLI 54027 Pontremoli (MS) Tel: 0039 (0)187 830511
SARZANA	Cattedrale Basilica S. Maria, 5, VIA NICOLO' V 19038 Sarzana (SP) Tel: 0039 (0)187 620017
	Parrocchia Di S. Venanzio? 33, VIA CROCIATA 19038 Sarzana (SP) Tel: 0039 (0)187 621036
PIETRASANTA	Circolo Anspi Renzo Tognetti, 163, VIA DUCA DELLA VITTORIA 55044 Marina Di Pietrasanta (LU) Tel: 0039 (0)584 267049
	Parrocchia Di S. Antonio? 161, VIA DUCA DELLA VITTORIA 55045 Marina Di Pietrasanta (LU) Tel: 0039 (0)584 20866
	Parrocchia S. Maria Assunta, 9, VIA MALTA 55044 Marina Di Pietrasanta (LU) Tel: 0039 (0)584 21312
LUCCA	Chiese Cattoliche Parrocchiali, 53, VIA TOGLIATTI PALMIRO 55100 Lucca (LU) Tel: 0039 (0)583 510933
	Chiese Cattoliche Parrocchiali Parrocchia Di S. Anna, 367, VIALE PUCCINI G. - S. ANNA 55100 Lucca (LU) Tel: 0039 (0)583 587593
GAMBASSI TERME	Caritas Parrocchiale, 50050 Gambassi Terme (FI) Tel: 0039 (0)571 638242

List of churches and religious organisations continued.

Parrocchia Di S. Maria A Le Grazie, 53034 Colle Di Val D'Elsa (SI) Tel: 0039 (0)577 959068

Parrocchia S. Caterina, 35, VIA DEL CAMPANA 53034 Colle Di Val D'Elsa (SI) Tel: 0039 (0)577 920647

Parrocchia S. Marziale, 1, LOCALITA' S. MARZIALE 53034 Colle Di Val D'Elsa (SI) Tel: 0039 (0)577 928677

SIENA *

Chiesa Cattolica Parrocchiale Maria Ss. Immacolata Abitazione Del Parroco,104, STRADA DEI CAPPUCCINI 53100 Siena (SI) Tel: 0039 (0)577 287240

Parrocchia Beata Anna Maria Taigi Abitazione Del Parroco, 6, VIA LIGURIA 53100 Siena (SI) Tel: 0039 (0)577 593562

Parrocchia Di S. Spirito Abitazione Del Parroco, 2, PIAZZA S. SPIRITO 53100 Siena (SI) Tel: 0039 (0)577 284353

BOLSENA

1 Parrocchia Basilica S. Cristina Pp. Sacramentini, 1, VIA MAZZINI 01023 Bolsena (VT) Tel: 0039 (0)761 799067

VITERBO *

Parrocchia della Crocetta, 4, PIAZZA DELLA CROCETTA 01100 Viterbo (VT) Tel: 0039 (0)761 343170

Parrocchia S. Giovanni Battista? 22, PIAZZA XX SETTEMBRE 01100 Viterbo (VT) Tel: 0039 (0)761 289826

Parrocchia S. Maria Dell'Edera, 5, VIA ZARA 01100 Viterbo (VT) Tel: 0039 (0)761 340925

Books published by LightFoot Guides

All LighFoot Publications are also available in ebook and kindle formats and can be ordered directly from www.pilgrimagepublications.com

LightFoot Guides to the Via Francigena 2012

The complete 2012 LightFoot Guide to the via Francigena consists of 4 books:
Canterbury to Besançon Besançon to Vercelli Vercelli to Rome Companion to the Via Francigena
In the 2012 edition the authors continue to use the official route in Italy, as approved and signed by the Italian Minister of Culture, but also offer additional opportunities where it is too challenging for one or more groups.

Information provided in each section:
Instruction sheet/s comprising:
  Detailed directions corresponding to GPS way point numbers on the maps
  Distance (in metres) between each way point Verification Point - additional verification of current position
Compass direction Maps comprising:
  A visual representation of the route with way point numbers and adjacent details
  Altitude Profile for the section
  Icons indicating places to stay, monuments etc
Each volume contains detailed routing instructions, route and town schematics and listings of accommodation and services. Purchasers of the books are entitled to receive GPS Way Point data and periodic route updates for the area covered.

LightFoot Guide to the Via Domitia - Arles to Vercelli

Even with the wealth of historical data available to us today, we can only offer an approximate version of yesterday's reality and we claim to do nothing more in this book. The route described runs roughly parallel with a section of the via Domitia between Arles and Montgenévre (a large portion of the original route having been subsumed by the A51), continues along a variety of roads and tracks that together form a modern-day branch of the via Francigena and rejoins the official main route (to Rome) in Vercelli.

The LightFoot Companion to the Via Domitia is an optional partner to the guide, providing the additional historical and cultural information that will enhance your experience of the Via Domitia/Via Francigena pilgrim road to Rome, while allowing you to choose how and when you use it.

The LightFoot Guide to the Three Saints' Way

The name, Three Saint's Way, has been created by the authors of the LightFoot guide, but is based on the three saints associated with this pilgrimage: St Swithin, St Michael and St James. Far from being a single route, it is in fact a collection of intersecting routes:
*The Millenium Footpath Trail starting in Winchester and ending in Portsmouth, England
*Chemin Anglais to Mont St Michel
*The Plantagenet Way to St Jean d'Angely, where it intersects with the St James Way (starting from Paris).

Information provided in each section:
Instruction sheet/s comprising:
   Detailed directions corresponding to GPS way point numbers on the maps
   Distance (in metres) between each way point Verification Point - additional verification of current position
Compass direction Maps comprising:
   A visual representation of the route with way point numbers and adjacent details
   Altitude Profile for the section
   Icons indicating places to stay, monuments etc
Each volume contains detailed routing instructions, route and town schematics and listings of accommodation and services. Purchasers of the books are entitled to receive GPS Way Point data and periodic route updates for the area covered.

Winchester to Mont St Michel
A medieval route that starts from the shrine of St Swithun at Winchester Cathedral, and continues by way of Bishop's Waltham and Southwick to Portsmouth in the footsteps of the Miquelots, pilgrims who made the long journey to worship St Michael in Normandy. Today's travellers have the advantage of special waymark signs - green in Hampshire, blue in France leading to the medieval sanctuary of Mont St Michel in Normandy France, 155 miles away. The cult of Saint Michael was widespread in the British Isles from the 9th century. By the time of the reformation in the 16th century, there were more than six hundred churches in England dedicated to Saint Michael. Saint Michael's day, Michaelmas, is celebrated on 29 September. The Norman sanctuary of Mont St Michel attracted pilgrims from Scandinavia, Italy and Germany, as well as from Britain. Most pilgrims stopped at the Mount on their way to Santiago de Compostela in northern Spain. They landed at Barfleur, near Cherbourg, walked to the Mount and continued to Santiago.

The Plantagenet Way
The route starts in Mont St Michel and ends in St Jean d'Angely at the intersection with the St James Way. The name Plantagenet is derived from the common broom plant, known as "planta genista" in Latin. The House of Plantagenet, also called the House of Anjou, or the First Angevin dynasty, was originally a noble family from France, which ruled the county of Anjou. The name was first associated with Geoffrey of Anjou, father of King Henry II of England, either because he wore a sprig of broom in his bonnet, or because he planted broom to improve his hunting covers.

LightFoot Guide to Your Camino

After years of answering frequently asked questions on Camino forums, the Internet, Camino workshops and on her Camino blog (amaWalker.blogspot.com) Sylvia Nilsen (aka Sillydoll), provides the answers to thousands of FAQs in a book called 'Your Camino – on foot, bicycle or horseback, in France and Spain'.

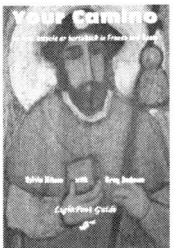

Besides providing information and maps on the many different Camino routes in France and Spain (with links to Jacobean routes in other countries) it offers advice on the best time to go and how to get there, planning daily stages, budgets and accommodation, pilgrim and trail etiquette.

She enlisted the help of Greg Dedman (Camino pilgrim and backpacking expert) to help with chapters on technology, weather, food and language. Many other experienced pilgrims shared their expertise on subjects as diverse as disabled pilgrims, cycling, trekking with children, horses, donkeys and dogs. There are chapters on clothing and equipment covering boots, shoes, backpacks and sleeping bags, as well as medical matters, relics, Santiago Holy Years and pilgrim statistics.

Illustrated with delightful pilgrim characters, this 280-page reference guide covers everything from learning about the Camino on the Internet, books and DVDs, Confraternities and Forums, to taking a donkey on the trail, and how to 'go' in the woods!

LightFoot Guide to Camino Lingo

If you only take one Spanish phrase book or dictionary with you on the Camino this is it!

Compiled by Sylvia Nilsen, an experienced Camino pilgrim, and her Spanish teacher Reinette Nóvoa, the Lightfoot Guide Camino Lingo - Spanish Words and Phrases for Pilgrims on el Camino de Santiago contains all the Spanish words you'll need while on a Camino pilgrimage in Spain.

No complicated verb conjugations or rules on diphthongs and grammar. This is a 'cheats' guide to speaking Spanish on the Camino.
Over 650 English/Spanish words relating specifically to the Camino pilgrimage with simplified pronunciation - including a few curse words should you need them!
Useful phrases for travelling, accommodation, eating out, shopping, walking the path, health and medical and emergencies, menu Reader including a list of Tapas and a list of words just for cyclists

"It's about time somebody wrote a book like this for pilgrims. I can't believe it hasn't been done before! The pronunciation is easy to read and I've learned a lot of words and phrases in just a few days. Can't wait to try it on my Camino!"

LightFoot Guide to Foraging

"Nowadays if I look at a meadow I think lunch." Heiko Vermeulen A guide to over 130 of the most common edible and medicinal plants in Western Europe, aimed at the long-distance or casual hiker along the main pilgrim routes through Western Europe. The author has had some 40 years of experience in foraging and though a Dutchman by birth, has been at home all over Europe including Germany, Ireland, England and for the last 8 years in Italy along the Via Francigena pilgrim route, where he feeds his family as a subsistence farmer, cultivating a small piece of Ligurian hillside along permaculture principles, and by gathering food from the wild.

Riding the Milky Way - Le Puy en Velay to Santiago de Compostela

Riding the Milky Way tells the story of Babette and Paul's journey, but it is not about hardships and heroes. In fact it was a motley and uninspiring crew that left Le Puy en Velay, France, in July 2005. The humans, broke, burnt-out and vaguely hoping that early retirement would save their health and sanity. The horses, plucked off the equine scrap-heap in France and still grappling with their new roles as something between mount and mountain goat. The dog, doing his best to understand why he was there. But 75 days later they reached their destination, overcoming the challenges, and most importantly, finding that they had become an inseparable team. Packed with sketches and photographs, this book will inspire even the most timid traveller, while also giving practical guidelines for someone wanting to do the same or a similar journey. And finally, it is quite simply an excellent, sometimes irreverent, guide to the St James Way. Much more than just a good read.

Riding the Roman Way

"We have good equipment, our horses are fit and we are fully prepared, so why this feeling of dread? Perhaps it has something to do with knowing what to expect." Babette and Paul have come a long way since their first horseback pilgrimage and not just in kilometres. They have learnt a great deal about themselves, their animals and some of the practicalities of long distance riding, but they continue to regard themselves as incompetent amateurs and are still in search of a rationale for their insatiable wanderlust. Common sense and the deteriorating east-west political situation put an end to their original plan, riding on from Santiago de Compostela to Jerusalem in 2006, but Paul has found an equally exciting alternative: the via Francigena pilgrimage to Rome. The good news is that there will be no war zones to contend with, but the bad news is that they will be travelling 2000 kilometres along a relatively unknown route, with a 2,469 metre climb over the Swiss Alps, often under snow, even in August. Riding the Roman Way takes you alongside this intrepid team every step of the way and shares the highs and lows with disarming honesty. It also provides a detailed account of the via Francigena and offers practical guidance for someone wanting to embark on a similar journey. But be warned, this book will inspire even the most timid traveller and you read it at your own risk.